GENERAL MOTORS
CHEVROLET 2004-11 REPAIR MANUAL

CHILTON'S

Covers all U.S. and Canadian models of Chevrolet Aveo
2004 through 2011

by Jeff Killingsworth

CHILTON *Automotive Books*
PUBLISHED BY **HAYNES NORTH AMERICA, Inc.**

Manufactured in USA
©2016 Haynes North America, Inc.
ISBN-13: 978-1-62092-253-8
ISBN-10: 1-62092-253-3
Library of Congress Control Number 2016952944

Haynes Publishing Group
Sparkford Nr Yeovil
Somerset BA22 7JJ England

Haynes North America, Inc
859 Lawrence Drive
Newbury Park
California 91320 USA

ABCDE
FGHIJ
KLMNO
PQRST

Contents

2007 Chevrolet Aveo in the Haynes workshop

ACKNOWLEDGEMENTS

Technical writers who contributed to this project include Demian Hurst and Scott "Gonzo" Weaver.

About this manual

ITS PURPOSE

The purpose of this manual is to help you get the best value from your vehicle. It can do so in several ways. It can help you decide what work must be done, even if you choose to have it done by a dealer service department or a repair shop; it provides information and procedures for routine maintenance and servicing; and it offers diagnostic and repair procedures to follow when trouble occurs.

We hope you use the manual to tackle the work yourself. For many simpler jobs, doing it yourself may be quicker than arranging an appointment to get the vehicle into a shop and making the trips to leave it and pick it up. More importantly, a lot of money can be saved by avoiding the expense the shop must pass on to you to cover its labor and overhead costs. An added benefit is the sense of satisfaction and accomplishment that you feel after doing the job yourself.

USING THE MANUAL

The manual is divided into Chapters. Each Chapter is divided into numbered Sections. Each Section consists of consecutively numbered paragraphs.

The reference numbers used in illustration captions pinpoint the pertinent Section and the Step within that Section. That is, illustration 3.2 means the illustration refers to Section 3 and Step (or paragraph) 2 within that Section.

Procedures, once described in the text, are not normally repeated. When it's necessary to refer to another Chapter, the reference will be given as Chapter and Section number. Cross references given without use of the word "Chapter" apply to Sections and/or paragraphs in the same Chapter. For example, "see Section 8" means in the same Chapter.

References to the left or right side of the vehicle assume you are sitting in the driver's seat, facing forward.

Even though we have prepared this manual with extreme care, neither the publisher nor the author can accept responsibility for any errors in, or omissions from, the information given.

➡ **NOTE**

A *Note* provides information necessary to properly complete a procedure or information which will make the procedure easier to understand.

✳✳ CAUTION

A *Caution* provides a special procedure or special steps which must be taken while completing the procedure where the Caution is found. Not heeding a Caution can result in damage to the assembly being worked on.

✳✳ WARNING

A *Warning* provides a special procedure or special steps which must be taken while completing the procedure where the Warning is found. Not heeding a Warning can result in personal injury.

Introduction

1   These models are available in sedan and hatchback body styles. They feature transversely mounted 1.6L four-cylinder engines.

2   The 1.6L four-cylinder DOHC or DOHC VVT engine transmits power to the front wheels through either a five-speed manual transaxle or an electronically controlled four-speed automatic transaxle, via independent driveaxles. All models are equipped with an electronically controlled Sequential Multi-Port Fuel Injection (MPI) system.

3   The front suspension is a MacPherson strut design. The rear suspension employs two trailing arms that pivot on bushings on the underbody, connected by a stamped-steel axle, with two coil springs and two shock absorbers.

4   The rack-and-pinion steering unit is mounted behind the engine on the front suspension subframe, and is power-assisted on all models by an engine mounted, belt-driven hydraulic power steering pump.

5   All models are equipped with power assisted front disc and rear drum brakes, with an Anti-lock Brake System (ABS) available as an option.

Vehicle identification numbers

Modifications are a continuing and unpublicized process in vehicle manufacturing. Since spare parts manuals and lists are compiled on a numerical basis, the individual vehicle numbers are essential to correctly identify the component required.

VEHICLE IDENTIFICATION NUMBER (VIN)

This very important identification number is stamped on a plate attached to the dashboard inside the windshield on the driver's side of the vehicle (see illustration). It can also be found on the certification label located on the driver's side door post. The VIN also appears on the Vehicle Certificate of Title and Registration. It contains information such as where and when the vehicle was manufactured, the model year and the body style.

On the models covered by this manual the model year codes are:

4	2004
5	2005
6	2006
7	2007
8	2008
9	2009
A	2010
B	2011

On the models covered by this manual the engine codes are:

6	1.6L (L91) four-cylinder 16-valve, DOHC engine - 2004 through 2007
6	1.6L (LXT) four-cylinder 16-valve, DOHC engine - 2008
E	1.6L (LXV) four-cylinder 16-valve, DOHC, VVT engine - 2009 through 2011

CERTIFICATION LABEL

The certification label is attached to the driver's door post (see illustration). The plate contains the name of the manufacturer, the month and year of production, the Gross Vehicle Weight Rating (GVWR), the Gross Axle Weight Rating (GAWR) and the certification statement.

ENGINE IDENTIFICATION NUMBERS

The engine serial number can be found on a machined surface at the rear of the engine, on the front side of the engine block (see illustration).

TRANSAXLE IDENTIFICATION

The transmission identification is listed on a Manufacturer's RPO code list or on a sticker attached to the transaxle (see illustration). The codes are as follows:

RPO code	Transaxle sticker	Transaxle
MLM	D16/D20	5-speed manual transaxle
MM5	Y4M	5-speed manual transaxle
MLQ	81-40LE	4-speed automatic transaxle

3.2 The Vehicle Identification Number (VIN) is visible through the driver's side of the windshield

3.5 The Manufacturer's Certification Regulation label is located on the driver's door opening

3.6 The engine identification code date can be found stamped on the front side of the engine block, under the exhaust manifold, next to the transaxle (1.6L L91 engine shown)

3.7 The transaxle identification label is affixed to the top of the transaxle

Recall information

Vehicle recalls are carried out by the manufacturer in the rare event of a possible safety-related defect. The vehicle's registered owner is contacted at the address on file at the Department of Motor Vehicles and given the details of the recall. Remedial work is carried out free of charge at a dealer service department.

If you are the new owner of a used vehicle which was subject to a recall and you want to be sure that the work has been carried out, it's best to contact a dealer service department and ask about your indi-

vidual vehicle - you'll need to furnish them your Vehicle Identification Number (VIN).

The table below is based on information provided by the National Highway Traffic Safety Administration (NHTSA), the body which oversees vehicle recalls in the United States. The recall database is updated constantly. For the latest information on vehicle recalls, check the NHTSA website at www.nhtsa.gov, or call the NHTSA hotline at 1-888-327-4236.

Recall date	Recall campaign number	Model(s) affected	Concern
Aug 17, 2004	04V407000	2004 - Aveo	On some models the rear safety belt can become twisted. If this happens, the safety belt retractor may lock in position so that the belt cannot be used. In the event of a crash, personal injury to the seat occupant could occur.
Oct 17, 2006	06V398000	2007 - Aveo	During crash tests, the fuel line in the engine compartment of some models developed a fracture. In addition, the crash damage caused four short circuits in the fuse block, the combination of which allowed the fuel pump to continue running and fuel leaked onto the ground. If these conditions occurred in an actual crash, a fire could occur.

Recall date	Recall campaign number	Model(s) affected	Concern
May 19, 2014	14V261000	2004, 2005, 2006, 2007, 2008 - Aveo	On some models equipped with daytime running lights (DRL), there may be heat generated within the DRL module located in the center console in the instrument panel, which could melt the DRL module. If the DRL module melts due to the heat generation, it could cause a fire.
July 29, 2014	14V460000	2009, 2010 - Aveo	Some models may contain brake fluid which does not protect against corrosion of the valves inside the Anti-lock Brake System (ABS) module, affecting the closing motion of the valves. If the ABS valve corrodes it may result in longer brake pedal travel or reduced performance, increasing the risk of a crash.

Buying parts

Replacement parts are available from many sources, which generally fall into one of two categories - authorized dealer parts departments and independent retail auto parts stores. Our advice concerning these parts is as follows:

Retail auto parts stores: Good auto parts stores will stock frequently needed components which wear out relatively fast, such as clutch components, exhaust systems, brake parts, tune-up parts, etc. These stores often supply new or reconditioned parts on an exchange basis, which can save a considerable amount of money. Discount auto parts stores are often very good places to buy materials and parts needed for general vehicle maintenance such as oil, grease, filters, spark plugs, belts, touch-up paint, bulbs, etc. They also usually sell

tools and general accessories, have convenient hours, charge lower prices and can often be found not far from home.

Authorized dealer parts department: This is the best source for parts which are unique to the vehicle and not generally available elsewhere (such as major engine parts, transmission parts, trim pieces, etc.).

Warranty information: If the vehicle is still covered under warranty, be sure that any replacement parts purchased - regardless of the source - do not invalidate the warranty!

To be sure of obtaining the correct parts, have engine and chassis numbers available and, if possible, take the old parts along for positive identification.

MAINTENANCE TECHNIQUES

There are a number of techniques involved in maintenance and repair that will be referred to throughout this manual. Application of these techniques will enable the home mechanic to be more efficient, better organized and capable of performing the various tasks properly, which will ensure that the repair job is thorough and complete.

Fasteners

Fasteners are nuts, bolts, studs and screws used to hold two or more parts together. There are a few things to keep in mind when working with fasteners. Almost all of them use a locking device of some type, either a lockwasher, locknut, locking tab or thread adhesive. All threaded fasteners should be clean and straight, with undamaged threads and undamaged corners on the hex head where the wrench fits. Develop the habit of replacing all damaged nuts and bolts with new ones. Special locknuts with nylon or fiber inserts can only be used once. If they are removed, they lose their locking ability and must be replaced with new ones.

Rusted nuts and bolts should be treated with a penetrating fluid to ease removal and prevent breakage. Some mechanics use turpentine in a spout-type oil can, which works quite well. After applying the rust penetrant, let it work for a few minutes before trying to loosen the nut or bolt. Badly rusted fasteners may have to be chiseled or sawed off or removed with a special nut breaker, available at tool stores.

If a bolt or stud breaks off in an assembly, it can be drilled and removed with a special tool commonly available for this purpose. Most automotive machine shops can perform this task, as well as other repair procedures, such as the repair of threaded holes that have been stripped out.

Flat washers and lockwashers, when removed from an assembly, should always be replaced exactly as removed. Replace any damaged washers with new ones. Never use a lockwasher on any soft metal surface (such as aluminum), thin sheet metal or plastic.

Fastener sizes

For a number of reasons, automobile manufacturers are making wider and wider use of metric fasteners. Therefore, it is important to be able to tell the difference between standard (sometimes called U.S. or SAE) and metric hardware, since they cannot be interchanged.

All bolts, whether standard or metric, are sized according to diameter, thread pitch and length. For example, a standard 1/2 - 13 x 1 bolt is 1/2 inch in diameter, has 13 threads per inch and is 1 inch long. An M12 - 1.75 x 25 metric bolt is 12 mm in diameter, has a thread pitch of 1.75 mm (the distance between threads) and is 25 mm long. The two bolts are nearly identical, and easily confused, but they are not interchangeable.

In addition to the differences in diameter, thread pitch and length, metric and standard bolts can also be distinguished by examining the bolt heads. To begin with, the distance across the flats on a standard bolt head is measured in inches, while the same dimension on a metric bolt is sized in millimeters (the same is true for nuts). As a result, a standard wrench should not be used on a metric bolt and a metric wrench should not be used on a standard bolt. Also, most standard bolts have slashes radiating out from the center of the head to denote the grade or strength of the bolt, which is an indication of the amount of torque that can be applied to it. The greater the number of slashes, the greater the strength of the bolt. Grades 0 through 5 are commonly used on automobiles. Metric bolts have a property class (grade) number, rather than a slash, molded into their heads to indicate bolt strength. In this case, the higher the number, the stronger the bolt. Property class numbers 8.8, 9.8 and 10.9 are commonly used on automobiles.

Strength markings can also be used to distinguish standard hex nuts from metric hex nuts. Many standard nuts have dots stamped into one side, while metric nuts are marked with a number. The greater the number of dots, or the higher the number, the greater the strength of the nut.

Metric studs are also marked on their ends according to property class (grade). Larger studs are numbered (the same as metric bolts), while smaller studs carry a geometric code to denote grade.

It should be noted that many fasteners, especially Grades 0 through 2, have no distinguishing marks on them. When such is the case, the only way to determine whether it is standard or metric is to measure the thread pitch or compare it to a known fastener of the same size.

Standard fasteners are often referred to as SAE, as opposed to metric. However, it should be noted that SAE technically refers to a non-metric fine thread fastener only. Coarse thread non-metric fasteners are referred to as USS sizes.

Since fasteners of the same size (both standard and metric) may have different strength ratings, be sure to reinstall any bolts, studs or nuts removed from your vehicle in their original locations. Also, when replacing a fastener with a new one, make sure that the new one has a strength rating equal to or greater than the original.

Tightening sequences and procedures

Most threaded fasteners should be tightened to a specific torque value (torque is the twisting force applied to a threaded component such as a nut or bolt). Overtightening the fastener can weaken it and cause it to break, while undertightening can cause it to eventually come loose. Bolts, screws and studs, depending on the material they are made of and their thread diameters, have specific torque values, many of which are noted in the Specifications at the end of each Chapter. Be sure to follow the torque recommendations closely. For fasteners not assigned a specific torque, a general torque value chart is presented here as a guide. These torque values are for dry (unlubricated) fasteners threaded into steel or cast iron (not aluminum). As was previously mentioned, the size and grade of a fastener determine the amount of torque that can safely be applied to it. The figures listed here are approximate for Grade 2 and Grade 3 fasteners. Higher grades can tolerate higher torque values.

Fasteners laid out in a pattern, such as cylinder head bolts, oil pan bolts, differential cover bolts, etc., must be loosened or tightened in sequence to avoid warping the component. This sequence will normally be shown in the appropriate Chapter. If a specific pattern is not given, the following procedures can be used to prevent warping.

Initially, the bolts or nuts should be assembled finger-tight only. Next, they should be tightened one full turn each, in a criss-cross or diagonal pattern. After each one has been tightened one full turn, return to the first one and tighten them all one-half turn, following the same

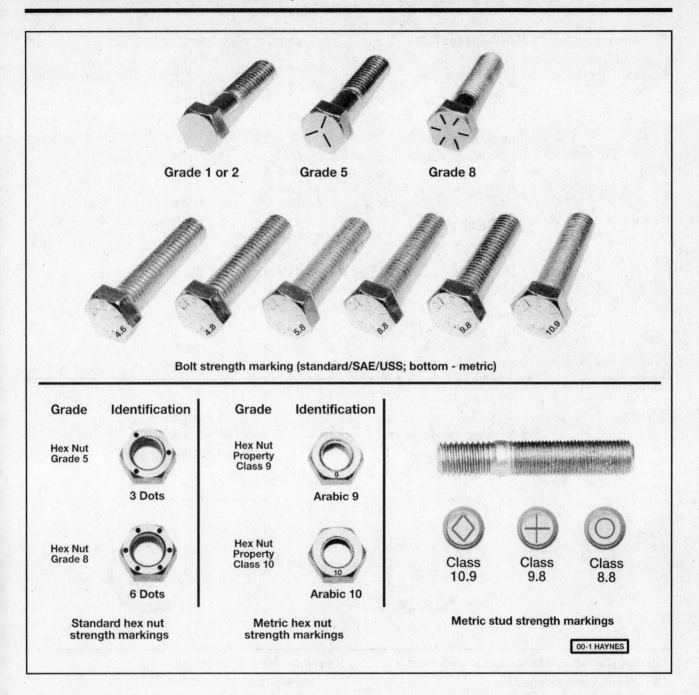

Grade 1 or 2   Grade 5   Grade 8

Bolt strength marking (standard/SAE/USS; bottom - metric)

Grade	Identification
Hex Nut Grade 5	3 Dots
Hex Nut Grade 8	6 Dots

Standard hex nut strength markings

Grade	Identification
Hex Nut Property Class 9	Arabic 9
Hex Nut Property Class 10	Arabic 10

Metric hex nut strength markings

Class 10.9   Class 9.8   Class 8.8

Metric stud strength markings

00-1 HAYNES

pattern. Finally, tighten each of them one-quarter turn at a time until each fastener has been tightened to the proper torque. To loosen and remove the fasteners, the procedure would be reversed.

Component disassembly

Component disassembly should be done with care and purpose to help ensure that the parts go back together properly. Always keep track of the sequence in which parts are removed. Make note of special characteristics or marks on parts that can be installed more than one way, such as a grooved thrust washer on a shaft. It is a good idea to lay the disassembled parts out on a clean surface in the order that they were removed. It may also be helpful to make sketches or take instant photos of components before removal.

When removing fasteners from a component, keep track of their locations. Sometimes threading a bolt back in a part, or putting the washers and nut back on a stud, can prevent mix-ups later. If nuts and bolts cannot be returned to their original locations, they should be kept in a compartmented box or a series of small boxes. A cupcake or muffin tin is ideal for this purpose, since each cavity can hold the bolts and nuts from a particular area (i.e. oil pan bolts, valve cover bolts, engine

Metric thread sizes

	Ft-lbs	Nm
M-6	6 to 9	9 to 12
M-8	14 to 21	19 to 28
M-10	28 to 40	38 to 54
M-12	50 to 71	68 to 96
M-14	80 to 140	109 to 154

Pipe thread sizes

1/8	5 to 8	7 to 10
1/4	12 to 18	17 to 24
3/8	22 to 33	30 to 44
1/2	25 to 35	34 to 47

U.S. thread sizes

1/4 - 20	6 to 9	9 to 12
5/16 - 18	12 to 18	17 to 24
5/16 - 24	14 to 20	19 to 27
3/8 - 16	22 to 32	30 to 43
3/8 - 24	27 to 38	37 to 51
7/16 - 14	40 to 55	55 to 74
7/16 - 20	40 to 60	55 to 81
1/2 - 13	55 to 80	75 to 108

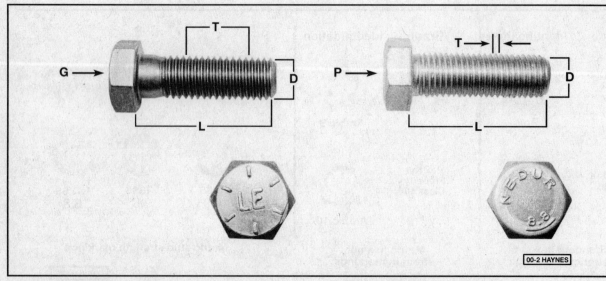

00-2 HAYNES

Standard (SAE and USS) bolt dimensions/grade marks

G   Grade marks (bolt strength)
L   Length (in inches)
T   Thread pitch (number of threads per inch)
D   Nominal diameter (in inches)

Metric bolt dimensions/grade marks

P   Property class (bolt strength)
L   Length (in millimeters)
T   Thread pitch (distance between threads in millimeters)
D   Diameter

mount bolts, etc.). A pan of this type is especially helpful when working on assemblies with very small parts, such as the carburetor, alternator, valve train or interior dash and trim pieces. The cavities can be marked with paint or tape to identify the contents.

Whenever wiring looms, harnesses or connectors are separated, it is a good idea to identify the two halves with numbered pieces of masking tape so they can be easily reconnected.

Gasket sealing surfaces

Throughout any vehicle, gaskets are used to seal the mating surfaces between two parts and keep lubricants, fluids, vacuum or pressure contained in an assembly.

Many times these gaskets are coated with a liquid or paste-type gasket sealing compound before assembly. Age, heat and pressure can sometimes cause the two parts to stick together so tightly that they are very difficult to separate. Often, the assembly can be loosened by striking it with a soft-face hammer near the mating surfaces. A regular hammer can be used if a block of wood is placed between the hammer and the part. Do not hammer on cast parts or parts that could be easily damaged. With any particularly stubborn part, always recheck to make sure that every fastener has been removed.

Avoid using a screwdriver or bar to pry apart an assembly, as

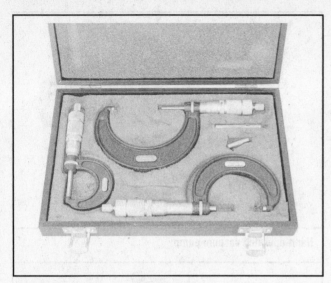

Micrometer set

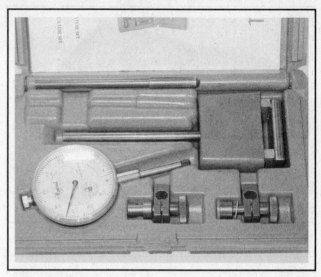

Dial indicator set

they can easily mar the gasket sealing surfaces of the parts, which must remain smooth. If prying is absolutely necessary, use an old broom handle, but keep in mind that extra clean up will be necessary if the wood splinters.

After the parts are separated, the old gasket must be carefully scraped off and the gasket surfaces cleaned. Stubborn gasket material can be soaked with rust penetrant or treated with a special chemical to soften it so it can be easily scraped off.

✳ CAUTION:

Never use gasket removal solutions or caustic chemicals on plastic or other composite components.

A scraper can be fashioned from a piece of copper tubing by flattening and sharpening one end. Copper is recommended because it is usually softer than the surfaces to be scraped, which reduces the chance of gouging the part. Some gaskets can be removed with a wire brush, but regardless of the method used, the mating surfaces must be left clean and smooth. If for some reason the gasket surface is gouged, then a gasket sealer thick enough to fill scratches will have to be used during reassembly of the components. For most applications, a non-drying (or semi-drying) gasket sealer should be used.

Hose removal tips

✳ WARNING:

If the vehicle is equipped with air conditioning, do not disconnect any of the A/C hoses without first having the system depressurized by a dealer service department or a service station.

Hose removal precautions closely parallel gasket removal precautions. Avoid scratching or gouging the surface that the hose mates against or the connection may leak. This is especially true for radiator hoses. Because of various chemical reactions, the rubber in hoses can bond itself to the metal spigot that the hose fits over. To remove a hose, first loosen the hose clamps that secure it to the spigot. Then, with slip-joint pliers, grab the hose at the clamp and rotate it around the spigot. Work it back and forth until it is completely free, then pull it off. Silicone or other lubricants will ease removal if they can be applied

between the hose and the outside of the spigot. Apply the same lubricant to the inside of the hose and the outside of the spigot to simplify installation.

As a last resort (and if the hose is to be replaced with a new one anyway), the rubber can be slit with a knife and the hose peeled from the spigot. If this must be done, be careful that the metal connection is not damaged.

If a hose clamp is broken or damaged, do not reuse it. Wire-type clamps usually weaken with age, so it is a good idea to replace them with screw-type clamps whenever a hose is removed.

TOOLS

A selection of good tools is a basic requirement for anyone who plans to maintain and repair his or her own vehicle. For the owner who has few tools, the initial investment might seem high, but when compared to the spiraling costs of professional auto maintenance and repair, it is a wise one.

To help the owner decide which tools are needed to perform the tasks detailed in this manual, the following tool lists are offered: *Maintenance and minor repair, Repair/overhaul and Special.*

The newcomer to practical mechanics should start off with the *maintenance and minor repair* tool kit, which is adequate for the simpler jobs performed on a vehicle. Then, as confidence and experience grow, the owner can tackle more difficult tasks, buying additional tools as they are needed. Eventually the basic kit will be expanded into the *repair and overhaul* tool set. Over a period of time, the experienced do-it-yourselfer will assemble a tool set complete enough for most repair and overhaul procedures and will add tools from the special category when it is felt that the expense is justified by the frequency of use.

Maintenance and minor repair tool kit

The tools in this list should be considered the minimum required for performance of routine maintenance, servicing and minor repair work. We recommend the purchase of combination wrenches (box-end and open-end combined in one wrench). While more expensive than open end wrenches, they offer the advantages of both types of wrench.

Combination wrench set (1/4-inch to 1 inch or 6 mm to 19 mm)
Adjustable wrench, 8 inch
Spark plug wrench with rubber insert

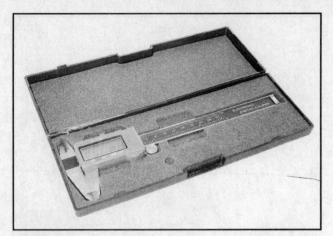

Dial caliper

Hand-operated vacuum pump

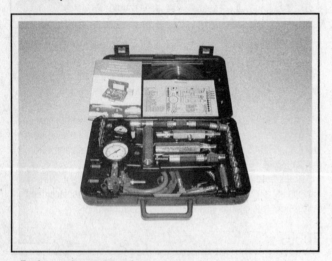

Fuel pressure gauge set

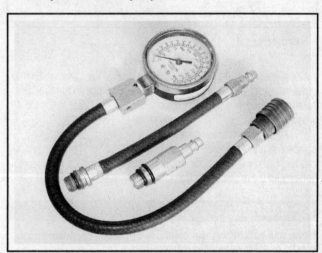

Compression gauge with spark plug hole adapter

Damper/steering wheel puller

General purpose puller

Hydraulic lifter removal tool

Spark plug gap adjusting tool
Feeler gauge set
Brake bleeder wrench
Standard screwdriver (5/16-inch x 6 inch)
Phillips screwdriver (No. 2 x 6 inch)
Combination pliers - 6 inch
Hacksaw and assortment of blades
Tire pressure gauge
Grease gun

Oil can
Fine emery cloth
Wire brush
Battery post and cable cleaning tool
Oil filter wrench
Funnel (medium size)
Safety goggles
Jackstands (2)
Drain pan

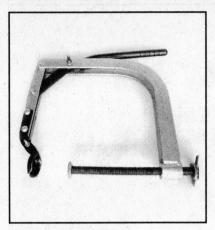

Valve spring compressor

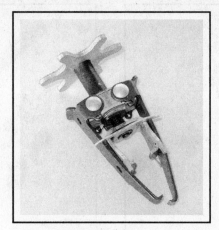

Valve spring compressor

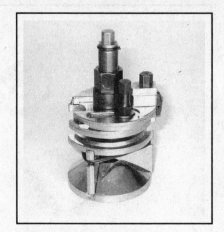

Ridge reamer

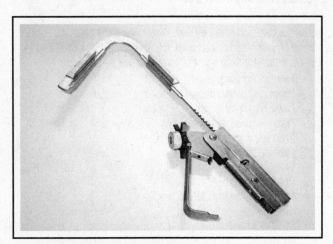

Piston ring groove cleaning tool

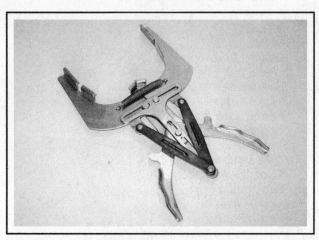

Ring removal/installation tool

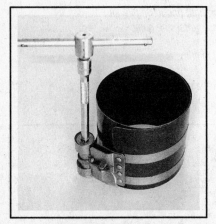

Ring compressor

Cylinder hone

Brake hold-down spring tool

➡ **Note: If basic tune-ups are going to be part of routine maintenance, it will be necessary to purchase a good quality stroboscopic timing light and combination tachometer/dwell meter. Although they are included in the list of special tools, it is mentioned here because they are absolutely necessary for tuning most vehicles properly.**

Repair and overhaul tool set

These tools are essential for anyone who plans to perform major repairs and are in addition to those in the maintenance and minor repair tool kit. Included is a comprehensive set of sockets which, though expensive, are invaluable because of their versatility, especially when various extensions and drives are available. We recommend the 1/2-inch drive over the 3/8-inch drive. Although the larger drive is bulky and more expensive, it has the capacity of accepting a very wide range of large sockets. Ideally, however, the mechanic should have a 3/8-inch drive set and a 1/2-inch drive set.

Torque angle gauge

Clutch plate alignment tool

Socket set(s)
Reversible ratchet
Extension - 10 inch
Universal joint
Torque wrench (same size drive as sockets)
Ball peen hammer - 8 ounce
Soft-face hammer (plastic/rubber)
Standard screwdriver (1/4-inch x 6 inch)
Standard screwdriver (stubby - 5/16-inch)
Phillips screwdriver (No. 3 x 8 inch)
Phillips screwdriver (stubby - No. 2)
Pliers - vise grip
Pliers - lineman's
Pliers - needle nose
Pliers - snap-ring (internal and external)
Cold chisel - 1/2-inch
Scribe
Scraper (made from flattened copper tubing)
Centerpunch
Pin punches (1/16, 1/8, 3/16-inch)
Steel rule/straightedge - 12 inch
Allen wrench set (1/8 to 3/8-inch or 4 mm to 10 mm)
A selection of files
Wire brush (large)
Jackstands (second set)
Jack (scissor or hydraulic type)

➡ **Note: Another tool which is often useful is an electric drill with a chuck capacity of 3/8-inch and a set of good quality drill bits.**

Special tools

The tools in this list include those which are not used regularly, are expensive to buy, or which need to be used in accordance with their manufacturer's instructions. Unless these tools will be used frequently, it is not very economical to purchase many of them. A consideration would be to split the cost and use between yourself and a friend or friends. In addition, most of these tools can be obtained from a tool rental shop on a temporary basis.

This list primarily contains only those tools and instruments widely available to the public, and not those special tools produced by the vehicle manufacturer for distribution to dealer service departments. Occasionally, references to the manufacturer's special tools are included in the text of this manual. Generally, an alternative method of doing the job without the special tool is offered. However, sometimes there is no alternative to their use. Where this is the case, and the tool cannot be purchased or borrowed, the work should be turned over to the dealer service department or an automotive repair shop.

Valve spring compressor
Piston ring groove cleaning tool
Piston ring compressor
Piston ring installation tool
Cylinder compression gauge
Cylinder ridge reamer
Cylinder surfacing hone
Cylinder bore gauge
Micrometers and/or dial calipers
Hydraulic lifter removal tool
Balljoint separator
Universal-type puller
Impact screwdriver
Dial indicator set
Stroboscopic timing light (inductive pick-up)
Hand operated vacuum/pressure pump
Tachometer/dwell meter
Universal electrical multimeter
Cable hoist
Brake spring removal and installation tools
Floor jack

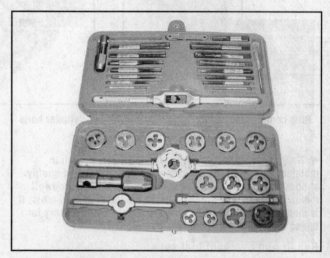

Tap and die set

Buying tools

For the do-it-yourselfer who is just starting to get involved in vehicle maintenance and repair, there are a number of options available when purchasing tools. If maintenance and minor repair is the extent of the work to be done, the purchase of individual tools is satisfactory. If, on the other hand, extensive work is planned, it would be a good idea to purchase a modest tool set from one of the large retail chain stores. A set can usually be bought at a substantial savings over the individual tool prices, and they often come with a tool box. As additional tools are needed, add-on sets, individual tools and a larger tool box can be purchased to expand the tool selection. Building a tool set gradually allows the cost of the tools to be spread over a longer period of time and gives the mechanic the freedom to choose only those tools that will actually be used.

Tool stores will often be the only source of some of the special tools that are needed, but regardless of where tools are bought, try to avoid cheap ones, especially when buying screwdrivers and sockets, because they won't last very long. The expense involved in replacing cheap tools will eventually be greater than the initial cost of quality tools.

Care and maintenance of tools

Good tools are expensive, so it makes sense to treat them with respect. Keep them clean and in usable condition and store them properly when not in use. Always wipe off any dirt, grease or metal chips before putting them away. Never leave tools lying around in the work area. Upon completion of a job, always check closely under the hood for tools that may have been left there so they won't get lost during a test drive.

Some tools, such as screwdrivers, pliers, wrenches and sockets, can be hung on a panel mounted on the garage or workshop wall, while others should be kept in a tool box or tray. Measuring instruments, gauges, meters, etc. must be carefully stored where they cannot be damaged by weather or impact from other tools.

When tools are used with care and stored properly, they will last a very long time. Even with the best of care, though, tools will wear out if used frequently. When a tool is damaged or worn out, replace it. Subsequent jobs will be safer and more enjoyable if you do.

HOW TO REPAIR DAMAGED THREADS

Sometimes, the internal threads of a nut or bolt hole can become stripped, usually from overtightening. Stripping threads is an all-too-common occurrence, especially when working with aluminum parts, because aluminum is so soft that it easily strips out.

Usually, external or internal threads are only partially stripped. After they've been cleaned up with a tap or die, they'll still work. Sometimes, however, threads are badly damaged. When this happens, you've got three choices:

1) *Drill and tap the hole to the next suitable oversize and install a larger diameter bolt, screw or stud.*

2) *Drill and tap the hole to accept a threaded plug, then drill and tap the plug to the original screw size. You can also buy a plug already threaded to the original size. Then you simply drill a hole to the specified size, then run the threaded plug into the hole with a bolt and jam nut. Once the plug is fully seated, remove the jam nut and bolt.*

3) *The third method uses a patented thread repair kit like Heli-Coil or Slimsert. These easy-to-use kits are designed to repair damaged threads in straight-through holes and blind holes. Both are available as kits which can handle a variety of sizes and thread patterns. Drill the hole, then tap it with the special included tap. Install the Heli-Coil and the hole is back to its original diameter and thread pitch.*

Regardless of which method you use, be sure to proceed calmly and carefully. A little impatience or carelessness during one of these relatively simple procedures can ruin your whole day's work and cost you a bundle if you wreck an expensive part.

WORKING FACILITIES

Not to be overlooked when discussing tools is the workshop. If anything more than routine maintenance is to be carried out, some sort of suitable work area is essential.

It is understood, and appreciated, that many home mechanics do not have a good workshop or garage available, and end up removing an engine or doing major repairs outside. It is recommended, however, that the overhaul or repair be completed under the cover of a roof.

A clean, flat workbench or table of comfortable working height is an absolute necessity. The workbench should be equipped with a vise that has a jaw opening of at least four inches.

As mentioned previously, some clean, dry storage space is also required for tools, as well as the lubricants, fluids, cleaning solvents, etc. which soon become necessary.

Sometimes waste oil and fluids, drained from the engine or cooling system during normal maintenance or repairs, present a disposal problem. To avoid pouring them on the ground or into a sewage system, pour the used fluids into large containers, seal them with caps and take them to an authorized disposal site or recycling center. Plastic jugs, such as old antifreeze containers, are ideal for this purpose.

Always keep a supply of old newspapers and clean rags available. Old towels are excellent for mopping up spills. Many mechanics use rolls of paper towels for most work because they are readily available and disposable. To help keep the area under the vehicle clean, a large cardboard box can be cut open and flattened to protect the garage or shop floor.

Whenever working over a painted surface, such as when leaning over a fender to service something under the hood, always cover it with an old blanket or bedspread to protect the finish. Vinyl covered pads, made especially for this purpose, are available at auto parts stores.

Jacking and towing

✴ WARNING:

The jack supplied with the vehicle should only be used for changing a tire or placing jackstands under the frame. Never work under the vehicle or start the engine while this jack is being used as the only means of support.

1   The vehicle should be on level ground. Place the shift lever in Park, if you have an automatic, or Reverse if you have a manual trans-

7.3 Front and rear jacking points

mission. Block the wheel diagonally opposite the wheel being changed. Set the parking brake.

2   Remove the spare tire and jack from stowage. Remove the wheel cover and trim ring (if so equipped) with the tapered end of the lug nut wrench by inserting and twisting the handle and then prying against the back of the wheel cover. Loosen, but do not remove, the lug nuts (one-half turn is sufficient).

3   Place the scissors-type jack under the vehicle and adjust the jack height until it engages with the proper jacking point on the unibody seam. There is a front and rear jacking point on each side of the vehicle (see illustration).

4   Turn the jack handle clockwise until the tire clears the ground. Remove the lug nuts and pull the wheel off, then install the spare.

5   Install the lug nuts with the beveled edges facing in. Tighten them snugly. Don't attempt to tighten them completely until the vehicle is lowered or it could slip off the jack. Turn the jack handle counter-clockwise to lower the vehicle. Remove the jack and tighten the lug nuts in a diagonal pattern.

6   Stow the tire, jack and wrench. Unblock the wheels.

TOWING

7   All models must be towed with the drive (front) wheels off the ground, using either a wheel-lift tow truck or a towing dolly. A flat-bed car carrier is the preferred method.

Booster battery (jump) starting

1   Observe these precautions when using a booster battery to start a vehicle:

a) *Before connecting the booster battery, make sure the ignition switch is in the Off position.*

b) *Turn off the lights, heater and other electrical loads.*

c) *Your eyes should be shielded. Safety goggles are a good idea.*

d) *Make sure the booster battery is the same voltage as the dead one in the vehicle.*

e) *The two vehicles MUST NOT TOUCH each other!*

f) *Make sure the transaxle is in Neutral (manual) or Park (automatic).*

g) *If the booster battery is not a maintenance-free type, remove the vent caps and lay a cloth over the vent holes.*

2   Connect the red jumper cable to the positive (+) terminals of each vehicle (see illustrations).

3   Connect one end of the black jumper cable to the negative (-) terminal of the booster battery. The other end of this cable should be connected to a good ground on the vehicle to be started, such as a bolt or bracket on the body.

4   Start the engine using the booster battery, then, with the engine running at idle speed, disconnect the jumper cables in the reverse order of connection.

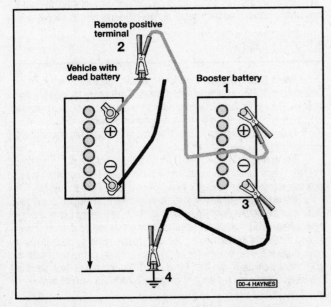

8.2a Make the booster battery connections in the numerical order shown

8.2b Positive (A) and negative (B) battery terminals

Automotive chemicals and lubricants

A number of automotive chemicals and lubricants are available for use during vehicle maintenance and repair. They include a wide variety of products ranging from cleaning solvents and degreasers to lubricants and protective sprays for rubber, plastic and vinyl.

CLEANERS

Carburetor cleaner and choke cleaner is a strong solvent for gum, varnish and carbon. Most carburetor cleaners leave a dry-type lubricant film which will not harden or gum up. Because of this film it is not recommended for use on electrical components.

Brake system cleaner is used to remove brake dust, grease and brake fluid from the brake system, where clean surfaces are absolutely necessary. It leaves no residue and often eliminates brake squeal caused by contaminants.

Electrical cleaner removes oxidation, corrosion and carbon deposits from electrical contacts, restoring full current flow. It can also be used to clean spark plugs, carburetor jets, voltage regulators and other parts where an oil-free surface is desired.

Demoisturants remove water and moisture from electrical components such as alternators, voltage regulators, electrical connectors and fuse blocks. They are non-conductive and non-corrosive.

Degreasers are heavy-duty solvents used to remove grease from the outside of the engine and from chassis components. They can be sprayed or brushed on and, depending on the type, are rinsed off either with water or solvent.

LUBRICANTS

Motor oil is the lubricant formulated for use in engines. It normally contains a wide variety of additives to prevent corrosion and reduce foaming and wear. Motor oil comes in various weights (viscosity ratings) from 0 to 50. The recommended weight of the oil depends on the season, temperature and the demands on the engine. Light oil is used in cold climates and under light load conditions. Heavy oil is used in hot climates and where high loads are encountered. Multi-viscosity oils are designed to have characteristics of both light and heavy oils and are available in a number of weights from 0W-20 to 20W-50.

Gear oil is designed to be used in differentials, manual transmissions and other areas where high-temperature lubrication is required.

Chassis and wheel bearing grease is a heavy grease used where increased loads and friction are encountered, such as for wheel bearings, ball-joints, tie-rod ends and universal joints.

High-temperature wheel bearing grease is designed to withstand the extreme temperatures encountered by wheel bearings in disc brake equipped vehicles. It usually contains molybdenum disulfide (moly), which is a dry-type lubricant.

White grease is a heavy grease for metal-to-metal applications where water is a problem. White grease stays soft under both low and high temperatures (usually from -100 to +190-degrees F), and will not wash off or dilute in the presence of water.

Assembly lube is a special extreme pressure lubricant, usually containing moly, used to lubricate high-load parts (such as main and rod bearings and cam lobes) for initial start-up of a new engine. The assembly lube lubricates the parts without being squeezed out or washed away until the engine oiling system begins to function.

Silicone lubricants are used to protect rubber, plastic, vinyl and nylon parts.

Graphite lubricants are used where oils cannot be used due to contamination problems, such as in locks. The dry graphite will lubricate metal parts while remaining uncontaminated by dirt, water, oil or acids. It is electrically conductive and will not foul electrical contacts in locks such as the ignition switch.

Moly penetrants loosen and lubricate frozen, rusted and corroded fasteners and prevent future rusting or freezing.

Heat-sink grease is a special electrically non-conductive grease that is used for mounting electronic ignition modules where it is essential that heat is transferred away from the module.

SEALANTS

RTV sealant is one of the most widely used gasket compounds. Made from silicone, RTV is air curing, it seals, bonds, waterproofs, fills surface irregularities, remains flexible, doesn't shrink, is relatively easy to remove, and is used as a supplementary sealer with almost all low and medium temperature gaskets.

Anaerobic sealant is much like RTV in that it can be used either to seal gaskets or to form gaskets by itself. It remains flexible, is solvent resistant and fills surface imperfections. The difference between an anaerobic sealant and an RTV-type sealant is in the curing. RTV cures when exposed to air, while an anaerobic sealant cures only in the absence of air. This means that an anaerobic sealant cures only after the assembly of parts, sealing them together.

Thread and pipe sealant is used for sealing hydraulic and pneumatic fittings and vacuum lines. It is usually made from a Teflon compound, and comes in a spray, a paint-on liquid and as a wrap-around tape.

CHEMICALS

Anti-seize compound prevents seizing, galling, cold welding, rust and corrosion in fasteners. High-temperature anti-seize, usually made with copper and graphite lubricants, is used for exhaust system and exhaust manifold bolts.

Anaerobic locking compounds are used to keep fasteners from vibrating or working loose and cure only after installation, in the absence of air. Medium strength locking compound is used for small nuts, bolts and screws that may be removed later. High-strength locking compound is for large nuts, bolts and studs which aren't removed on a regular basis.

Oil additives range from viscosity index improvers to chemical treatments that claim to reduce internal engine friction. It should be noted that most oil manufacturers caution against using additives with their oils.

Gas additives perform several functions, depending on their chemical makeup. They usually contain solvents that help dissolve gum and varnish that build up on carburetor, fuel injection and intake parts. They also serve to break down carbon deposits that form on the inside surfaces of the combustion chambers. Some additives contain upper cylinder lubricants for valves and piston rings, and others contain chemicals to remove condensation from the gas tank.

MISCELLANEOUS

Brake fluid is specially formulated hydraulic fluid that can withstand the heat and pressure encountered in brake systems. Care must be taken so this fluid does not come in contact with painted surfaces or plastics. An opened container should always be resealed to prevent contamination by water or dirt.

Weatherstrip adhesive is used to bond weatherstripping around doors, windows and trunk lids. It is sometimes used to attach trim pieces.

Undercoating is a petroleum-based, tar-like substance that is designed to protect metal surfaces on the underside of the vehicle from corrosion. It also acts as a sound-deadening agent by insulating the bottom of the vehicle.

Waxes and polishes are used to help protect painted and plated surfaces from the weather. Different types of paint may require the use of different types of wax and polish. Some polishes utilize a chemical or abrasive cleaner to help remove the top layer of oxidized (dull) paint on older vehicles. In recent years many non-wax polishes that contain a wide variety of chemicals such as polymers and silicones have been introduced. These non-wax polishes are usually easier to apply and last longer than conventional waxes and polishes.

CONVERSION FACTORS

LENGTH (distance)

Inches (in)	X	25.4	= Millimeters (mm)	X 0.0394	= Inches (in)
Feet (ft)	X	0.305	= Meters (m)	X 3.281	= Feet (ft)
Miles	X	1.609	= Kilometers (km)	X 0.621	= Miles

VOLUME (capacity)

Cubic inches (cu in; in^3)	X	16.387	= Cubic centimeters (cc; cm^3)	X 0.061	= Cubic inches (cu in; in^3)
Imperial pints (Imp pt)	X	0.568	= Liters (l)	X 1.76	= Imperial pints (Imp pt)
Imperial quarts (Imp qt)	X	1.137	= Liters (l)	X 0.88	= Imperial quarts (Imp qt)
Imperial quarts (Imp qt)	X	1.201	= US quarts (US qt)	X 0.833	= Imperial quarts (Imp qt)
US quarts (US qt)	X	0.946	= Liters (l)	X 1.057	= US quarts (US qt)
Imperial gallons (Imp gal)	X	4.546	= Liters (l)	X 0.22	= Imperial gallons (Imp gal)
Imperial gallons (Imp gal)	X	1.201	= US gallons (US gal)	X 0.833	= Imperial gallons (Imp gal)
US gallons (US gal)	X	3.785	= Liters (l)	X 0.264	= US gallons (US gal)

MASS (weight)

Ounces (oz)	X	28.35	= Grams (g)	X 0.035	= Ounces (oz)
Pounds (lb)	X	0.454	= Kilograms (kg)	X 2.205	= Pounds (lb)

FORCE

Ounces-force (ozf; oz)	X	0.278	= Newtons (N)	X 3.6	= Ounces-force (ozf; oz)
Pounds-force (lbf; lb)	X	4.448	= Newtons (N)	X 0.225	= Pounds-force (lbf; lb)
Newtons (N)	X	0.1	= Kilograms-force (kgf; kg)	X 9.81	= Newtons (N)

PRESSURE

Pounds-force per square inch (psi; lbf/in^2; lb/in^2)	X	0.070	= Kilograms-force per square centimeter (kgf/cm^2; kg/cm^2)	X 14.223	= Pounds-force per square inch (psi; lbf/in^2; lb/in^2)
Pounds-force per square inch (psi; lbf/in^2; lb/in^2)	X	0.068	= Atmospheres (atm)	X 14.696	= Pounds-force per square inch (psi; lbf/in^2; lb/in^2)
Pounds-force per square inch (psi; lbf/in^2; lb/in^2)	X	0.069	= Bars	X 14.5	= Pounds-force per square inch (psi; lbf/in^2; lb/in^2)
Pounds-force per square inch (psi; lbf/in^2; lb/in^2)	X	6.895	= Kilopascals (kPa)	X 0.145	= Pounds-force per square inch (psi; lbf/in^2; lb/in^2)
Kilopascals (kPa)	X	0.01	= Kilograms-force per square centimeter (kgf/cm^2; kg/cm^2)	X 98.1	= Kilopascals (kPa)

TORQUE (moment of force)

Pounds-force inches (lbf in; lb in)	X	1.152	= Kilograms-force centimeter (kgf cm; kg cm)	X 0.868	= Pounds-force inches (lbf in; lb in)
Pounds-force inches (lbf in; lb in)	X	0.113	= Newton meters (Nm)	X 8.85	= Pounds-force inches (lbf in; lb in)
Pounds-force inches (lbf in; lb in)	X	0.083	= Pounds-force feet (lbf ft; lb ft)	X 12	= Pounds-force inches (lbf in; lb in)
Pounds-force feet (lbf ft; lb ft)	X	0.138	= Kilograms-force meters (kgf m; kg m)	X 7.233	= Pounds-force feet (lbf ft; lb ft)
Pounds-force feet (lbf ft; lb ft)	X	1.356	= Newton meters (Nm)	X 0.738	= Pounds-force feet (lbf ft; lb ft)
Newton meters (Nm)	X	0.102	= Kilograms-force meters (kgf m; kg m)	X 9.804	= Newton meters (Nm)

VACUUM

Inches mercury (in. Hg)	X	3.377	= Kilopascals (kPa)	X 0.2961	= Inches mercury
Inches mercury (in. Hg)	X	25.4	= Millimeters mercury (mm Hg)	X 0.0394	= Inches mercury

POWER

Horsepower (hp)	X	745.7	= Watts (W)	X 0.0013	= Horsepower (hp)

VELOCITY (speed)

Miles per hour (miles/hr; mph)	X	1.609	= Kilometers per hour (km/hr; kph)	X 0.621	= Miles per hour (miles/hr; mph)

FUEL CONSUMPTION *

Miles per gallon, Imperial (mpg)	X	0.354	= Kilometers per liter (km/l)	X 2.825	= Miles per gallon, Imperial (mpg)
Miles per gallon, US (mpg)	X	0.425	= Kilometers per liter (km/l)	X 2.352	= Miles per gallon, US (mpg)

TEMPERATURE

Degrees Fahrenheit = (°C x 1.8) + 32   Degrees Celsius (Degrees Centigrade; °C) = (°F - 32) x 0.56

*It is common practice to convert from miles per gallon (mpg) to liters/100 kilometers (l/100km), where mpg (Imperial) x l/100 km = 282 and mpg (US) x l/100 km = 235

FRACTION/DECIMAL/MILLIMETER EQUIVALENTS

DECIMALS TO MILLIMETERS

Decimal	mm	Decimal	mm
0.001	0.0254	0.500	12.7000
0.002	0.0508	0.510	12.9540
0.003	0.0762	0.520	13.2080
0.004	0.1016	0.530	13.4620
0.005	0.1270	0.540	13.7160
0.006	0.1524	0.550	13.9700
0.007	0.1778	0.560	14.2240
0.008	0.2032	0.570	14.4780
0.009	0.2286	0.580	14.7320
		0.590	14.9860
0.010	0.2540		
0.020	0.5080		
0.030	0.7620		
0.040	1.0160	0.600	15.2400
0.050	1.2700	0.610	15.4940
0.060	1.5240	0.620	15.7480
0.070	1.7780	0.630	16.0020
0.080	2.0320	0.640	16.2560
0.090	2.2860	0.650	16.5100
		0.660	16.7640
0.100	2.5400	0.670	17.0180
0.110	2.7940	0.680	17.2720
0.120	3.0480	0.690	17.5260
0.130	3.3020		
0.140	3.5560		
0.150	3.8100		
0.160	4.0640	0.700	17.7800
0.170	4.3180	0.710	18.0340
0.180	4.5720	0.720	18.2880
0.190	4.8260	0.730	18.5420
		0.740	18.7960
0.200	5.0800	0.750	19.0500
0.210	5.3340	0.760	19.3040
0.220	5.5880	0.770	19.5580
0.230	5.8420	0.780	19.8120
0.240	6.0960	0.790	20.0660
0.250	6.3500		
0.260	6.6040		
0.270	6.8580	0.800	20.3200
0.280	7.1120	0.810	20.5740
0.290	7.3660	0.820	21.8280
		0.830	21.0820
0.300	7.6200	0.840	21.3360
0.310	7.8740	0.850	21.5900
0.320	8.1280	0.860	21.8440
0.330	8.3820	0.870	22.0980
0.340	8.6360	0.880	22.3520
0.350	8.8900	0.890	22.6060
0.360	9.1440		
0.370	9.3980		
0.380	9.6520		
0.390	9.9060		
		0.900	22.8600
0.400	10.1600	0.910	23.1140
0.410	10.4140	0.920	23.3680
0.420	10.6680	0.930	23.6220
0.430	10.9220	0.940	23.8760
0.440	11.1760	0.950	24.1300
0.450	11.4300	0.960	24.3840
0.460	11.6840	0.970	24.6380
0.470	11.9380	0.980	24.8920
0.480	12.1920	0.990	25.1460
0.490	12.4460	1.000	25.4000

FRACTIONS TO DECIMALS TO MILLIMETERS

Fraction	Decimal	mm	Fraction	Decimal	mm
1/64	0.0156	0.3969	33/64	0.5156	13.0969
1/32	0.0312	0.7938	17/32	0.5312	13.4938
3/64	0.0469	1.1906	35/64	0.5469	13.8906
1/16	0.0625	1.5875	9/16	0.5625	14.2875
5/64	0.0781	1.9844	37/64	0.5781	14.6844
3/32	0.0938	2.3812	19/32	0.5938	15.0812
7/64	0.1094	2.7781	39/64	0.6094	15.4781
1/8	0.1250	3.1750	5/8	0.6250	15.8750
9/64	0.1406	3.5719	41/64	0.6406	16.2719
5/32	0.1562	3.9688	21/32	0.6562	16.6688
11/64	0.1719	4.3656	43/64	0.6719	17.0656
3/16	0.1875	4.7625	11/16	0.6875	17.4625
13/64	0.2031	5.1594	45/64	0.7031	17.8594
7/32	0.2188	5.5562	23/32	0.7188	18.2562
15/64	0.2344	5.9531	47/64	0.7344	18.6531
1/4	0.2500	6.3500	3/4	0.7500	19.0500
17/64	0.2656	6.7469	49/64	0.7656	19.4469
9/32	0.2812	7.1438	25/32	0.7812	19.8438
19/64	0.2969	7.5406	51/64	0.7969	20.2406
5/16	0.3125	7.9375	13/16	0.8125	20.6375
21/64	0.3281	8.3344	53/64	0.8281	21.0344
11/32	0.3438	8.7312	27/32	0.8438	21.4312
23/64	0.3594	9.1281	55/64	0.8594	21.8281
3/8	0.3750	9.5250	7/8	0.8750	22.2250
25/64	0.3906	9.9219	57/64	0.8906	22.6219
13/32	0.4062	10.3188	29/32	0.9062	23.0188
27/64	0.4219	10.7156	59/64	0.9219	23.4156
7/16	0.4375	11.1125	15/16	0.9375	23.8125
29/64	0.4531	11.5094	61/64	0.9531	24.2094
15/32	0.4688	11.9062	31/32	0.9688	24.6062
31/64	0.4844	12.3031	63/64	0.9844	25.0031
1/2	0.5000	12.7000	1	1.0000	25.4000

Safety first!

Regardless of how enthusiastic you may be about getting on with the job at hand, take the time to ensure that your safety is not jeopardized. A moment's lack of attention can result in an accident, as can failure to observe certain simple safety precautions. The possibility of an accident will always exist, and the following points should not be considered a comprehensive list of all dangers. Rather, they are intended to make you aware of the risks and to encourage a safety conscious approach to all work you carry out on your vehicle.

ESSENTIAL DOS AND DON'TS

DON'T rely on a jack when working under the vehicle. Always use approved jackstands to support the weight of the vehicle and place them under the recommended lift or support points.

DON'T attempt to loosen extremely tight fasteners (i.e. wheel lug nuts) while the vehicle is on a jack - it may fall.

DON'T start the engine without first making sure that the transmission is in Neutral (or Park where applicable) and the parking brake is set.

DON'T remove the radiator cap from a hot cooling system - let it cool or cover it with a cloth and release the pressure gradually.

DON'T attempt to drain the engine oil until you are sure it has cooled to the point that it will not burn you.

DON'T touch any part of the engine or exhaust system until it has cooled sufficiently to avoid burns.

DON'T siphon toxic liquids such as gasoline, antifreeze and brake fluid by mouth, or allow them to remain on your skin.

DON'T inhale brake lining dust - it is potentially hazardous (see Asbestos below).

DON'T allow spilled oil or grease to remain on the floor - wipe it up before someone slips on it.

DON'T use loose fitting wrenches or other tools which may slip and cause injury.

DON'T push on wrenches when loosening or tightening nuts or bolts. Always try to pull the wrench toward you. If the situation calls for pushing the wrench away, push with an open hand to avoid scraped knuckles if the wrench should slip.

DON'T attempt to lift a heavy component alone - get someone to help you.

DON'T rush or take unsafe shortcuts to finish a job.

DON'T allow children or animals in or around the vehicle while you are working on it.

DO wear eye protection when using power tools such as a drill, sander, bench grinder, etc. and when working under a vehicle.

DO keep loose clothing and long hair well out of the way of moving parts.

DO make sure that any hoist used has a safe working load rating adequate for the job.

DO get someone to check on you periodically when working alone on a vehicle.

DO carry out work in a logical sequence and make sure that everything is correctly assembled and tightened.

DO keep chemicals and fluids tightly capped and out of the reach of children and pets.

DO remember that your vehicle's safety affects that of yourself and others. If in doubt on any point, get professional advice.

STEERING, SUSPENSION AND BRAKES

These systems are essential to driving safety, so make sure you have a qualified shop or individual check your work. Also, compressed suspension springs can cause injury if released suddenly - be sure to use a spring compressor.

AIRBAGS

Airbags are explosive devices that can CAUSE injury if they deploy while you're working on the vehicle. Follow the manufacturer's instructions to disable the airbag whenever you're working in the vicinity of airbag components.

ASBESTOS

Certain friction, insulating, sealing, and other products - such as brake linings, brake bands, clutch linings, torque converters, gaskets, etc. - may contain asbestos or other hazardous friction material. Extreme care must be taken to avoid inhalation of dust from such products, since it is hazardous to health. If in doubt, assume that they do contain asbestos.

FIRE

Remember at all times that gasoline is highly flammable. Never smoke or have any kind of open flame around when working on a vehicle. But the risk does not end there. A spark caused by an electrical short circuit, by two metal surfaces contacting each other, or even by static electricity built up in your body under certain conditions, can ignite gasoline vapors, which in a confined space are highly explosive. Do not, under any circumstances, use gasoline for cleaning parts. Use an approved safety solvent.

Always disconnect the battery ground (-) cable at the battery before working on any part of the fuel system or electrical system. Never risk spilling fuel on a hot engine or exhaust component. It is strongly recommended that a fire extinguisher suitable for use on fuel and electrical fires be kept handy in the garage or workshop at all times. Never try to extinguish a fuel or electrical fire with water.

FUMES

Certain fumes are highly toxic and can quickly cause unconsciousness and even death if inhaled to any extent. Gasoline vapor falls into this category, as do the vapors from some cleaning solvents. Any draining or pouring of such volatile fluids should be done in a well ventilated area.

When using cleaning fluids and solvents, read the instructions on the container carefully. Never use materials from unmarked containers.

Never run the engine in an enclosed space, such as a garage. Exhaust fumes contain carbon monoxide, which is extremely poisonous. If you need to run the engine, always do so in the open air, or at least have the rear of the vehicle outside the work area.

THE BATTERY

Never create a spark or allow a bare light bulb near a battery. They normally give off a certain amount of hydrogen gas, which is highly explosive.

Always disconnect the battery ground (-) cable at the battery before working on the fuel or electrical systems.

If possible, loosen the filler caps or cover when charging the battery from an external source (this does not apply to sealed or maintenance-free batteries). Do not charge at an excessive rate or the battery may burst.

Take care when adding water to a non maintenance-free battery and when carrying a battery. The electrolyte, even when diluted, is very corrosive and should not be allowed to contact clothing or skin.

Always wear eye protection when cleaning the battery to prevent the caustic deposits from entering your eyes.

HOUSEHOLD CURRENT

When using an electric power tool, inspection light, etc., which operates on household current, always make sure that the tool is correctly connected to its plug and that, where necessary, it is properly grounded. Do not use such items in damp conditions and, again, do not create a spark or apply excessive heat in the vicinity of fuel or fuel vapor.

SECONDARY IGNITION SYSTEM VOLTAGE

A severe electric shock can result from touching certain parts of the ignition system (such as the spark plug wires) when the engine is running or being cranked, particularly if components are damp or the insulation is defective. In the case of an electronic ignition system, the secondary system voltage is much higher and could prove fatal.

HYDROFLUORIC ACID

This extremely corrosive acid is formed when certain types of synthetic rubber, found in some O-rings, oil seals, fuel hoses, etc. are exposed to temperatures above 750-degrees F (400-degrees C). The rubber changes into a charred or sticky substance containing the acid. *Once formed, the acid remains dangerous for years. If it gets onto the skin, it may be necessary to amputate the limb concerned.*

When dealing with a vehicle which has suffered a fire, or with components salvaged from such a vehicle, wear protective gloves and discard them after use.

Troubleshooting

CONTENTS

Section   Symptom

Engine

1   Engine will not rotate when attempting to start
2   Engine rotates but will not start
3   Engine hard to start when cold
4   Engine hard to start when hot
5   Starter motor noisy or excessively rough in engagement
6   Engine starts but stops immediately
7   Oil puddle under engine
8   Engine lopes while idling or idles erratically
9   Engine misses at idle speed
10   Engine misses throughout driving speed range
11   Engine stumbles on acceleration
12   Engine surges while holding accelerator steady
13   Engine stalls
14   Engine lacks power
15   Engine backfires
16   Pinging or knocking engine sounds during acceleration or uphill
17   Engine runs with oil pressure light on
18   Engine continues to run after switching off

Engine electrical systems

19   Battery will not hold a charge
20   Alternator light fails to go out
21   Alternator light fails to come on when key is turned on

Fuel system

22   Excessive fuel consumption
23   Fuel leakage and/or fuel odor

Cooling system

24   Overheating
25   Overcooling
26   External coolant leakage
27   Internal coolant leakage
28   Coolant loss
29   Poor coolant circulation

Clutch

30   Pedal travels to floor - no pressure or very little resistance
31   Fluid in area of master cylinder dust cover and on pedal
32   Fluid on release cylinder
33   Pedal feels spongy when depressed
34   Unable to select gears
35   Clutch slips (engine speed increases with no increase in vehicle speed)
36   Grabbing (chattering) as clutch is engaged
37   Transaxle rattling (clicking)
38   Noise in clutch area
39   Clutch pedal stays on floor
40   High pedal effort

Section   Symptom

Manual transaxle

41   Knocking noise at low speeds
42   Noise most pronounced when turning
43   Clunk on acceleration or deceleration
44   Clicking noise in turns
45   Vibration
46   Noisy in neutral with engine running
47   Noisy in one particular gear
48   Noisy in all gears
49   Slips out of gear
50   Leaks lubricant
51   Locked in gear

Automatic transaxle

52   Fluid leakage
53   Transmission fluid brown or has a burned smell
54   General shift mechanism problems
55   Transaxle slips, shifts roughly, is noisy or has no drive in forward or reverse gears

Driveaxles

56   Clicking noise in turns
57   Shudder or vibration during acceleration
58   Vibration at highway speeds
59   Vehicle pulls to one side during braking
60   Noise (high-pitched squeal or grinding when the brakes are applied)
61   Brake roughness or chatter (pedal pulsates)
62   Excessive brake pedal effort required to stop vehicle
63   Excessive brake pedal travel
64   Dragging brakes
65   Grabbing or uneven braking action
66   Brake pedal feels spongy when depressed
67   Brake pedal travels to the floor with little resistance
68   Parking brake does not hold

Suspension and steering systems

69   Vehicle pulls to one side
70   Abnormal or excessive tire wear
71   Wheel makes a thumping noise
72   Shimmy, shake or vibration
73   Hard steering
74   Poor returnability of steering to center
75   Abnormal noise at the front end
76   Wander or poor steering stability
77   Erratic steering when braking
78   Excessive pitching and/or rolling around corners or during braking
79   Suspension bottoms
80   Cupped tires
81   Excessive tire wear on outside edge
82   Excessive tire wear on inside edge
83   Tire tread worn in one place
84   Excessive play or looseness in steering system
85   Rattling or clicking noise in steering gear

This section provides an easy reference guide to the more common problems which may occur during the operation of your vehicle. These problems and their possible causes are grouped under headings denoting various components or systems, such as Engine, Cooling system, etc. They also refer you to the chapter and/or section which deals with the problem.

Remember that successful troubleshooting is not a mysterious black art practiced only by professional mechanics. It is simply the result of the right knowledge combined with an intelligent, systematic approach to the problem. Always work by a process of elimination, starting with the simplest solution and working through to the most complex - and never overlook the obvious. Anyone can run the gas tank dry or leave the lights on overnight, so don't assume that you are exempt from such oversights.

Finally, always establish a clear idea of why a problem has occurred and take steps to ensure that it doesn't happen again. If the electrical system fails because of a poor connection, check the other connections in the system to make sure that they don't fail as well. If a particular fuse continues to blow, find out why - don't just replace one fuse after another. Remember, failure of a small component can often be indicative of potential failure or incorrect functioning of a more important component or system.

ENGINE

1   Engine will not rotate when attempting to start

1   Battery terminal connections loose or corroded (Chapter 1).
2   Battery discharged or faulty (Chapters 1 and 5).
3   Automatic transaxle not completely engaged in Park (Chapter 7A) or clutch pedal not completely depressed (Chapter 6).
4   Broken, loose or disconnected wiring in the starting circuit (Chapters 5 and 12).
5   Starter motor pinion jammed in flywheel ring gear (Chapter 5).
6   Starter solenoid faulty (Chapter 5).
7   Starter motor faulty (Chapter 5).
8   Ignition switch faulty (Chapter 12).
9   Starter pinion or flywheel teeth worn or broken (Chapter 5).

2   Engine rotates but will not start

1   Fuel tank empty.
2   Battery discharged (engine rotates slowly) (Chapter 5).
3   Battery terminal connections loose or corroded (Chapter 1).
4   Leaking fuel injector(s), faulty fuel pump, pressure regulator, etc. (Chapter 4).
5   Broken timing belt (Chapter 2A).
6   Ignition components damp or damaged (Chapter 5).
7   Worn, faulty or incorrectly-gapped spark plugs (Chapter 1).
8   Broken, loose or disconnected wiring in the starting circuit (Chapter 5).
9   Broken, loose or disconnected wires at the ignition coil or faulty coil (Chapter 5).
10 Defective crankshaft or camshaft sensor (Chapter 6).

3   Engine hard to start when cold

1   Battery discharged or low (Chapter 1).
2   Malfunctioning fuel system (Chapter 4).
3   Faulty coolant temperature sensor or intake air temperature sensor (Chapter 6).
4   Faulty ignition system (Chapter 5).

4   Engine hard to start when hot

1   Air filter clogged (Chapter 1).
2   Fuel not reaching the fuel injection rail (Chapter 4).

3   Corroded battery connections (Chapter 1).
4   Faulty coolant temperature sensor or intake air temperature sensor (Chapter 6).

5   Starter motor noisy or excessively rough in engagement

1   Pinion or flywheel gear teeth worn or broken (Chapter 5).
2   Starter motor mounting bolts loose or missing (Chapter 5).

6   Engine starts but stops immediately

1   Insufficient fuel reaching the fuel injector(s) (Chapters 1 and 4).
2   Vacuum leak at the gasket between the intake manifold/plenum and throttle body (Chapter 4).

7   Oil puddle under engine

1   Oil pan gasket and/or oil pan drain bolt washer leaking (Chapter 2A).
2   Oil pressure sending unit leaking (Chapter 2A).
3   Valve cover leaking (Chapter 2A).
4   Engine oil seals leaking (Chapter 2A).
5   Timing chain cover leaking (Chapter 2A).

8   Engine lopes while idling or idles erratically

1   Vacuum leakage (Chapters 2A and 4).
2   Leaking EGR valve (Chapter 6).
3   Air filter clogged (Chapter 1).
4   Malfunction in the fuel injection or engine control system (Chapters 4 and 6).
5   Leaking head gasket (Chapter 2A).
6   Timing chain and/or sprockets worn (Chapter 2A).
7   Camshaft lobes worn (Chapter 2A).

9   Engine misses at idle speed

1   Spark plugs worn or not gapped properly (Chapter 1).
2   Faulty coil(s) (Chapter 1).
3   Vacuum leaks (Chapter 1).
4   Uneven or low compression (Chapter 2A).
5   Problem with the fuel injection system (Chapter 4).

10 Engine misses throughout driving speed range

1   Fuel filter clogged and/or impurities in the fuel system (Chapters 1 and 4).
2   Low fuel pressure (Chapter 4).
3   Faulty or incorrectly gapped spark plugs (Chapter 1).
4   Faulty engine management system components (Chapter 6).
5   Low or uneven cylinder compression pressures (Chapter 2A).
6   Weak or faulty ignition system (Chapter 5).
7   Vacuum leak in fuel injection system, intake manifold, air control valve or vacuum hoses (Chapters 4 and 6).

11 Engine stumbles on acceleration

1   Spark plugs fouled (Chapter 1).
2   Problem with fuel injection or engine control system (Chapters 4 and 6).
3   Fuel filter clogged (Chapters 1 and 4).
4   Intake manifold air leak (Chapters 2A and 4).
5   Problem with the emissions control system (Chapter 6).

12 Engine surges while holding accelerator steady

1   Intake air leak (Chapter 4).
2   Fuel pump or fuel pressure regulator faulty (Chapter 4).
3   Problem with the fuel injection system (Chapter 4).
4   Problem with the emissions control system (Chapter 6).

13 Engine stalls

1   Idle speed incorrect (Chapter 1).
2   Fuel filter clogged and/or water and impurities in the fuel system (Chapters 1 and 4).
3   Faulty emissions system components (Chapter 6).
4   Faulty or incorrectly gapped spark plugs (Chapter 1).
5   Vacuum leak in the fuel injection system, intake manifold or vacuum hoses (Chapters 2A and 4).

14 Engine lacks power

1   Obstructed exhaust system (Chapter 4).
2   Faulty or incorrectly gapped spark plugs (Chapter 1).
3   Problem with the fuel injection system (Chapter 4).
4   Dirty air filter (Chapter 1).
5   Brakes binding (Chapter 9).
6   Automatic transaxle fluid level incorrect (Chapter 1).
7   Clutch slipping (Chapter 8).
8   Fuel filter clogged and/or impurities in the fuel system (Chapters 1 and 4).
9   Emission control system not functioning properly (Chapter 6).
10 Low or uneven cylinder compression pressures (Chapter 2A).

15 Engine backfires

1   Emission control system not functioning properly (Chapter 6).
2   Problem with the fuel injection system (Chapter 4).
3   Vacuum leak at fuel injector(s), intake manifold or vacuum hoses (Chapters 2A and 4).
4   Valve sticking (Chapter 2A).

16 Pinging or knocking engine sounds during acceleration or uphill

1   Incorrect grade of fuel.
2   Fuel injection system faulty (Chapter 4).
3   Improper or damaged spark plugs or wires (Chapter 1).
4   Knock sensor defective (Chapter 6).
5   EGR valve not functioning (Chapter 6).
6   Vacuum leak (Chapters 2A and 4).

17 Engine runs with oil pressure light on

1   Low oil level (Chapter 1).
2   Idle rpm below specification (Chapter 1).
3   Short in wiring circuit (Chapter 12).
4   Faulty oil pressure sender (Chapter 2A).
5   Worn engine bearings and/or oil pump (Chapter 2A).

18 Engine continues to run after switching off

1   Defective ignition switch (Chapter 12).
2   Faulty Powertrain Control Module (Chapter 6).
3   Faulty Body Control Module.
4   Leaking fuel injector (Chapter 4).

ENGINE ELECTRICAL SYSTEMS

19 Battery will not hold a charge

1   Drivebelt or tensioner defective (Chapter 1).
2   Battery electrolyte level low (Chapter 1).
3   Battery terminals loose or corroded (Chapter 1).
4   Alternator not charging properly (Chapter 5).
5   Loose, broken or faulty wiring in the charging circuit (Chapter 5).
6   Short in vehicle wiring (Chapter 12).
7   Internally defective battery (Chapters 1 and 5).

20 Alternator light fails to go out

1   Faulty alternator or charging circuit (Chapter 5).
2   Drivebelt or tensioner defective (Chapter 1).

21 Alternator light fails to come on when key is turned on

1   Instrument cluster defective (Chapter 12).
2   Fault in the wiring harness (Chapter 12).

FUEL SYSTEM

22 Excessive fuel consumption

1   Dirty air filter element (Chapter 1).
2   Emissions system not functioning properly (Chapter 6).
3   Fuel injection system not functioning properly (Chapter 4).
4   Low tire pressure or incorrect tire size (Chapter 1).

23 Fuel leakage and/or fuel odor

1 Leaking fuel line (Chapters 1 and 4).
2 Tank overfilled.
3 Evaporative emissions control system problem (Chapters 1 and 6).
4 Problem with the fuel injection system (Chapter 4).

COOLING SYSTEM

24 Overheating

1 Insufficient coolant in system (Chapter 1).
2 Water pump drivebelt defective or out of adjustment (Chapter 1).
3 Radiator core blocked or grille restricted (Chapter 3).
4 Thermostat faulty (Chapter 3).
5 Electric cooling fan inoperative or blades broken (Chapter 3).
6 Expansion tank cap not maintaining proper pressure (Chapter 3).

25 Overcooling

1 Faulty thermostat (Chapter 3).
2 Inaccurate temperature gauge sending unit (Chapter 3).

26 External coolant leakage

1 Deteriorated/damaged hoses; loose clamps (Chapters 1 and 3).
2 Water pump defective (Chapter 3).
3 Leakage from radiator core or coolant expansion tank (Chapter 3).
4 Engine drain or water jacket core plugs leaking (Chapter 2A).

27 Internal coolant leakage

1 Leaking cylinder head gasket (Chapter 2A).
2 Cracked cylinder bore or cylinder head (Chapter 2A).

28 Coolant loss

1 Too much coolant in reservoir (Chapter 1).
2 Coolant boiling away because of overheating (Chapter 3).
3 Internal or external leakage (Chapter 3).
4 Faulty radiator cap (Chapter 3).

29 Poor coolant circulation

1 Inoperative water pump (Chapter 3).
2 Restriction in cooling system (Chapters 1 and 3).
3 Drivebelt or tensioner defective (Chapter 1).
4 Thermostat sticking (Chapter 3).

CLUTCH

30 Pedal travels to floor - no pressure or very little resistance

1 Master or release cylinder faulty (Chapter 8).
2 Hose/pipe burst or leaking (Chapter 8).
3 Connections leaking (Chapter 8).

4 No fluid in reservoir (Chapter 8).
5 If fluid level in reservoir rises as pedal is depressed, master cylinder center valve seal is faulty (Chapter 8).
6 Broken release bearing or fork (Chapter 8).
7 Faulty pressure plate diaphragm spring (Chapter 8).

31 Fluid in area of master cylinder dust cover and on pedal

Piston primary seal failure in master cylinder (Chapter 8).

32 Fluid on release cylinder

Release cylinder plunger seal faulty (Chapter 8).

33 Pedal feels spongy when depressed

Air in system (Chapter 8).

34 Unable to select gears

1 Faulty transaxle (Chapter 7A).
2 Faulty clutch disc or pressure plate (Chapter 8).
3 Faulty release lever or release bearing (Chapter 8).
4 Faulty shift lever assembly or control cables (Chapter 8).

35 Clutch slips (engine speed increases with no increase in vehicle speed)

1 Clutch plate worn (Chapter 8).
2 Clutch plate is oil soaked by leaking rear main seal (Chapters 2A and 8).
3 Clutch plate not seated (Chapter 8).
4 Warped pressure plate or flywheel (Chapter 8).
5 Weak diaphragm springs (Chapter 8).
6 Clutch plate overheated. Allow to cool.

36 Grabbing (chattering) as clutch is engaged

1 Oil on clutch plate lining, burned or glazed facings (Chapter 8).
2 Worn or loose engine or transaxle mounts (Chapter 2A).
3 Worn splines on clutch plate hub (Chapter 8).
4 Warped pressure plate or flywheel (Chapter 8).
5 Burned or smeared resin on flywheel or pressure plate (Chapter 8).

37 Transaxle rattling (clicking)

1 Release lever loose (Chapter 8).
2 Clutch plate damper spring failure (Chapter 8).

38 Noise in clutch area

1 Fork shaft improperly installed (Chapter 8).
2 Faulty bearing (Chapter 8).

39 Clutch pedal stays on floor

1 Clutch master cylinder piston binding in bore (Chapter 8).
2 Broken release bearing or fork (Chapter 8).

40 High pedal effort

1 Piston binding in bore (Chapter 8).
2 Pressure plate faulty (Chapter 8).
3 Incorrect size master or release cylinder (Chapter 8).

MANUAL TRANSAXLE

41 Knocking noise at low speeds

Worn input shaft bearing (Chapter 7A).*

42 Noise most pronounced when turning

Rear differential gear noise (Chapter 10).*

43 Clunk on acceleration or deceleration

1 Loose engine or transaxle mounts (Chapter 2A).
2 Worn differential pinion shaft in case.*
3 Worn side gear shaft counterbore in rear differential case (Chapter 10).*

44 Clicking noise in turns

Worn or damaged outboard CV joint (Chapter 8).

45 Vibration

1 Rough wheel bearing (Chapter 10).
2 Damaged driveshaft (Chapter 8).
3 Out-of-round tires (Chapter 1).
4 Tire out of balance (Chapters 1 and 10).
5 Worn driveshaft joints (Chapter 8).

46 Noisy in neutral with engine running

1 Damaged input gear bearing (Chapter 7A).*
2 Damaged clutch release bearing (Chapter 8).

Although the corrective action necessary to remedy the symptoms described is beyond the scope of this manual, the above information should be helpful in isolating the cause of the condition so that the owner can communicate clearly with a professional mechanic.

47 Noisy in one particular gear

1 Damaged or worn constant mesh gears (Chapter 7A).*
2 Damaged or worn synchronizers (Chapter 7A).*
3 Bent reverse fork (Chapter 7A).*
4 Damaged fourth/fifth speed gear or output gear (Chapter 7A).*
5 Worn or damaged reverse idler gear or idler bushing (Chapter 7A).*

48 Noisy in all gears

1 Insufficient lubricant (Chapter 7A).
2 Damaged or worn bearings (Chapter 7A).*
3 Worn or damaged input gear shaft and/or output gear shaft (Chapter 7A).*

49 Slips out of gear

1 Worn or improperly adjusted linkage (Chapter 7A).
2 Shift linkage does not work freely, binds (Chapter 7A).
3 Input gear bearing retainer broken or loose (Chapter 7A).*
4 Worn or bent shift fork (Chapter 7A).*

50 Leaks lubricant

1 Side gear shaft seals worn (Chapter 7A).
2 Excessive amount of lubricant in transaxle (Chapters 1 and 7A).
3 Loose or broken input gear shaft bearing retainer (Chapter 7A).*
4 Input gear bearing retainer O-ring and/or lip seal damaged (Chapter 7A).*

51 Locked in gear

1 Lock pin or interlock pin missing (Chapter 7A).*

Although the corrective action necessary to remedy the symptoms described is beyond the scope of this manual, the above information should be helpful in isolating the cause of the condition so that the owner can communicate clearly with a professional mechanic.

AUTOMATIC TRANSAXLE

52 Fluid leakage

1 Automatic transmission fluid is a deep red color. Fluid leaks should not be confused with engine oil, which can easily be blown onto the transaxle by air flow.
2 To pinpoint a leak, first remove all built-up dirt and grime from the transaxle housing with degreasing agents and/or steam cleaning. Then drive the vehicle at low speeds so air flow will not blow the leak far from its source. Raise the vehicle and determine where the leak is coming from. Common areas of leakage are:

a) *Transaxle oil lines (Chapter 7A).*
b) *Speed sensor (Chapter 6).*
c) *Driveaxle oil seal (Chapter 7A).*

53 Transmission fluid brown or has a burned smell

Transmission fluid overheated (Chapter 1).

54 General shift mechanism problems

1 Chapter 7B deals with checking and adjusting the shift linkage on automatic transaxles. Common problems which may be attributed to poorly adjusted linkage are:

a) *Engine starting in gears other than Park or Neutral.*
b) *Indicator on shifter pointing to a gear other than the one actually being used.*
c) *Vehicle moves when in Park.*

2 Refer to Chapter 7B for the shift linkage adjustment procedure.

55 Transaxle slips, shifts roughly, is noisy or has no drive in forward or reverse gears

There are many probable causes for the above problems, but the home mechanic should be concerned with only one possibility - fluid level. Before taking the vehicle to a repair shop, check the level and condition of the fluid as described in Chapter 1. Correct the fluid level as necessary or change the fluid and filter if needed. If the problem persists, have a professional diagnose the cause.

DRIVEAXLES

56 Clicking noise in turns

Worn or damaged outboard CV joint (Chapter 8).

57 Shudder or vibration during acceleration

1 Excessive toe-in (Chapter 10).
2 Worn or damaged inboard or outboard CV joints (Chapter 8).
3 Sticking inboard CV joint assembly (Chapter 8).

58 Vibration at highway speeds

1 Out-of-balance front wheels and/or tires (Chapters 1 and 10).
2 Out-of-round front tires (Chapters 1 and 10).
3 Worn CV joint(s) (Chapter 8).

BRAKES

59 Vehicle pulls to one side during braking

1 Incorrect tire pressures (Chapter 1).
2 Front end out of alignment (have the front end aligned).
3 Front, or rear, tire sizes not matched to one another.
4 Restricted brake lines or hoses (Chapter 9).
5 Malfunctioning caliper assembly (Chapter 9).
6 Loose suspension parts (Chapter 10).
7 Excessive wear of pad material or disc on one side (Chapter 9).
8 Contamination (grease or brake fluid) of brake pad material or disc on one side (Chapter 9).

60 Noise (high-pitched squeal or grinding when the brakesare applied)

Brake pads or shoes worn out. Replace pads or shoes with new ones immediately. Also inspect the discs/drums (Chapter 9).

61 Brake roughness or chatter (pedal pulsates)

1 Excessive lateral runout (Chapter 9).
2 Uneven pad wear (Chapter 9).
3 Defective disc (Chapter 9).

62 Excessive brake pedal effort required to stop vehicle

1 Malfunctioning power brake booster (Chapter 9).
2 Partial system failure (Chapter 9).
3 Excessively worn pads (Chapter 9).
4 Piston in caliper stuck or sluggish (Chapter 9).
5 Brake pads contaminated with oil or grease (Chapter 9).
6 Brake disc grooved and/or glazed (Chapter 9).

63 Excessive brake pedal travel

1 Partial brake system failure (Chapter 9).
2 Insufficient fluid in master cylinder (Chapters 1 and 9).
3 Air trapped in system (Chapter 9).

64 Dragging brakes

1 Incorrect adjustment of brake light switch (Chapter 9).
2 Master cylinder pistons not returning correctly (Chapter 9).
3 Caliper piston stuck (Chapter 9).
4 Restricted brakes lines or hoses (Chapter 9).
5 Incorrect parking brake adjustment (Chapter 9).

65 Grabbing or uneven braking action

1 Malfunction of proportioning valve (Chapter 9).
2 Binding brake pedal mechanism (Chapter 9).
3 Contaminated brake linings (Chapter 9).

66 Brake pedal feels spongy when depressed

1 Air in hydraulic lines (Chapter 9).
2 Master cylinder mounting bolts loose (Chapter 9).
3 Master cylinder defective (Chapter 9).

67 Brake pedal travels to the floor with little resistance

1 Little or no fluid in the master cylinder reservoir caused by leaking caliper piston(s) or wheel cylinder(s) (Chapter 9).
2 Loose, damaged or disconnected brake lines (Chapter 9).

68 Parking brake does not hold

Parking brake improperly adjusted (Chapter 9).

SUSPENSION AND STEERING SYSTEMS

69 Vehicle pulls to one side

1 Mismatched or uneven tires (Chapter 10).
2 Broken or sagging springs (Chapter 10).
3 Wheel alignment incorrect. Have the wheels professionally aligned.
4 Front brake dragging (Chapter 9).

70 Abnormal or excessive tire wear

1 Wheel alignment out-of-specification. Have the wheels aligned.
2 Sagging or broken springs (Chapter 10).
3 Tire out-of-balance (Chapter 10).
4 Worn strut damper or shock absorber (Chapter 10).
5 Overloaded vehicle.
6 Tires not rotated regularly.

71 Wheel makes a thumping noise

1 Blister or bump on tire (Chapter 10).
2 Improper strut damper action (Chapter 10).

72 Shimmy, shake or vibration

1 Tire or wheel out-of-balance or out-of-round (Chapter 10).
2 Loose or worn wheel bearings (Chapter 10).
3 Worn tie-rod ends (Chapter 10).
4 Worn balljoints (Chapters 1 and 10).
5 Excessive wheel runout (Chapter 10).
6 Blister or bump on tire (Chapter 10).

73 Hard steering

1 Defective power steering pump (Chapter 10).
2 Worn balljoints and/or tie-rod ends (Chapter 10).
3 Wheel alignment out-of-specifications. Have the wheels professionally aligned.
4 Low tire pressure(s) (Chapter 1).
5 Worn steering gear (Chapter 10).

74 Poor returnability of steering to center

1 Worn balljoints or tie-rod ends (Chapter 10).
2 Worn steering gear assembly (Chapter 10).
3 Wheel alignment out-of-specifications. Have the wheels professionally aligned.

75 Abnormal noise at the front end

1 Worn balljoints or tie-rod ends (Chapter 10).
2 Damaged shock absorber mounting (Chapter 10).
3 Worn control arm bushings or tie-rod ends (Chapter 10).
4 Loose stabilizer bar (Chapter 10).
5 Loose wheel nuts (Chapter 1).
6 Loose suspension bolts (Chapter 10).

76 Wander or poor steering stability

1 Mismatched or uneven tires (Chapter 10).
2 Worn balljoints or tie-rod ends (Chapters 1 and 10).
3 Worn struts or shock absorbers (Chapter 10).
4 Broken or sagging springs (Chapter 10).
5 Wheels out of alignment. Have the wheels professionally aligned.

77 Erratic steering when braking

1 Wheel bearings worn (Chapter 10).
2 Broken or sagging springs (Chapter 10).

3 Leaking wheel cylinder or caliper (Chapter 10).
4 Excessive brake disc runout (Chapter 9).

78 Excessive pitching and/or rolling around corners or during braking

1 Loose stabilizer bar or worn stabilizer bar bushings (Chapter 10).
2 Worn strut dampers or mountings (Chapter 10).
3 Broken or sagging springs (Chapter 10).
4 Overloaded vehicle.

79 Suspension bottoms

1 Overloaded vehicle.
2 Sagging springs (Chapter 10).

80 Cupped tires

1 Wheel alignment out-of-specifications. Have the wheels professionally aligned.
2 Worn shock absorbers (Chapter 10).
3 Wheel bearings worn (Chapter 10).
4 Excessive tire or wheel runout (Chapter 10).
5 Worn balljoints (Chapter 10).

81 Excessive tire wear on outside edge

1 Inflation pressures incorrect (Chapter 1).
2 Excessive speed in turns.
3 Wheel alignment incorrect (excessive toe-in). Have professionally aligned.
4 Suspension arm bent or twisted (Chapter 10).

82 Excessive tire wear on inside edge

1 Inflation pressures incorrect (Chapter 1).
2 Wheel alignment incorrect (toe-out). Have professionally aligned.
3 Loose or damaged steering components (Chapter 10).

83 Tire tread worn in one place

1 Tires out-of-balance.
2 Damaged or buckled wheel. Inspect and replace if necessary.
3 Defective tire (Chapter 1).

84 Excessive play or looseness in steering system

1 Wheel bearing(s) worn (Chapter 10).
2 Tie-rod end loose (Chapter 10).
3 Steering gear loose (Chapter 10).
4 Worn or loose steering intermediate shaft U-joint (Chapter 10).

85 Rattling or clicking noise in steering gear

1 Steering gear loose (Chapter 10).
2 Steering gear defective (Chapter 10).

TUNE-UP AND ROUTINE MAINTENANCE

Section

1 Maintenance schedule

The maintenance intervals in this manual are provided with the assumption that you, not the dealer, will be doing the work. These are the minimum maintenance intervals recommended by the factory for vehicles that are driven daily. If you wish to keep your vehicle in peak condition at all times, you may wish to perform some of these procedures even more often. Because frequent maintenance enhances the efficiency, performance and resale value of your car, we encourage you to do so. If you drive in dusty areas, tow a trailer, idle or drive at low speeds for extended periods or drive for short distances (less than four miles) in below freezing temperatures, shorter intervals are also recommended.

When your vehicle is new, it should be serviced by a factory authorized dealer service department to protect the factory warranty. In many cases, the initial maintenance check is done at no cost to the owner.

EVERY 250 MILES (400 KM) OR WEEKLY, WHICHEVER COMES FIRST

Check the engine oil level (Section 4)
Check the engine coolant level (Section 4)
Check the brake and clutch fluid level (Section 4)
Check the windshield washer fluid level (Section 4)
Check the power steering fluid level (Section 4)
Check the tires and tire pressures (Section 5)

EVERY 3000 MILES (4800 KM) OR 3 MONTHS, WHICHEVER COMES FIRST

All items listed above plus:
Change the engine oil and oil filter (Section 6)

EVERY 6000 MILES (10,000 KM) OR 6 MONTHS, WHICHEVER COMES FIRST

All items listed above plus:
Inspect (and replace, if necessary) the windshield wiper blades (Section 7)
Check and service the battery (Section 8)
Check the cooling system (Section 9)
Rotate the tires (Section 10)
Check the seat belts (Section 11)
Inspect the brake system (Section 12)

EVERY 15,000 MILES (24,000 KM) OR 12 MONTHS, WHICHEVER COMES FIRST

All items listed above plus:
Replace the interior ventilation filter (2007 and later models only) (Section 13)

Check all underhood hoses (Section 14)
Inspect the suspension, steering components and driveaxle boots (Section 15)
Check the exhaust system (Section 16)
Check the fuel system (Section 17)
Check the engine drivebelts (Section 18)

EVERY 30,000 MILES (48,000 KM) OR 24 MONTHS, WHICHEVER COMES FIRST

All items listed above plus:
Check (and replace, if necessary) the air filter (Section 19)*
Service the cooling system (drain, flush and refill) (Section 20)
Change the brake fluid (Section 21)

EVERY 60,000 MILES (96,000 KM)

Replace the timing belt (2008 and earlier models) (Chapter 2A)

EVERY 90,000 MILES (145,000 KM)

Fuel filter replacement (Section 23).

EVERY 100,000 MILES (166,000 KM)

Replace the timing belt (2009 and later models) (Chapter 2A)
Replace the automatic transaxle fluid (Section 22)**
Replace the manual transaxle lubricant (Section 24)
Replace the spark plugs (Section 25)

This item is affected by "severe" operating conditions as described below. If your vehicle is operated under "severe" conditions, perform all maintenance indicated with an asterisk (*) at 3000 mile/3 month intervals. Severe conditions are indicated if you mainly operate your vehicle under one or more of the following conditions:
    a) Operating in dusty areas
    b) Idling for extended periods and/or low speed operation

** *If operated under one or more of the following conditions, change the manual or automatic transaxle fluid lubricant every 50,000 miles:*
    a) In heavy city traffic where the outside temperature regularly reaches 90-degrees F (32-degrees C) or higher
    b) In hilly or mountainous terrain

Engine compartment layout -1.6L (L91) engine shown, others similar

1	Engine oil dipstick	5	Brake fluid reservoir	8	Windshield washer fluid reservoir
2	Engine oil filler cap	6	Engine coolant expansion tank	9	Battery
3	Air filter housing	7	Underhood fuse/relay block	10	Power steering fluid reservoir
4	PCV hose				

Under vehicle engine compartment layout - L91 engine shown, others similar

1	Driveaxle inner boot	4	Brake disc	6	Engine oil pan drain plug
2	Strut and coil spring assembly	5	Front brake caliper and brake pads	7	Engine oil filter
3	Driveaxle outer boot				

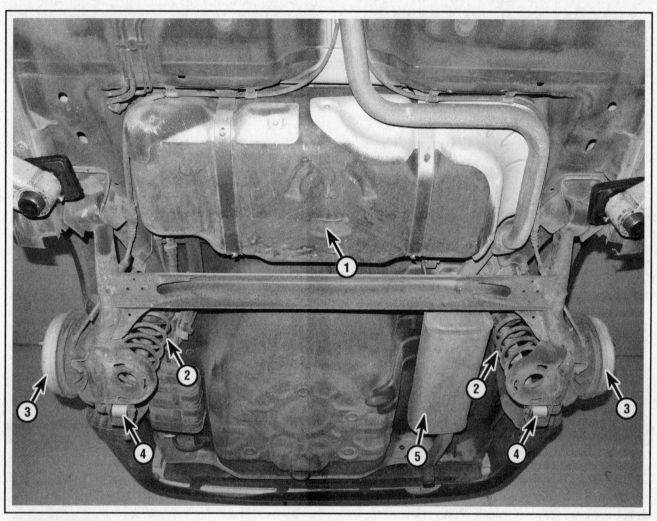

Typical rear underside components

1	Fuel tank	3	Brake drum	5	Muffler
2	Coil spring	4	Shock absorber		

2 Introduction

1   This Chapter is designed to help the home mechanic maintain the Chevrolet Aveo with the goals of maximum performance, economy, safety and reliability in mind.

2   Included is a master maintenance schedule, followed by procedures dealing specifically with each item on the schedule. Visual checks, adjustments, component replacement and other helpful items are included. Refer to the accompanying illustrations of the engine compartment and under the vehicle, for the locations of various components.

3   Servicing the vehicle, in accordance with the mileage/time maintenance schedule and the step-by-step procedures will result in a planned maintenance program that should produce a long and reliable service life. Keep in mind that it is a comprehensive plan, so maintaining some items but not others at the specified intervals will not produce the same results.

4   As you service the vehicle, you will discover that many of the procedures can - and should - be grouped together because of the nature of the particular procedure you're performing or because of the close proximity of two otherwise unrelated components to one another.

5   For example, if the vehicle is raised for chassis lubrication, you should inspect the exhaust, suspension, steering and fuel systems while you're under the vehicle. When you're rotating the tires, it makes good sense to check the brakes since the wheels are already removed. Finally, let's suppose you have to borrow or rent a torque wrench. Even if you only need it to tighten the spark plugs, you might as well check the torque of as many critical fasteners as time allows.

6   The first step in this maintenance program is to prepare yourself before the actual work begins. Read through all the procedures you're planning to do, then gather up all the parts and tools needed. If it looks like you might run into problems during a particular job, seek advice from a mechanic or an experienced do-it-yourselfer.

OWNER'S MANUAL AND VECI LABEL INFORMATION

7   Your vehicle owner's manual was written for your year and model and contains very specific information on component locations, specifications, fuse ratings, part numbers, etc. The Owner's Manual is an important resource for the do-it-yourselfer to have; if one was not supplied with your vehicle, it can generally be ordered from a dealer parts department.

8   Among other important information, the Vehicle Emissions Control Information (VECI) label contains specifications and procedures for applicable tune-up adjustments and, in some instances, spark plugs (see Chapter 6 for more information on the VECI label). The information on this label is the exact maintenance data recommended by the manufacturer. This data often varies by intended operating altitude, local emissions regulations, month of manufacture, etc.

9   This Chapter contains procedural details, safety information and more ambitious maintenance intervals than you might find in manufacturer's literature. However, you may also find procedures or specifications in your Owner's Manual or VECI label that differ with what's printed here. In these cases, the Owner's Manual or VECI label can be considered correct, since it is specific to your particular vehicle.

3 Tune-up general information

1   The term tune-up is used in this manual to represent a combination of individual operations rather than one specific procedure.

2   If, from the time the vehicle is new, the routine maintenance schedule is followed closely and frequent checks are made of fluid levels and high wear items, as suggested throughout this manual, the engine will be kept in relatively good running condition and the need for additional work will be minimized.

3   More likely than not, however, there will be times when the engine is running poorly due to lack of regular maintenance. This is even more likely if a used vehicle, which has not received regular and frequent maintenance checks, is purchased. In such cases, an engine tune-up will be needed outside of the regular routine maintenance intervals.

4   The first step in any tune-up or diagnostic procedure to help correct a poor running engine is a cylinder compression check. A compression check (see Chapter 2B) will help determine the condition of internal engine components and should be used as a guide for tune-up and repair procedures. If, for instance, a compression check indicates serious internal engine wear, a conventional tune-up will not improve the performance of the engine and would be a waste of time and money. Because of its importance, the compression check should be done by someone with the right equipment and the knowledge to use it properly.

5   The following procedures are those most often needed to bring a generally poor running engine back into a proper state of tune.

MINOR TUNE-UP

Check all engine related fluids (Section 4).
Clean, inspect and test the battery (Section 8).
Check the cooling system (Section 9).
Check all underhood hoses (Section 14).
Check the fuel system (Section 17).
Check the drivebelt (Section 18).
Check the air filter (Section 19).

MAJOR TUNE-UP

All items listed under Minor tune-up, plus. . .
Replace the air filter (Section 19).
Replace the fuel filter (Section 23).
Replace the spark plugs (Section 25).

4 Fluid level checks (every 250 miles [400 km] or weekly)

1 Fluids are an essential part of the lubrication, cooling, brake and windshield washer systems. Because the fluids gradually become depleted and/or contaminated during normal operation of the vehicle, they must be periodically replenished. See *Recommended lubricants and fluids* in this Chapter's Specifications before adding fluid to any of the following components.

➡ Note: The vehicle must be on level ground when fluid levels are checked.

ENGINE OIL

2 The oil level is checked with a dipstick, which extends down into the oil pan (see illustration).

3 The oil level should be checked before the vehicle has been driven, or about 5 minutes after the engine has been shut off. If the oil is checked immediately after driving the vehicle, some of the oil will remain in the upper part of the engine, resulting in an inaccurate reading on the dipstick.

4 Pull the dipstick out and wipe all the oil from the end with a clean rag or paper towel. Insert the clean dipstick all the way back in and pull it out again. Note the oil at the end of the dipstick. At its highest point, the level should be between the MIN and MAX marks on the dipstick (see illustration).

5 It takes about one quart of oil to raise the level from the MIN mark to the MAX mark on the dipstick. Do not allow the level to drop below the MIN mark or oil starvation may cause engine damage. Conversely, overfilling the engine (adding oil above the MAX mark) may cause oil fouled spark plugs, oil leaks or oil seal failures. Maintaining the oil level above the MAX mark can cause excessive oil consumption.

6 To add oil, remove the filler cap from the valve cover (see illustration). After adding oil, wait a few minutes to allow the level to stabilize, then pull out the dipstick and check the level again. Add more oil if required. Install the filler cap and tighten it by hand only.

7 Checking the oil level is an important preventive maintenance step. A consistently low oil level indicates oil leakage through damaged seals, defective gaskets or past worn rings or valve guides. If the oil looks milky in color or has water droplets in it, the cylinder head gasket(s) may be blown or the head(s) or block may be cracked. The engine should be checked immediately. The condition of the oil should also be checked. Whenever you check the oil level, slide your thumb and index finger up the dipstick before wiping off the oil. If you see small dirt or metal particles clinging to the dipstick, the oil should be changed (see Section 6).

ENGINE COOLANT

⁂ WARNING:

Do not allow antifreeze to come in contact with your skin or painted surfaces of the vehicle. Flush contaminated areas immediately with plenty of water. Don't store new coolant or leave old coolant lying around where it's accessible to children or pets - they're attracted by its sweet smell. Ingestion of even a small amount of coolant can be fatal! Wipe up garage floor and drip pan spills immediately. Keep antifreeze containers covered and repair cooling system leaks as soon as they're noticed.

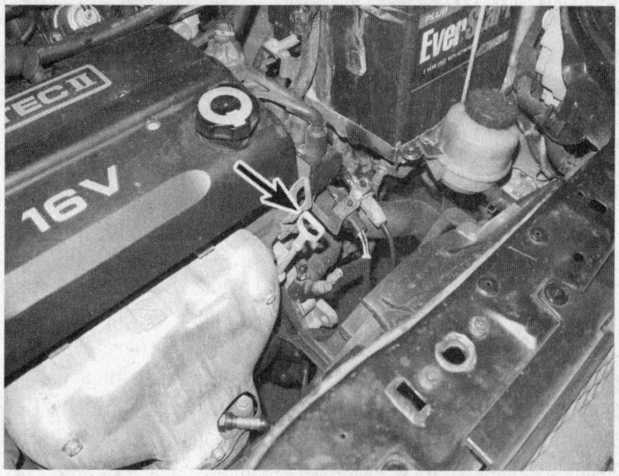

4.2 The engine oil dipstick is located on the forward side of the engine

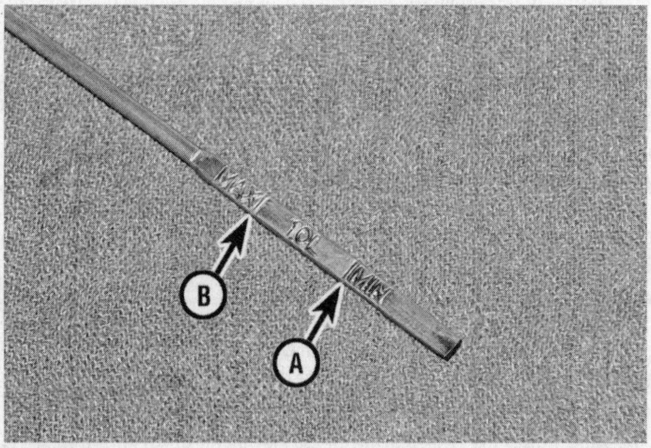

4.4 The oil level should be in the safe range - if it's below the MIN or ADD area (A), add enough oil to bring it up to or near the MAX or FULL area (B)

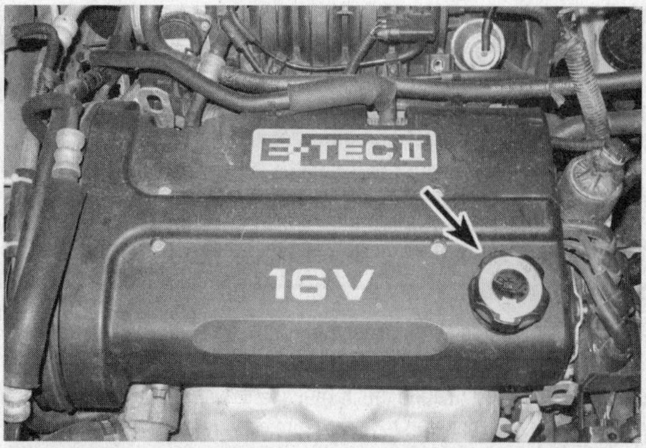

4.6 The oil filler cap is located on the valve cover - always make sure the area around the opening is clean before unscrewing the cap to prevent dirt from contaminating the engine

4.8 The coolant expansion tank is located at the rear of the engine compartment

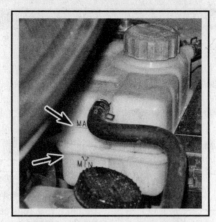

4.9 When the engine is cold, the engine coolant level should be below the MAX line and above the MIN line

4.14 The brake fluid level should be kept between the MIN and MAX marks on the translucent plastic reservoir; with manual transaxles, the brake fluid reservoir is connected to the clutch master cylinder by a hose

⁕⁕ WARNING:

Do not remove the expansion tank cap when the engine is warm!

8   All models covered by this manual are equipped with a pressurized coolant recovery system. The coolant expansion tank is located at the left rear of the engine compartment and is connected by hoses to the cooling system (see illustration). As the engine heats up during operation, the level in the tank rises.

9   The coolant level should be checked regularly. It must be between the MAX and MIN lines on the tank when the engine is cold (see illustration). If it isn't, allow the fluid in the tank to cool, then remove the expansion tank cap and add coolant to bring the level up to the line. Use only the type of coolant listed in this Chapter's Specifications. Do not use supplemental inhibitors or additives. If only a small amount of coolant is required to bring the system up to the proper level, water can be used. However, repeated additions of water will dilute the recommended antifreeze and water solution. In order to maintain the proper ratio of antifreeze and water, it is advisable to top up the coolant level with the correct mixture.

⁕⁕ WARNING:

Never remove the pressure cap when the engine is running or has just been shut down, because the cooling system is hot. Escaping steam and scalding liquid could cause serious injury. If it is necessary to open the pressure cap, wait until the system has cooled completely, then wrap a thick cloth around the cap and slowly unscrew it. If you hear hissing or any steam escapes, wait until the system has cooled further, then remove the cap.

10 If the coolant level drops within a short time after replenishment, there may be a leak in the system. Inspect the radiator, hoses, engine expansion tank pressure cap, drain plugs, and water pump. If no leak is evident, have the expansion tank pressure cap pressure tested.

11 When checking the coolant level, always note its condition. It should be relatively clear. If it is brown or rust colored, the system should be drained, flushed and refilled. Even if the coolant appears to be normal, the corrosion inhibitors wear out with use, so it must be

replaced at the specified intervals.

12 Do not allow antifreeze to come in contact with your skin or painted surfaces of the vehicle. Flush contacted areas immediately with plenty of water.

BRAKE AND CLUTCH FLUID

13 The brake master cylinder is mounted on the front of the power booster unit in the engine compartment. The hydraulic clutch master cylinder used on manual transaxle models is located to the left and below the coolant expansion tank.

14 The brake master cylinder and the clutch master cylinder share a common reservoir. To check the fluid level of either system, simply look at the MAX and MIN marks on the brake fluid reservoir (see illustration).

15 If the level is low, wipe the top of the reservoir cover with a clean rag to prevent contamination of the brake system before lifting the cover.

16 Add only the specified brake fluid to the reservoir (refer to *Recommended lubricants and fluids* in this Chapter's Specifications or to your owner's manual). Mixing different types of brake fluid can damage the system. Fill the brake master cylinder reservoir only to the MAX line.

⁕⁕ WARNING:

Be careful when filling the reservoir - brake fluid can harm your eyes and damage painted surfaces. Do not use brake fluid that is more than one year old or has been left open. Brake fluid absorbs moisture from the air. Excess moisture can cause a dangerous loss of braking.

17 While the reservoir cap is removed, inspect the master cylinder reservoir for contamination. If deposits, dirt particles or water droplets are present, the system should be drained and refilled.

18 After filling the reservoir to the proper level, make sure the cap is properly seated to prevent fluid leakage.

19 The fluid in the brake master cylinder will drop slightly as the brake pads at each wheel wear down during normal operation. If the master cylinder requires repeated replenishing to keep it at the proper

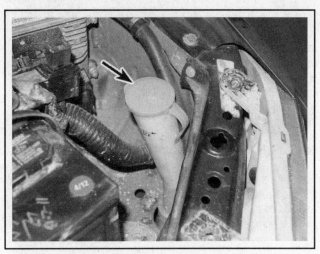

4.21 The windshield washer fluid reservoir is located in the left front corner of the engine compartment

4.27 On a translucent reservoir, the power steering fluid level can be checked through the translucent section of the reservoir

level, this is an indication of leakage in the brake or clutch system, which should be corrected immediately. If the brake system shows an indication of leakage check all brake lines and connections, along with the calipers, wheel cylinders and booster (see Section 12 for more information). If the hydraulic clutch system shows an indication of leakage, check all clutch lines and connections, along with the clutch release cylinder (see Chapter 8 for more information).

20 If, upon checking the brake or clutch master cylinder fluid level, you discover the reservoir empty or nearly empty, the systems should be checked, repaired and bled (see Chapters 8 and 9).

WINDSHIELD WASHER FLUID

21 Fluid for the windshield washer system is stored in a plastic reservoir located at the left side of the engine compartment (see illustration).

22 In milder climates, plain water can be used in the reservoir, but it should be kept no more than 2/3 full to allow for expansion if the water freezes. In colder climates, use windshield washer system antifreeze, available at any auto parts store, to lower the freezing point of the fluid. Mix the antifreeze with water in accordance with the manufacturer's directions on the container.

❄ **CAUTION:**

Do not use cooling system antifreeze - it will damage the vehicle's paint.

POWER STEERING FLUID LEVEL CHECK (EVERY 3000 MILES OR 3 MONTHS)

23 The power steering system relies on fluid which may, over a period of time, require replenishing.

24 All models have a remote power steering fluid reservoir mounted to a bracket on the left (driver's) front corner of the engine compartment. There are two types of reservoirs; a translucent reservoir allows the

fluid to be checked without removing the cap and reservoir that has a dipstick attached to the cap. For the check, the front wheels should be pointed straight ahead and the engine should be off.

25 Use a clean rag to wipe off the reservoir and the area around the cap. This will help prevent any foreign matter from entering the reservoir during the check.

26 Feel the reservoir to check the temperature of the fluid.

27 On translucent type reservoirs, check the level of the fluid on the side of the reservoir (see illustration).

28 On reservoirs with dipsticks, twist off the cap and check the temperature of the fluid at the end of the dipstick with your finger. Wipe off the fluid with a clean rag, reinsert it, then withdraw it and read the fluid level.

29 On both types, the level should be at the HOT or MAX mark if the reservoir was hot to the touch. If the reservoir felt cool, the level should be at the COLD mark (but not below the MIN level).

30 The fluid should be at the proper level, depending on whether it was checked hot or cold. Never allow the fluid level to drop below the MIN mark on the reservoir.

31 If additional fluid is required, pour the specified type directly into the reservoir, using a funnel to prevent spills.

32 If the reservoir requires frequent fluid additions, all power steering hoses, hose connections, steering gear and the power steering pump should be carefully checked for leaks.

AUTOMATIC TRANSAXLE FLUID

33 The level of the automatic transaxle fluid should be carefully maintained. Low fluid level can lead to slipping or loss of drive, while overfilling can cause foaming, loss of fluid and transmission damage.

❄ **CAUTION:**

If the vehicle has just been driven for a long time at high speed or in city traffic in hot weather, an accurate fluid level reading cannot be obtained. Allow the fluid to cool down for about 30 minutes.

34 The fluid level should only be checked when the transaxle is hot (at its normal operating temperature). If the vehicle has just been driven over 10 miles (15 miles in a frigid climate), and the fluid temperature is 160 to 175-degrees F, the transaxle is hot.

35 If the vehicle has not just been driven, park the vehicle on level ground, set the parking brake and start the engine.

36 While the engine is idling, depress the brake pedal and move the selector lever through all the gear ranges, beginning and ending in Park.

37 With the engine still idling, remove the dipstick from the case. Check the level of the fluid on the dipstick and note its condition.

➡ **Note: The automatic transaxel fluid dipstick is located in the front of the engine compartment near the battery and power steering fluid reservoir.**

38 Wipe the fluid from the dipstick with a clean rag and reinsert it back into the case until the cap seats.

39 Pull the dipstick out again and note the fluid level. If the transaxle is cold, the level should be between marks 3 cold maximumand 4 cold minimum on the dipstick. If it is hot, the fluid level should be in the HOT range,mark 1 is hot maximum and mark 2 is hot minimum. If the level is at the low side of either range, add the specified automatic transmission fluid through the dipstick tube with a funnel.

40 Add just enough of the recommended fluid to fill the transaxle to the proper level. It takes about one pint to raise the level from the low mark to the high mark when the fluid is hot, so add the fluid a little at a time and keep checking the level until it is correct.

41 The condition of the fluid should also be checked along with the level. If the fluid at the end of the dipstick is black or a dark reddish brown color, or if it emits a burned smell, the fluid should be changed (see Section 22). If you are in doubt about the condition of the fluid, purchase some new fluid and compare the two for color and smell.

5   Tire and tire pressure checks (every 250 miles [400 km] or weekly)

1   Periodic inspection of the tires may spare you the inconvenience of being stranded with a flat tire. It can also provide you with vital information regarding possible problems in the steering and suspension systems before major damage occurs.

2   The original tires on this vehicle are equipped with 1/2-inch wide bands that will appear when tread depth reaches 1/16-inch, at which point they can be considered worn out. Tread wear can be monitored with a simple, inexpensive device known as a tread depth indicator (see illustration).

3   Note any abnormal tread wear (see illustration). Tread pattern irregularities such as cupping, flat spots and more wear on one side than the other are indications of front end alignment and/or balance problems. If any of these conditions are noted, take the vehicle to a tire

shop or service station to correct the problem.

4   Look closely for cuts, punctures and embedded nails or tacks. Sometimes a tire will hold air pressure for a short time or leak down very slowly after a nail has embedded itself in the tread. If a slow leak persists, check the valve stem core to make sure it is tight (see illustration). Examine the tread for an object that may have embedded itself in the tire or for a "plug" that may have begun to leak (radial tire punctures are repaired with a plug that is installed in a puncture). If a puncture is suspected, it can be easily verified by spraying a solution of soapy water onto the puncture area (see illustration). The soapy solution will bubble if there is a leak. Unless the puncture is unusually large, a tire shop or service station can usually repair the tire.

5   Carefully inspect the inner sidewall of each tire for evidence of brake fluid leakage. If you see any, inspect the brakes immediately.

6   Correct air pressure adds miles to the life span of the tires, improves mileage and enhances overall ride quality. Tire pressure cannot be accurately estimated by looking at a tire, especially if it's a radial. A tire pressure gauge is essential. Keep an accurate gauge in the glove compartment. The pressure gauges attached to the nozzles of air hoses at gas stations are often inaccurate.

7   Always check tire pressure when the tires are cold. Cold, in this case, means the vehicle has not been driven over a mile in the three hours preceding a tire pressure check. A pressure rise of four to eight pounds is not uncommon once the tires are warm.

8   Unscrew the valve cap protruding from the wheel or hubcap and push the gauge firmly onto the valve stem (see illustration). Note the reading on the gauge and compare the figure to the recommended tire pressure shown on the tire placard on the driver's side door. Reinstall the valve cap to keep dirt and moisture out of the valve stem mechanism. Check all four tires and, if necessary, add enough air to bring them up to the recommended pressure.

9   Don't forget to keep the spare tire inflated to the specified pressure (refer to the pressure molded into the tire sidewall).

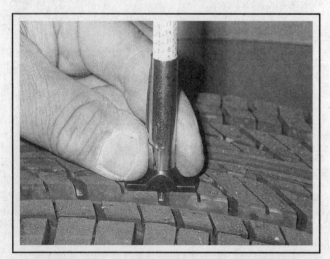

5.2 A tire tread depth indicator should be used to monitor tire wear - they are available at auto parts stores and service stations and cost very little

UNDERINFLATION

CUPPING

OVERINFLATION

Cupping may be caused by:

• Underinflation and/or mechanical irregularities such as out-of-balance condition of wheel and/or tire, and bent or damaged wheel.

• Loose or worn steering tie-rod or steering idler arm.

• Loose, damaged or worn front suspension parts.

INCORRECT TOE-IN OR EXTREME CAMBER

FEATHERING DUE TO MISALIGNMENT

5.3 This chart will help you determine the condition of your tires, the probable cause(s) of abnormal wear and the corrective action necessary

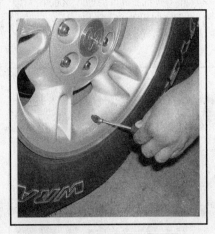

5.4a If a tire loses air on a steady basis, check the valve core first to make sure it's snug (special inexpensive wrenches are commonly available at auto parts stores)

5.4b If the valve core is tight, raise the corner of the vehicle with the low tire and spray a soapy water solution onto the tread as the tire is turned slowly - slow leaks will cause small bubbles to appear

5.8 To extend the life of your tires, check the air pressure at least once a week with an accurate gauge (don't forget the spare!)

6 Engine oil and filter change (every 3000 miles [5000 km] or 3 months)

➡ Note: 2009 and later models are equipped with an oil life indicator system that illuminates a light or message on the instrument panel when the system deems it necessary to change the oil. A number of factors are taken into consideration to determine when the oil should be considered worn out. Generally, this system will allow the vehicle to accumulate more miles between oil changes than the traditional 3000 mile interval, but we believe that frequent oil changes are cheap insurance and will prolong engine life. If you do decide not to change your oil every 3000 miles and rely on the oil life indicator instead, make sure you don't exceed 7,500 miles before the oil is changed, regardless of what the oil life indicator shows.

1 Frequent oil changes are the most important preventive maintenance procedures that can be done by the home mechanic. As engine oil ages, it becomes diluted and contaminated, which leads to premature engine wear.

2 Make sure that you have all the necessary tools before you begin this procedure. You should also have plenty of rags or newspapers handy for mopping up oil spills.

3 Access to the oil drain plug and filter will be improved if the vehicle can be lifted on a hoist, driven onto ramps or supported by jackstands.

✳ WARNING:

Do not work under a vehicle supported only by a jack - always use jackstands!

4 If you haven't changed the oil on this vehicle before, get under it and locate the oil drain plug and the oil filter. The exhaust components will be warm as you work, so note how they are routed to avoid touching them when you are under the vehicle.

5 Start the engine and allow it to reach normal operating temperature - oil and sludge will flow out more easily when warm. If new oil, a filter or tools are needed, use the vehicle to go get them and warm up the engine/oil at the same time. Park on a level surface and shut off the engine when it's warmed up. Remove the oil filler cap from the valve cover.

6 Raise the vehicle and support it securely on jackstands.

7 Being careful not to touch the hot exhaust components, position a drain pan under the plug in the bottom of the engine, then remove the plug (see illustration). It's a good idea to wear a rubber glove while unscrewing the plug the final few turns to avoid being scalded by hot oil.

➡ Note: 2009 and later (LXV) models use a Torx type drain plug.

8 It may be necessary to move the drain pan slightly as oil flow slows to a trickle. Inspect the old oil for the presence of metal particles.

9 After all the oil has drained, wipe off the drain plug with a clean rag. Any small metal particles clinging to the plug would immediately contaminate the new oil.

10 Clean the area around the drain plug opening, reinstall the plug and tighten it to the torque listed in this Chapter's Specifications.

11 Move the drain pan into position under the oil filter.

2008 AND EARLIER MODELS (L91 AND LXT ENGINES)

✳ WARNING:

The engine exhaust manifold may still be hot, so be careful.

12 The oil filter is visible from underneath the engine (see illustration). Loosen the oil filter by turning it counterclockwise with an oil filter wrench. On most engines you will have to use the type of wrench that slips over the bottom of the filter and is turned with a ratchet. Just as the filter is detached from the block, immediately tilt the open end up to prevent the oil inside the filter from spilling out. Make sure that the old filter gasket does not remain stuck to the block.

13 With a clean rag, wipe off the mounting surface on the block. If a residue of old oil is allowed to remain, it will smoke when the block is heated up. It will also prevent the new filter from seating properly. Also make sure that none of the old gasket remains stuck to the mounting surface. It can be removed with a scraper if necessary.

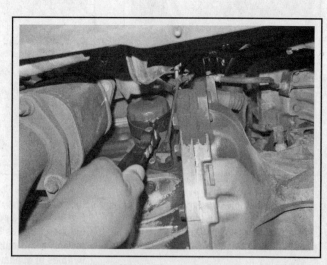

6.7 On 2008 and earlier models (L91 and LXT engines), use a proper size box-end wrench or socket to remove the oil drain plug and avoid rounding it off

6.12 Typical oil filter location

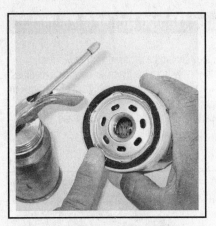

6.14 Lubricate the oil filter gasket with clean engine oil before installing the filter on the engine

6.15 Unscrew the cap. . .

6.16a. . . remove the filter cartridge. . .

14 Compare the old filter with the new one to make sure they are the same type. Smear some engine oil on the rubber gasket of the new filter and screw it into place (see illustration). Overtightening the filter will damage the gasket, so don't use a filter wrench. Most filter manufacturers recommend tightening the filter by hand only. Normally they should be tightened 3/4-turn after the gasket contacts the block, but be sure to follow the directions on the filter or container. Once the filter is installed, lower the vehicle and proceed to Step 20.

2009 AND LATER MODELS (LXV ENGINES)

15 The canister-type oil filter is located at the left end of the engine. Unscrew the filter cap with a wrench (see illustration).

16 Unscrew the oil filter cap (using a large socket, not an open-end wrench) and withdraw it, together with the element (see illustrations).

17 Use a clean rag to remove all oil, dirt and sludge from the oil filter housing and cap.

18 Install a new O-ring seal in the groove on the retaining cap, then install the new element in the cap and insert them both in the filter housing. Screw on the cap and tighten it to the torque listed in this Chapter's Specifications.

19 Remove all tools and materials from under the vehicle, being careful not to spill the oil in the drain pan, then lower the vehicle.

ALL MODELS

20 Add new oil to the engine through the oil filler cap. Use a funnel to prevent oil from spilling onto the top of the engine. Pour four quarts of fresh oil into the engine, wait a few minutes to allow the oil to drain into the pan, then check the level on the dipstick (see Section 4 if necessary). If the oil level is in the OK range, install the filler cap.

21 Start the engine and run it for about a minute. Check for leaks at the oil pan drain plug and around the oil filter.

22 Wait a few minutes, then recheck the level on the dipstick. Add oil as necessary to bring the level into the OK range.

23 During the first few trips after an oil change, make it a point to check frequently for leaks and proper oil level.

24 The old oil drained from the engine cannot be reused in its

6.16b. . . then separate the element from the cap - typical filter cartridge shown

present state and should be disposed of. Check with your local auto parts store, disposal facility or environmental agency to see if they will accept the oil for recycling. After the oil has cooled it can be drained into a container (capped plastic jugs, topped bottles, milk cartons, etc.) for transport to one of these disposal sites. Don't dispose of the oil by pouring it on the ground or down a drain!

ENGINE OIL LIFE SYSTEM RESET

25 Reset the "Change Engine Oil" light by turning the ignition key to the RUN position, with the engine off.

26 Depress the accelerator pedal to the floor and release the pedal three times within five seconds.

27 Turn the key to the OFF/LOCK position.

➡ **Note: If the "CHANGE OIL" light appears, the system was not reset and the procedure must be repeated.**

7 Windshield wiper blade inspection and replacement (every 6000 miles [10,000 km] or 6 months)

1   The windshield wiper and blade assembly should be inspected periodically for damage, loose components and cracked or worn blade elements.

2   Road film can build up on the wiper blades and affect their efficiency, so they should be washed regularly with a mild detergent solution.

3   If the wiper blade elements are cracked, worn or warped, or no longer clean adequately, they should be replaced with new ones.

4   Lift the arm assembly away from the glass for clearance, depress the release lever, then slide the wiper blade assembly out of the hook in the end of the arm (see illustrations).

5   Attach the new wiper to the arm and push it into place. Connection can be confirmed by an audible click.

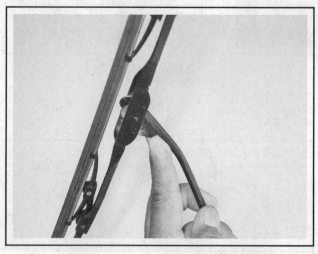

7.4a To release the blade holder, depress the release tab. . .

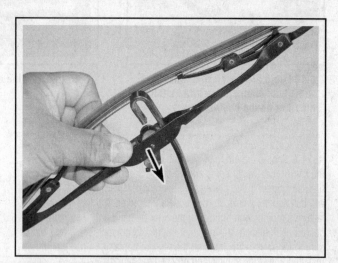

7.4b. . . and pull the wiper blade in the direction of the windshield to separate it from the arm

8 Battery check, maintenance and charging (every 6000 miles [10,000 km] or 6 months)

✳✳ WARNING:

Certain precautions must be followed when checking and servicing the battery. Hydrogen gas, which is highly flammable, is always present in the battery cells, so keep lighted tobacco and all other open flames and sparks away from the battery. The electrolyte inside the battery is actually dilute sulfuric acid, which will cause injury if splashed on your skin or in your eyes. It will also ruin clothes and painted surfaces. When removing the battery cables, always detach the negative cable first and hook it up last!

CHECK AND MAINTENANCE

1   A routine preventive maintenance program for the battery in your vehicle is the only way to ensure quick and reliable starts. But before performing any battery maintenance, make sure that you have the proper equipment necessary to work safely around the battery (see illustration).

2   There are also several precautions that should be taken whenever battery maintenance is performed. Before servicing the battery, always turn the engine and all accessories off and disconnect the cable from the negative terminal of the battery.

3   The battery produces hydrogen gas, which is both flammable and explosive. Never create a spark, smoke or light a match around the battery. Always charge the battery in a ventilated area.

4   Electrolyte contains poisonous and corrosive sulfuric acid. Do not allow it to get in your eyes, on your skin on your clothes. Never ingest it. Wear protective safety glasses when working near the battery. Keep children away from the battery.

5   Note the external condition of the battery. If the positive terminal and cable clamp on your vehicle's battery is equipped with a rubber protector, make sure that it's not torn or damaged. It should completely cover the terminal. Look for any corroded or loose connections, cracks in the case or cover or loose hold-down clamps. Also check the entire length of each cable for cracks and frayed conductors.

6   If corrosion, which looks like white, fluffy deposits (see illustration) is evident, particularly around the terminals, the battery should be removed for cleaning. Loosen the cable clamp bolts with a wrench, being careful to remove the ground cable first, and slide them off the terminals (see illustration). Then disconnect the hold-down clamp bolt and nut, remove the clamp and lift the battery from the compartment (see Chapter 5).

7   Clean the cable clamps thoroughly with a battery brush or a terminal cleaner and a solution of warm water and baking soda (see illustration). Wash the terminals and the top of the battery case with the

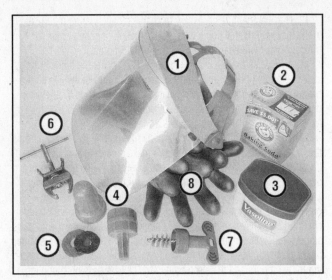

8.6a Battery terminal corrosion usually appears as light, fluffy powder

8.1 Tools and materials required for battery maintenance

1   *Face shield/safety goggles* - *When removing corrosion with a brush, the acidic particles can easily fly up into your eyes*

2   *Baking soda* - *A solution of baking soda and water can be used to neutralize corrosion*

3   *Petroleum jelly* - *A layer of this on the battery posts will help prevent corrosion*

4   *Battery post/cable cleaner* - *This wire brush cleaning tool will remove all traces of corrosion from the battery posts and cable clamps*

5   *Treated felt washers* - *Placing one of these on each post, directly under the cable clamps, will help prevent corrosion*

6   *Puller* - *Sometimes the cable clamps are very difficult to pull off the posts, even after the nut/bolt has been completely loosened. This tool pulls the clamp straight up and off the post without damage*

7   *Battery post/cable cleaner* - *Here is another cleaning tool which is a slightly different version of Number 4 above, but it does the same thing*

8   *Rubber gloves* - *Another safety item to consider when servicing the battery; remember that's acid inside the battery!*

same solution but make sure that the solution doesn't get into the battery. When cleaning the cables, terminals and battery top, wear safety goggles and rubber gloves to prevent any solution from coming in contact with your eyes or hands. Wear old clothes too - even diluted, sulfuric acid splashed onto clothes will burn holes in them. If the terminals have been extensively corroded, clean them up with a terminal cleaner (see illustration). Thoroughly wash all cleaned areas with plain water.

8   Make sure that the battery tray is in good condition and the hold-down clamp bolts are tight. If the battery is removed from the tray, make sure no parts remain in the bottom of the tray when the battery is reinstalled. When reinstalling the hold-down clamp bolts, do not over-tighten them.

9   Any metal parts of the vehicle damaged by corrosion should be covered with a zinc-based primer, then painted.

10 Information on removing and installing the battery can be found in Chapter 5. Information on jump starting can be found at the front of this manual.

8.6b Removing a cable from the battery post with a wrench - sometimes a pair of special battery pliers are required for this procedure if corrosion has caused deterioration of the nut hex (always remove the ground (-) cable first and hook it up last!)

8.7a When cleaning the cable clamps, all corrosion must be removed

8.7b Regardless of the type of tool used to clean the battery posts, a clean, shiny surface should be the result

CHARGING

➡ Note: The manufacturer recommends the battery be removed from the vehicle for charging because the gas that escapes during this procedure can damage the paint. Fast charging with the battery cables connected can result in damage to the electrical system.

11 Slow-rate charging is the best way to restore a battery that's discharged to the point where it will not start the engine. It's also a good way to maintain the battery charge in a vehicle that's only driven a few miles between starts. Maintaining the battery charge is particularly important in the winter when the battery must work harder to start the engine and electrical accessories that drain the battery are in greater use.

12 It's best to use a one or two-amp battery charger (sometimes called a "trickle" charger). They are the safest and put the least strain on the battery. They are also the least expensive. For a faster charge, you can use a higher amperage charger, but don't use one rated more than 1/10th the amp/hour rating of the battery. Rapid boost charges that claim to restore the power of the battery in one to two hours are hardest on the battery and can damage batteries not in good condition. This type of charging should only be used in emergency situations.

13 The average time necessary to charge a battery should be listed in the instructions that come with the charger. As a general rule, a trickle charger will charge a battery in 12 to 16 hours.

14 Remove all the cell caps (if equipped) and cover the holes with a clean cloth to prevent spattering electrolyte. Disconnect the negative battery cable and hook the battery charger cable clamps up to the battery posts (positive to positive, negative to negative), then plug in the charger. Make sure it is set at 12-volts if it has a selector switch.

15 If you're using a charger with a rate higher than two amps, check the battery regularly during charging to make sure it doesn't overheat. If you're using a trickle charger, you can safely let the battery charge overnight after you've checked it regularly for the first couple of hours.

16 If the battery has removable cell caps, measure the specific gravity with a hydrometer every hour during the last few hours of the charging cycle. Hydrometers are available inexpensively from auto parts stores - follow the instructions that come with the hydrometer. Consider the battery charged when there's no change in the specific gravity reading for two hours and the electrolyte in the cells is gassing (bubbling) freely. The specific gravity reading from each cell should be very close to the others. If not, the battery probably has a bad cell(s).

17 Some batteries with sealed tops have built-in hydrometers on the top that indicate the state of charge by the color displayed in the hydrometer window. Normally, a brightly-colored hydrometer indicates a full charge and a dark hydrometer indicates the battery still needs charging.

18 If the battery has a sealed top and no built-in hydrometer, you can hook up a digital voltmeter across the battery terminals to check the charge. A fully charged battery should read at least 12.66 volts.

19 Further information on the battery and jump-starting can be found in Chapter 5 and at the front of this manual.

9   Cooling system check (every 6000 miles [10,000 km] or 6 months)

1   Many major engine failures can be caused by a faulty cooling system.
2   The engine must be cold for the cooling system check, so perform the following procedure before the vehicle is driven for the day or after it has been shut off for at least three hours.
3   Remove the pressure cap from the coolant expansion tank. Clean the cap thoroughly, inside and out, with clean water. The presence of corrosion on the underside of the cap means the coolant should be changed (see Section 20). The coolant inside the reservoir should be relatively clean and transparent. If it's not, drain the system and refill it with new coolant of the proper type.

If it is necessary to open the pressure cap, wait until the system has cooled completely, then wrap a thick cloth around the cap and slowly unscrew it. If you hear hissing or any steam escapes, wait until the system has cooled further, then remove the cap.

4   Carefully check the radiator hoses and the smaller diameter heater hoses. Inspect each coolant hose along its entire length, replacing any hose which is cracked, swollen or deteriorated (see illustration). Cracks will show up better if the hose is squeezed. Pay close attention to hose clamps that secure the hoses to cooling system components. Hose clamps can pinch and puncture hoses, resulting in coolant leaks.
5   Make sure that all hose connections are tight. A leak in the cooling system will usually show up as white, bluish or brown colored deposits on the area adjoining the leak.
6   Clean the front of the radiator and air conditioning condenser with compressed air, if available, or a soft brush. Remove all bugs, leaves, etc. embedded in the radiator fins. Be extremely careful not to damage the cooling fins or cut your fingers on them.
7   If the coolant level has been dropping consistently and no leaks are detectable, have the expansion tank cap and cooling system pressure checked at a service station.

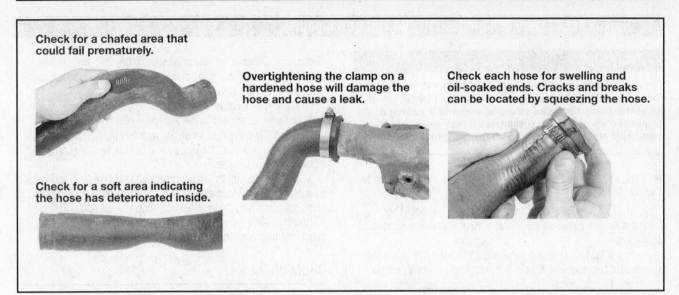

Check for a chafed area that could fail prematurely.

Check for a soft area indicating the hose has deteriorated inside.

Overtightening the clamp on a hardened hose will damage the hose and cause a leak.

Check each hose for swelling and oil-soaked ends. Cracks and breaks can be located by squeezing the hose.

9.4 Hoses, like drivebelts, have a habit of failing at the worst possible time - to prevent the inconvenience of a blown radiator or heater hose, inspect them carefully as shown here

10 Tire rotation (every 6000 miles [10,000 km] or 6 months)

1   The tires should be rotated at the specified intervals and whenever uneven wear is noticed. Since the vehicle will be raised and the tires removed anyway, check the brakes also (see Section 12).

2   Radial tires must be rotated in a specific pattern (see illustration).

3   Refer to the information in *Jacking and towing* at the front of this manual for the proper procedure to follow when raising the vehicle and changing a tire. If the brakes must be checked, don't apply the parking brake as stated.

4   The vehicle must be raised on a hoist or supported on jackstands to get all four wheels off the ground. Make sure the vehicle is safely supported!

5   After the rotation procedure is finished, check and adjust the tire pressures as necessary and check the lug nut tightness.

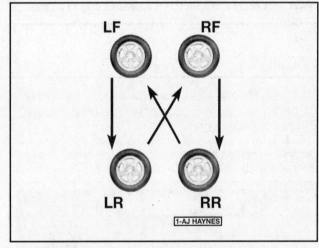

10.2 The recommended four-tire rotation pattern

11 Seat belt check (every 6000 miles [10,000 km] or 6 months)

1   Check seat belts, buckles, latch plates and guide loops for obvious damage and signs of wear.

2   See if the seat belt reminder light comes on when the key is turned to the Run or Start position. A chime should also sound.

3   The seat belts are designed to lock up during a sudden stop or impact, yet allow free movement during normal driving. Make sure the retractors return the belt against your chest while driving and rewind the belt fully when the buckle is unlatched.

4   If any of the above checks reveal problems with the seat belt system, replace parts as necessary.

12 Brake check (every 6000 miles [10,000 km] or 6 months)

✳ WARNING:

The dust created by the brake system is harmful to your health. Never blow it out with compressed air and don't inhale any of it. An approved filtering mask should be worn when working on the brakes. Do not, under any circumstances, use petroleum-based solvents to clean brake parts. Use brake system cleaner only!

➡ **Note: For detailed photographs of the brake system, refer to Chapter 9.**

1   In addition to the specified intervals, the brakes should be inspected every time the wheels are removed or whenever a defect is suspected.

2   Any of the following symptoms could indicate a potential brake system defect: The vehicle pulls to one side when the brake pedal is depressed, the brakes make squealing or dragging noises when applied, brake pedal travel is excessive, the pedal pulsates, or brake fluid leaks, usually onto the inside of the tire or wheel.

3   Disc brakes can be visually checked without removing any parts except the wheels. To check the drum brake shoe linings, the brake drums will have to be removed. Remove the hub caps (if applicable) and loosen the wheel lug nuts a quarter turn each.

4   Raise the vehicle and place it securely on jackstands.

✳ WARNING:

Never work under a vehicle that is supported only by a jack!

DISC BRAKES

5   Remove the front wheels. Now visible is the disc brake caliper that contains the pads. There is an outer brake pad and an inner pad. Both must be checked for wear.

6   Measure the thickness of the outer pad at each end of the caliper and the inner pad through the inspection hole in the caliper body (see

illustration). Compare the measurement with the limit given in this Chapter's Specifications; if any brake pad thickness is less than specified, then all brake pads must be replaced (see Chapter 9).

7   If you're in doubt as to the exact pad thickness or quality, remove them for measurement and further inspection (see Chapter 9).

8   Check the disc for score marks, wear and burned spots. If any of these conditions exist, the disc should be removed for servicing or replacement (see Chapter 9).

9   Before installing the wheels, check all the brake lines and hoses for damage, wear, deformation, cracks, corrosion, leakage, bends and twists, particularly in the vicinity of the rubber hoses and calipers.

10   Install the wheels, lower the vehicle and tighten the wheel lug nuts to the torque given in this Chapter's Specifications.

DRUM BRAKES

➡ **Note: On 2005 (with VIN number 5B426447 and lower) and all earlier models, the rear drum cannot be removed without removing the rear hub nut (see Chapter 10).**

11   Remove the rear wheels, make sure the parking brake is off, then tap on the outside of the drum with a rubber mallet to loosen it.

12   Remove the brake drums. If the drum still won't come off, refer to Chapter 9.

13   With the drums removed, carefully clean the brake assembly with brake system cleaner.

✳ WARNING:

Don't blow the dust out with compressed air and don't inhale any of it (it is harmful to your health).

14   Note the thickness of the lining material on both front and rear brake shoes (see illustration). Compare the measurement with the limit given in this Chapter's Specifications; if any lining thickness is less than specified, then all of the brake shoes must be replaced (see Chapter 9). The shoes should also be replaced if they're cracked,

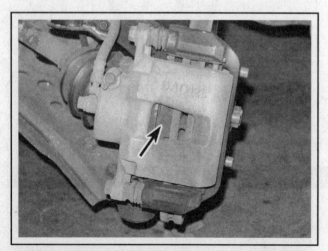

12.6 You will find an inspection hole like this in each caliper through which you can view the thickness of remaining friction material for the inner pad

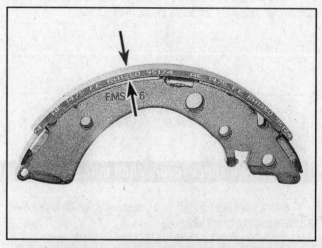

12.14 If the lining is bonded to the brake shoe, measure the lining thickness from the outer surface to the metal shoe, as shown here; if the lining is riveted to the shoe, measure from the lining outer surface to the rivet head

glazed (shiny areas), or covered with brake fluid.

15 Make sure all the brake assembly springs are connected and in good condition.

16 Check the brake components for signs of fluid leakage. With your finger or a small screwdriver, carefully pry back the rubber cups on the wheel cylinder located at the top of the brake shoes (see illustration). Any leakage here is an indication that the wheel cylinders should be replaced immediately (see Chapter 9). Also, check all hoses and connections for signs of leakage.

17 Wipe the inside of the drum with a clean rag and denatured alcohol or brake cleaner. Again, be careful not to breathe the dangerous brake dust.

18 Check the inside of the drum for cracks, score marks, deep scratches and hard spots which will appear as small discolored areas. If imperfections cannot be removed with fine emery cloth, the drum must be taken to an automotive machine shop for resurfacing.

19 Repeat the procedure for the remaining wheel. If the inspection reveals that all parts are in good condition, reinstall the brake drums, install the wheels and lower the vehicle to the ground.

BRAKE BOOSTER CHECK

20 Sit in the driver's seat and perform the following sequence of tests.

21 With the brake fully depressed, start the engine - the pedal should move down a little when the engine starts.

22 With the engine running, depress the brake pedal several times - the travel distance should not change.

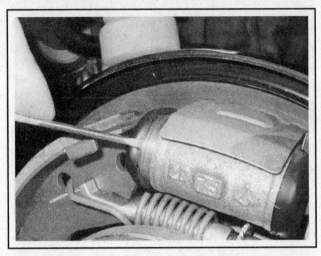

12.16 Carefully peel back the wheel cylinder boot and check for leaking fluid, indicating that the cylinder must be replaced

23 Depress the brake, stop the engine and hold the pedal in for about 30 seconds - the pedal should neither sink nor rise.

24 Restart the engine, run it for about a minute and turn it off. Then firmly depress the brake several times - the pedal travel should decrease with each application.

25 If your brakes do not operate as described, the brake booster has failed. Refer to Chapter 9 for the replacement procedure.

13 Interior ventilation filter replacement (every 15,000 miles [24,000 km] or 12 months)

➡ **Note: 2006 and earlier models are not equipped with an interior ventilation system filter.**

1 2007 and later models are equipped with an air filtering element for the interior ventilation system. The access panel is located behind the glove box.

2 Release the stops and lower the glove box door (see Chapter 11, if necessary).

3 Remove the glove box support screws and remove the support (see illustration).

4 Release the tab on the filter cover, pulling on the bottom retaining tab and lifting the cover away from the housing (see illustration).

13.3 Remove the glove box support mounting screws

13.4 Release the tab on the ventilation filter housing and pull the cover out

13.5 Remove the element from the housing

13.7 Install the filter with the airflow arrow pointing toward the left

5   Slide the filter straight out (see illustration).
6   Clean out any leaves or other debris from the housing.
7   Installation is the reverse of the removal procedure. Make sure

the arrow indicating airflow is pointing toward the left when you push the new filter in (see illustration).

---

14 Underhood hose check and replacement (every 15,000 miles [24,000 km] or 12 months)

✳✳ WARNING:

Never remove air conditioning components or hoses until the refrigerant has been recovered by a licensed air conditioning technician.

GENERAL

1   High temperatures under the hood can cause deterioration of the rubber and plastic hoses used for engine, accessory and emission systems operation. Periodic inspection should be made for cracks, loose clamps, material hardening and leaks.

2   Information specific to the cooling system hoses can be found in Section 9.

3   Most (but not all) hoses are secured to the fittings with clamps. Where clamps are used, check to be sure they haven't lost their tension, allowing the hose to leak. If clamps aren't used, make sure the hose has not expanded and/or hardened where it slips over the fitting, allowing it to leak.

PCV SYSTEM HOSE

4   To reduce hydrocarbon emissions, crankcase blow-by gas is vented through the PCV valve in the valve arm cover to the intake manifold via a rubber hose on most models. The blow-by gases mix with incoming air in the intake manifold before being burned in the combustion chambers.

5   Check the PCV hose for cracks, leaks and other damage. Disconnect it from the valve cover and the intake manifold and check the inside for obstructions. If it's clogged, clean it out with solvent.

VACUUM HOSES

6   It's quite common for vacuum hoses, especially those in the emissions system, to be color coded or identified by colored stripes molded into them. Various systems require hoses with different wall thickness, collapse resistance and temperature resistance. When replacing hoses, be sure the new ones are made of the same material.

7   Often the only effective way to check a hose is to remove it completely from the vehicle. If more than one hose is removed, label the hoses and fittings to ensure correct installation.

8   When checking vacuum hoses, include any plastic T-fittings in the check. Inspect the fittings for cracks and the hose where it fits over each fitting for distortion, which could cause leakage.

9   A small piece of vacuum hose (1/4-inch inside diameter) can be used as a stethoscope to detect vacuum leaks. Hold one end of the hose to your ear and probe around vacuum hoses and fittings, listening for the hissing sound characteristic of a vacuum leak.

✳✳ WARNING:

When probing with the vacuum hose stethoscope, be careful not to come into contact with moving engine components such as drivebelts, the cooling fan, etc.

FUEL HOSE

> ### ✳✳ WARNING:
>
> **Gasoline is flammable, so take extra precautions when you work on any part of the fuel system. Don't smoke or allow open flames or bare light bulbs near the work area, and don't work in a garage where a gas-type appliance (such as a water heater or clothes dryer) is present. Since fuel is carcinogenic, wear fuel-resistant gloves when there's a possibility of being exposed to fuel, and, if you spill any fuel on your skin, rinse it off immediately with soap and water. Mop up any spills immediately and do not store fuel-soaked rags where they could ignite. The fuel system is under constant pressure, so, if any fuel lines are to be disconnected, the fuel pressure in the system must be relieved first (see Chapter 4 for more information). When you perform any kind of work on the fuel system, wear safety glasses and have a Class B type fire extinguisher on hand.**

10 The fuel lines are usually under pressure, so if any fuel lines are to be disconnected be prepared to catch spilled fuel.

> ### ✳✳ WARNING:
>
> **Your vehicle is equipped with fuel injection and you must relieve the fuel system pressure before servicing the fuel lines. Refer to Chapter 4 for the fuel system pressure relief procedure.**

11 Check all flexible fuel lines for deterioration and chafing. Check especially for cracks in areas where the hose bends and just before fittings, such as where a hose attaches to the fuel pump, fuel filter and fuel injection unit.

12 When replacing a hose, use only hose that is specifically designed for your fuel injection system.

13 Spring-type clamps are sometimes used on fuel return or vapor lines. These clamps often lose their tension over a period of time, and can be sprung during removal. Replace all spring-type clamps with screw clamps whenever a hose is replaced. Some fuel lines use spring-lock type couplings, which require a special tool to disconnect. See Chapter 4 for more information on this type of coupling.

METAL LINES

14 Sections of metal line are often used for fuel line between the fuel pump and the fuel injection unit. Check carefully to make sure the line isn't bent, crimped or cracked.

15 If a section of metal fuel line must be replaced, use seamless steel tubing only, since copper and aluminum tubing do not have the strength necessary to withstand vibration caused by the engine.

16 Check the metal brake lines where they enter the master cylinder and brake proportioning unit (if used) for cracks in the lines and loose fittings. Any sign of brake fluid leakage calls for an immediate thorough inspection of the brake system.

15 Steering, suspension and driveaxle boot check (every 15,000 miles [24,000 km] or 12 months)

➡ **Note: For detailed illustrations of the steering and suspension components, refer to Chapter 10.**

WITH THE WHEELS ON THE GROUND

1 With the vehicle stopped and the front wheels pointed straight ahead, rock the steering wheel gently back and forth. If freeplay is excessive, a front wheel bearing, steering shaft universal joint or lower arm balljoint is worn or the steering gear is out of adjustment or broken. Refer to Chapter 10 for the appropriate repair procedure.

2 Other symptoms, such as excessive vehicle body movement over rough roads, swaying (leaning) around corners and binding as the steering wheel is turned, may indicate faulty steering and/or suspension components.

3 Check the shock absorbers by pushing down and releasing the vehicle several times at each corner. If the vehicle does not come back to a level position within one or two bounces, the shocks/struts are worn and must be replaced. When bouncing the vehicle up and down, listen for squeaks and noises from the suspension components.

4 Check the struts and shock absorbers for evidence of fluid leakage (see illustration). A light film of fluid is no cause for concern. Make sure that any fluid noted is from the struts/shocks and not from some other source. If leakage is noted, replace the struts/shocks as a set.

5 Check the struts and shocks to be sure they are securely mounted and undamaged. Check the upper mounts for damage and wear. If damage or wear is noted, replace the shocks as a set (front and rear).

6 If the shocks must be replaced, refer to Chapter 10 for the procedure.

UNDER THE VEHICLE

7 Raise the vehicle with a floor jack and support it securely on jackstands.

8 Check the tires for irregular wear patterns and proper inflation. See Section 5 for information regarding tire wear and Chapter 10 for information on wheel bearing replacement.

9 Inspect the universal joint between the steering shaft and the steering gear housing. Check the steering gear housing for lubricant leakage. Make sure that the dust seals and boots are not damaged

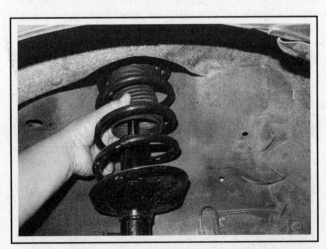

15.4 Check the struts and shock absorbers for leakage

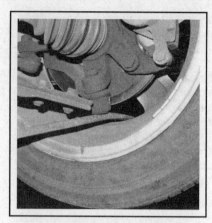

15.10 To check a balljoint for wear, try to pry the control arm up and down to make sure there is no play in the balljoint (if there is, replace it)

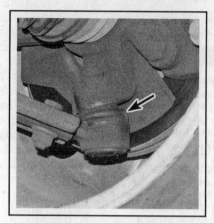

15.11 Check the balljoint boot for damage

15.14 Flex the driveaxle boots by hand to check for cracks and/or leaking grease

and that the boot clamps are not loose. Check the steering linkage for looseness or damage. Check the tie-rod ends for excessive play. Look for loose bolts, broken or disconnected parts and deteriorated rubber bushings on all suspension and steering components. While an assistant turns the steering wheel from side to side, check the steering components for free movement, chafing and binding. If the steering components do not seem to be reacting with the movement of the steering wheel, try to determine where the slack is located.

10 Check the balljoints for wear by trying to move each control arm up and down with a prybar (see illustration) to ensure that its balljoint has no play. If any balljoint does have play, replace it. See Chapter 10 for the balljoint replacement procedure.

11 Inspect the balljoint boots for damage and leaking grease (see illustration). Replace the balljoints with new ones if they are damaged (see Chapter 10).

12 At the rear of the vehicle, inspect the suspension arm bushings

for deterioration. Additional information on suspension components can be found in Chapter 10.

DRIVEAXLE BOOT CHECK

➡ **Note: For detailed illustrations of the driveaxles, refer to Chapter 8.**

13 The driveaxle boots are very important because they prevent dirt, water and foreign material from entering and damaging the constant velocity (CV) joints. Because it constantly pivots back and forth following the steering action of the front hub, the outer CV boot wears out sooner and should be inspected regularly.

14 Inspect the boots for tears and cracks as well as loose clamps (see illustration). If there is any evidence of cracks or leaking lubricant, they must be replaced as described in Chapter 8.

16 Exhaust system check (every 15,000 miles [24,000 km] or 12 months)

1 With the engine cold (at least three hours after the vehicle has been driven), check the complete exhaust system from the engine to the end of the tailpipe. Ideally, the inspection should be done with the vehicle on a hoist to permit unrestricted access. If a hoist isn't available, raise the vehicle and support it securely on jackstands.

2 Check the exhaust pipes and connections for evidence of leaks, severe corrosion and damage. Make sure that all brackets and hangers are in good condition and tight (see illustration).

3 At the same time, inspect the underside of the body for holes, corrosion, open seams, etc., which may allow exhaust gases to enter the passenger compartment. Seal all body openings with silicone or body putty.

4 Rattles and other noises can often be traced to the exhaust system, especially the mounts and hangers. Try to move the pipes, muffler and catalytic converter. If the components can come in contact with the body or suspension parts, secure the exhaust system with new mounts.

5 Check the running condition of the engine by inspecting inside the end of the tailpipe. The exhaust deposits here are an indication of engine state-of-tune. If the pipe is black and sooty or coated with white deposits, the engine may need a tune-up, including a thorough engine management and fuel system inspection.

16.2 Check all the exhaust system rubber hangers for damage

17 Fuel system check (every 15,000 miles [24,000 km] or 12 months)

✷✷ WARNING:

Gasoline is flammable, so take extra precautions when you work on any part of the fuel system. Don't smoke or allow open flames or bare light bulbs near the work area, and don't work in a garage where a gas-type appliance (such as a water heater or clothes dryer) is present. Since fuel is carcinogenic, wear fuel-resistant gloves when there's a possibility of being exposed to fuel, and, if you spill any fuel on your skin, rinse it off immediately with soap and water. Mop up any spills immediately and do not store fuel-soaked rags where they could ignite. When you perform any kind of work on the fuel system, wear safety glasses and have a Class B type fire extinguisher on hand. The fuel system is under constant pressure, so before any lines are disconnected, the fuel system pressure must be relieved (see Chapter 4).

1   If you smell gasoline while driving or after the vehicle has been sitting in the sun, inspect the fuel system immediately.

2   Remove the fuel filler cap and inspect it for damage and corrosion. The gasket should have an unbroken sealing imprint. If the gasket is damaged or corroded, install a new cap.

3   Inspect the fuel feed line for cracks. Make sure that the connections between the fuel lines and the fuel injection system and between the fuel lines and the in-line fuel filter are tight.

✷✷ WARNING:

Your vehicle is fuel injected, so you must relieve the fuel system pressure before servicing fuel system components. The fuel system pressure relief procedure is outlined in Chapter 4.

4   Since some components of the fuel system - the fuel tank and part of the fuel feed line, for example - are underneath the vehicle, they can be inspected more easily with the vehicle raised on a hoist. If that's not possible, raise the vehicle and support it on jackstands.

5   With the vehicle raised and safely supported, inspect the gas tank and filler neck for punctures, cracks and other damage. The connection between the filler neck and the tank is particularly critical. Sometimes a rubber filler neck will leak because of loose clamps or deteriorated rubber. Inspect all fuel tank mounting brackets and straps to be sure that the tank is securely attached to the vehicle.

✷✷ WARNING:

Do not, under any circumstances, try to repair a fuel tank (except rubber components). A welding torch or any open flame can easily cause fuel vapors inside the tank to explode.

6   Carefully check all rubber hoses and metal lines leading away from the fuel tank. Check for loose connections, deteriorated hoses, crimped lines and other damage. Repair or replace damaged sections as necessary (see Chapter 4).

18 Drivebelt check and replacement/tensioner replacement (every 15,000 miles [24,000 km] or 12 months)

DRIVEBELT

1   A drivebelt (2008 and earlier models) or two drivebelts (2009 and later models) are located at the front of the engine and play an important role in the overall operation of the engine and its components. Due to its function and material make up, the belt is prone to wear and should be periodically inspected. Although the belt(s) should be inspected at the recommended intervals, replacement may not be necessary for more than 100,000 miles.

Check

2   With the engine stopped, inspect the full length of the drivebelt for cracks and separation of the belt plies. It will be necessary to turn the engine (using a wrench or socket and bar on the crankshaft pulley bolt) in order to move the belt from the pulleys so that the belt can be inspected thoroughly. Twist the belt between the pulleys so that both sides can be viewed. Also check for fraying, and glazing which gives the belt a shiny appearance. Check the pulleys for nicks, cracks, distortion and corrosion.

3   Note that it is not unusual for a ribbed belt to exhibit small cracks in the edges of the belt ribs, and unless these are extensive or very deep, belt replacement is not essential (see illustration).

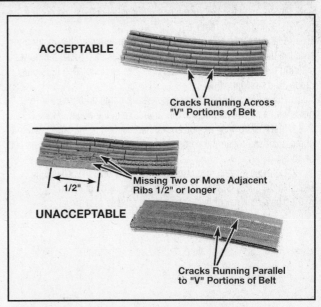

18.3 Here are some of the more common problems associated with drivebelts (check the belts very carefully to prevent an untimely breakdown)

18.14 Remove the inner fender front half splash shield fasteners

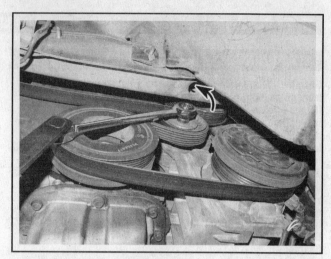

18.15 Rotate the arm counterclockwise to release the tension on the belt - L91 and LXT models shown

Replacement

Power steering pump belt - 2009 and later models (LXV engines) only

➡ **Note: The power steering belt doesn't use a tensioner and must be pried or "pushed" off. It can also be cut off to be removed.**

4 Remove the right side headlight housing (see Chapter 12) and the air filter housing (see Chapter 4).

5 Remove the main drivebelt as described in this Section.

6 Place a long flat bar or screwdriver between the belt and pump pulley.

7 Insert a 3/8-inch hex bit socket into the end of the power steering pump shaft and rotate the pump pulley clockwise while pushing the belt off of the pulley.

8 If replacing the belt, use a pair of diagonal cutters and cut the power steering belt to remove it.

9 Place the new belt or belt over the water pump pulley, making sure the belt is fully seated in the pulley grooves then rotate the power steering pump pulley so that one of the three large holes in the pulley is in the 12 o'clock position.

10 Place the belt onto the power steering pump and secure it in place with a plastic tie through the large hole in the pulley.

11 Insert a 3/8-inch hex bit socket into the end of the power steering pump shaft and rotate the pump pulley clockwise while pushing the belt on to the pulley.

12 Continue rotating the power steering pulley until the belt is fully seated in the pulley grooves, then cut the plastic tie off of the pulley.

13 The remainder of installation is the reverse of removal.

Drivebelt

14 Loosen the right front wheel lug nuts, then raise the front of the vehicle and support it on jackstands. Remove the right front wheel and the front half of the inner fender splash shield (see illustration).

15 Note how the drivebelt is routed, then place a twelve point socket with a 3/8-inch drive breaker bar onto the tensioner center bolts (L91 and LXT models) or knob (LXV models). Rotate the arm counterclockwise and release tension on the belt (see illustration). Slip the belt from the pulleys while the tension is released.

16 Fit the new drivebelt onto the crankshaft, alternator, power steering pump (2008 and earlier models) and air conditioning compressor pulleys, as applicable, then turn the tensioner and locate the drivebelt on the tensioner pulley. Make sure that the drivebelt is correctly seated in all of the pulley grooves, then release the tensioner.

17 Install the fenderwell splash shield and wheel, then lower the car to the ground. Tighten the lug nuts to the torque listed in this Chapter's Specifications.

18 Remaining installation is the reverse of removal.

TENSIONER REPLACEMENT

19 Remove the drivebelt and power steering belt, if equipped as described previously, then rotate the tensioner back until all the pressure is released and remove the socket and breaker bar.

20 On L91 and LXT engines, remove the air filter housing (see Chapter 4) to access the tensioner mounting bolts. Remove the tensioner mounting bolts and tensioner from the bottom of the vehicle.

21 On LXV engines, unscrew the tensioner reverse Torx mounting bolt and remove the tensioner from the bottom of the vehicle.

22 Installation is the reverse of removal. Tighten the tensioner bolt(s) to the torque listed in this Chapter's Specifications.

19 Air filter check and replacement (every 30,000 miles [48,000 km] or 24 months)

✲✲ CAUTION:

Never drive the vehicle with the air filter element removed. Excessive engine wear could result and backfiring could even cause a fire under the hood.

1   Unscrew the filter housing cover screws (see illustration).
2   Lift up the cover and remove the filter element from the housing (see illustration).
3   Inspect the outer surface of the filter element. If it is dirty, replace it. If it is only moderately dusty, it can be reused by blowing it clean from the back to the front surface with compressed air. Because it is a pleated paper type filter, it cannot be washed or oiled. If it cannot be cleaned satisfactorily with compressed air, discard it and install a new one. While the cover is off, be careful not to drop anything down into the housing.
4   Wipe out the inside of the filter housing.
5   Place the new filter into the housing, making sure it seats properly (see illustration).
6   The remainder of installation is the reverse of removal.

19.1 Filter housing cover screws

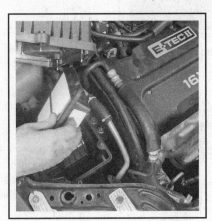

19.2 Lift the housing cover up, then remove the filter from the housing

19.5 Make sure the filter is seated and the holes in the filter are aligned with the mounting screw holes

20 Cooling system servicing (draining, flushing and refilling) (every 30,000 miles [48,000 km] or 24 months)

✲✲ WARNING:

Do not allow antifreeze to come in contact with your skin or painted surfaces of the vehicle. Rinse off spills immediately with plenty of water. Antifreeze is highly toxic if ingested. Never leave antifreeze lying around in an open container or in puddles on the floor; children and pets are attracted by its sweet smell and may drink it. Check with local authorities on disposing of used antifreeze. Many communities have collection centers that will see that antifreeze is disposed of safely.

✲✲ WARNING:

Wait until the engine is completely cool before beginning this procedure.

➡ Note: Non-toxic antifreeze is now manufactured and available at local auto parts stores, but even this type should be disposed of properly.

DRAINING

1   Periodically, the cooling system should be drained, flushed and refilled to replenish the antifreeze mixture and prevent formation of rust and corrosion, which can impair the performance of the cooling system and cause engine damage. When the cooling system is serviced, all hoses and the expansion tank cap should be checked and replaced if necessary.
2   Apply the parking brake and block the wheels. Raise the front of the vehicle and support it securely on jackstands, then remove the under-vehicle splash shield.

✲✲ WARNING:

If the vehicle has just been driven, wait several hours to allow the engine to cool down before beginning this procedure.

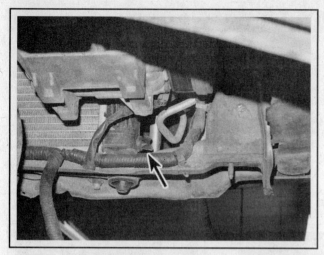

20.3 The radiator drain valve is located on the right end of the radiator

3   Move a large container under the radiator drain to catch the coolant. The coolant is drained by turning the knob on the radiator drain valve (see illustration). Remove the expansion tank cap and allow the coolant to drain. When the flow of coolant has stopped, close the drain plug.

4   While the coolant is draining, check the condition of the radiator hoses, heater hoses and clamps (refer to Section 9 if necessary). Replace any damaged clamps or hoses.

FLUSHING

5   Fill the cooling system with clean water, following the Refilling procedure (see Step 11).

6   Start the engine and allow it to reach normal operating temperature, then rev up the engine a few times.

7   Turn the engine off and allow it to cool completely, then drain the system as described earlier.

8   Repeat Steps 3, 6 and 7 until the water being drained is free of contaminants.

9   In severe cases of contamination or clogging of the radiator, remove the radiator (see Chapter 3) and have a radiator repair facility clean and repair it if necessary.

10   When the coolant is regularly drained and the system refilled with the correct antifreeze/water mixture, there should be no need to use chemical cleaners or descalers. The manufacturer states that chemical flushing solutions should not be used.

REFILLING

11   Close and tighten the radiator drain.

12   Place the heater temperature control in the maximum heat position.

13   Slowly add new coolant (a 50/50 mixture of water and DEX-COOL antifreeze) to the coolant expansion tank until the level is at the MIN mark.

14   Install the expansion tank cap and run the engine at idle in a well-ventilated area for five minutes.

15   Turn the engine off and let it cool. Remove the pressure cap from the expansion tank and add more coolant mixture to the reservoir until it's level with the MIN mark.

16   Squeeze the upper radiator hose to expel air, then add more coolant mixture if necessary. Reinstall the expansion tank cap.

17   Start the engine and run it at idle for another five minutes. Also, set the heater and blower controls to the maximum setting and check to see that the heater output from the air ducts is warm. This is a good indication that all air has been purged from the cooling system.

21   Brake fluid change (every 30,000 miles [48,000 km] or 24 months)

⁂ WARNING:

Brake fluid can harm your eyes and damage painted surfaces, so use extreme caution when handling or pouring it. Do not use brake fluid that has been standing open or is more than one year old. Brake fluid absorbs moisture from the air. Excess moisture can cause a dangerous loss of braking effectiveness.

1   At the specified intervals, the brake fluid should be drained and replaced. Since the brake fluid may drip or splash when pouring it, place plenty of rags around the master cylinder to protect any surrounding painted surfaces.

2   Before beginning work, purchase the specified brake fluid (see *Recommended lubricants and fluids* in this Chapter's Specifications).

3   Remove the cap from the master cylinder reservoir.

4   Using a hand-operated suction pump or similar device, withdraw the fluid from the master cylinder reservoir.

5   Add new fluid to the master cylinder until it rises to the base of the filler neck.

6   Bleed the brake system as described in Chapter 9 at all four brakes until new and uncontaminated fluid is expelled from the bleeder screw. Maintain the fluid level in the master cylinder as you perform the bleeding process. If you allow the master cylinder to run dry, air will enter the system.

7   Refill the master cylinder with fluid and check the operation of the brakes. The pedal should feel solid when depressed, with no sponginess.

⁂ WARNING:

Do not operate the vehicle if you are in doubt about the effectiveness of the brake system.

22 Automatic transaxle fluid change and screen cleaning (60,000 miles [96,000 km] or 72 months)

1   At the specified time intervals, the automatic transmission or automatic transaxle and differential fluid should be drained and replaced.

➡ **Note: The manufacturer recommends changing the automatic transmission fluid and filter change for severe service only, which are for vehicles mainly driven in heavy city traffic in hot weather, in hilly or mountain areas, taxi or if the vehicle is used as for deliveries. Although the manufacturer doesn't specify it for other driving situations, it is a good idea to replace the transaxle fluid filter periodically to remove accumulated dirt and metal particles.**

2   Before beginning work, purchase the specified fluid (see *Recommended lubricants and fluids* in this Chapter's Specifications).

3   Other tools necessary for this job include jackstands to support the vehicle in a raised position, an appropriate wrench, a drain pan, newspapers and clean rags.

✳ WARNING:

Fluid temperature can exceed 350-degrees F in a hot transaxle. Wear protective gloves.

4   The fluid should be drained immediately after the vehicle has been driven. Hot fluid is more effective than cold fluid at removing built up sediment.

5   After the vehicle has been driven to warm up the fluid, raise it and place it on jackstands.

6   Move the necessary equipment under the vehicle, being careful not to touch any of the hot exhaust components.

7   Place the drain pan under the drain plug and remove the drain plug. Once the fluid is drained, reinstall the drain plug and tighten it to the torque listed in this Chapter's Specifications.

8   Remove the transmission oil pan bolts, pan and gasket. Carefully clean the gasket surface of the transmission to remove all traces of old gasket and sealant.

9   Drain any fluid still left in the transmission pan, clean it with solvent and dry it.

10 Remove the strainer bolts and from the valve body and lower the strainer.

11 Remove and replace the strainer gasket.

12 Clean the strainer using brake cleaner or solvent, then completely dry the strainer.

13 Install the cleaned strainer and a new gasket and tighten the bolts to the torque listed in this Chapter's Specifications.

14 Make sure the gasket surface on the transmission pan is clean, then fit a new gasket on the pan. Put the pan in place against the transmission and working around the pan, tighten each bolt a little at a time until the final torque is reached (see this Chapter's Specifications). Keep in mind that the correct torque to avoid leaks is very low.

15 Add new fluid to the transmission/transaxle through the dipstick hole opening (see *Recommended lubricants and fluids* in this Chapter's Specifications for the recommended fluid type and capacity). Use a funnel to prevent spills. It is best to add a little fluid at a time, continually checking the level with the dipstick (see Section 4).

✳ WARNING:

It's important not to overfill the transaxle.

16 Start the engine and shift into all positions from P through L, then shift into N and apply the parking brake.

17 With the engine idling, check the fluid level. Add fluid up to the level mark 3 (maximum cold) on the dipstick.

18 Drive the vehicle to warm up the transaxle to normal operating temperature, then recheck the fluid level.

23 Fuel filter replacement - LXV engines (every 90,000 miles [145,000 km])

✳ WARNING:

Gasoline is flammable, so take extra precautions when you work on any part of the fuel system. Don't smoke or allow open flames or bare light bulbs near the work area; and don't work in a garage where a gas-type appliance (such as a water heater or clothes dryer) is present. Since fuel is carcinogenic, wear fuel-resistant gloves when there's a possibility of being exposed to fuel, and, if you spill any fuel on your skin, rinse it off immediately with soap and water. Mop up any spills immediately and do not store fuel-soaked rags where they could ignite. When you perform any kind of work on the fuel system, wear safety glasses and have a Class B type fire extinguisher on hand. The fuel system is under constant pressure, so, before any lines are disconnected, the fuel system pressure must be relieved (see Chapter 4).

➡ **Note: The fuel filter is located under the vehicle, near the right-rear wheel.**

1   Relieve the fuel pressure (see Chapter 4).

2   Disconnect the cable from the negative battery terminal (see Chapter 5).

3   Raise the rear of the vehicle and support it securely on jackstands.

4   Disconnect the fuel filter inlet and outlet line quick-connect fitting (see Chapter 4, Section 5) from the filter.

5   Remove the fuel filter bracket mounting bolts and filter assembly.

6   Separate the fuel filter from the bracket.

7   Insert the new fuel filter into the bracket making sure the filter is pointing in the correct fuel flow direction.

8   Installation is the reverse of removal.

24 Manual transaxle lubricant level check and change (every 100,000 miles [166,000 km])

CHECK

1 Raise the vehicle and support it securely on jackstands.

2 Remove the transaxle the check/fill plug from the side of the case (see illustration), the lubricant should be up to the bottom of the check/fill plug hole.

3 If it isn't, add the recommended lubricant with a syringe or squeeze bottle until there is a slight flow out of the bottom edge of the hole.

4 Install the check/fill plug and tighten the plug to the torque listed in this Chapter's Specifications.

CHANGE

❋ WARNING:

The manufacturer recommends changing the fluid only after it has been warmed to operating temperature. Be careful when draining the hot fluid.

5 Loosen the left front wheel lug nuts, raise the vehicle and support it securely on jackstands.

6 Move a drain pan, rags, newspapers and wrenches under the transaxle.

D16/D20 transaxles

7 Loosen all the differential cover bolts (see illustration) and carefully pry the cover down and allow the lubricant to drain.

8 Once the fluid has stopped draining, remove the cover bolts and cover. Remove the gasket from the cover, or transaxle.

9 Clean the cover and the transaxle surface area, then install a new gasket to the cover.

10 Place the cover against the transaxle and install the bolts. Tighten the differential cover bolts to the torque listed in this Chapter's Specifications.

Y4M transaxles

11 Remove the transaxle drain plug from the lower side of the case, then allow the lubricant to drain into the pan for approximately 10 minutes.

12 After the lubricant has drained completely, measure the amount of fluid that has been drained (if there was no apparent leak). Coat the drain plug with thread locking compound, install it, then tighten it to the torque listed in this Chapter's Specifications.

All models

13 Clean the area around the transaxle check/fill plug, then remove it.

14 Insert a funnel into the fill plug hole.

15 Compare the measured amount of fluid that was drained to the quantity listed in the Specifications and refill the transaxle to the correct level.

16 Reinstall the check/fill plug and tighten it securely.

17 Lower the vehicle.

18 Drive the vehicle for a short distance, then check for leakage.

19 The old lubricant drained from the transaxle cannot be reused in its present state and should be disposed of. Check with your local auto parts store, disposal facility or environmental agency to see if they will accept the lubricant for recycling. After the lubricant has cooled it can be drained into a container (capped plastic jugs, topped bottles, milk cartons, etc.) for transport to one of these disposal sites. Don't dispose of the lubricant by pouring it on the ground or down a drain!

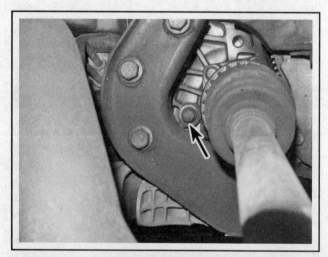

24.2 The transaxle check/fill plug on D16/D20 transaxles (shown) is located on the passenger's side of the transaxle. On Y4M models the plug is located on the driver's side of the transaxle

24.7 Loosen the differential cover bolts and allow the fluid to drain

25 Spark plug check and replacement (every 100,000 miles [166,000 km])

✳✳ WARNING:

Because of the very high voltage generated by the ignition system, use extreme care when you're servicing ignition components such as the ignition coil(s) and spark plugs.

✳✳ CAUTION:

Don't remove the spark plugs when the engine is hot; damage to the threads in the cylinder head might result.

1   Disconnect the cable from the negative battery terminal (see Chapter 5).

2   On L91 and LXT models, remove the engine cover (see illustration).

3   On LXV engines, unclip the ignition coil cover, then remove the ignition coil assembly (see Chapter 5).

4   On L91 and LXT engines, remove the spark plug wire from one spark plug (see illustration). Pull only on the boot at the end of the wire - do not pull on the wire. A plug wire removal tool should be used if available.

5   In most cases, the tools necessary for spark plug replacement include a spark plug socket which fits onto a ratchet (spark plug sockets are padded inside to prevent damage to the porcelain insulators on the new plugs), various extensions and a gap gauge to check and adjust the gaps on the new plugs (see illustration). A torque wrench should be used to tighten the new plugs.

6   The best approach when replacing the spark plugs is to purchase the new ones in advance, adjust them to the proper gap and replace the plugs one at a time. When buying the new spark plugs, obtain the correct plug type for your particular engine. This information can be found in the Specifications Section in this Chapter or in your Owner's Manual.

7   Allow the engine to cool completely before attempting to remove any of the plugs. These engines are equipped with aluminum cylinder heads, which can be damaged if the spark plugs are removed when the engine is hot. While you are waiting for the engine to cool, check the new plugs for defects and adjust the gaps.

25.2 Remove the engine cover mounting screws

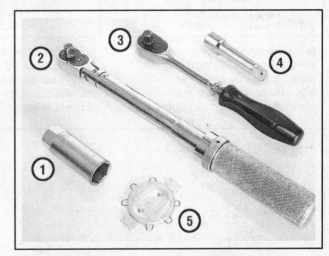

25.5 Tools required for changing spark plugs

1   *Spark plug socket* - This will have special padding inside to protect the spark plug's porcelain insulator
2   *Torque wrench* - Although not mandatory, using this tool is the best way to ensure the plugs are tightened properly
3   *Ratchet* - Standard hand tool to fit the spark plug socket
4   *Extension* - Depending on model and accessories, you may need special extensions and universal joints to reach one or more of the plugs
5   *Spark plug gap gauge* - This gauge for checking the gap comes in a variety of styles. Make sure the gap for your engine is included

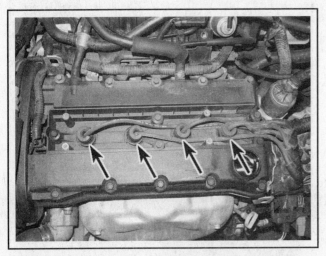

25.4 Label and remove the spark plug wires from the spark plugs one at a time

8   The gap is checked by inserting the proper-thickness gauge between the electrodes at the tip of the plug (see illustration). The gap between the electrodes should be the same as the one specified on the Emissions Control Information label or in this Chapter's Specifications. The gauge should just fit between the electrodes. If the gap is incorrect, use the adjuster on the gauge body to bend the curved side electrode slightly until the proper gap is obtained (see illustration). If the side electrode is not exactly over the center electrode, bend it with the adjuster until it is. Check for cracks in the porcelain insulator (if any are found, the plug should not be used).

✳✳ CAUTION:

Don't force the gauge into the gap, as the coating on the electrodes could be scraped.

➥ **Note: The manufacturer recommends using a wire-type thickness gauge when checking platinum or iridium-type spark plugs. Other types of gauges may scrape the thin coating from the electrodes, thus dramatically shortening the life of the plugs.**

9   If compressed air is available, use it to blow any dirt or foreign material away from the spark plug hole. The idea here is to eliminate the possibility of debris falling into the cylinder as the spark plug is removed.

10   Place the spark plug socket over the plug and remove it from the engine by turning it in a counterclockwise direction (see illustration).

11   Compare the spark plug with the chart shown (see illustration) to get an indication of the general running condition of the engine. Before installing the new plugs, it is a good idea to apply a thin coat of anti-seize compound to the threads.

12   Install one of the new plugs into the hole until you can no longer

25.8a The manufacturer recommends using a wire-type thickness gauge when checking the gap - if the wire does not just fit between the electrodes, adjustment is required

25.8b To change the gap, bend the side electrode only, and be very careful not to crack or chip the porcelain insulator surrounding the center electrode

25.10 Use a ratchet and extension to remove the spark plugs

A **normally worn** spark plug should have light tan or gray deposits on the firing tip.

A **carbon fouled** plug, identified by soft, sooty, black deposits, may indicate an improperly tuned vehicle. Check the air cleaner, ignition components and engine control system.

An **oil fouled** spark plug indicates an engine with worn piston rings and/or bad valve seals allowing excessive oil to enter the chamber.

This spark plug has been **left in the engine too long,** as evidenced by the extreme gap- Plugs with such an extreme gap can cause misfiring and stumbling accompanied by a noticeable lack of power.

A **physically damaged** spark plug may be evidence of severe detonation in that cylinder. Watch that cylinder carefully between services, as a continued detonation will not only damage the plug, but could also damage the engine.

A **bridged or almost bridged** spark plug, identified by a build-up between the electrodes caused by excessive carbon or oil build-up on the plug.

25.11 Inspect the spark plug to determine engine running conditions

turn it with your fingers, then tighten it with a torque wrench (if available) to the torque listed in this Chapter's Specifications, or the ratchet. It is a good idea to slip a length of rubber hose over the end of the plug to use as a tool to thread it into place (see illustration). The hose will grip the plug well enough to turn it, but will start to slip if the plug begins to cross-thread in the hole - this will prevent damaged threads and the accompanying repair costs.

13 Repeat the procedure for the remaining spark plugs.

14 After replacing all the plugs, install the spark plug wires or ignition coil pack (see Chapter 5).

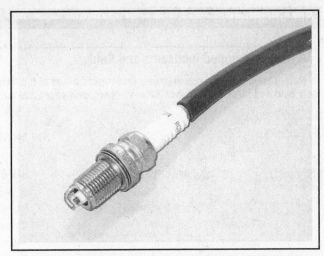

25.12 A length of snug-fitting rubber hose will save time and prevent damaged threads when installing the spark plugs

26 Spark plug wire check and replacement (L91 and LXT engines) (every 30,000 miles or 30 months)

1 The spark plug wires should be checked at the recommended intervals or whenever new spark plugs are installed.

2 Begin this procedure by making a visual check of the spark plug wires while the engine is running. In a darkened garage (make sure there is adequate ventilation) or at night while using a flashlight, start the engine and observe each plug wire. Be careful not to come into contact with any moving engine parts. If possible, use an insulated or non-conductive object to wiggle each wire. If there is a break in the wire, you will see arcing or a small blue spark coming from the damaged area. Secondary ignition voltage increases with engine speed and sometimes a damaged wire will not produce an arc at idle speed. Have an assistant press the accelerator pedal to raise the engine speed to approximately 2000 rpm. Check the spark plug wires for arcing as stated previously. If arcing is noticed, replace all spark plug wires.

3 Perform the following checks with the engine OFF. The wires should be inspected one at a time to prevent mixing up the order that is essential for proper engine operation.

4 With the engine cool, disconnect the spark plug wire from the ignition coil pack. Pull only on the boot at the end of the wire; don't pull on the wire itself. Special pliers are available to help grip the cable boot securely. Use a twisting motion to free the boot/wire from the coil. Disconnect the same spark plug wire from the spark plug, using the same twisting method while pulling on the boot. Disconnect the spark plug wire from any retaining clips as necessary and remove it from the engine.

5 Check inside the boot for corrosion, which will look like a white, crusty powder (don't mistake the white dielectric grease used on some plug wire boots for corrosion protection).

6 Push the wire and boot back onto the end of the spark plug. It should be a tight fit on the plug end. If not, remove the wire and use a pair of pliers to carefully crimp the metal connector inside the wire boot until the fit is snug.

7 Push the wire and boot back into the end of the ignition coil terminal. It should be a tight fit in the terminal. If not, remove the wire and use a pair of pliers to carefully crimp the metal connector inside the wire boot until the fit is snug.

8 Now, using a cloth, clean each wire along its entire length. Remove all built-up dirt and grease. As this is done, inspect for burned areas, cracks and any other form of damage. Bend the wires in several places to ensure that the conductive material inside hasn't hardened. Repeat the procedure for the remaining wires.

9 If new spark plug wires are required, purchase a complete set for your particular engine. The terminals and rubber boots should already be installed on the wires. Replace the wires one at a time to avoid mixing up the firing order and make sure the terminals are securely seated on the coil pack and the spark plugs.

10 Attach the plug wire to the new spark plug and to the ignition coil pack using a twisting motion on the boot until it is firmly seated. Attach the spark plug wire to any retaining clips to keep the wires in their proper location on the valve cover.

Specifications

Recommended lubricants and fluids

➡ Note: Listed here are manufacturer recommendations at the time this manual was written. Manufacturers occasionally upgrade their fluid and lubricant specifications, so check with your local auto parts store for current recommendations.

Engine oil	
Type	API "certified for gasoline engines"
Viscosity	
2007 and earlier models	SAE-5W-30, SAE-10W-30, SAE-15W-40 (SAE 5W-30 for cold area or SAE 15W-40 for hot areas)
2008 and later models	SAE-5W-30
Fuel	Unleaded gasoline, 87 octane minimum
Automatic transaxle fluid	T-IV automatic transmission fluid
Manual transaxle lubricant	Synthetic Manual Transmission Fluid or equivalent SAE 75W-85 GL-4 gear oil
Brake fluid	DOT 3 brake fluid
Clutch fluid	DOT 3 brake fluid
Engine coolant	50/50 mixture of DEX-COOL coolant and de-ionized water

Capacities*

Engine oil (including filter)	
2008 and earlier models	4.0 quarts (3.75 liters)
2009 and larter models	4.8 quarts (4.5 liters)
Coolant	
2008 and earlier models	6.3 quarts (5.9 liters)
2009 and larter models	6.7 quarts (6.3 liters)
Automatic transaxle (drain and refill)	6.2 quarts (5.87 liters)
Manual transaxle	1.9 quarts (1.8 liters)

➡ Note: *All capacities approximate. Add as necessary to bring up to appropriate level.

Ignition system

Spark plug type and gap	
Type	
L91 engine	NGK - BKR6E-11 or equivalent
LXT engine	NGK - ZFR6U-9 or equivalent
LXV engine	NGK - ZFR6U-11 or equivalent
Gap	
L91 and LXT engines	0.039 to 0.043 inch (1.0 to 1.1 mm)
LXV engine	0.035 inch (0.9 mm)
Engine firing order, all models	1-3-4-2

FRONT OF VEHICLE ① ② ③ ④

Cylinder locations and firing order

Brakes

Disc brake pad lining thickness (minimum)	1/8 inch (3 mm)
Drum brake shoe lining thickness (minimum)	1/16 inch (1.5 mm)
Parking brake adjustment	3 to 4 clicks

Torque specifications	Ft-lbs (unless otherwise indicated)	Nm

➡ **Note: One foot-pound (ft-lb) of torque is equivalent to 12 inch-pounds (in-lbs) of torque. Torque values below approximately 15 ft-lbs are expressed in inch-pounds, because most foot-pound torque wrenches are not accurate at these smaller values.**

Engine oil drain plug		
L91 engine	26	35
LXT engine	40	55
LXV engine	80 in-lbs	9
Engine oil filter (L91 and LXT engine)	124 in-lbs	14
Engine oil filter cap (LXV engine)	18	25
Automatic transaxle fluid drain plug	156 in-lbs	17
Automatic transaxle strainer bolts	89 in-lbs	10
Automatic transaxle pan bolts	65 in-lbs	7.5
Transaxle differential cover bolts - (D16/D20 models)	30	40
Manual transaxle check/fill plug	21	28
Manual transaxle drain plug (Y4M models)	21	28
Spark plugs	18	25
Drivebelt tensioner bolt		
LXV engine	37	50
Wheel lug nuts		
2009 and earlier models	88	120
2010 models	92	125
2011 models	103	140

Notes

2A

ENGINES

Section

1 General Information

1 The Chevrolet Aveo has been equipped with either a 1.6L 16-valve DOHC or DOHC VVT engine. This Part of Chapter 2 is devoted to in-vehicle repair procedures for these DOHC (Double Overhead Camshaft) four-cylinder engines. Information concerning engine removal and installation and engine overhaul can be found in Chapter 2B.

2 The engine is equipped with a single timing belt to drive the camshafts. On 2009 and later (LXV) engines a variable valve timing VVT system was added (see Chapter 6).

3 The Specifications included in this Part of Chapter 2 apply only to the procedures contained in this Part. Specifications related to engine removal and installation or overhaul can be found in Chapter 2B.

2 Repair operations possible with the engine in the vehicle

1 Many major repair operations can be accomplished without removing the engine from the vehicle.

2 Clean the engine compartment and the exterior of the engine with some type of degreaser before any work is done. It will make the job easier and help keep dirt out of the internal areas of the engine.

3 Depending on the components involved, it may be helpful to remove the hood to improve access to the engine as repairs are performed (refer to Chapter 11 if necessary). Cover the fenders to prevent damage to the paint. Special pads are available, but an old bedspread or blanket will also work.

4 If vacuum, exhaust, oil or coolant leaks develop, indicating a need for gasket or seal replacement, the repairs can generally be made with the engine in the vehicle. The intake and exhaust manifold gaskets, oil pan gasket, crankshaft oil seals and cylinder head gasket are all accessible with the engine in place.

5 Exterior engine components, such as the intake and exhaust manifolds, the oil pan, the oil pump, the water pump, the starter motor, the alternator and the fuel system components can be removed for repair with the engine in place.

6 Since the cylinder head can be removed without pulling the engine, camshaft and valve component servicing can also be accomplished with the engine in the vehicle. Replacement of the timing chain or timing belt, and sprockets is also possible with the engine in the vehicle.

7 In extreme cases caused by a lack of necessary equipment, repair or replacement of crankshaft, piston rings, pistons, connecting rods and rod bearings is possible with the engine in the vehicle. However, this practice is not recommended because of the cleaning and preparation work that must be done to the components involved.

3 Top Dead Center (TDC) for number one piston - locating

1 Top Dead Center (TDC) is the highest point in the cylinder that each piston reaches as it travels up-and-down during crankshaft rotation. Each piston reaches TDC on the compression stroke and again on the exhaust stroke, but TDC generally refers to piston position on the compression stroke.

2 Positioning the piston(s) at TDC is an essential part of certain other repair procedures discussed in this manual.

3 Before beginning this procedure, place the transmission in Park or Neutral and apply the parking brake or block the rear wheels. Remove the spark plugs (see Chapter 1).

4 Insert a compression gauge into the number one cylinder spark plug hole. Turn the crankshaft using a ratchet or breaker bar and socket (normal direction of rotation is clockwise) until compression registers on the gauge, then turn it slowly until the TDC mark on the timing belt cover is aligned with the hole or notch on the crankshaft pulley (see illustration).

➡ **Note: On LXV engines, the notch on the crankshaft pulley must align with the notch in the lower timing belt cover at the 6 o'clock position.**

5 After the number one piston has been positioned at TDC on the compression stroke, TDC for any of the remaining pistons can be located by turning the crankshaft and following the firing order. Divide the crankshaft pulley into two equal sections with chalk marks at each

3.4 Align the notch on the crankshaft pulley (1) with the pointer on the timing belt cover (2) - L91 and LXT models

point, each indicating 180-degrees of crankshaft rotation. Rotating the engine past TDC no. 1 to the next mark will place the engine at TDC for cylinder no. 3.

4 Valve cover - removal and installation

REMOVAL

1 Disconnect the cable from the negative battery terminal (see Chapter 5).

2 On L91 and LXT engines, disconnect the spark plug wires from the spark plugs (see Chapter 1).

3 On LXV engines, remove the ignition coil assembly from the valve cover (see Chapter 5).

4 Detach the PCV hose from the valve cover.

5 Detach the electrical connectors to the sensors routed in the main wiring harness and reposition the harness away from the valve cover.

6 Remove the valve cover bolts, then lift the valve cover off. Tap gently with a soft-face hammer, if necessary, to break the gasket seal.

7 Remove the valve cover gasket (see illustration) and the O-rings around each bolt hole opening (see illustration).

INSTALLATION

8 Clean the gasket surfaces on the intake manifold, cylinder head and valve cover. Use a shop rag and brake cleaner to wipe off all residue and gasket material from the sealing surfaces.

9 Insert a new valve cover gasket into the grooved recess in the valve cover. Make sure the gasket is positioned properly in the groove (see illustration), then install the O-rings around each of the bolt holes.

10 Apply a bead of RTV sealant to the joints where the front camshaft bearing caps meet the cylinder head and to the semi-circular cutouts (see illustration).

11 The remainder of installation is the reverse of removal. Tighten the valve cover bolts evenly, starting with the center bolts and working outward (see illustration), to the torque listed in this Chapter's Specifications.

12 Reconnect the battery (see Chapter 5).

4.7a Remove the valve cover gasket. . .

4.7b. . . then remove the O-rings around each bolt hole

4.9 Install the gasket into the grooved recess in the valve cover

4.10 Apply a bead of sealant to the joints

4.11 Valve cover tightening sequence - L91 models, other models similar

5 Intake manifold - removal and installation

※ WARNING:

Wait until the engine is completely cool before beginning this procedure.

L91 AND LXT ENGINES

Removal

1 Relieve the system fuel pressure (see Chapter 4).
2 Disconnect the cable from the negative battery terminal (see Chapter 5).
3 Raise the vehicle and support it securely on jackstands.
4 Remove the engine cover.
5 Disconnect any electrical connectors that would interfere with manifold removal. Open the wiring harness clips and detach all wiring harnesses from the manifold.
6 Disconnect any vacuum hoses connected to the manifold, including the hose leading to the brake booster. Mark the hoses, if necessary, to ensure correct reassembly.
7 Drain the cooling system (see Chapter 1).
8 Disconnect the throttle cable from the throttle body (see Chapter 4), if equipped.
9 Disconnect the PCV hose from the intake manifold.
10 Detach the fuel feed line from the fuel rail then remove the fuel rail and fuel injectors as an assembly (see Chapter 4).
11 Disconnect the vent line from the EVAP canister purge solenoid valve (see Chapter 6).
12 Remove the alternator mounting bolts (see Chapter 5) then remove the alternator bracket-to-intake manifold bolt.
13 From under the vehicle, remove the intake manifold support bracket from under the intake manifold (see illustration).
14 Remove the intake manifold lower mounting bolts (see illustrations).
15 Remove the intake manifold mounting bolts (see illustration).
16 Detach the intake manifold from the cylinder head.
17 Once the intake manifold is removed the alternator and intake manifold support bracket can be removed.

5.13 Intake manifold support bracket bolt locations

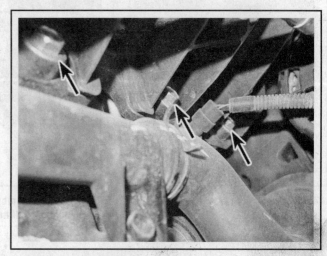

5.14a Remove the lower mounting bolts. . .

5.14b . . . along the bottom of the intake manifold

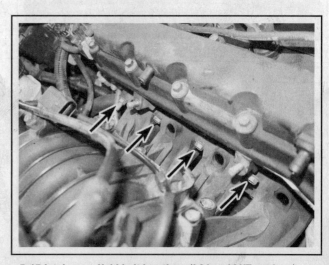

5.15 Intake manifold bolt locations (L91 and LXT engines)

Installation

18 Place the intake manifold support bracket and alternator into the engine compartment, if they were completely removed.

19 Install a new gasket to the manifold.

→ **Note: Make sure the mating surfaces of the manifold and cylinder head are clean.**

20 Place the manifold against the cylinder head and install the bolts, but only finger-tight.

21 Tighten the bolts in sequence (see illustration) to the torque listed in this Chapter's Specifications, starting with the center bolts and working toward the ends.

22 The remainder of installation is the reverse of removal.

23 Reconnect the battery (see Chapter 5).

24 Refill the cooling system (see Chapter 1).

25 Run the engine and check for vacuum and fuel leaks.

LXV ENGINES

Removal

26 Relieve the fuel system pressure (see Chapter 4), then disconnect the cable from the negative battery terminal (see Chapter 5).

27 Remove the air filter housing, air intake duct and throttle body (see Chapter 4).

28 Disconnect any electrical connectors that would interfere with manifold removal. Open the wiring harness clips and detach all wiring harnesses from the manifold.

29 Disconnect any vacuum hoses connected to the manifold, including the hose leading to the brake booster. Mark the hoses, if necessary, to ensure correct reassembly.

30 Remove the valve cover (see Section 4).

31 Remove the intake manifold mounting bolts.

32 Detach the intake manifold from the cylinder head.

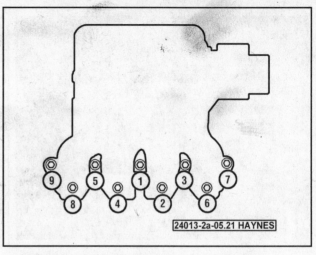

5.21 Intake manifold tightening sequence - L91 and LXT models

Installation

33 Install new gaskets to the manifold.

→ **Note: Make sure the mating surfaces of the manifold and cylinder head are clean.**

34 Place the manifold against the cylinder head and install the bolts, but only finger-tight.

35 Tighten the bolts to the torque listed in this Chapter's Specifications, starting with the center bolts and working toward the ends.

36 The remainder of installation is the reverse of removal.

37 Reconnect the battery (see Chapter 5).

38 Run the engine and check for vacuum and fuel leaks.

6 Exhaust manifold - removal and installation

✳ WARNING:

Wait until the engine is completely cool before starting this procedure.

→ **Note: On LXV engines the catalytic converter is integrated into the exhaust manifold and cannot be serviced separately.**

REMOVAL

1 Disconnect the cable from the negative battery terminal (see Chapter 5).

2 Remove the exhaust manifold heat shield (see illustration).

3 Remove the dipstick tube mounting bolt and tube.

4 Raise the vehicle and support it securely on jackstands.

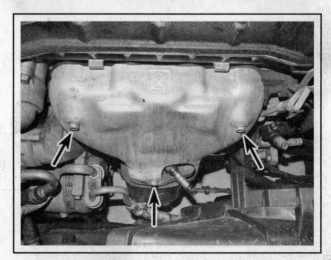

6.2 Heat shield mounting bolt locations - L91 engine shown, others similar

6.5 Remove the exhaust manifold-to-catalytic converter nuts

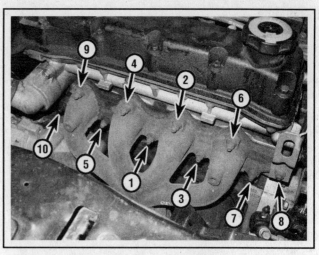

6.11 L91 and LXT model exhaust manifold tightening sequence

5 On L91 and LXT models, remove the exhaust manifold-to-catalytic converter nuts (see illustration).

6 On LXV models, detach the exhaust pipe from the manifold/catalytic coverter.

7 Follow the lead from the oxygen sensor up to its electrical connector, then unplug the connector. Also detach the lead from its retaining clip.

8 On LXV models, remove the exhaust manifold support bracket-to-engine block bolts, but leave the support bracket attached to the converter, if equipped.

9 Remove the exhaust manifold mounting nuts; on L91 and LXT models, loosen them in the reverse order of the tightening sequence (see illustration 6.11). Detach the manifold assembly from the cylinder head.

INSTALLATION

10 Using a scraper, thoroughly clean the mating surfaces on the cylinder head, manifold and exhaust pipe. Remove the residue with brake system cleaner.

11 Check that the mating surfaces are perfectly flat and not damaged in any way. A warped or damaged manifold may require machining or, if severe enough, replacement. Install the new gasket to the cylinder head studs and place the manifold on the cylinder head. On L91 and LXT models, tighten the nuts in sequence (see illustration) to the torque listed in this Chapter's Specifications. On LXV models, tighten the nuts evenly, working from the center outward, to the torque listed in this Chapter's Specifications.

12 Connect the exhaust pipe to the manifold and tighten the nuts evenly to the torque listed in this Chapter's Specifications.

13 The remainder of installation is the reverse of removal.

14 Reconnect the battery (see Chapter 5).

15 Run the engine and check for exhaust leaks.

7 Timing belt and sprockets - removal, inspection and installation

⁑ CAUTION:

The timing system is complex. Severe engine damage will occur if you make any mistakes. Do not attempt this procedure unless you are highly experienced with this type of repair. If you are at all unsure of your abilities, consult an expert. Double-check all your work and be sure everything is correct before you attempt to start the engine.

➡ Note: This is a difficult procedure, involving special tools. Read through the entire Section and obtain the necessary tools before beginning the procedure. New camshaft sprocket bolts must be purchased ahead of time.

➡ Note: Because the timing belt drives the water pump on 2008 and earlier models (L91 and LXT engines), it is a good idea to replace the water pump whenever changing the timing belt.

REMOVAL

1 Disconnect the cable from the negative terminal of the battery (see Chapter 5).

2 Remove the engine cover.

3 Remove the air filter housing (see Chapter 4).

4 Loosen the right front wheel lug nuts, then raise the front of the vehicle and support it securely on jackstands. Apply the parking brake and block the rear wheels. Remove the wheel.

7.7 Upper timing belt cover bolt locations

7.9 Lower timing belt cover bolt locations

7.11 Verify that the mark on the crankshaft sprocket (1) is aligned with the mark on the rear timing belt cover (2)

5 Remove the inner fender splash shield (see Chapter 1, Section 18). Also remove the under-vehicle splash shield.

6 Remove the drivebelt and drivebelt tensioner (see Chapter 1).

L91 and LXT models

7 Remove the upper timing belt cover bolts and cover (see illustration).

8 Set the engine at TDC for number one cylinder (see Section 3).

9 Remove the crankshaft pulley (see Section 8) and the lower timing belt cover (see illustration).

10 Remove the power steering pump bolts and place the pump out of the way, if equipped.

11 Install the crankshaft bolt and rotate the engine clockwise for TDC number one cylinder if not already done and verify that the crankshaft sprocket is aligned with the timing mark on the bottom of the rear timing belt cover (see illustration).

12 Slightly loosen the water pump mounting bolts (see Chapter 3).

13 Using special tool J 42492-A or a thin 41 mm open-end wrench, turn the water pump counterclockwise to release the tension on the timing belt (see illustration).

✳✳ WARNING:

Failure to use the correct tool for rotating the water pump or trying to set the timing belt tension while the engine is hot can cause the premature failure of the water pump or automatic tensioner.

14 Support the engine with a floor jack and a block of wood, then carefully raise the engine just enough to take the weight off the mount.

15 Remove the right-side mount (see Section 15).

16 If you intend to reuse the belt, mark it with an arrow indicating direction of travel and put match marks from the belt to the sprockets so it can be realigned easily.

17 Remove the timing belt.

18 Using a wrench on the flat spot on the camshaft(s), hold the camshaft from turning, then use a socket and ratchet to loosen the camshaft gear mounting bolt.

19 Slide the camshaft sprocket off of the end of the camshaft.

20 To remove the timing belt rear cover, remove the timing tensioner

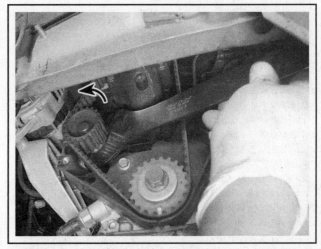

7.13 Rotate the water pump counterclockwise to release the tension on the timing belt

bolts, idler pulley center bolts and crankshaft gear. Then remove the rear cover bolts and lower the cover out of the vehicle.

LXV models

21 Rotate the crankshaft pulley until the notch on the pulley is aligned with the notch on the timing belt cover.

22 Remove the valve cover (see Section 4). Confirm that the camshaft sprocket timing marks are aligned (see illustration 7.28). If they aren't, rotate the crankshaft one complete revolution and realign the notch on the pulley with the notch on the timing belt cover.

23 Place a block of wood between the jack head and the oil pan, then carefully raise the engine just enough to take the weight off the mount.

24 Remove the right-side mount (see Section 15).

25 Install a flywheel/driveplate locking tool. If you're working on a model with a manual transaxle, remove the transaxle-to-engine nut and bolt from the front of the bellhousing, mid-way up, near the catalytic converter. If you're working on a model with an automatic transaxle, remove the engine-to-transaxle bolt near the transaxle front mount. On all models, engage flywheel/driveplate locking tool no. KM-6625 (or

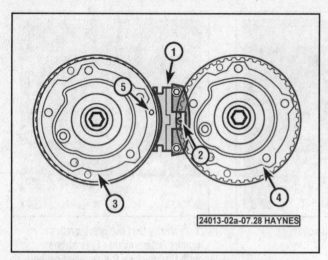

7.28 Install the special tool to lock the camshaft adjuster sprockets in place

1   Special tool KM-6340
2   Exhaust camshaft
    alignment mark
3   Intake camshaft
4   Exhaust camshaft
5   Intake camshaft
    alignment mark

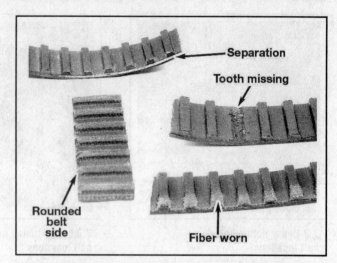

7.36 Check the timing belt for cracked or missing teeth; if the belt is cracked or worn, also check the pulleys for nicks or burrs - wear on one side of the belt indicates pulley misalignment problems

equivalent) with the ring gear teeth, then reinstall the bolt and tighten it securely.

26 Remove the upper timing belt cover, then the right side mount engine mount bracket.

27 Remove the crankshaft pulley (see Section 8) and the lower timing belt cover.

28 If you're just removing the timing belt, install special tool KM-6340 (or equivalent) in between the camshaft adjuster sprockets (see illustration) to lock the sprockets/adjuster wheels in place. Make sure the mark on the exhaust camshaft adjuster is aligned with the groove in the special tool.

29 Insert an Allen wrench into the timing belt tensioner and rotate the tensioner clockwise until lock pin tool EN-6333 (or equivalent) can be inserted into the back side of the tensioner.

30 Remove the idler pulley center bolt and idler pulley.

➡ **Note: The timing belt tensioner bolt and idler pulley bolt must be replaced.**

31 If you intend to reuse the belt, mark it with an arrow indicating direction of travel and put match marks from the belt to the sprockets so it can be realigned easily.

32 Remove the timing belt and the tensioner. Always replace the tensioner bolt with a new one during reassembly.

33 Insert locking tool KM-6628 into the horizontal slots in both camshafts or a metal bar that can be inserted into the slots with little play, and long enough to reach to both camshafts. The tool should lay flat against the valve cover sealing surface of the cylinder head and into both horizontal slots on the camshafts.

34 The camshaft adjuster sprockets can be removed now, if necessary. Hold the hex area of the camshaft securely with a wrench, remove the outer closure plugs (the sealing "caps" over the sprocket bolts), then remove the camshaft adjuster sprocket bolts. Replace the sprocket bolts with new ones.

35 Remove the camshaft adjuster sprockets from the end of the camshafts.

INSPECTION

36 Check the belt for the presence of oil or dirt, and inspect for visible defects (see illustration).

37 Check that the tensioner and idler pulley turn smoothly.

INSTALLATION

38 Remove all dirt, oil and grease from the timing belt area at the front of the engine.

39 Install the camshaft sprocket(s) (if they were removed) on the camshaft(s) with new bolts, finger-tight.

L91 and LXT models

40 Verify that the crankshaft sprocket is aligned with the timing mark on the bottom of the rear timing belt cover (see illustration 7.11).

41 Hold the hex area of the camshaft securely with a wrench, then tighten the sprocket bolts to the torque listed in this Chapter's Specifications.

42 Position the mark on the intake camshaft gear at the 3 o'clock position and the mark on the exhaust gear at the 9 o'clock position (see illustration), making sure the exhaust camshaft gear dowel pin is at the 11 o'clock position.

➡ **Note: The exhaust camshaft gear has two marks but only one is used. To verify that you're using the correct mark when the gear is installed, the dowel pin on the exhaust camshaft should be in the 11 o'clock position.**

43 Install the timing belt over the gears.

44 Using special tool J 42492-A or a 41 mm open-end wrench, turn the water pump clockwise until the adjuster arm pointer of the timing belt tensioner is aligned with the notch in the tensioner bracket (see illustrations), approximately at the 11 o'clock position.

45 Tighten the water pump mounting bolts to 89 in-lbs (10 Nm).

7.42 The mark on the intake camshaft gear should be at the 3 o'clock position (1), the mark on the exhaust gear should be at the 9 o'clock position (2), with the exhaust camshaft gear dowel pin at the 11 o'clock position (3)

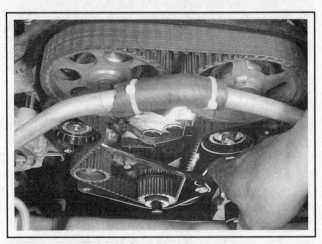

7.44a Use a 41 mm open-end wrench, to rotate the water pump clockwise. . .

7.44b. . . until the adjuster arm pointer of the timing belt tensioner is aligned with the notch in the tensioner bracket (approximately at the 11 o'clock position); this is the Stage 1 setting

7.47 Turn the water pump clockwise until the pointer on the tensioner arm is aligned with the pointer on the tensioner body

46 Using a socket and breaker bar on the crankshaft pulley bolt, turn the crankshaft slowly (clockwise) through two complete revolutions (720-degrees) then loosen the water pump mounting bolts slightly.

✳ CAUTION:

Stop turning the crankshaft immediately if you feel resistance; the valves could be contacting the pistons.

47 Using special tool J 42492-A or a 41 mm open-end wrench, turn the water pump clockwise until the adjuster arm pointer of the timing belt tensioner is aligned with the pointer on the tensioner bracket (see illustration).

48 Tighten the water pump mounting bolts to 89 in-lbs (10 Nm).

49 If the timing marks are not aligned exactly, repeat the timing belt installation procedure. DO NOT start the engine until you're absolutely certain that the timing belt is installed correctly. Serious and costly engine damage could occur if the belt is installed incorrectly.

50 The remainder of installation is the reverse of removal.

LXV models

51 Install special tool KM-6628 into the horizontal slots in the ends of the camshafts, if removed.

52 Install special tool KM-6340 onto the camshaft adjuster sprockets (see illustration 7.28),making sure the intake and exhaust camshaft adjuster marks are aligned.

➡ **Note: The intake camshaft sprocket mark does align with the groove on KM-6628 locking tool during the installation of KM-6340 but is very close.**

53 Hold the hex area of the camshaft securely with a wrench, then tighten the adjuster sprocket bolts to the torque listed in this Chapter's Specifications.

✳ CAUTION:

Do not use special tool KM-6628 to hold the camshafts while tightening the bolts - the camshafts could be damaged.

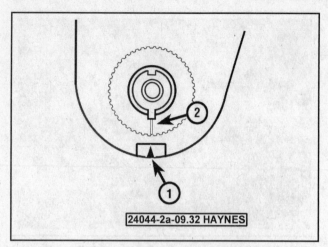

24044-2a-09.32 HAYNES

7.58 Align the crankshaft sprocket mark with the TDC mark on the oil pump housing

1   *TDC mark on the oil pump housing*
2   *Crankshaft alignment mark*

54 Hold the hex area of the camshaft securely with a wrench, then install and tighten the adjuster sprocket closure plugs to the torque listed in this Chapter's Specifications.

55 Remove special tool KM-6628 from the ends of the camshafts.

56 Install the timing belt tensioner with a new bolt and tighten the bolt to the torque listed in this Chapter's Specifications.

57 Install the idler pulley with a new bolt and tighten the bolt to the torque listed in this Chapter's Specifications.

58 Slide the crankshaft sprocket onto the end of the crankshaft, making sure the keyway (and sprocket mark) and TDC marks are aligned

(see illustration).

59 Cover half of the timing belt with tape, then thread the timing belt through the engine mount bracket. Once the belt is through the bracket you can remove the tape.

➡ **Note: The timing belt can be cut when threading it through the engine mount bracket; it is a good idea to cover the belt before trying to slide it through the bracket.**

60 Verify the crankshaft timing mark is at 6 o'clock position (see illustration 7.58). Now align the camshaft sprockets with special tool KM-6340 (see illustration 7.28) and install the timing belt.

61 Insert an Allen wrench into the front of the tensioner and rotate the tensioner clockwise until the locking pin installed in Step 8 can be removed.

62 Using a socket and breaker bar on the crankshaft pulley bolt, turn the crankshaft slowly (clockwise) through two complete revolutions (720-degrees), positioning the crankshaft sprocket timing mark at the 6 o'clock position, with the marks lined up (see illustration 7.58). Insert special tool KM-6340 between the camshaft adjuster sprockets, then try to install special tool KM-6628 into the slots at the rear of the camshafts.

※ **CAUTION:**

Stop turning the crankshaft immediately if you feel resistance; the valves could be contacting the pistons.

63 If the timing marks are not aligned exactly, repeat the timing belt installation procedure. DO NOT start the engine until you're absolutely certain that the timing belt is installed correctly. Serious and costly engine damage could occur if the belt is installed incorrectly.

64 The remainder of installation is the reverse of removal.

8   Crankshaft pulley and front oil seal - removal and installation

CRANKSHAFT PULLEY

1   Disconnect the cable from the negative battery terminal (see Chapter 5).

2   Remove the drivebelt (see Chapter 1).

3   Raise the vehicle and support it securely on jackstands.

4   Remove the under-vehicle splash shield.

5   Remove the inner fender splash shield (see Chapter 11).

6   If you're removing the crankshaft pulley as part of the timing belt removal procedure, set the engine at TDC for cylinder no. 1 (see Section 3).

L91 and LXT engines

7   Remove the bolt from the front of the crankshaft. A breaker bar will be necessary, since the bolt is very tight. Have an assistant lock the flywheel in place with a prybar.

8   Slide the pulley off the nose of the crankshaft.

9   If you're replacing the crankshaft front oil seal, proceed to Step 24.

10 Lubricate the hub of the pulley with clean engine oil, then slide it onto the crankshaft.

11 Install the bolt and, holding the pulley with a strap wrench, tighten the bolt to the torque listed in this Chapter's Specifications.

12 The remainder of installation is the reverse of removal.

13 Reconnect the battery (see Chapter 5).

LXV engine

14 Place a large block of wood between the jack head and the oil pan, then carefully raise the engine just enough to take the weight off the front engine mount, then remove the front engine mount (see Section 15).

15 Install a flywheel/driveplate locking tool. If you're working on a model with a manual transaxle, remove the transaxle-to-engine nut and bolt from the front of the bellhousing, mid-way up, near the catalytic converter. If you're working on a model with an automatic transaxle, remove the engine-to-transaxle bolt near the transaxle front mount. On all models, engage flywheel/driveplate locking tool no. EN-6625 (or equivalent) with the ring gear teeth, then reinstall the bolt and tighten it securely.

16 Using a large ratchet or breaker bar and socket, unscrew the crankshaft pulley center bolt. Discard the bolt and obtain a new one for installation.

17 Lower the front of the engine enough to slide the pulley off the nose of the crankshaft.

18 If you are going to replace the crankshaft front oil seal, remove the timing belt (see Section 7) and slide the crankshaft sprocket off the nose of the crankshaft, then proceed to Step 24.

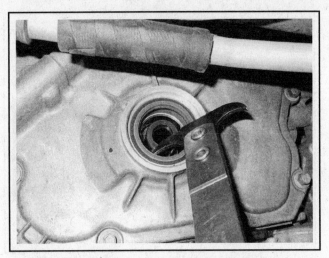

8.25 Use a seal puller to remove the old crankshaft seal, taking care not to damage the crankshaft or the seal bore in the cover

8.27 Driving the new seal in with a seal driver until the seal is flush with the surface of the oil pump

19 Lubricate the hub of the pulley with clean engine oil, then slide it onto the crankshaft.

20 Install a NEW bolt and tighten it to the torque listed in this Chapter's Specifications.

21 The remainder of installation is the reverse of removal.

22 Reconnect the battery (see Chapter 5).

CRANKSHAFT FRONT OIL SEAL REPLACEMENT

23 Remove the crankshaft pulley.

24 Remove the timing belt (see Section 7).

25 Use a seal removal tool to pry the seal out (see illustration).

26 Clean the seal bore and check it for nicks or gouges. Also examine the area of the hub that rides in the seal for signs of abnormal wear or scoring.

27 Coat the lip of the new seal with clean engine oil and drive it into the bore with a seal driver (see illustration). The open side of the seal faces into the engine.

28 Using clean engine oil, lubricate the sealing surface of the crankshaft pulley hub.

29 Install the crankshaft pulley.

9   Camshafts and lifters - removal, inspection and installation

➡ **Note: This is a difficult procedure, involving special tools. Read through the entire Section and obtain the necessary tools before beginning the procedure. New camshaft sprocket bolts must be purchased ahead of time.**

1 Disconnect the cable from the negative battery terminal (see Chapter 5).

2 Remove the valve cover (see Section 4).

REMOVAL

L91 and LXT engines

3 Remove the timing belt and camshaft sprockets (see Section 7).

4 If not already removed, remove the camshaft position sensor (see Chapter 6).

5 Each camshaft cap should be marked for location and direction. Loosen each bearing cap bolt slowly and evenly, a half turn at a time in the order of the removal sequence (see illustration). Lift the camshaft

9.5 Camshaft bearing cap removal order sequence

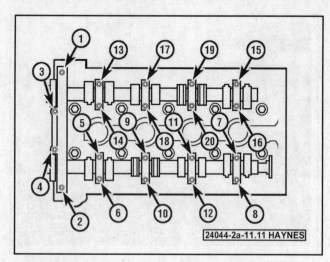

9.10 Camshaft bearing cap removal order sequence - LXV engines

9.14 Check the cam lobes for pitting, excessive wear, and scoring. If scoring is excessive, as shown here, replace the camshaft

9.15 Measure each camshaft lobe height with a micrometer

from the cylinder head, parallel to the head surface, then remove the oil seal from the front of the camshafts.

✳ CAUTION:

The caps must be installed in their original locations. Keep all parts from each camshaft together; never mix parts from one camshaft with those for another.

6 Remove the lifters (tappets) from their bores in the cylinder head. Identify and arrange the lifters so they can be reinstalled in their original locations.

LXV engine

7 Remove the timing belt, timing belt tensioner and camshaft adjuster sprockets (see Section 7).

8 If not already removed, remove both camshaft position sensors (see Chapter 6).

9 Remove the timing belt rear cover bolts and cover.

10 Each camshaft cap should be marked for location and direction. Loosen each bearing cap bolt slowly and evenly, a half turn at a time in the order of the removal sequence (see illustration). Lift the camshaft from the cylinder head, parallel to the head surface and remove the camshaft seal from the camshafts.

✳ CAUTION:

The caps must be installed in their original locations. Keep all parts from each camshaft together; never mix parts from one camshaft with those for another.

11 Remove the lifters (tappets) from their bores in the cylinder head. Identify and arrange the lifters so they can be reinstalled in their original locations.

INSPECTION

12 Check the lifters for scuffing and wear marks and replace as necessary.

13 If the adjusters or the cylinder head bores are excessively worn, new adjusters or a new cylinder head, or both, may be required. If the valve train is noisy, particularly if the noise persists after a cold start, you can suspect a faulty lash adjuster.

14 Examine the camshaft lobes for scoring, pitting, galling (wear due to rubbing), and evidence of overheating (blue, discolored areas). Look for flaking of the hardened surface layer of each lobe (see illustration). If any such wear is evident, replace the camshaft.

15 Measure the lobe height of each cam lobe on the intake camshaft, and record your measurements (see illustration). Compare the measurements for excessive variation; if the lobe heights vary more than 0.005 inch (0.125 mm), replace the camshaft. Compare the lobe height measurements on the exhaust camshaft and follow the same procedure. Do not compare intake camshaft lobe heights with exhaust camshaft lobe heights, as they are different. Only compare intake lobes with intake lobes and exhaust lobes with exhaust lobes.

16 Inspect the camshaft bearing journals and the cylinder head bearing surfaces for pitting or excessive wear. If any such wear is evident, replace the component concerned.

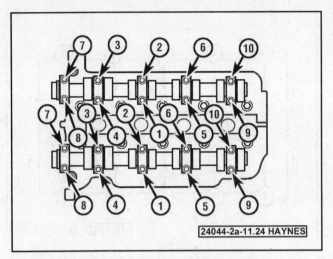

9.19a Camshaft bearing cap tightening sequence - L91 and LXT engines

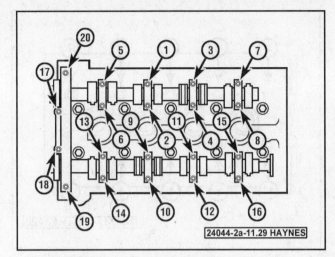

9.19b Camshaft bearing cap tightening sequence - LXV engines

INSTALLATION

17 Lubricate the lifters with engine assembly lubricant or fresh engine oil. Install the lifters into their original bores.

18 Lubricate the camshafts with camshaft installation lubricant and install them in their correct locations. The camshaft lobes for cylinder no. 1 must be pointing away from the lifters, and the slots at the rear of the shafts must be parallel (or nearly parallel with the surface of the cylinder head.

19 Install the camshaft bearing caps in order, and tighten the caps slowly and evenly in order of the tightening sequence (see illustrations). When installing the first camshaft bearing cap, apply anaerobic sealant to the sealing surfaces of the cap, making sure the sealant does not block the oil passages.

20 Coat the lips of the new camshaft oil seals with clean engine oil and drive them into their bores with a seal driver or a socket slightly smaller in diameter than the seal. The open side of the seal faces into the cylinder head.

21 On LXV models, place a wrench on the hex section of the camshaft, rotate the intake camshaft counterclockwise and install special tool EN-6628-A into the rear of the intake camshaft, then rotate the exhaust camshaft counterclockwise until special tool EN-6628-A can be installed into the end of the camshaft. The tool should fit into both camshafts and be flush against the cylinder head.

➡ **Note: It may be necessary to use a second wrench on the intake camshaft and slightly take the pressure off of the special tool to allow it to seat in both camshafts.**

22 The remainder of installation is the reverse of removal.

23 If you're working on an LXV engine, check and adjust the valve clearances (see Section 16).

24 Reconnect the battery (see Chapter 5).

10 Cylinder head - removal and installation

✳ CAUTION:

The engine must be completely cool when the head is removed. Failure to allow the engine to cool off could result in head warpage. New head bolts should be purchased ahead of time.

REMOVAL

1 Disconnect the cable from the negative battery terminal (see Chapter 5).

2 Wait until the engine is completely cool, then drain the cooling system (see Chapter 1).

3 Remove the drivebelt and the drivebelt tensioner (see Chapter 1).

4 Remove the exhaust manifold (see Section 6).

5 Remove the intake manifold (see Section 5).

6 Remove the timing belt (see Section 7).

7 Place a large block of wood between the jack head and the oil pan, then carefully raise the engine just enough to take the weight off the front engine mount. Then remove the front engine mount (see Section 15).

8 Remove the timing belt (see Section 7) and the timing belt covers.

9 On LXV engines remove the camshafts (see Section 9).

10 Label and disconnect the electrical connectors from the cylinder head that will interfere with removal. Use tape and mark each connector to insure correct reassembly.

11 Remove the cylinder head bolts and discard them, following the reverse of the tightening sequence (see illustration 10.19a or 10.19b). Loosen the bolts in sequence 1/4-turn then a 1/2-turn at a time. If the head is to be completely overhauled, refer to Section 9 for removal of the camshafts, rocker arms, (if equipped) and hydraulic lash adjusters or lifters.

12 Use a prybar at the corners of the head-to-block mating surface to break the gasket seal. Do not pry between the cylinder head and engine block in the gasket sealing area.

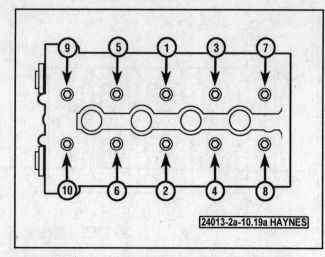

10.19a Cylinder head bolt tightening sequence - L91 and LXT engines

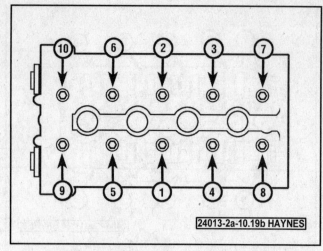

10.19b Cylinder head bolt tightening sequence - LXV engines

13 Lift the cylinder head off the engine. If resistance is felt, place a wood block against the end and strike the wood block with a hammer. Store the cylinder head on wood blocks to prevent damage to the gasket sealing surfaces.

14 Remove the old cylinder head gasket. Before removing, note the correct orientation of the gasket for correct installation.

INSTALLATION

15 The mating surfaces of the cylinder head and block must be perfectly clean when the head is installed. Use a gasket scraper to remove all traces of carbon and old gasket material, then clean the mating surfaces with brake system cleaner. If there's oil on the mating surfaces when the cylinder head is installed, the gasket may not seal correctly and leaks may develop. When working on the engine block, cover the open areas of the engine with shop rags to keep debris out during repair and reassembly. Use a vacuum cleaner to remove any debris that falls into the cylinders.

16 Check the engine block and cylinder head mating surfaces for nicks, deep scratches and other damage.

17 Use a tap of the correct size to chase the threads in the cylinder head bolt holes. Dirt, corrosion, sealant and damaged threads will affect torque readings.

18 Make sure the new gasket is located on the dowels in the block.

19 Carefully position the cylinder head on the engine block without disturbing the gasket. Install new cylinder head bolts and, following the recommended sequence (see illustrations), tighten the bolts to the torque listed in this Chapter's Specifications.

➡ **Note: The method used for the head bolt tightening procedure is referred to as a "torque-angle" method. A special torque angle gauge (available at most auto parts stores) is available to attach to a breaker bar and socket for better accuracy during the tightening procedure.**

20 Install the timing belt (see Section 7).

21 Install the exhaust manifold (see Section 6).

22 Install the intake manifold (see Section 5).

23 The remaining installation steps are the reverse of removal.

24 If you're working on an LXV engine and any of the following work has been performed, check and adjust the valve clearances:

  a) *Camshaft replacement*
  b) *Lifter replacement*
  c) *Valve job*

25 Reconnect the battery (see Chapter 5).

26 Change the engine oil and filter and refill the cooling system (see Chapter 1), then start the engine and check carefully for oil and coolant leaks.

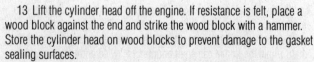

11 Oil pan - removal and installation

REMOVAL

1   Raise the front of the vehicle and support it securely on jackstands.

2   Drain the engine oil (see Chapter 1).

3   Disconnect the exhaust pipe/catalytic converter from the exhaust manifold (see Section 6).

4   On automatic transmission models, remove the transmission rear mounting bracket bolts.

5   Remove the oil pan-to-transaxle bolts.

6   Loosen the oil pan bolts a little at a time, in a criss-cross pattern, until they can be removed.

7   Carefully remove the oil pan from the lower crankcase.

❋❋ CAUTION:

If the oil pan is difficult to separate from the lower crankcase, use a rubber mallet or a block of wood and a hammer to jar it loose. If it's stubborn and still won't come off, pry carefully on casting protrusions (not the mating surfaces!).

INSTALLATION

8   Using a gasket scraper, thoroughly clean all old gasket material from the lower crankcase and oil pan. Remove residue and oil film with a solvent such as brake system cleaner.

9   On LXV engines, make sure the oil screen is seated properly in the oil pan.

10   Apply a 1/8-inch (3.5 mm) bead of sealant to the perimeter of the oil pan, inboard of the bolt holes. Allow the sealant to set-up before installing the oil pan to the engine (but be sure to install the pan within the time given by the sealant manufacturer).

11   Apply extra beads of sealant to the joints where the oil pump and rear main oil seal retainer meet the engine block.

12   Install the oil pan and bolts, tightening them to approximately 18 in-lbs (2 Nm), then tighten the oil pan-to-transaxle bolts to the torque listed in this Chapter's Specifications. Finally, tighten the oil pan bolts a little at a time, starting from the center bolts and working outward, to the torque listed in this Chapter's Specifications.

13   The remaining installation is the reverse of removal.

14   Refill the engine with oil and install a new oil filter (see Chapter 1), then run the engine and check for leaks.

12 Oil pump - removal, inspection and installation

REMOVAL

1   Drain the engine oil (see Chapter 1).

2   Remove the drivebelt (see Chapter 1).

3   Loosen the right-front wheel lug nuts, raise the front of the vehicle and support it securely on jackstands. Remove the right front wheel.

L91 and LXT engines

4   Remove the timing belt, timing belt rear cover and timing belt sprocket (see Section 7).

5   Remove the crankshaft position sensor (see Chapter 6).

6   Remove the oil pan (see Section 11), then remove the oil pump pickup tube and bracket bolts, and remove the tube.

7   Remove the oil pump mounting bolts (see illustration) and carefully separate the oil pump from the engine block.

LXV engines

8   Drain the engine coolant (see Chapter 1).

9   Remove the exhaust manifold (see Section 6).

10   Remove the air conditioning compressor mounting bolts (see Chapter 3), without disconnecting the lines, and secure the compressor out of the way.

11   Remove the alternator (see Chapter 5).

12   Remove the camshaft actuator sprockets (see Section 7).

13   Remove the timing belt and slide the crankshaft sprocket from the end of the crankshaft (see Section 7), then remove the timing belt rear cover bolts and cover.

14   Remove the oil pan (see Section 11).

12.7 Oil pump-to-engine block mounting bolts

15   Loosen the hose clamp and detach the radiator hose from the water pump.

16   Remove the engine oil cooler inlet and outlet pipe bolts and push the pipes toward the oil cooler housing.

17   Remove the oil pump/front cover bolts, then remove the pump assembly from the front of the engine block and discard the gaskets.

INSPECTION

LXV engines

18   Note any identification marks on the rotors and withdraw the rotors from the pump body. If no marks can be seen, use a permanent marker and make your own to ensure that they will be installed correctly.

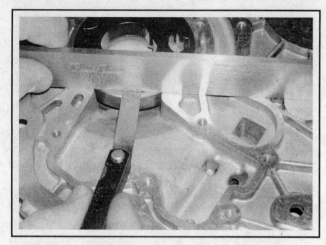

12.20 Use a straightedge and a feeler gauge to check the rotor-to-cover clearance

19 Thoroughly clean and dry the components.

20 Inspect the rotors for obvious wear or damage. If either rotor, the pump body or the cover is scored or damaged, the complete oil pump assembly must be replaced. Also check the rotor-to-cover side clearance (see illustration).

21 If the oil pump components are in acceptable condition, dip the rotors in clean engine oil and install them into the pump body with any identification marks positioned as noted during disassembly.

INSTALLATION

All models

22 Install the rotors into the housing with the hub of the inner rotor facing the housing. The inner rotor hub must be installed correctly or the housing/gerotor cover will not fasten properly.

23 Pack the recesses between the rotors with petroleum jelly.

24 Install the oil pump cover and screws and tighten the screws securely.

25 Install the front cover and oil pump assembly, using a new gasket. Tighten the bolts a little at a time to the torque listed in this Chapter's Specifications.

26 Remaining installation is the reverse of removal.

27 Fill the engine with fresh engine oil (see Chapter 1). Install a new oil filter.

28 If you're working on a LXV model, refill the cooling system (see Chapter 1).

29 Start the engine and check for leaks.

30 Run the engine and make sure oil pressure comes up to normal quickly. If it doesn't, stop the engine and find out the cause. Severe engine damage can result from running an engine with insufficient oil pressure!

13 Flywheel/driveplate - removal and installation

REMOVAL

1 Remove the transaxle (see Chapter 7A or 7B). If it's leaking, now would be a very good time to replace the front pump seal/O-ring (automatic transaxle only).

2 If you're working on a manual transaxle equipped vehicle, remove the pressure plate and clutch disc (see Chapter 8). Now is a good time to check/replace the clutch components.

3 Use a center punch or paint to make alignment marks on the flywheel/driveplate and crankshaft to ensure correct alignment during reinstallation.

4 Remove the bolts that secure the flywheel/driveplate to the crankshaft. Wedge a screwdriver in the ring gear teeth to prevent the crankshaft from turning.

5 Remove the flywheel/driveplate from the crankshaft. Since the flywheel is fairly heavy, support it while removing the last bolt. If an automatic transaxle-equipped vehicle has a spacer between the crankshaft and the driveplate, note which way it was installed.

INSTALLATION

6 Clean the flywheel to remove grease and oil. Inspect the surface for cracks, rivet grooves, burned areas and score marks. Light scoring can be removed with emery cloth. Check for cracked and broken ring gear teeth. Lay the flywheel on a flat surface and use a straightedge to check for warpage.

7 Clean and inspect the mating surfaces of the flywheel/driveplate and the crankshaft. If the crankshaft rear seal is leaking, replace it before reinstalling the flywheel/driveplate (see Section 14).

8 Position the flywheel/driveplate against the crankshaft, installing the spacer if one was present originally. Align the mating marks made during removal. Note that some engines have an alignment dowel or staggered bolt holes to ensure correct installation. Before installing the bolts, apply thread locking compound to the threads.

9 Wedge a screwdriver in the ring gear teeth to keep the flywheel/driveplate from turning and tighten the bolts to the torque listed in this Chapter's Specifications. Work up to the final torque in three or four steps.

10 The remainder of installation is the reverse of removal.

14 Rear main oil seal - replacement

1 The one-piece rear main oil seal is pressed into the engine block and the crankcase reinforcement section. Remove the transaxle (see Chapter 7A or 7B), the clutch components, if equipped (see Chapter 8) and the flywheel/driveplate (see Section 13).

2 On LXV engines, remove the crankshaft position sensor (see Chapter 6). Once the flywheel is removed, remove the crankshaft position sensor mounting bracket from the end of the cylinder block.

3 Pry out the old seal with a special seal removal tool or a flat-blade screwdriver.

❋❋ CAUTION:

To prevent an oil leak after the new seal is installed, be very careful not to scratch or otherwise damage the crankshaft sealing surface or the bore in the engine block.

4 Clean the crankshaft and seal bore in the block thoroughly, then de-grease these areas by wiping them with a rag soaked in brake system cleaner. Lubricate the lip of the new seal and the outer diameter of the crankshaft with clean engine oil.

5 Position the new seal and housing, if equipped, onto the crankshaft. Make sure the edges of the new oil seal are not rolled over. Use a special rear main oil seal installation tool or a socket with the exact diameter of the seal to drive the seal in place. Make sure the seal is not offset; it must be flush along the entire circumference of the engine block and the crankcase reinforcement section.

❋❋ CAUTION:

When installing the new seal, if so marked, the words THIS SIDE OUT on the seal must face out, toward the rear of the engine.

6 The remainder of installation is the reverse of removal.

15 Powertrain mounts - check and replacement

CHECK

1 Engine mounts seldom require attention, but broken or deteriorated mounts should be replaced immediately or the added strain placed on the driveline components may cause damage or wear.

2 During the check, the engine must be raised slightly to remove the weight from the mounts.

3 Raise the vehicle and support it securely on jackstands, then position a jack under the engine oil pan. Place a large block of wood between the jack head and the oil pan, then carefully raise the engine just enough to take the weight off the mounts.

❋❋ WARNING:

DO NOT place any part of your body under the engine when it's supported only by a jack!

4 Check the mounts to see if the rubber is cracked, hardened or separated from the bushing in the center of the mount.

5 Check for relative movement between the mount and the engine or frame (use a large screwdriver or prybar to attempt to move the mounts). If movement is noted, tighten the mount fasteners.

REPLACEMENT

6 Disconnect the negative battery cable (see Chapter 5). If you're replacing the right-side engine mount, remove the air filter housing (see Chapter 4). if you're removing the left-side transaxle mount, remove the battery and the battery tray (see Chapter 5).

7 If you're replacing the front or rear transaxle mount, raise the vehicle and support it securely on jackstands.

8 Place a block of wood between the jack head and the oil pan, then carefully raise the engine or transaxle just enough to take the weight off the mounts.

❋❋ CAUTION:

Do not disconnect more than one mount at a time unless the engine will be removed from the vehicle.

9 Refer to the accompanying illustrations for the locations of the powertrain mount fasteners (see illustrations).

15.9a Right-side engine mounting fasteners
1   *Mount-to-body bolts*
2   *Mount-to-mount bracket bolt/nuts*

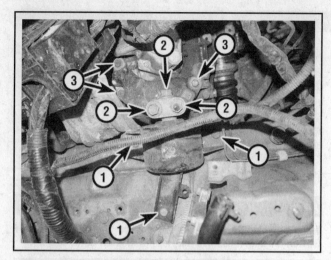

15.9b Left-side transaxle mounting fasteners
1   Mount-to-body bolts
2   Mount-to-mount bracket bolts/nut
3   Mount bracket-to-transaxle bolts

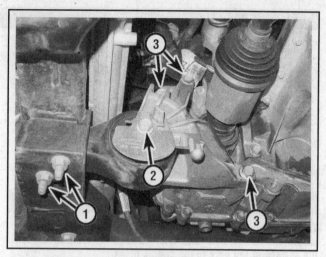

15.9c Transaxle rear mount fasteners
1   Mount-to-subframe bolts
2   Through-bolt and nut
3   Bracket-to-transaxle bolts (2 of 3 bolts shown)

10 Remove the fasteners holding the mount to the bracket.
11 Installation is the reverse of removal. Proceed to Step 12.

POWERTRAIN/MOUNT BALANCING

➡ **Note: The engine/transaxle assembly must be aligned and balanced in its weight distribution among the powertrain mounts, before the mounting bolts are tightened.**

12 Raise the vehicle and support it securely on jackstands, if not already done.
13 Loosen the left and rear transaxle mount through-bolts (see illustrations 15.19b and 15.19c).
14 Lower the vehicle, then using two floor jacks, support the engine and transaxle.

❉❉ **CAUTION:**

Place blocks of wood on the heads of the floor jacks to protect the engine and transaxle.

15 Loosen the transaxle mount-to-transaxle bolts (see illustration 15.19b).
16 Loosen the engine mount-to-mount bracket bolts (see illustration 15.19a).
17 Lower the floor jacks so there is a 1/4-inch gap between the engine mount and its bracket and the transaxle mount and the transaxle.
18 The front and rear transaxle mounts must be centered in their brackets; if not, use a prybar to adjust the powertrain to achieve this.
19 Once alignment has been achieved, tighten the transaxle mount-to-transaxle bolts to the torque listed in this Chapter's Specifications.
20 Tighten the engine mount-to-mount bracket to the torque listed in this Chapter's Specifications.
21 Lower the floor jacks, then raise the vehicle and support it securely on jackstands.
22 Shake the engine and transaxle back and forth, then tighten the transaxle rear through-bolt, then the left through-bolt, in that order, to the torque listed in this Chapter's Specifications.
23 Install the under-vehicle splash shield, then lower the vehicle.
24 Reconnect the battery (see Chapter 5).

16 Valve clearance (LXV engine) - check and adjustment

➡ **Note: This procedure applies to 2009 and later models only. 2008 and earlier models (L91 and LXT engines) have hydraulic lash adjusters that don't require checking or adjustment.**

CHECK

1   Disconnect the cable from the negative terminal of the battery (see Chapter 5).
2   Remove the spark plugs (see Chapter 1).
3   Remove the valve cover (see Section 4).
4   Turn the crankshaft pulley so the mark on the crankshaft pulley is

aligned with the mark on the engine at the 6 o'clock position. Verify that the camshaft sprocket marks are aligned as shown in illustration 7.28.
5   Measure the clearances of the valves marked B and F with feeler gauges (see illustration). Record the measurements. They will be used later to determine the required replacement lifters.
6   Turn the crankshaft clockwise 180-degrees and measure the clearances of the valves marked C and G, recording the measurements.
7   Turn the crankshaft clockwise 180-degrees and measure the clearances of the valves marked D and H, recording the measurements.
8   Turn the crankshaft clockwise 180-degrees and measure the clearances of the valves marked A and E, recording the measurements.

16.5 Valve identification for clearance checking and adjustment

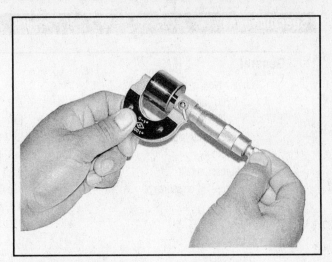

16.10 Measure the thickness of the lifter head with a micrometer

ADJUSTMENT

9   If any of the valve clearances were out of adjustment, remove the camshaft(s) from over the lifter(s) that was/were out of the specified clearance range (see Section 9).

10   Measure the thickness of the lifter with a micrometer (see illustration). To calculate the correct thickness of a replacement lifter that will place the valve clearance within the specified value, use the following formula:

$N = T + (A - V)$

T = thickness of the old shim or lifter

A = valve clearance measured

N = thickness of the new shim or lifter

V = desired valve clearance

See this Chapter's Specifications.

11   Select a lifter with a thickness as close as possible to provide the desired valve clearance calculated. The lifters are available in 33 sizes in various increments.

12   Install the proper thickness lifter(s) in position, making sure to lubricate them with clean engine oil first.

➡ **Note: Apply the lubricant to the underside of the lifter where it contacts the valve stem, the walls of the lifter and the face of the lifter.**

13   Install the camshaft(s) (see Section 9).

14   Install the timing belt (see Section 7).

15   Re-check the valve clearances.

Specifications

General

Engine type

2007 and earlier models	L91
2008 models	LXT
2009 and later models	LXV
Firing order	1-3-4-2
Compression ratio	9.5:1
Compression pressure	See Chapter 2B
Bore	3.1 inches (79.0 mm)
Stroke	3.21 inches (81.5 mm)
Displacement	97.5 cubic inches (1.6L)
Oil pressure	See Chapter 2B

FRONT OF
VEHICLE

Cylinder locations and firing order

Camshafts

Lobe lift (2008 and earlier models)	0.283 inch (7.2 mm)
Lobe height (2009 and later models)	
Intake	1.8228 inches (46.3 mm)
Exhaust	1.7835 inches (45.3 mm)
Allowable lobe lift variation	0.005 inch (0.127 mm)
Endplay	
2008 and earlier models	0.0039 to 0.0079 inch (0.1 to 0.25 mm)
2009 and later models	0.0051 to 0.0085 inch (0.13 to 0.215 mm)
Journal diameter - 2008 and earlier models	
No. 1 journal	1.1785 to 1.1791 inches (29.935 to 29.95 mm)
No. 2 through 5 journal	1.0604 to 1.0610 inches (26.935 to 26.95 mm)
Journal diameter - 2009 and later models	1.1000 to-1.1008 inches (27.939 to 27.960 mm)
Camshaft bearing oil clearance	Not available

Valve clearance, cold (LXV engine)

Intake	0.0083 to 0.0114 inch (0.21 to 0.29 mm)
Exhaust	0.0106 to 0.0138 inch (0.27 to 0.35 mm)

Oil pump

2008 and earlier models	
Oil pump body-to-outer rotor clearance	0.0157 to 0.0191 inch (0.4 to 0.484 mm)
Outer rotor-to-body side clearance	0.0018 to 0.0039 inch (0.045 to 0.1 mm)
Inner rotor-to-body side clearance	0.0014 to 0.0033 inch (0.035 to 0.085 mm)
2009 and later models	
Oil pump body-to-outer rotor clearance	0.0008 to 0.0023 inch (0.02 to 0.058 mm)

Torque specifications	Ft-lbs (unless otherwise indicated)	Nm

➡ **Note: One foot-pound (ft-lb) of torque is equivalent to 12 inch-pounds (in-lbs) of torque. Torque values below approximately 15 foot-pounds are expressed in inch-pounds, because most foot-pound torque wrenches are not accurate at these smaller values.**

Camshaft position actuator bolts (intake and exhaust)		
LXV engines		
Step 1	48	65
Step 2	Tighten an additional 120-degrees	
Step 3	Tighten an additional 15-degrees	
Camshaft adjuster sprocket closure plugs (LXV engine)	37	50
Camshaft bearing cap bolts (in sequence - see illustrations 9.19a or 9.19b)		
L91 and LXT engines	144 in-lbs	16
LXV engines	71 in-lbs	8
Camshaft sprocket bolt (L91 and LXT) engines	49	67.5
Crankshaft pulley bolt*		
L91 and LXT engines		
Step 1	70	95
Step 2	Tighten an additional 30-degrees	
Step 3	Tighten an additional 15-degrees	
LXV engine		
Step 1	70	95
Step 2	Tighten an additional 45-degrees	
Step 3	Tighten an additional 15-degrees	
Cylinder head bolts*		
L91 and LXT engines (in sequence - see illustration 10.19a)		
Step 1	18	25
Step 2	Tighten an additional 60-degrees	
Step 3	Tighten an additional 60-degrees	
Step 4	Tighten an additional 60-degrees	
Step 5	Tighten an additional 10-degrees	
LXV engine (in sequence - see illustration 10.19b)		
Step 1	18	25
Step 2	Tighten an additional 90-degrees	
Step 3	Tighten an additional 90-degrees	
Step 4	Tighten an additional 90-degrees	
Step 5	Tighten an additional 45-degrees	
Drivebelt tensioner bolt	See Chapter 1	
Driveplate bolts* (automatic transaxle)		
L91 and LXT engines	44	60
LXV engine		
Step 1	25	35
Step 2	Tighten an additional 30-degrees	
Step 3	Tighten an additional 15-degrees	
Flywheel bolts* (manual transaxle)		
Step 1	25	35
Step 2	Tighten an additional 30-degrees	
Step 3	Tighten an additional 15-degrees	

→ **Note:** One foot-pound (ft-lb) of torque is equivalent to 12 inch-pounds (in-lbs) of torque. Torque values below approximately 15 foot-pounds are expressed in inch-pounds, because most foot-pound torque wrenches are not accurate at these smaller values.

Exhaust manifold/catalytic converter-to-cylinder head nuts

	Ft-lbs	Nm
L91 and LXT engines		
(in sequence - see illustration 6.11)	18	25
LXV engines	15	20
Exhaust pipe-to-manifold nuts	30	40
Engine mount (passenger's side)		
Mount-to-body bolts/nut	46	62
Mount-to-engine mount bracket bolts		
Step 1	37	50
Step 2	Tighten an additional 60 to 70-degrees	
Engine mount bracket bolts		
Step 1	45	60
Step 2	Tighten an additional 45 to 60-degrees	
Transaxle mount fasteners (rear)		
Mount-to-subframe bolts/nuts	44	60
Mount-to-transaxle bracket through-bolt/nut	59	80
Transaxle mount bracket bolts	74	100
Transaxle mount (driver's side)		
Mount-to-body bolts and nut	46	62
Mount-to-transaxle bolts		
Step 1	37	50
Step 2	Tighten an additional 60 to 75-degrees	
Intake manifold bolts/nuts	15	20
Oil pan		
Oil pan-to-engine block bolts		
L91 and LXT engines	89 in-lbs	10
LXV engines	126 in-lbs	14
Oil pan-to-transaxle bolts		
L91 and LXT engines	18	25
LXV engines	30	40
Oil pump-to-engine bolts (L91 and LXT engines)	89 in-lbs	10
Oil pump/front cover-to-engine bolts (LXV engines)	15	20
Timing belt		
Idler pulley bolt		
L91 and LXT engines	30	40
LXV engines*	18	25
Tensioner bolt(s)		
L91 and LXT engines	18	25
LXV engines*	15	20
Timing belt cover bolts	53 in-lbs	6
Valve cover bolts	71 in-lbs	8
Valve cover ground strap bolt	89 in-lbs	10
Water pump bolts	See Chapter 3	

Bolt(s) must be replaced.

Notes

Notes

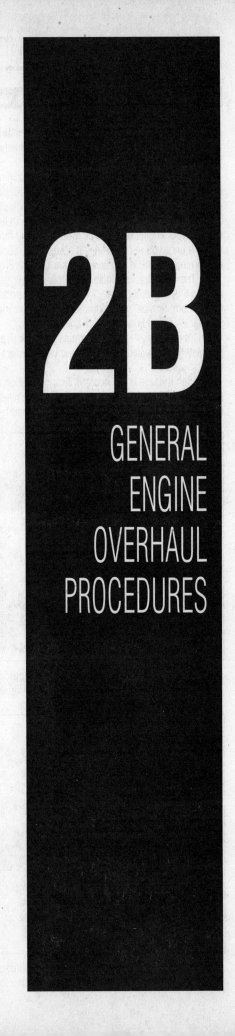

2B

GENERAL ENGINE OVERHAUL PROCEDURES

Section

1   General information - engine overhaul

1   Included in this Chapter are general information and diagnostic testing procedures for determining the overall mechanical condition of your engine.

2   The information ranges from advice concerning preparation for an overhaul and the purchase of replacement parts and/or components to detailed, step-by-step procedures covering removal and installation.

3   The following Sections have been written to help you determine whether your engine needs to be overhauled and how to remove and install it once you've determined it needs to be rebuilt. For information concerning in-vehicle engine repair, see Chapter 2A.

4   The Specifications included in this Part are general in nature and include only those necessary for testing the oil pressure, checking the engine compression, and bottom-end torque specifications. Refer to Chapter 2A for additional engine Specifications.

5   It's not always easy to determine when, or if, an engine should be completely overhauled, because a number of factors must be considered.

6   High mileage is not necessarily an indication that an overhaul is needed, while low mileage doesn't preclude the need for an overhaul. Frequency of servicing is probably the most important consideration.

An engine that's had regular and frequent oil and filter changes, as well as other required maintenance, will most likely give many thousands of miles of reliable service. Conversely, a neglected engine may require an overhaul very early in its service life.

7   Excessive oil consumption is an indication that piston rings, valve seals and/or valve guides are in need of attention. Make sure that oil leaks aren't responsible before deciding that the rings and/or guides are bad. Perform a cylinder compression check to determine the extent of the work required (see Section 3). Also check the vacuum readings under various conditions (see Section 4).

8   Check the oil pressure with a gauge installed in place of the oil pressure sending unit and compare it to this Chapter's Specifications (see Section 2). If it's extremely low, the bearings and/or oil pump are probably worn out.

9   Loss of power, rough running, knocking or metallic engine noises, excessive valve train noise and high fuel consumption rates may also point to the need for an overhaul, especially if they're all present at the same time.

10 An engine overhaul involves restoring the internal parts to the specifications of a new engine. During an overhaul, the piston rings are replaced and the cylinder walls are reconditioned (rebored and/or honed) (see illustrations 1.10a and 1.10b). If a rebore is done by an automotive machine shop, new oversize pistons will also be installed. The main bearings, connecting rod bearings and camshaft bearings are generally replaced with new ones and, if necessary, the crankshaft may be reground to restore the journals (see illustration 1.10c). Generally, the valves are serviced as well, since they're usually in less-than-perfect condition at this point. While the engine is being overhauled, other components, such as the distributor, starter and alternator, can be rebuilt as well. The end result should be similar to a new engine that will give many trouble free miles.

➡ **Note: Critical cooling system components such as the hoses, drivebelts, thermostat and water pump should be replaced with new parts when an engine is overhauled. The radiator should be checked carefully to ensure that it isn't clogged or leaking (see Chapter 3). If you purchase a rebuilt engine or short block, some rebuilders will not warranty their engines unless the radiator has been professionally flushed. Also, we don't recommend overhauling the oil pump - always install a new one when an engine is rebuilt.**

1.10a An engine block being bored. An engine rebuilder will use special machinery to recondition the cylinder bores

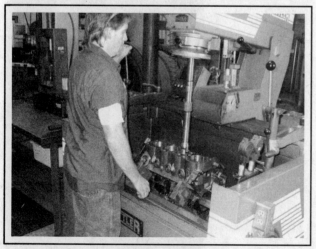

1.10b If the cylinders are bored, the machine shop will normally hone the engine on a machine like this

1.10c A crankshaft having a main bearing journal ground

1.11a A machinist checks for a bent connecting rod, using specialized equipment

1.11b A bore gauge being used to check a cylinder bore

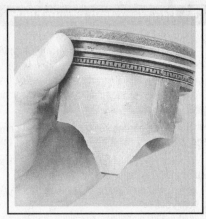

1.11c Uneven piston wear like this indicates a bent connecting rod

11 Overhauling the internal components on today's engines is a difficult and time-consuming task which requires a significant amount of specialty tools and is best left to a professional engine rebuilder (see illustrations 1.11a, 1.11b and 1.11c). A competent engine rebuilder will handle the inspection of your old parts and offer advice concerning the reconditioning or replacement of the original engine; never purchase parts or have machine work done on other components until the block has been thoroughly inspected by a professional machine shop. As a general rule, time is the primary cost of an overhaul, especially since the vehicle may be tied up for a minimum of two weeks or more. Be aware that some engine builders only have the capability to rebuild the engine you bring them while other rebuilders have a large inventory of rebuilt exchange engines in stock. Also be aware that many machine shops could take as much as two weeks time to completely rebuild your engine depending on shop workload. Sometimes it makes more sense to simply exchange your engine for another engine that's already rebuilt to save time.

2 Oil pressure check

1 Low engine oil pressure can be a sign of an engine in need of rebuilding. A low oil pressure indicator (often called an "idiot light") is not a test of the oiling system. Such indicators only come on when the oil pressure is dangerously low. Even a factory oil pressure gauge in the instrument panel is only a relative indication, although much better for driver information than a warning light. A better test is with a mechanical (not electrical) oil pressure gauge.

2008 AND EARLIER MODELS

2 On 2008 and earlier models, the oil pressure switch is located on the right rear corner of the engine, near the crankshaft pulley (see illustration).

3 Unscrew and remove the oil pressure sending unit and screw in the hose for your oil pressure gauge. If necessary, install an adapter fitting. Use Teflon tape or thread sealant on the threads of the adapter and/or the fitting on the end of your gauge's hose.

2009 AND LATER MODELS

4 On these models, the oil pressure switch is also located on the right end of the engine, but there is also a plug in the center of the front side of the cylinder head that can be removed and a pressure gauge adapter can be installed. Remove the exhaust manifold heat shield for access to the plug. Remove the plug and install an adapter and pressure gauge.

ALL MODELS

5 Check the oil pressure with the engine running (normal operating temperature) at the specified engine speed, and compare it to this Chapter's Specifications. If it's extremely low, the bearings and/or oil pump are probably worn out.

2.2 The oil pressure sending unit is located on the right rear corner of the engine (2008 and earlier models)

3 Cylinder compression check

1 A compression check will tell you what mechanical condition the upper end of your engine (pistons, rings, valves, head gaskets) is in. Specifically, it can tell you if the compression is down due to leakage caused by worn piston rings, defective valves and seats or a blown head gasket.

➡ **Note: The engine must be at normal operating temperature and the battery must be fully charged for this check.**

2 Begin by cleaning the area around the spark plugs before you remove them (compressed air should be used, if available). The idea is to prevent dirt from getting into the cylinders as the compression check is being done.

3 Remove all of the spark plugs from the engine (see Chapter 1). Disable the ignition system by disconnecting the electrical connector from the Crankshaft Position (CKP) sensor (see Chapter 6).

4 Disable the fuel system by removing the fuel pump relay (see Chapter 4, Section 2).

5 Install a compression gauge in the spark plug hole (see illustration).

6 Have an assistant hold the accelerator pedal to the floor and crank the engine over at least seven compression strokes while you watch the gauge. The compression should build up quickly in a healthy engine. Low compression on the first stroke, followed by gradually increasing pressure on successive strokes, indicates worn piston rings. A low compression reading on the first stroke, which doesn't build up during successive strokes, indicates leaking valves or a blown head gasket (a cracked head could also be the cause). Deposits on the undersides of the valve heads can also cause low compression. Record the highest gauge reading obtained.

7 Repeat the procedure for the remaining cylinders and compare the results to this Chapter's Specifications.

8 Add some engine oil (about three squirts from a plunger-type oil can) to each cylinder, through the spark plug hole, and repeat the test.

9 If the compression increases after the oil is added, the piston rings are definitely worn. If the compression doesn't increase significantly, the leakage is occurring at the valves or head gasket. Leakage past the valves may be caused by burned valve seats and/or faces or

3.5 Use a compression gauge with a threaded fitting for the spark plug hole, not the type that requires hand pressure to maintain the seal

warped, cracked or bent valves.

10 If two adjacent cylinders have equally low compression, there's a strong possibility that the head gasket between them is blown. The appearance of coolant in the combustion chambers or the crankcase would verify this condition.

11 If one cylinder is slightly lower than the others, and the engine has a slightly rough idle, a worn lobe on the camshaft could be the cause.

12 If the compression is unusually high, the combustion chambers are probably coated with carbon deposits. If that's the case, the cylinder head(s) should be removed and decarbonized.

13 If compression is way down or varies greatly between cylinders, it would be a good idea to have a leak-down test performed by an automotive repair shop. This test will pinpoint exactly where the leakage is occurring and how severe it is.

4 Vacuum gauge diagnostic checks

1 A vacuum gauge provides inexpensive but valuable information about what is going on in the engine. You can check for worn rings or cylinder walls, leaking head or intake manifold gaskets, incorrect carburetor adjustments, restricted exhaust, stuck or burned valves, weak valve springs, improper ignition or valve timing and ignition problems.

2 Unfortunately, vacuum gauge readings are easy to misinterpret, so they should be used in conjunction with other tests to confirm the diagnosis.

3 Both the absolute readings and the rate of needle movement are important for accurate interpretation. Most gauges measure vacuum in inches of mercury (in-Hg). The following references to vacuum assume the diagnosis is being performed at sea level. As elevation increases (or atmospheric pressure decreases), the reading will decrease. For every 1,000 foot increase in elevation above approximately 2,000 feet, the gauge readings will decrease about one inch of mercury.

4 Connect the vacuum gauge directly to intake manifold vacuum, not to ported (throttle body) vacuum (see illustration). Be sure no hoses are left disconnected during the test or false readings will result.

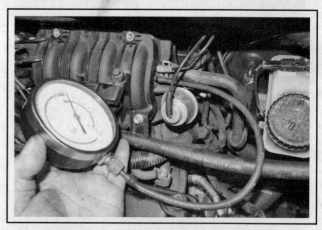

4.4 A simple vacuum gauge connected to manifold vacuum can be handy in diagnosing engine condition and performance

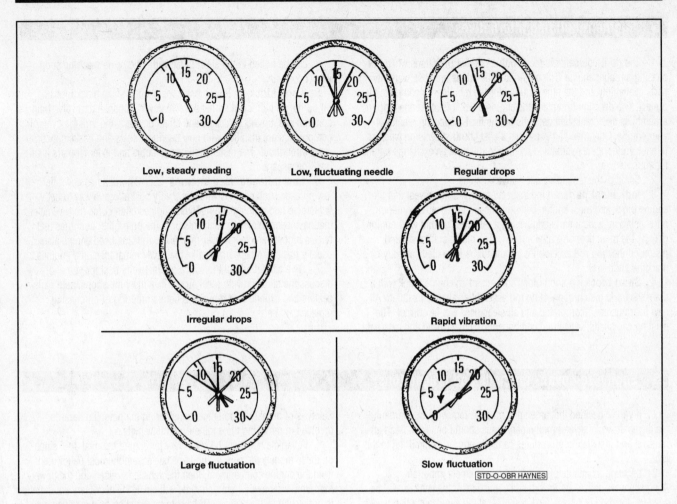

Low, steady reading   Low, fluctuating needle   Regular drops

Irregular drops   Rapid vibration

Large fluctuation   Slow fluctuation

STD-O-OBR HAYNES

4.6 Typical vacuum gauge readings

5   Before you begin the test, allow the engine to warm up completely. Block the wheels and set the parking brake. With the transaxle in Park, start the engine and allow it to run at normal idle speed.

※※ WARNING:

Keep your hands and the vacuum gauge clear of the fans.

6   Read the vacuum gauge; an average, healthy engine should normally produce about 17 to 22 in-Hg with a fairly steady needle (see illustration). Refer to the following vacuum gauge readings and what they indicate about the engine's condition:

7   A low steady reading usually indicates a leaking gasket between the intake manifold and cylinder head(s) or throttle body, a leaky vacuum hose, late ignition timing or incorrect camshaft timing. Check ignition timing with a timing light and eliminate all other possible causes, utilizing the tests provided in this Chapter before you remove the timing chain cover to check the timing marks.

8   If the reading is three to eight inches below normal and it fluctuates at that low reading, suspect an intake manifold gasket leak at an intake port or a faulty fuel injector.

9   If the needle has regular drops of about two-to-four inches at a steady rate, the valves are probably leaking. Perform a compression check or leak-down test to confirm this.

10   An irregular drop or down-flick of the needle can be caused by a sticking valve or an ignition misfire. Perform a compression check or leak-down test and read the spark plugs.

11   A rapid vibration of about four in-Hg vibration at idle combined with exhaust smoke indicates worn valve guides. Perform a leak-down test to confirm this. If the rapid vibration occurs with an increase in engine speed, check for a leaking intake manifold gasket or head gasket, weak valve springs, burned valves or ignition misfire.

12   A slight fluctuation, say one inch up and down, may mean ignition problems. Check all the usual tune-up items and, if necessary, run the engine on an ignition analyzer.

13   If there is a large fluctuation, perform a compression or leak-down test to look for a weak or dead cylinder or a blown head gasket.

14   If the needle moves slowly through a wide range, check for a clogged PCV system, incorrect idle fuel mixture, throttle body or intake manifold gasket leaks.

15   Check for a slow return after revving the engine by quickly snapping the throttle open until the engine reaches about 2,500 rpm and let it shut. Normally the reading should drop to near zero, rise above normal idle reading (about 5 in-Hg over) and return to the previous idle reading. If the vacuum returns slowly and doesn't peak when the throttle is snapped shut, the rings may be worn. If there is a long delay, look for a restricted exhaust system (often the muffler or catalytic converter). An easy way to check this is to temporarily disconnect the exhaust ahead of the suspected part and redo the test.

5 Engine rebuilding alternatives

1   The do-it-yourselfer is faced with a number of options when purchasing a rebuilt engine. The major considerations are cost, warranty, parts availability and the time required for the rebuilder to complete the project. The decision to replace the engine block, piston/connecting rod assemblies and crankshaft depends on the final inspection results of your engine. Only then can you make a cost effective decision whether to have your engine overhauled or simply purchase an exchange engine for your vehicle.

2   Some of the rebuilding alternatives include:

3   **Individual parts** - If the inspection procedures reveal that the engine block and most engine components are in reusable condition, purchasing individual parts and having a rebuilder rebuild your engine may be the most economical alternative. The block, crankshaft and piston/connecting rod assemblies should all be inspected carefully by a machine shop first.

4   **Short block** - A short block consists of an engine block with a crankshaft and piston/connecting rod assemblies already installed. All new bearings are incorporated and all clearances will be correct. The existing camshafts, valve train components, cylinder head and external parts can be bolted to the short block with little or no machine shop work necessary.

5   **Long block** - A long block consists of a short block plus an oil pump, oil pan, cylinder head, valve cover, camshaft and valve train components, timing sprockets and chain or gears and timing cover. All components are installed with new bearings, seals and gaskets incorporated throughout. The installation of manifolds and external parts is all that's necessary.

6   **Low mileage used engines** - Some companies now offer low mileage used engines which is a very cost effective way to get your vehicle up and running again. These engines often come from vehicles that have been totaled in accidents or come from other countries that have a higher vehicle turnover rate. A low mileage used engine also usually has a similar warranty like the newly remanufactured engines.

7   Give careful thought to which alternative is best for you and discuss the situation with local automotive machine shops, auto parts dealers and experienced rebuilders before ordering or purchasing replacement parts.

6 Engine removal - methods and precautions

1   If you've decided that an engine must be removed for overhaul or major repair work, several preliminary steps should be taken. Read all removal and installation procedures carefully prior to committing to this job.

2   Locating a suitable place to work is extremely important. Adequate work space, along with storage space for the vehicle, will be needed. If a shop or garage isn't available, at the very least a flat, level, clean work surface made of concrete or asphalt is required.

3   Cleaning the engine compartment and engine before beginning the removal procedure will help keep tools clean and organized (see illustrations).

4   An engine hoist will also be necessary. Make sure the hoist is rated in excess of the combined weight of the engine and transaxle.

Safety is of primary importance, considering the potential hazards involved in removing the engine from the vehicle.

5   A vehicle hoist will be necessary for engine removal, too, since on these models the engine and transaxle assembly must be lowered from the engine compartment, then the vehicle is raised and the powertrain unit is removed from under the vehicle. If the necessary equipment is not available, the engine will have to be removed by a qualified automotive repair facility.

6   If you're a novice at engine removal, get at least one helper. One person cannot easily do all the things you need to do to remove a big heavy engine and transaxle assembly from the engine compartment. Also helpful is to seek advice and assistance from someone who's experienced in engine removal.

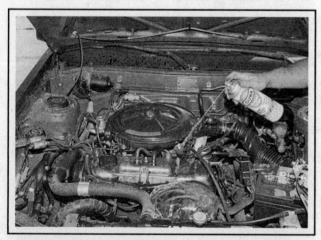

6.3a After tightly wrapping water-vulnerable components, use a spray cleaner on everything, with particular concentration on the greasiest areas, usually around the valve cover and lower edges of the block. If one section dries out, apply more cleaner

6.3b Depending on how dirty the engine is, let the cleaner soak in according to the directions and hose off the grime and cleaner. Get the rinse water down into every area you can get at; then dry important components with a hair dryer or paper towels

6.7a Get an engine stand sturdy enough to firmly support the engine while you're working on it. Stay away from three-wheeled models; they have a tendency to tip over more easily, so get a four-wheeled unit

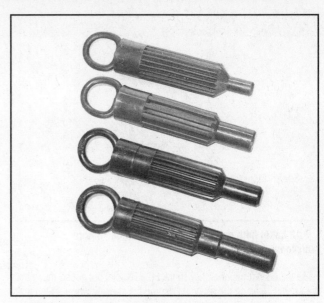

6.7b A clutch alignment tool will be necessary if you're working on a model with a manual transaxle

7   Plan the operation ahead of time. Arrange for or obtain all of the tools and equipment you'll need prior to beginning the job (see illustrations). Some of the equipment necessary to perform engine removal and installation safely and with relative ease are (in addition to a vehicle hoist and an engine hoist) a heavy duty floor jack (preferably fitted with a transaxle jack head adapter), complete sets of wrenches and sockets as described in the front of this manual, wooden blocks, plenty of rags and cleaning solvent for mopping up spilled oil, coolant and gasoline.

8   Plan for the vehicle to be out of use for quite a while. A machine shop can do the work that is beyond the scope of the home mechanic. Machine shops often have a busy schedule, so before removing the engine, consult the shop for an estimate of how long it will take to rebuild or repair the components that may need work.

7   Engine - removal and installation

> ☀☀ **WARNING:**

Gasoline is extremely flammable, so take extra precautions when you work on any part of the fuel system. Don't smoke or allow open flames or bare light bulbs near the work area, and don't work in a garage where a gas-type appliance (such as a water heater or clothes dryer) is present. Since gasoline is carcinogenic, wear fuel-resistant gloves when there's a possibility of being exposed to fuel, and, if you spill any fuel on your skin, rinse it off immediately with soap and water. Mop up any spills immediately and do not store fuel-soaked rags where they could ignite. The fuel system is under constant pressure, so, if any fuel lines are to be disconnected, the fuel pressure in the system must be relieved first (see Chapter 4 for more information). When you perform any kind of work on the fuel system, wear safety glasses and have a Class B type fire extinguisher on hand.

> ☀☀ **WARNING:**

The engine must be completely cool before beginning this procedure.

➡ Note: Engine removal on these models is a difficult job, especially for the do-it-yourself mechanic working at home. Because of the vehicle's design, the manufacturer states that the engine and transaxle have to be removed as a unit from the bottom of the vehicle, not the top. With a floor jack and jackstands, the vehicle can't be raised high enough or supported safely enough for the engine/transaxle assembly to slide out from underneath. The manufacturer recommends that removal of the engine/transaxle assembly only be performed with the use of a frame-contact type vehicle hoist.

➡ Note: Read through the entire Section before beginning this procedure. The engine and transaxle are removed as a unit from below, then separated outside the vehicle.

REMOVAL

1   Have the air conditioning refrigerant recovered by a qualified air conditioning technician.

2   Park the vehicle on a frame-contact type vehicle hoist, then engage the arms of the hoist with the jacking points of the vehicle.

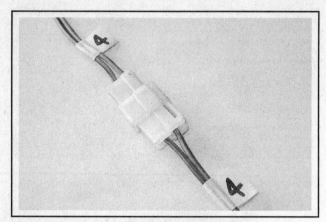

7.13 Label both ends of each wire and hose before disconnecting it

7.33 Locations of the engine lifting brackets

Raise the hoist arms until they contact the vehicle, but not so much that the wheels come off the ground. Position the steering wheel so the front wheels point straight ahead.

3 Disconnect the cable from the negative terminal of the battery (see Chapter 5), then relieve the fuel system pressure (see Chap-ter 4).

4 Remove the hood (see Chapter 11). Cover the fenders with fender covers.

5 Remove the air filter housing and the air intake duct (see Chapter 4).

6 Disconnect the breather tube from the valve cover.

7 Remove the spark plug cover (see Chapter 1) then remove the spark plug wires.

8 Disconnect the fuel line from the fuel rail (see Chapter 4).

9 Disconnect the throttle cable from the throttle body and the cable bracket from the intake manifold (see Chapter 4).

10 Drain the cooling system (see Chapter 1). Remove the radiator and cooling fan assembly (see Chapter 3).

11 Remove the upper radiator hose and disconnect the coolant hoses at the engine oil cooler, then remove the coolant expansion tank (see Chapter 3).

12 Follow the heater hoses from the firewall and detach them from the pipes on the engine.

13 Clearly label and disconnect all vacuum lines, emissions hoses, wiring harness connectors, fuel lines and the electrical connectors to the transaxle. Masking tape and/or a touch up paint applicator work well for marking items (see illustration). Take photos or sketch the locations of components and brackets. Move the wiring harness out of the way.

14 Loosen the wheel lug nuts and the driveaxle/hub nuts (see Chapter 8), then raise the vehicle on the hoist. Remove the wheels then remove the inner fender splash shield (see Chapter 11, Section 10).

15 Remove the drivebelt and drain the engine oil (see Chapter 1).

16 Disconnect the electrical connector to the oil pressure sending unit (see Section 2).

17 Disconnect the power steering hoses from the power steering pump (see Chapter 10).

18 Remove the driveaxles (see Chapter 8).

19 Disconnect the automatic transmission cooler lines (see Chapter 7B).

20 Remove the air conditioning compressor (see Chapter 3).

21 Remove the intake manifold support bracket bolts and bracket (see Chapter 2A).

22 Detach the battery cable and the electrical connectors from the alternator and starter, then remove the starter motor (see Chapter 5). With the starter removed, pull the lower section of the engine harness away from the engine and secure it out of the way.

23 Remove the upper radiator hose from the thermostat housing and the lower radiator hose.

24 Remove the battery and battery tray (see Chapter 5) then remove the battery tray support bolts and tray support.

25 Unbolt the front exhaust pipe from the exhaust manifold (see Chapter 2A) then remove the exhaust pipe bracket bolts. Disconnect the oxygen sensor electrical connectors. Remove the front exhaust pipe to muffler pipe bolts and remove the exhaust pipe from the vehicle. Make sure to check the exhaust pipe gaskets and replace the gaskets if there is any damage.

26 Disconnect the shift cable(s) from the transaxle (see Chapter 7A). Also disconnect any wiring harness connectors from the transaxle and cable brackets from the engine.

27 On D16 manual transaxle models, remove the release cylinder mounting bolts (see Chapter 8) and cylinder and secure the cylinder out of the way.

28 On Y4M manual transaxle models, remove the clutch cable adjustment nut from the clutch pivot arm (see Chapter 8).

29 Remove the damping block-to-transaxle mounting bolts/nuts (see Chapter 2A) then remove the rear mounting bracket bolts and bracket.

30 Disconnect the stabilizer bar links from the stabilizer bar, the tie-rod ends from the steering knuckles, and the steering intermediate shaft from the steering gear (see Chapter 10).

✳✳ CAUTION:

Don't allow the steering shaft to rotate after the intermediate shaft has been disconnected, as damage to the airbag clockspring could occur.

31 Disconnect the pressure and return lines from the power steering gear.

32 Disconnect the control arms from the steering knuckles (see Chapter 10).

33 Support the engine/transaxle assembly from above with an engine hoist securely attached by heavy-duty chains to the engine lifting brackets (see illustration). With the hoist taking the weight off the mounts, remove the engine/transaxle mounts.

✳✳ WARNING:

DO NOT place any part of your body under the engine when it's supported only by a hoist or other lifting device.

34 Remove the subframe (see Chapter 10).

35 Inspect the engine/transaxle assembly thoroughly once more to make sure that nothing is still attached, then slowly lower the powertrain down out of the engine compartment and onto the floor. Check carefully to make sure nothing is hanging up as this is done.

36 Once the powertrain is on the floor, disconnect the engine lifting chains and move the engine hoist out of the way, then raise the vehicle hoist until the vehicle clears the powertrain.

37 Reconnect the engine hoist to the engine, raise the engine/transaxle up a little and support the engine with blocks of wood. Support the transaxle with a floor jack; preferably one with a transmission adapter. Secure the transaxle to the jack with safety chains.

38 On automatic transaxle models, mark the torque converter to the driveplate and remove the driveplate-to-torque converter bolts.

39 Remove the bolts and the engine-to-transaxle brace, if equipped. Remove engine-to-transaxle mounting bolts and separate the engine from the transaxle.

40 Remove the driveplate/flywheel (see Chapter 2A) and mount the engine on an engine stand (see illustration 6.7a).

INSTALLATION

41 Installation is the reverse of removal, noting the following points:

a) *Check the engine/transaxle mounts. If they're worn or damaged, replace them.*

b) *Attach the transaxle to the engine following the procedure described in Chapter 7A or 7B.*

c) *Add coolant, oil and transaxle fluids as needed (see Chapter 1).*

d) *Reconnect the battery (see Chapter 5).*

e) *Run the engine and check for proper operation and leaks. Shut off the engine and recheck fluid levels.*

f) *Have the air conditioning system re-charged and leak tested, if it was discharged.*

8 Engine overhaul - disassembly sequence

1 It's much easier to remove the external components if the engine is mounted on a portable engine stand. A stand can often be rented quite cheaply from an equipment rental yard. Before the engine is mounted on a stand, the flywheel/driveplate should be removed from the engine.

2 If a stand isn't available, it's possible to remove the external engine components with it blocked up on the floor. Be extra careful not to tip or drop the engine when working without a stand.

3 If you're going to obtain a rebuilt engine, all external components must come off first, to be transferred to the replacement engine. These components include:

- *Clutch and flywheel (models with manual transaxle)*
- *Driveplate (models with automatic transaxle)*
- *Ignition system components*
- *Emissions-related components*
- *Engine mounts and mount brackets*
- *Engine rear cover (spacer plate between flywheel/driveplate and engine block)*

- *Intake/exhaust manifolds*
- *Fuel injection components*
- *Oil filter*
- *Spark plugs and ignition coil*
- *Thermostat and housing assembly*
- *Water pump*

➡ **Note: When removing the external components from the engine, pay close attention to details that may be helpful or important during installation. Note the installed position of gaskets, seals, spacers, pins, brackets, washers, bolts and other small items.**

4 If you're going to obtain a short block (assembled engine block, crankshaft, pistons and connecting rods), then remove the timing chain, cylinder head, oil pan, oil pump pick-up tube, oil pump and water pump from your engine so that you can turn in your old short block to the rebuilder as a core. See *Engine rebuilding alternatives* for additional information regarding the different possibilities to be considered.

9 Pistons and connecting rods - removal and installation

REMOVAL

➡ **Note: Prior to removing the piston/connecting rod assemblies, remove the cylinder head and oil pan (see Chapter 2A).**

1 Use your fingernail to feel if a ridge has formed at the upper limit of ring travel (about 1/4-inch down from the top of each cylinder). If carbon deposits or cylinder wear have produced ridges, they must be completely removed with a special tool (see illustration). Follow the manufacturer's instructions provided with the tool. Failure to remove the ridges before attempting to remove the piston/connecting rod assemblies may result in piston breakage.

2 After the cylinder ridges have been removed, turn the engine so the crankshaft is facing up.

3 Before the main bearing cap assembly and connecting rods are removed, check the connecting rod endplay with feeler gauges. Slide

9.1 Before you try to remove the pistons, use a ridge reamer to remove the raised material (ridge) from the top of the cylinders

9.3 Checking the connecting rod endplay (side clearance)

9.4 If the connecting rods and caps are not marked, use permanent ink to mark the caps to the rods by cylinder number (for example, this would be the No. 4 connecting rod)

9.13 Install the piston ring into the cylinder then push it down into position using a piston so the ring will be square in the cylinder

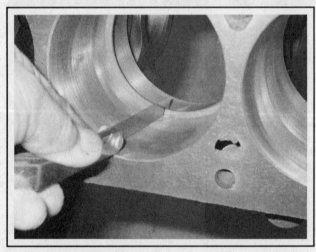

9.14 With the ring square in the cylinder, measure the ring end gap with a feeler gauge

them between the first connecting rod and the crankshaft throw until the play is removed (see illustration). Repeat this procedure for each connecting rod. The endplay is equal to the thickness of the feeler gauge(s). Check with an automotive machine shop for the endplay service limit (a typical endplay limit should measure between 0.005 to 0.015 inch [0.127 to 0.381 mm]). If the play exceeds the service limit, new connecting rods will be required. If new rods (or a new crankshaft) are installed, the endplay may fall under the minimum allowable. If it does, the rods will have to be machined to restore it. If necessary, consult an automotive machine shop for advice.

4   Check the connecting rods and caps for identification marks. If they aren't plainly marked, use paint or marker to clearly identify each rod and cap (1, 2, 3, etc., depending on the cylinder they're associated with) (see illustration).

5   Remove the connecting rod cap bolts from the number one connecting rod.

➡ **Note: New connecting rod cap bolts must be used when reassembling the engine, but save the old bolts - they'll be used during the bearing oil clearance check during reassembly.**

6   Remove the number one connecting rod cap and bearing insert. Don't drop the bearing insert out of the cap.

7   Remove the bearing insert and push the connecting rod/piston assembly out through the top of the engine. Use a wooden dowel to push on the connecting rod. If resistance is felt, double-check to make sure that all of the ridge was removed from the cylinder.

8   Repeat the procedure for the remaining cylinders.

9   After removal, reassemble the connecting rod caps and bearing inserts in their respective connecting rods and install the cap bolts finger-tight. Leaving the old bearing inserts in place until reassembly will help prevent the connecting rod bearing surfaces from being accidentally nicked or gouged.

10   The pistons and connecting rods are now ready for inspection and overhaul at an automotive machine shop.

PISTON RING INSTALLATION

11   Before installing the new piston rings, the ring end gaps must be checked. It's assumed that the piston ring side clearance has been checked and verified correct.

12   Lay out the piston/connecting rod assemblies and the new ring sets so the ring sets will be matched with the same piston and cylinder during the end gap measurement and engine assembly.

13   Insert the top (number one) ring into the first cylinder and square it up with the cylinder walls by pushing it in with the top of the piston (see illustration). The ring should be near the bottom of the cylinder, at the lower limit of ring travel.

14   To measure the end gap, slip feeler gauges between the ends of the ring until a gauge equal to the gap width is found (see illustration). The feeler gauge should slide between the ring ends with a slight amount of drag. A typical ring gap should fall between 0.010 and 0.020 inch [0.25 to 0.50 mm] for compression rings and up to 0.030 inch [0.76 mm] for the oil ring steel rails. If the gap is larger or smaller than specified, double-check to make sure you have the correct rings before proceeding.

15   If the gap is too small, it must be enlarged or the ring ends may come in contact with each other during engine operation, which can cause serious damage to the engine. If necessary, increase the end gaps by filing the ring ends very carefully with a fine file. Mount the file in a vise equipped with soft jaws, slip the ring over the file with the ends

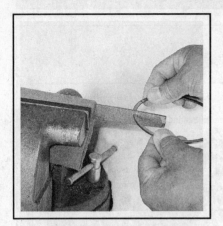

9.15 If the ring end gap is too small, clamp a file in a vise as shown and file the piston ring ends - remove all raised material

9.19a Installing the spacer/expander in the oil ring groove

9.19b DO NOT use a piston ring installation tool when installing the oil ring side rails

contacting the file face and slowly move the ring to remove material from the ends. When performing this operation, file only by pushing the ring from the outside end of the file towards the vise (see illustration).

16 Excess end gap isn't critical unless it's greater than 0.040 inch (1.01 mm). Again, double-check to make sure you have the correct ring type.

17 Repeat the procedure for each ring that will be installed in the first cylinder and for each ring in the remaining cylinders. Remember to keep rings, pistons and cylinders matched up.

18 Once the ring end gaps have been checked/corrected, the rings can be installed on the pistons.

19 The oil control ring (lowest one on the piston) is usually installed first. It's composed of three separate components. Slip the spacer/expander into the groove (see illustration). If an anti-rotation tang is used, make sure it's inserted into the drilled hole in the ring groove. Next, install the upper side rail in the same manner (see illustration). Don't use a piston ring installation tool on the oil ring side rails, as they may be damaged. Instead, place one end of the side rail into the groove between the spacer/expander and the ring land, hold it firmly in place and slide a finger around the piston while pushing the rail into the groove. Finally, install the lower side rail.

20 After the three oil ring components have been installed, check to make sure that both the upper and lower side rails can be rotated smoothly inside the ring grooves.

21 The number two (middle) ring is installed next. It's usually stamped with a mark, which must face up, toward the top of the piston. Do not mix up the top and middle rings, as they have different cross-sections.

➡ **Note: Always follow the instructions printed on the ring package or box - different manufacturers may require different approaches.**

22 Use a piston ring installation tool and make sure the identification mark is facing the top of the piston, then slip the ring into the middle groove on the piston (see illustration). Don't expand the ring any more than necessary to slide it over the piston.

23 Install the number one (top) ring in the same manner. Make sure the mark is facing up. Be careful not to confuse the number one and number two rings.

24 Repeat the procedure for the remaining pistons and rings.

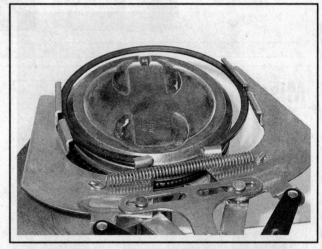

9.22 Use a piston ring installation tool to install the number 2 and the number 1 (top) rings - be sure the directional mark on the piston ring(s) is facing toward the top of the piston

INSTALLATION

➡ **Note: For final assembly, the pistons and rods are installed after the lower crankcase (or bedplate) has been installed and torqued in sequence.**

25 Before installing the piston/connecting rod assemblies, the cylinder walls must be perfectly clean, the top edge of each cylinder bore must be chamfered, and the crankshaft must be in place.

26 Remove the cap from the end of the number one connecting rod (refer to the marks made during removal). Remove the original bearing inserts and wipe the bearing surfaces of the connecting rod and cap with a clean, lint-free cloth. They must be kept spotlessly clean.

Connecting rod bearing oil clearance check

27 Clean the back side of the new upper bearing insert, then lay it in place in the connecting rod.

28 Make sure the tab on the bearing fits into the recess in the rod. Don't hammer the bearing insert into place and be very careful not to

ENGINE BEARING ANALYSIS

Debris

Babbitt bearing embedded with debris from machinings

Microscopic detail of debris

Microscopic detail of gouges

Overplated copper alloy bearing gouged by cast iron debris

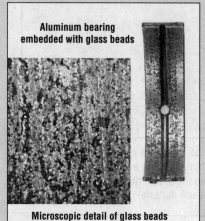

Aluminum bearing embedded with glass beads

Microscopic detail of glass beads

Damaged lining caused by dirt left on the bearing back

Misassembly

Result of a lower half assembled as an upper - blocking the oil flow

Excessive oil clearance is indicated by a short contact arc

Polished and oil-stained backs are a result of a poor fit in the housing bore

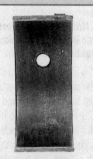

Result of a wrong, reversed, or shifted cap

Overloading

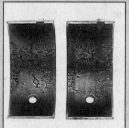

Damage from excessive idling which resulted in an oil film unable to support the load imposed

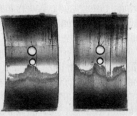

Damaged upper connecting rod bearings caused by engine lugging; the lower main bearings (not shown) were similarly affected

The damage shown in these upper and lower connecting rod bearings was caused by engine operation at a higher-than-rated speed under load

Misalignment

A warped crankshaft caused this pattern of severe wear in the center, diminishing toward the ends

A poorly finished crankshaft caused the equally spaced scoring shown

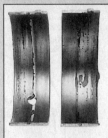

A tapered housing bore caused the damage along one edge of this pair

A bent connecting rod led to the damage in the "V" pattern

Lubrication

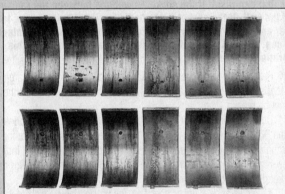

Result of dry start: The bearings on the left, farthest from the oil pump, show more damage

Result of a low oil supply or oil starvation

Severe wear as a result of inadequate oil clearance

Corrosion

Microscopic detail of corrosion

Corrosion is an acid attack on the bearing lining generally caused by inadequate maintenance, extremely hot or cold operation, or inferior oils or fuels

Microscopic detail of cavitation

Example of cavitation - a surface erosion caused by pressure changes in the oil film

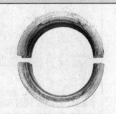

Damage from excessive thrust or insufficient axial clearance

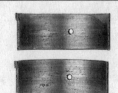

Bearing affected by oil dilution caused by excessive blow-by or a rich mixture

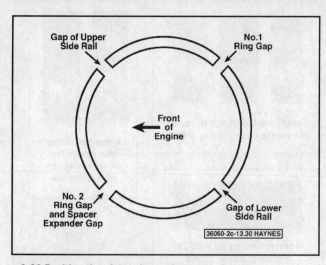

9.30 Position the piston ring end gaps as shown

nick or gouge the bearing face. Don't lubricate the bearing at this time.

29 Clean the back side of the other bearing insert and install it in the rod cap. Again, make sure the tab on the bearing fits into the recess in the cap, and don't apply any lubricant. It's critically important that the mating surfaces of the bearing and connecting rod are perfectly clean and oil free when they're assembled.

30 Position the piston ring gaps at the specified intervals around the piston as shown (see illustration).

31 Lubricate the piston and rings with clean engine oil and attach a piston ring compressor to the piston. Leave the skirt protruding about 1/4-inch to guide the piston into the cylinder. The rings must be compressed until they're flush with the piston.

32 Rotate the crankshaft until the number one connecting rod journal is at BDC (Bottom Dead Center) and apply a liberal coat of engine oil to the cylinder walls.

33 With the arrow on top of the piston facing the front (timing belt end) of the engine, gently insert the piston/connecting rod assembly into the number one cylinder bore and rest the bottom edge of the ring compressor on the engine block. Install the pistons with the cavity mark(s) or arrow facing toward the timing belt or timing chain end of the engine.

34 Tap the top edge of the ring compressor to make sure it's contacting the block around its entire circumference.

35 Gently tap on the top of the piston with the end of a wooden or plastic hammer handle (see illustration) while guiding the end of the connecting rod into place on the crankshaft journal (a pair of wooden dowels would be helpful for this). The piston rings may try to pop out of the ring compressor just before entering the cylinder bore, so keep some downward pressure on the ring compressor. Work slowly, and if any resistance is felt as the piston enters the cylinder, stop immediately. Find out what's hanging up and fix it before proceeding. Do not force the piston into the cylinder - you might break a ring and/or the piston.

36 Once the piston/connecting rod assembly is installed, the connecting rod bearing oil clearance must be checked before the rod cap is permanently installed.

37 Cut a piece of the appropriate size Plastigage slightly shorter than the width of the connecting rod bearing and lay it in place on the number one connecting rod journal, parallel with the journal axis (see illustration).

38 Clean the connecting rod cap bearing face and install the rod cap. Make sure the mating mark on the cap is on the same side as the mark on the connecting rod (see illustration 9.4).

39 Install the old rod bolts at this time and tighten them to the torque listed in this Chapter's Specifications.

➡ **Note: Use a thin-wall socket to avoid erroneous torque readings that can result if the socket is wedged between the rod cap and the bolt. If the socket tends to wedge itself between the fastener and the cap, lift up on it slightly until it no longer contacts the cap. DO NOT rotate the crankshaft at any time during this operation.**

40 Remove the fasteners and detach the rod cap, being very careful not to disturb the Plastigage. Discard the cap bolts at this time as they cannot be reused.

41 Compare the width of the crushed Plastigage to the scale printed on the Plastigage envelope to obtain the oil clearance (see illustration). The connecting rod oil clearance is usually about 0.001 to 0.002 inch. Consult an automotive machine shop for the clearance specified for the rod bearings on your engine.

42 If the clearance is not as specified, the bearing inserts may be the wrong size (which means different ones will be required). Before deciding that different inserts are needed, make sure that no dirt or oil was between

9.35 Use a plastic or wooden hammer handle to push the piston into the cylinder

9.37 Place Plastigage on each connecting rod bearing journal, parallel to the crankshaft centerline

9.41 Use the scale on the Plastigage package to determine the bearing oil clearance - measure the widest part of the Plastigage and use the correct scale; it comes with both standard and metric scales

the bearing inserts and the connecting rod or cap when the clearance was measured. Also, recheck the journal diameter. If the Plastigage was wider at one end than the other, the journal may be tapered. If the clearance still exceeds the limit specified, the bearing will have to be replaced with an undersize bearing.

➡ **Note: When installing a new crankshaft always use a standard size bearing.**

Final installation

43 Carefully scrape all traces of the Plastigage material off the rod journal and/or bearing face. Be very careful not to scratch the bearing – use your fingernail or the edge of a plastic card.

44 Make sure the bearing faces are perfectly clean, then apply a uniform layer of clean moly-base grease or engine assembly lube to both of them. You'll have to push the piston into the cylinder to expose the face of the bearing insert in the connecting rod.

45 Slide the connecting rod back into place on the journal, install the rod cap, install the new bolts and tighten them to the torque listed in this Chapter's Specifications.

➡ **Note: Install new connecting rod cap bolts. Do NOT reuse old bolts - they have stretched and cannot be reused.**

46 Repeat the entire procedure for the remaining pistons/connecting rods.

47 The important points to remember are:

a) *Keep the back sides of the bearing inserts and the insides of the connecting rods and caps perfectly clean when assembling them.*

b) *Make sure you have the correct piston/rod assembly for each cylinder.*

c) *The arrow or mark on the piston must face the front (timing belt end) of the engine.*

d) *Lubricate the cylinder walls liberally with clean oil.*

e) *Lubricate the bearing faces when installing the rod caps after the oil clearance has been checked.*

48 After all the piston/connecting rod assemblies have been correctly installed, rotate the crankshaft a number of times by hand to check for any obvious binding.

49 As a final step, check the connecting rod endplay, as described in Step 3. If it was correct before disassembly and the original crankshaft and rods were reinstalled, it should still be correct. If new rods or a new crankshaft were installed, the endplay may be inadequate. If so, the rods will have to be removed and taken to an automotive machine shop for resizing.

10 Crankshaft - removal and installation

REMOVAL

➡ **Note: It's assumed that the flywheel or driveplate, crankshaft pulley, timing belt, oil pan, oil pump body, oil filter and piston/connecting rod assemblies have already been removed. The rear main oil seal is removed.**

1 Before the crankshaft is removed, measure the endplay. Mount a dial indicator with the indicator in line with the crankshaft and just touching the end of the crankshaft as shown (see illustration).

2 Pry the crankshaft all the way to the rear and zero the dial indicator. Next, pry the crankshaft to the front as far as possible and check the reading on the dial indicator. The distance traveled is the endplay. A typical crankshaft endplay will fall between 0.003 to 0.010 inch (0.076 to 0.254 mm). If it is greater than that, check the crankshaft thrust sur-

faces for wear after it's removed. If no wear is evident, new main bearings should correct the endplay.

3 If a dial indicator isn't available, feeler gauges can be used. Gently pry the crankshaft all the way to the front of the engine. Slip feeler gauges between the crankshaft and the front face of the thrust bearing or washer to determine the clearance (see illustration).

4 Loosen the main bearing cap bolts 1/4-turn at a time each, until they can be removed by hand. Follow the reverse of the tightening sequence (see illustration 10.19).

❊❊ CAUTION:

All main bearing cap bolts must be replaced with new ones upon installation. Save the old bolts, however, as they will be used for the main bearing oil clearance check.

10.1 Checking crankshaft endplay with a dial indicator

10.3 Checking the crankshaft endplay with feeler gauges at the thrust bearing journal

10.17 Place the Plastigage onto the crankshaft bearing journal as shown

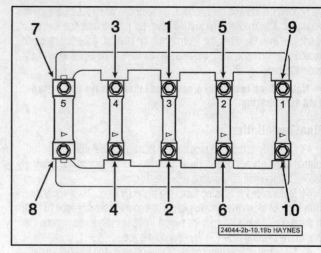

10.19 Main bearing cap bolt tightening sequence

5 Remove each individual bearing cap, while keeping them in order. Try not to drop the bearing inserts if they come out with the lower crankcase or bearing caps.

6 Carefully lift the crankshaft out of the engine. It may be a good idea to have an assistant available, since the crankshaft is quite heavy and awkward to handle. Apply black RTV to the groove on each side of the rear bearing cap, then install the main bearing caps with the bearing inserts onto the engine block in their original locations.

INSTALLATION

7 Crankshaft installation is the first step in engine reassembly. It's assumed at this point that the engine block and crankshaft have been cleaned, inspected and repaired or reconditioned.

8 Position the engine block with the bottom facing up.

9 Remove the mounting bolts and lift off the lower crankcase or bearing caps.

10 If they're still in place, remove the original bearing inserts from the block and from the lower crankcase. Wipe the bearing surfaces of the block and lower crankcase saddle with a clean, lint-free cloth. They must be kept spotlessly clean. This is critical for determining the correct bearing oil clearance.

MAIN BEARING OIL CLEARANCE CHECK

11 Without mixing them up, clean the back sides of the new upper main bearing inserts (with grooves and oil holes) and lay one in each main bearing saddle in the engine block. Each upper bearing (engine block) has an oil groove and oil hole in it.

✳✳ CAUTION:

The oil holes in the block must line up with the oil holes in the engine block inserts. The thrust washer or thrust bearing insert must be installed in the correct location.

✳✳ CAUTION:

Do not hammer the bearing insert into place and don't nick or gouge the bearing faces. DO NOT apply any lubrication at this time.

➡ Note: The thrust bearing is located on the engine block number 3 journal. Clean the back sides of the lower main bearing inserts and lay them in the corresponding location in the lower crankcase saddles. Make sure the tab on the bearing insert fits into the recess in the block or lower crankcase saddles.

12 Clean the faces of the bearing inserts in the block and the crankshaft main bearing journals with a clean, lint-free cloth.

13 Check or clean the oil holes in the crankshaft, as any dirt here can go only one way - straight through the new bearings.

14 Once you're certain the crankshaft is clean, carefully lay it in position in the cylinder block.

15 Before the crankshaft can be permanently installed, the main bearing oil clearance must be checked.

16 Cut several strips of the appropriate size of Plastigage. They must be slightly shorter than the width of the main bearing journal.

17 Place one piece on each crankshaft main bearing journal, parallel with the journal axis as shown (see illustration).

18 Clean the faces of the bearing inserts in the lower crankcase. Hold the bearing inserts in place and install the lower crankcase onto the crankshaft and cylinder block. DO NOT disturb the Plastigage.

19 Apply clean engine oil to all bolt threads prior to installation, then install all bolts finger-tight. Tighten the main bearing cap bolts in the sequence shown (see illustration) progressing in steps, to the torque listed in this Chapter's Specifications. DO NOT rotate the crankshaft at any time during this operation.

20 Remove the bolts in the reverse order of the tightening sequence and carefully lift the lower crankcase straight up and off the block. Do not disturb the Plastigage or rotate the crankshaft.

21 Compare the width of the crushed Plastigage on each journal to the scale printed on the Plastigage envelope to determine the main

bearing oil clearance (see illustration). Check with an automotive machine shop for the oil clearance for your engine.

22 If the clearance is not correct, the bearing inserts may be the wrong size (which means different ones will be required). Before deciding if different inserts are needed, make sure that no dirt or oil was between the bearing inserts and the caps or block when the clearance was measured. If the Plastigage was wider at one end than the other, the crankshaft journal may be tapered. If the clearance still exceeds the limit specified, the bearing insert(s) will have to be replaced with an undersize bearing insert(s).

❈❈ CAUTION:

When installing a new crankshaft always install a standard bearing insert set.

23 Carefully scrape all traces of the Plastigage material off the main bearing journals and/or the bearing insert faces. Remove all residue from the oil holes. Use your fingernail or the edge of a plastic card - don't nick or scratch the bearing faces.

FINAL INSTALLATION

24 Carefully lift the crankshaft out of the cylinder block. If the crankshaft position sensor reluctor wheel ring was removed, install the ring and tighten the bolts to the torque listed in this Chapter's Specifications.

25 Clean the bearing insert faces in the cylinder block, then apply a thin, uniform layer of moly-base grease or engine assembly lube to each of the bearing surfaces. Coat the thrust faces as well as the journal face of the thrust bearing.

26 Make sure the crankshaft journals are clean, then lay the crankshaft back in place in the cylinder block.

27 Clean the bearing insert faces and apply the same lubricant to them. Clean the engine block and the mating surface of the lower crankcase thoroughly. The surfaces must be free of oil residue. Install the lower crankcase.

28 Prior to installation, apply clean engine oil to all bolt threads,

10.21 Use the scale on the Plastigage package to determine the bearing oil clearance - measure the widest part of the Plastigage and use the correct scale; it comes with both standard and metric scales

wiping off any excess, then install all bolts finger-tight.

❈❈ CAUTION:

Remember, new bolts must be used.

29 Tighten the bolts to the torque listed in this Chapter's Specifications following the correct torque sequence (see illustration 10.19).

30 Recheck the crankshaft endplay with a feeler gauge or a dial indicator. The endplay should be correct if the crankshaft thrust faces aren't worn or damaged and if new bearings have been installed.

31 Rotate the crankshaft a number of times by hand to check for any obvious binding. It should rotate with a running torque of 50 in-lbs or less. If the running torque is too high, correct the problem at this time.

32 Install the new rear main oil seal (see Chapter 2A).

11 Engine overhaul - reassembly sequence

1   Before beginning engine reassembly, make sure you have all the necessary new parts, gaskets and seals as well as the following items on hand:

Common hand tools
A 1/2-inch drive torque wrench
New engine oil
Gasket sealant
Thread locking compound

2   If you obtained a short block it will be necessary to install the cylinder head, the oil pump and pick-up tube, the oil pan, the water pump, the timing belt and timing cover, and the valve cover (see Chapter 2A). In order to save time and avoid problems, the external components

must be installed in the following general order:

Thermostat and housing cover
Water pump
Intake and exhaust manifolds
Fuel injection components
Emission control components
Spark plugs and spark plug wires (2008 and earlier models)
Ignition coil pack
Oil filter
Engine mounts and mount brackets
Clutch and flywheel (manual transaxle)
Driveplate (automatic transaxle)

12 Initial start-up and break-in after overhaul

✳✳ WARNING:

Have a fire extinguisher handy when starting the engine for the first time.

1 Once the engine has been installed in the vehicle, double-check the engine oil and coolant levels.

2 With the spark plugs out of the engine and the ignition system and fuel pump disabled, crank the engine until oil pressure registers on the gauge or the light goes out.

3 Install the spark plugs, coil pack or coils and restore the ignition system and fuel pump functions.

4 Start the engine. It may take a few moments for the fuel system to build up pressure, but the engine should start without a great deal of effort.

5 After the engine starts, it should be allowed to warm up to normal operating temperature. While the engine is warming up, make a thorough check for fuel, oil and coolant leaks.

6 Shut the engine off and recheck the engine oil and coolant levels.

7 Drive the vehicle to an area with minimum traffic, accelerate from 30 to 50 mph, then allow the vehicle to slow to 30 mph with the throttle closed. Repeat the procedure 10 or 12 times. This will load the piston rings and cause them to seat properly against the cylinder walls. Check again for oil and coolant leaks.

8 Drive the vehicle gently for the first 500 miles (no sustained high speeds) and keep a constant check on the oil level. It is not unusual for an engine to use oil during the break-in period.

9 At approximately 500 to 600 miles, change the oil and filter.

10 For the next few hundred miles, drive the vehicle normally. Do not pamper it or abuse it.

11 After 2,000 miles, change the oil and filter again and consider the engine broken in.

Specifications

General

Displacement	97.51 cubic inches (1.6L)
Bore	3.1 inches (79.0 mm)
Stroke	3.21 inches (81.5 mm)
Cylinder compression	Minimum compression of 100 psi (689 kPa).
	No more than 14.5 psi (100 kPa) variation between cylinders.
Minimum oil pressure (at idle, engine at operating temperature)	
2008 and earlier models	
(RPO L91 and LXT engines)	5 psi (30 kPa)
2009 and later models	18.85 psi (130 kPa)

Torque specifications

	Ft-lbs (unless otherwise indicated)	Nm
Connecting rod bearing cap bolts*		
2008 and earlier models (L91 and LXT engines)		
Step 1	18	25
Step 2	Tighten an additional 30-degrees	
Step 3	Tighten an additional 15-degrees	
2009 and later models (LXV engine)		
Step 1	26	35
Step 2	Tighten an additional 45-degrees	
Step 3	Tighten an additional 15-degrees	
Main bearing cap bolts* (see illustration 10.19)		
2008 and earlier models (L91 and LXT engines)		
Step 1	37	50
Step 2	Tighten an additional 45-degrees	
Step 3	Tighten an additional 15-degrees	
2009 and later models (LXV engine)		
Step 1	37	50
Step 2	Tighten an additional 50-degrees	

Bolt(s) must be replaced.

GLOSSARY

B

Backlash - The amount of play between two parts. Usually refers to how much one gear can be moved back and forth without moving the gear with which it's meshed.

Bearing Caps - The caps held in place by nuts or bolts which, in turn, hold the bearing surface. This space is for lubricating oil to enter.

Bearing clearance - The amount of space left between shaft and bearing surface. This space is for lubricating oil to enter.

Bearing crush - The additional height which is purposely manufactured into each bearing half to ensure complete contact of the bearing back with the housing bore when the engine is assembled.

Bearing knock - The noise created by movement of a part in a loose or worn bearing.

Blueprinting - Dismantling an engine and reassembling it to EXACT specifications.

Bore - An engine cylinder, or any cylindrical hole; also used to describe the process of enlarging or accurately refinishing a hole with a cutting tool, as to bore an engine cylinder. The bore size is the diameter of the hole.

Boring - Renewing the cylinders by cutting them out to a specified size. A boring bar is used to make the cut.

Bottom end - A term which refers collectively to the engine block, crankshaft, main bearings and the big ends of the connecting rods.

Break-in - The period of operation between installation of new or rebuilt parts and time in which parts are worn to the correct fit. Driving at reduced and varying speed for a specified mileage to permit parts to wear to the correct fit.

Bushing - A one-piece sleeve placed in a bore to serve as a bearing surface for shaft, piston pin, etc. Usually replaceable.

C

Camshaft - The shaft in the engine, on which a series of lobes are located for operating the valve mechanisms. The camshaft is driven by gears or sprockets and a timing chain. Usually referred to simply as the cam.

Carbon - Hard, or soft, black deposits found in combustion chamber, on plugs, under rings, on and under valve heads.

Cast iron - An alloy of iron and more than two percent carbon, used for engine blocks and heads because it's relatively inexpensive and easy to mold into complex shapes.

Chamfer - To bevel across (or a bevel on) the sharp edge of an object.

Chase - To repair damaged threads with a tap or die.

Combustion chamber - The space between the piston and the cylinder head, with the piston at top dead center, in which air-fuel mixture is burned.

Compression ratio - The relationship between cylinder volume (clearance volume) when the piston is at top dead center and cylinder volume when the piston is at bottom dead center.

Connecting rod - The rod that connects the crank on the crankshaft with the piston. Sometimes called a con rod.

Connecting rod cap - The part of the connecting rod assembly that attaches the rod to the crankpin.

Core plug - Soft metal plug used to plug the casting holes for the coolant passages in the block.

Crankcase - The lower part of the engine in which the crankshaft rotates; includes the lower section of the cylinder block and the oil pan.

Crank kit - A reground or reconditioned crankshaft and new main and connecting rod bearings.

Crankpin - The part of a crankshaft to which a connecting rod is attached.

Crankshaft - The main rotating member, or shaft, running the length of the crankcase, with offset throws to which the connecting rods are attached; changes the reciprocating motion of the pistons into rotating motion.

Cylinder sleeve - A replaceable sleeve, or liner, pressed into the cylinder block to form the cylinder bore.

D

Deburring - Removing the burrs (rough edges or areas) from a bearing.

Deglazer - A tool, rotated by an electric motor, used to remove glaze from cylinder walls so a new set of rings will seat.

E

Endplay - The amount of lengthwise movement between two parts. As applied to a crankshaft, the distance that the crankshaft can move forward and back in the cylinder block.

F

Face - A machinist's term that refers to removing metal from the end of a shaft or the face of a larger part, such as a flywheel.

Fatigue - A breakdown of material through a large number of loading and unloading cycles. The first signs are cracks followed shortly by breaks.

Feeler gauge - A thin strip of hardened steel, ground to an exact thickness, used to check clearances between parts.

Free height - The unloaded length or height of a spring.

Freeplay - The looseness in a linkage, or an assembly of parts, between the initial application of force and actual movement. Usually perceived as slop or slight delay.

Freeze plug - See Core plug.

G

Gallery - A large passage in the block that forms a reservoir for engine oil pressure.

Glaze - The very smooth, glassy finish that develops on cylinder walls while an engine is in service.

H

Heli-Coil - A rethreading device used when threads are worn or damaged. The device is installed in a retapped hole to reduce the thread size to the original size.

I

Installed height - The spring's measured length or height, as installed on the cylinder head. Installed height is measured from the spring seat to the underside of the spring retainer.

J

Journal - The surface of a rotating shaft which turns in a bearing.

K

Keeper - The split lock that holds the valve spring retainer in position on the valve stem.

Key - A small piece of metal inserted into matching grooves machined into two parts fitted together - such as a gear pressed onto a shaft - which prevents slippage between the two parts.

Knock - The heavy metallic engine sound, produced in the combustion chamber as a result of abnormal combustion - usually detonation. Knock is usually caused by a loose or worn bearing. Also referred to as detonation, pinging and spark knock. Connecting rod or main bearing knocks are created by too much oil clearance or insufficient lubrication.

L

Lands - The portions of metal between the piston ring grooves.

Lapping the valves - Grinding a valve face and its seat together with lapping compound.

Lash - The amount of free motion in a gear train, between gears, or in a mechanical assembly, that occurs before movement can begin. Usually refers to the lash in a valve train.

Lifter - The part that rides against the cam to transfer motion to the rest of the valve train.

M

Machining - The process of using a machine to remove metal from a metal part.

Main bearings - The plain, or babbitt, bearings that support the crankshaft.

Main bearing caps - The cast iron caps, bolted to the bottom of the block, that support the main bearings.

O

O.D. - Outside diameter.

Oil gallery - A pipe or drilled passageway in the engine used to carry engine oil from one area to another.

Oil ring - The lower ring, or rings, of a piston; designed to prevent excessive amounts of oil from working up the cylinder walls and into the combustion chamber. Also called an oil-control ring.

Oil seal - A seal which keeps oil from leaking out of a compartment. Usually refers to a dynamic seal around a rotating shaft or other moving part.

O-ring - A type of sealing ring made of a special rubberlike material; in use, the O-ring is compressed into a groove to provide the sealing action.

Overhaul - To completely disassemble a unit, clean and inspect all parts, reassemble it with the original or new parts and make all adjustments necessary for proper operation.

P

Pilot bearing - A small bearing installed in the center of the flywheel (or the rear end of the crankshaft) to support the front end of the input shaft of the transmission.

Pip mark - A little dot or indentation which indicates the top side of a compression ring.

Piston - The cylindrical part, attached to the connecting rod, that moves up and down in the cylinder as the crankshaft rotates. When the fuel charge is fired, the piston transfers the force of the explosion to the connecting rod, then to the crankshaft.

Piston pin (or wrist pin) - The cylindrical and usually hollow steel pin that passes through the piston. The piston pin fastens the piston to the upper end of the connecting rod.

Piston ring - The split ring fitted to the groove in a piston. The ring contacts the sides of the ring groove and also rubs against the cylinder wall, thus sealing space between piston and wall. There are two types of rings: Compression rings seal the compression pressure in the combustion chamber; oil rings scrape excessive oil off the cylinder wall.

Piston ring groove - The slots or grooves cut in piston heads to hold piston rings in position.

Piston skirt - The portion of the piston below the rings and the piston pin hole.

Plastigage - A thin strip of plastic thread, available in different sizes, used for measuring clearances. For example, a strip of plastigage is laid across a bearing journal and mashed as parts are assembled. Then parts are disassembled and the width of the strip is measured to determine clearance between journal and bearing. Commonly used to measure crankshaft main-bearing and connecting rod bearing clearances.

Press-fit - A tight fit between two parts that requires pressure to force the parts together. Also referred to as drive, or force, fit.

Prussian blue - A blue pigment; in solution, useful in determining the area of contact between two surfaces. Prussian blue is commonly used to determine the width and location of the contact area between the valve face and the valve seat.

R

Race (bearing) - The inner or outer ring that provides a contact surface for balls or rollers in bearing.

Ream - To size, enlarge or smooth a hole by using a round cutting tool with fluted edges.

Ring job - The process of reconditioning the cylinders and installing new rings.

Runout - Wobble. The amount a shaft rotates out-of-true.

S

Saddle - The upper main bearing seat.

Scored - Scratched or grooved, as a cylinder wall may be scored by abrasive particles moved up and down by the piston rings.

Scuffing - A type of wear in which there's a transfer of material between parts moving against each other; shows up as pits or grooves in the mating surfaces.

Seat - The surface upon which another part rests or seats. For example, the valve seat is the matched surface upon which the valve face rests. Also used to refer to wearing into a good fit; for example, piston rings seat after a few miles of driving.

Short block - An engine block complete with crankshaft and piston and, usually, camshaft assemblies.

Static balance - The balance of an object while it's stationary.

Step - The wear on the lower portion of a ring land caused by excessive side and back-clearance. The height of the step indicates the ring's extra side clearance and the length of the step projecting from the back wall of the groove represents the ring's back clearance.

Stroke - The distance the piston moves when traveling from top dead center to bottom dead center, or from bottom dead center to top dead center.

Stud - A metal rod with threads on both ends.

T

Tang - A lip on the end of a plain bearing used to align the bearing during assembly.

Tap - To cut threads in a hole. Also refers to the fluted tool used to cut threads.

Taper - A gradual reduction in the width of a shaft or hole; in an engine cylinder, taper usually takes the form of uneven wear, more pronounced at the top than at the bottom.

Throws - The offset portions of the crankshaft to which the connecting rods are affixed.

Thrust bearing - The main bearing that has thrust faces to prevent excessive endplay, or forward and backward movement of the crankshaft.

Thrust washer - A bronze or hardened steel washer placed between two moving parts. The washer prevents longitudinal movement and provides a bearing surface for thrust surfaces of parts.

Tolerance - The amount of variation permitted from an exact size of measurement. Actual amount from smallest acceptable dimension to largest acceptable dimension.

U

Umbrella - An oil deflector placed near the valve tip to throw oil from the valve stem area.

Undercut - A machined groove below the normal surface.

Undersize bearings - Smaller diameter bearings used with re-ground crankshaft journals.

V

Valve grinding - Refacing a valve in a valve-refacing machine.

Valve train - The valve-operating mechanism of an engine; includes all components from the camshaft to the valve.

Vibration damper - A cylindrical weight attached to the front of the crankshaft to minimize torsional vibration (the twist-untwist actions of the crankshaft caused by the cylinder firing impulses). Also called a harmonic balancer.

W

Water jacket - The spaces around the cylinders, between the inner and outer shells of the cylinder block or head, through which coolant circulates.

Web - A supporting structure across a cavity.

Woodruff key - A key with a radiused backside (viewed from the side).

Notes

Notes

3

COOLING, HEATING AND AIR CONDITIONING SYSTEMS

Section

1 General Information

ENGINE COOLING SYSTEM

1   The cooling system consists of a radiator, a coolant expansion tank, a pressure cap (located on the expansion tank), a thermostat, an electric cooling fan, and either a drivebelt driven water pump (2009 and later models [LXV engine]) or timing belt driven water pump (2008 and earlier models [L91 and LXT engines]).

2   When the engine is cold, the thermostat restricts the circulation of coolant to the engine. When the minimum operating temperature is reached, the thermostat begins to open, allowing coolant to flow through the radiator.

TRANSAXLE COOLING SYSTEM

3   Vehicles with an automatic transaxle are equipped with a transaxle fluid cooler, located inside the radiator.

ENGINE OIL COOLING SYSTEM

4   Besides the engine and transaxle cooling systems described above, engine heat on 2009 and later models is also dissipated through an external oil cooler that's integrated into the lubrication system. The oil cooler helps keep engine and oil temperatures within design limits under extreme load conditions.

HEATING SYSTEM

5   The heating system consists of the heater controls, the heater core, the heater blower assembly (which houses the blower motor and the blower motor resistor), and the hoses connecting the heater core to the engine cooling system. Hot engine coolant is circulated through the heater core. When the heater mode is activated, a flap door opens to expose the heater box to the passenger compartment. A fan switch on the heater control panel activates the blower motor, which forces air through the core, heating the air.

AIR CONDITIONING SYSTEM

6   The air conditioning system consists of the condenser, which is mounted in front of the radiator, the evaporator case assembly under the dash, a compressor mounted on the engine, and the plumbing connecting all of the above components.

7   A blower fan forces the warmer air of the passenger compartment through the evaporator core (sort of a radiator-in-reverse), transferring the heat from the air to the refrigerant. The liquid refrigerant boils off into low pressure vapor, taking the heat with it when it leaves the evaporator.

2 Troubleshooting

COOLANT LEAKS

1   A coolant leak can develop anywhere in the cooling system, but the most common causes are:

   a) A loose or weak hose clamp
   b) A defective hose
   c) A faulty pressure cap
   d) A damaged radiator
   e) A bad heater core
   f) A faulty water pump
   g) A leaking gasket at any joint that carries coolant

2   Coolant leaks aren't always easy to find. Sometimes they can only be detected when the cooling system is under pressure. Here's where a cooling system pressure tester comes in handy. After the engine has cooled completely, the tester is attached in place of the pressure cap, then pumped up to the pressure value equal to that of the pressure cap rating (see illustration). Now, leaks that only exist when the engine is fully warmed up will become apparent. The tester can be left connected to locate a nagging slow leak.

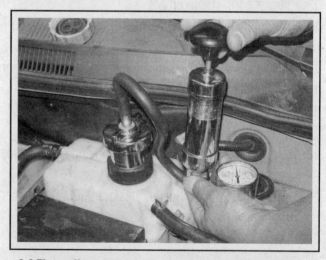

2.2 The cooling system pressure tester is connected in place of the pressure cap on the coolant expansion tank, then pumped up to pressurize the system

2.5a The combustion leak detector consists of a bulb, syringe and test fluid

2.5b Place the tester over the cooling system filler neck and use the bulb to draw a sample into the tester

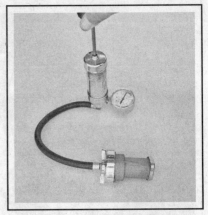

2.8 Checking the cooling system expansion tank pressure cap with a cooling system pressure tester

COOLANT LEVEL DROPS, BUT NO EXTERNAL LEAKS

3   If you find it necessary to keep adding coolant, but there are no external leaks, the probable causes include:

a) A blown head gasket
b) A leaking intake manifold gasket (only on engines that have coolant passages in the manifold)
c) A cracked cylinder head or cylinder block

4   Any of the above problems will also usually result in contamination of the engine oil, which will cause it to take on a milkshake-like appearance. A bad head gasket or cracked head or block can also result in engine oil contaminating the cooling system.

5   Combustion leak detectors (also known as block testers) are available at most auto parts stores. These work by detecting exhaust gases in the cooling system, which indicates a compression leak from a cylinder into the coolant. The tester consists of a large bulb-type syringe and bottle of test fluid (see illustration). A measured amount of the fluid is added to the syringe. The syringe is placed over the cooling system filler neck and, with the engine running, the bulb is squeezed and a sample of the gases present in the cooling system are drawn up through the test fluid (see illustration). If any combustion gases are present in the sample taken, the test fluid will change color.

6   If the test indicates combustion gas is present in the cooling system, you can be sure that the engine has a blown head gasket or a crack in the cylinder head or block, and will require disassembly to repair.

PRESSURE CAP

✷✷ WARNING:

Wait until the engine is completely cool before beginning this check.

7   The cooling system is sealed by a spring-loaded cap, which raises the boiling point of the coolant. If the cap's seal or spring are worn out, the coolant can boil and escape past the cap. With the engine completely cool, remove the cap and check the seal; if it's cracked, hardened or deteriorated in any way, replace it with a new one.

8   Even if the seal is good, the spring might not be; this can be checked with a cooling system pressure tester (see illustration). If the

cap can't hold a pressure within approximately 1-1/2 lbs. of its rated pressure (which is marked on the cap), replace it with a new one.

9   The cap is also equipped with a vacuum relief spring. When the engine cools off, a vacuum is created in the cooling system. The vacuum relief spring allows air back into the system, which will equalize the pressure and prevent damage to the radiator (the radiator tanks could collapse if the vacuum is great enough). If, after turning the engine off and allowing it to cool down you notice any of the cooling system hoses collapsing, replace the expansion tank pressure cap with a new one.

THERMOSTAT

10   Before assuming the thermostat (see illustration) is responsible for a cooling system problem, check the coolant level (see Chapter 1), drivebelt tension (see Chapter 1) and temperature gauge (or light) operation.

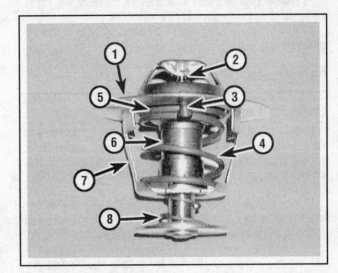

2.10 Typical thermostat:

1	Flange	5	Valve seat
2	Piston	6	Valve
3	Jiggle valve	7	Frame
4	Main coil spring	8	Secondary coil spring

2.28 The water pump weep hole is generally located on the underside of the pump

11 If the engine takes a long time to warm up (as indicated by the temperature gauge or heater operation), the thermostat is probably stuck open. Replace the thermostat with a new one.

12 If the engine runs hot or overheats, a thorough test of the thermostat should be performed.

13 Definitive testing of the thermostat can only be made when it is removed from the vehicle. If the thermostat is stuck in the open position at room temperature, it is faulty and must be replaced.

✳✳ CAUTION:

Do not drive the vehicle without a thermostat. The computer may stay in open loop and emissions and fuel economy will suffer.

14 To test a thermostat, suspend the (closed) thermostat on a length of string or wire in a pot of cold water.

15 Heat the water on a stove while observing the thermostat. The thermostat should fully open before the water boils.

16 If the thermostat doesn't open and close as specified, or sticks in any position, replace it.

COOLING FAN

Electric cooling fan

17 If the engine is overheating and the cooling fan is not coming on when the engine temperature rises to an excessive level, unplug the fan motor electrical connector(s) and connect the motor directly to the battery with fused jumper wires. If the fan motor doesn't come on, replace the motor.

18 If the radiator fan motor is okay, but it isn't coming on when the engine gets hot, the fan relay might be defective. A relay is used to control a circuit by turning it on and off in response to a control decision by the Powertrain Control Module (PCM). These control circuits are fairly complex, and checking them should be left to a qualified automotive technician. Sometimes, the control system can be fixed by simply identifying and replacing a bad relay.

19 Locate the fan relays in the engine compartment fuse/relay box.

20 Test the relay (see Chapter 12).

21 If the relay is okay, check all wiring and connections to the fan motor. Refer to the wiring diagrams at the end of Chapter 12. If no obvious problems are found, the problem could be the Engine Coolant

Temperature (ECT) sensor or the Powertrain Control Module (PCM). Have the cooling fan system and circuit diagnosed by a dealer service department or repair shop with the proper diagnostic equipment.

Belt-driven cooling fan

22 Disconnect the cable from the negative terminal of the battery and rock the fan back and forth by hand to check for excessive bearing play.

23 With the engine cold (and not running), turn the fan blades by hand. The fan should turn freely.

24 Visually inspect for substantial fluid leakage from the clutch assembly. If problems are noted, replace the clutch assembly.

25 With the engine completely warmed up, turn off the ignition switch and disconnect the negative battery cable from the battery. Turn the fan by hand. Some drag should be evident. If the fan turns easily, replace the fan clutch.

WATER PUMP

26 A failure in the water pump can cause serious engine damage due to overheating.

Drivebelt-driven water pump

27 There are two ways to check the operation of the water pump while it's installed on the engine. If the pump is found to be defective, it should be replaced with a new or rebuilt unit.

28 Water pumps are equipped with weep (or vent) holes (see illustration). If a failure occurs in the pump seal, coolant will leak from the hole.

29 If the water pump shaft bearings fail, there may be a howling sound at the pump while it's running. Shaft wear can be felt with the drivebelt removed if the water pump pulley is rocked up and down (with the engine off). Don't mistake drivebelt slippage, which causes a squealing sound, for water pump bearing failure.

Timing belt-driven water pump

30 Water pumps driven by the timing belt are located underneath the timing belt cover.

31 Checking the water pump is limited because of where it is located. However, some basic checks can be made before deciding to remove the water pump. If the pump is found to be defective, it should be replaced with a new or rebuilt unit.

32 One sign that the water pump may be failing is that the heater (climate control) may not work well. Warm the engine to normal operating temperature, confirm that the coolant level is correct, then run the heater and check for hot air coming from the ducts.

33 Check for noises coming from the water pump area. If the water pump impeller shaft or bearings are failing, there may be a howling sound at the pump while the engine is running.

34 If you suspect water pump failure due to noise, wear can be confirmed by feeling for play at the pump shaft. This can be done by rocking the drive sprocket on the pump shaft up and down. To do this you will need to remove the tension on the timing chain or belt as well as access the water pump.

All water pumps

35 In rare cases or on high-mileage vehicles, another sign of water pump failure may be the presence of coolant in the engine oil. This condition will adversely affect the engine in varying degrees.

➡ **Note: Finding coolant in the engine oil could indicate other serious issues besides a failed water pump, such as a blown head gasket or a cracked cylinder head or block.**

36 Even a pump that exhibits no outward signs of a problem, such as noise or leakage, can still be due for replacement. Removal for close examination is the only sure way to tell. Sometimes the fins on the back of the impeller can corrode to the point that cooling efficiency is diminished significantly.

HEATER SYSTEM

37 Little can go wrong with a heater. If the fan motor will run at all speeds, the electrical part of the system is okay. The three basic heater problems fall into the following general categories:

  a) *Not enough heat*
  b) *Heat all the time*
  c) *No heat*

38 If there's not enough heat, the control valve or door is stuck in a partially open position, the coolant coming from the engine isn't hot enough, or the heater core is restricted. If the coolant isn't hot enough, the thermostat in the engine cooling system is stuck open, allowing coolant to pass through the engine so rapidly that it doesn't heat up quickly enough. If the vehicle is equipped with a temperature gauge instead of a warning light, watch to see if the engine temperature rises to the normal operating range after driving for a reasonable distance.

39 If there's heat all the time, the control valve or the door is stuck wide open.

40 If there's no heat, coolant is probably not reaching the heater core, or the heater core is plugged. The likely cause is a collapsed or plugged hose, core, or a frozen heater control valve. If the heater is the type that flows coolant all the time, the cause is a stuck door or a broken or kinked control cable.

AIR CONDITIONING SYSTEM

41 If the cool air output is inadequate:

  a) *Inspect the condenser coils and fins to make sure they're clear.*
  b) *Check the compressor clutch for slippage.*
  c) *Check the blower motor for proper operation.*
  d) *Inspect the blower discharge passage for obstructions.*
  e) *Check the system air intake filter for clogging.*

42 If the system provides intermittent cooling air:

  a) *Check the circuit breaker, blower switch and blower motor for a malfunction.*

  b) *Make sure the compressor clutch isn't slipping.*
  c) *Inspect the plenum door to make sure it's operating properly.*
  d) *Inspect the evaporator to make sure it isn't clogged.*
  e) *If the unit is icing up, it may be caused by excessive moisture in the system, incorrect super heat switch adjustment or low thermostat adjustment.*

43 If the system provides no cooling air:

  a) *Inspect the compressor drivebelt. Make sure it's not loose or broken.*
  b) *Make sure the compressor clutch engages. If it doesn't, check for a blown fuse.*
  c) *Inspect the wire harness for broken or disconnected wires.*
  d) *If the compressor clutch doesn't engage, bridge the terminals of the A/C pressure switch(es) with a jumper wire; if the clutch now engages, and the system is properly charged, the pressure switch is bad.*
  e) *Make sure the blower motor is not disconnected or burned out.*
  f) *Make sure the compressor isn't partially or completely seized.*
  g) *Inspect the refrigerant lines for leaks.*
  h) *Check the components for leaks.*
  i) *Inspect the receiver-drier/accumulator or expansion valve/tube for clogged screens.*

44 If the system is noisy:

  a) *Look for loose panels in the passenger compartment.*
  b) *Inspect the compressor drivebelt. It may be loose or worn.*
  c) *Check the compressor mounting bolts. They should be tight.*
  d) *Listen carefully to the compressor. It may be worn out.*
  e) *Listen to the idler pulley and bearing and the clutch. Either may be defective.*
  f) *The winding in the compressor clutch coil or solenoid may be defective.*
  g) *The compressor oil level may be low.*
  h) *The blower motor fan bushing or the motor itself may be worn out.*
  i) *If there is an excessive charge in the system, you'll hear a rumbling noise in the high pressure line, a thumping noise in the compressor, or see bubbles or cloudiness in the sight glass.*
  j) *If there's a low charge in the system, you might hear hissing in the evaporator case at the expansion valve, or see bubbles or cloudiness in the sight glass.*

3   Air conditioning and heating system - check and maintenance

AIR CONDITIONING SYSTEM

⁂ WARNING:

The air conditioning system is under high pressure. Do not loosen any hose fittings or remove any components until after the system has been discharged. Air conditioning refrigerant should be properly discharged into an EPA-approved recovery/recycling unit at a dealer service department or an automotive air conditioning repair facility. Always wear eye protection when disconnecting air conditioning system fittings.

⁂ CAUTION:

All models covered by this manual use environmentally friendly R-134a. This refrigerant (and its appropriate refrigerant oils) are not compatible with R-12 refrigerant system components and must never be mixed or the components will be damaged.

⁂ CAUTION:

When replacing entire components, additional refrigerant oil should be added equal to the amount that is removed with the component being replaced. Be sure to read the can before adding any oil to the system, to make sure it is compatible with the R-134a system.

3.1 The evaporator drain hose is located on the center lower part of the firewall

3.9 Insert a thermometer in the center vent, turn on the air conditioning system and wait for it to cool down; depending on the humidity, the output air should be 35 to 40 degrees cooler than the ambient air temperature

3.11 R-134a automotive air conditioning charging kit

1   The following maintenance checks should be performed on a regular basis to ensure that the air conditioning continues to operate at peak efficiency.

 a) *Inspect the condition of the compressor drivebelt. If it is worn or deteriorated, replace it (see Chapter 1).*
 b) *Check the drivebelt tension (see Chapter 1).*
 c) *Inspect the system hoses. Look for cracks, bubbles, hardening and deterioration. Inspect the hoses and all fittings for oil bubbles or seepage. If there is any evidence of wear, damage or leakage, replace the hose(s).*
 d) *Inspect the condenser fins for leaves, bugs and any other foreign material that may have embedded itself in the fins. Use a fin comb or compressed air to remove debris from the condenser.*
 e) *Make sure the system has the correct refrigerant charge.*
 f) *If you hear water sloshing around in the dash area or have water dripping on the carpet, check the evaporator housing drain tube (see illustration) and insert a piece of wire into the opening to check for blockage.*

2   It's a good idea to operate the system for about ten minutes at least once a month. This is particularly important during the winter months because long term non-use can cause hardening, and subsequent failure, of the seals. Note that using the Defrost function operates the compressor.

3   If the air conditioning system is not working properly, proceed to Step 6 and perform the general checks outlined below.

4   Because of the complexity of the air conditioning system and the special equipment necessary to service it, in-depth troubleshooting and repairs beyond checking the refrigerant charge and the compressor clutch operation are not included in this manual. However, simple checks and component replacement procedures are provided in this Chapter.

5   The most common cause of poor cooling is simply a low system refrigerant charge. If a noticeable drop in system cooling ability occurs, one of the following quick checks will help you determine if the refrigerant level is low.

Checking the refrigerant charge

6   Warm the engine up to normal operating temperature.

7   Place the air conditioning temperature selector at the coldest setting and put the blower at the highest setting.

8   After the system reaches operating temperature, feel the larger pipe exiting the evaporator at the firewall. The outlet pipe should be cold (the tubing that leads back to the compressor). If the evaporator outlet pipe is warm, the system probably needs a charge.

9   Insert a thermometer in the center air distribution duct (see illustration) while operating the air conditioning system at its maximum setting - the temperature of the output air should be 35 to 40 degrees F below the ambient air temperature (down to approximately 40 degrees F). If the ambient (outside) air temperature is very high, say 110 degrees F, the duct air temperature may be as high as 60 degrees F, but generally the air conditioning is 35 to 40 degrees F cooler than the ambient air.

10 Further inspection or testing of the system requires special tools and techniques and is beyond the scope of the home mechanic.

Adding refrigerant

✳✳ CAUTION:

Make sure any refrigerant, refrigerant oil or replacement component you purchase is designated as compatible with R-134a systems.

11 Purchase an R-134a automotive charging kit at an auto parts store (see illustration). A charging kit includes a can of refrigerant, a tap valve and a short section of hose that can be attached between the tap valve and the system low side service valve.

✳✳ CAUTION:

Never add more than one can of refrigerant to the system. If more refrigerant than that is required, the system should be evacuated and leak tested.

12 Back off the valve handle on the charging kit and screw the kit onto the refrigerant can, making sure first that the O-ring or rubber seal inside the threaded portion of the kit is in place.

13 Remove the dust cap from the low-side charging port and attach

the hose's quick-connect fitting to the port (see illustration). The fittings on the charging kit are designed to fit only on the low side of the system.

❄❄ WARNING:

DO NOT hook the charging kit hose to the system high side!

❄❄ WARNING:

Wear protective eyewear when dealing with pressurized refrigerant cans.

14 Warm up the engine and turn On the air conditioning. Keep the charging kit hose away from the fan and other moving parts.

➡ **Note: The charging process requires the compressor to be running. If the clutch cycles off, you can put the air conditioning switch on High and leave the car doors open to keep the clutch on and compressor working. The compressor can be kept on during the charging by removing the connector from the pressure switch and bridging it with a paper clip or jumper wire during the procedure.**

15 Turn the valve handle on the kit until the stem pierces the can, then back the handle out to release the refrigerant. You should be able to hear the rush of gas. Keep the can upright at all times, but shake it occasionally. Allow stabilization time between each addition.

➡ **Note: The charging process will go faster if you wrap the can with a hot-water-soaked rag to keep the can from freezing up.**

16 If you have an accurate thermometer, you can place it in the center air conditioning duct inside the vehicle and keep track of the output air temperature. A charged system that is working properly should cool down to approximately 40 degrees F. If the ambient (outside) air temperature is very high, say 110 degrees F, the duct air temperature may be as high as 60 degrees F, but generally the air conditioning is 35 to 40 degrees F cooler than the ambient air.

17 When the can is empty, turn the valve handle to the closed position and release the connection from the low-side port. Reinstall the dust cap.

18 Remove the charging kit from the can and store the kit for future use with the piercing valve in the UP position, to prevent inadvertently piercing the can on the next use.

HEATING SYSTEMS

19 If the carpet under the heater core is damp, or if antifreeze vapor or steam is coming through the vents, the heater core is leaking. Remove it (see Section 13) and install a new unit (most radiator shops will not repair a leaking heater core).

20 If the air coming out of the heater vents isn't hot, the problem could stem from any of the following causes:

  a) *The thermostat is stuck open, preventing the engine coolant from warming up enough to carry heat to the heater core. Replace the thermostat (see Section 4).*
  b) *There is a blockage in the system, preventing the flow of coolant through the heater core. Feel both heater hoses at the firewall. They should be hot. If one of them is cold, there is an obstruction in one of the hoses or in the heater core, or the heater control valve is shut. Detach the hoses and back flush the heater core with a water hose. If the heater core is clear but circulation is impeded, remove the two hoses and flush them out with a water hose.*
  c) *If flushing fails to remove the blockage from the heater core, the core must be replaced (see Section 13).*

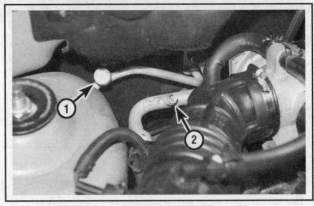

3.13 Air conditioning charging port locations
1   *High-side charging port*
2   *Low-side charging port*

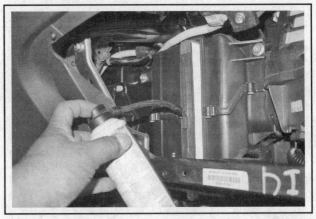

3.24 On models so equipped, remove the cabin air filter (see Chapter 1) and insert the nozzle of the disinfectant can into the housing

ELIMINATING AIR CONDITIONING ODORS

21 Unpleasant odors that often develop in air conditioning systems are caused by the growth of a fungus, usually on the surface of the evaporator core. The warm, humid environment there is a perfect breeding ground for mildew to develop.

22 The evaporator core on most vehicles is difficult to access, and factory dealerships have a lengthy, expensive process for eliminating the fungus by opening up the evaporator case and using a powerful disinfectant and rinse on the core until the fungus is gone. You can service your own system at home, but it takes something much stronger than basic household germ-killers or deodorizers.

23 Aerosol disinfectants for automotive air conditioning systems are available in most auto parts stores, but remember when shopping for them that the most effective treatments are also the most expensive. The basic procedure for using these sprays is to start by running the system in the RECIRC mode for ten minutes with the blower on its highest speed. Use the highest heat mode to dry out the system and keep the compressor from engaging by disconnecting the wiring connector at the compressor.

24 The disinfectant can usually comes with a long spray hose. Insert the nozzle into an intake port inside the cabin, and spray according to the manufacturer's recommendations (see illustration). Try to cover the

whole surface of the evaporator core, by aiming the spray up, down and sideways. Follow the manufacturer's recommendations for the length of spray and waiting time between applications.

25 Once the evaporator has been cleaned, the best way to prevent the mildew from coming back again is to make sure your evaporator housing drain tube is clear (see illustration 3.1).

AUTOMATIC HEATING AND AIR CONDITIONING SYSTEMS

26 Some vehicles are equipped with an optional automatic climate control system. This system has its own computer that receives inputs from various sensors in the heating and air conditioning system. This computer, like the PCM, has self-diagnostic capabilities to help pinpoint problems or faults within the system. Vehicles equipped with automatic heating and air conditioning systems are very complex and considered beyond the scope of the home mechanic. Vehicles equipped with automatic heating and air conditioning systems should be taken to dealer service department or other qualified facility for repair.

4   Thermostat - check and replacement

CHECK

➡ Note: On 2008 and earlier models (L91 and LXT engines), the thermostat is mounted to the front right end of the cylinder head. On 2009 and later models (LXV engines), the thermostat is mounted in a housing at the left end of the cylinder head above the transaxle.

1 Before assuming the thermostat is to blame for a cooling system problem, check the coolant level, drivebelt tension (see Chapter 1) and temperature gauge operation.

2 If the engine seems to be taking a long time to warm up, based on heater output or temperature gauge operation, the thermostat is probably stuck open. Replace the thermostat with a new one.

3 If the engine runs hot, use your hand to check the temperature of the radiator hose attached to the thermostat housing. If the hose isn't hot, but the engine is, the thermostat is probably stuck closed, preventing the coolant inside the engine from escaping to the radiator. Replace the thermostat.

✳ CAUTION:

Don't drive the vehicle without a thermostat. The computer may stay in open loop and emissions and fuel economy will suffer.

4 If the radiator hose is hot, it means that the coolant is flowing and the thermostat is open. Consult the Troubleshooting section at the front of this manual for cooling system diagnosis.

REPLACEMENT

✳ WARNING:

The engine must be completely cool before beginning this procedure.

5 Disconnect the cable from the negative terminal of the battery (see Chapter 5). Drain the cooling system (see Chapter 1).

2008 and earlier models (L91 and LXT engines)

6 Disconnect the upper radiator hose clamp (see illustration) and detach the hose from the thermostat housing.

7 Remove the fasteners and detach the thermostat housing (see illustration). If the housing is stuck, tap it with a soft-face hammer to jar it loose. Be prepared for some coolant to spill as the gasket seal is broken.

8 Disconnect the throttle body hose (see illustration) or bypass hose from the thermostat housing.

4.6 Loosen the clamp and disconnect the radiator hose

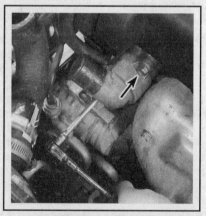

4.7 Remove the thermostat mounting bolts (L91 engine shown)

4.8 With the housing removed, disconnect the hose from the back side of the housing

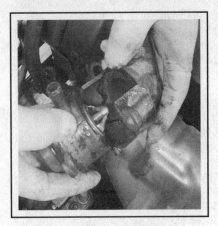

4.9a Separate the two housings...

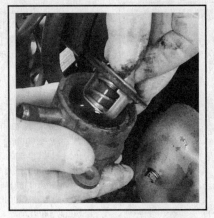

4.9b. . .and remove the thermostat

4.11a Install a new gasket onto the thermotat, then. . .

4.11b. . .place the thermostat into the housing, spring-end first - L91 engine shown

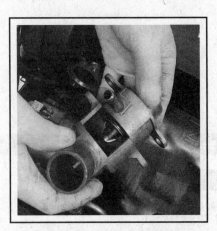

4.12 Assemble the cover and housing

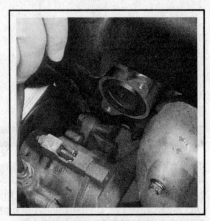

4.13 Make sure the gasket seal is seated into the recess in the engine

9 Separate the two housings (see illustration) then remove the thermostat (see illustration).

10 Clean the mating surfaces of the housing and cover.

11 Install a new gasket onto the thermostat and place the thermostat into the housing (see illustrations).

12 With both housings clean, slide the cover onto the thermostat housing (see illustration).

13 Install a new gasket seal into the groove in the engine block (see illustration).

14 Reconnect the throttle body inlet hose to the thermostat housing. Proceed to Step 20.

2009 and later models (LXV engine)

➡ **Note: On LXV models, the thermostat is an integral part of the housing; the complete assembly must be replaced when servicing the thermostat.**

15 Disconnect the upper radiator hose clamp and detach the hose from the thermostat housing.

16 Remove the fasteners and detach the thermostat housing (see illustration). If the housing is stuck, tap it with a soft-face hammer to jar it loose. Be prepared for some coolant to spill as the gasket seal is broken.

4.16 Remove the three thermostat housing bolts

4.18 Make sure the gasket is completely seated around the housing

17 Remove and discard the thermostat housing gasket.

18 Install a new thermostat housing gasket making sure it is seated correctly around the housing (see illustration).

19 Reattach the radiator hose to the outlet pipe on the thermostat cover and clamp.

All models

20 Install the thermostat housing and bolts, then tighten the bolts to the torque listed in this Chapter's Specifications.

21 The remaining installation is the reverse of the removal.

22 Refill the cooling system (see Chapter 1).

23 Reconnect the battery (see Chapter 5).

24 Start the engine and allow it to reach normal operating temperature, then check for leaks and proper thermostat operation (as described in Steps 3 and 4).

5 Engine cooling fan - replacement

✳ WARNING:

To avoid possible injury or damage, DO NOT operate the engine with a damaged fan. Do not attempt to repair fan blades - replace a damaged fan with a new one.

✳ WARNING:

The engine must be completely cool before beginning this procedure.

1 Disconnect the cable from the negative battery terminal (see Chapter 5).

2 Disconnect the fan motor electrical connector (see illustration), then separate the harness from the clips on the fan shroud and position the harness off to the side.

➡ Note: Depending on clearance, it may be necessary to raise the front of the vehicle and support it on jackstands.

3 Remove the fan shroud mounting bolts (see illustration) and maneuver the fan shroud out of the vehicle.

4 Installation is the reverse of removal.

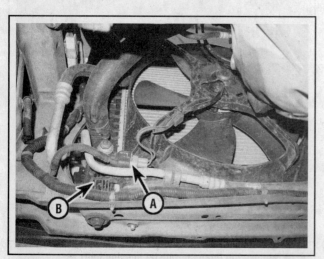

5.2 Cooling fan electrical connector (A). When installing the fan and shroud assembly, make sure the tabs at the bottom (B) are properly engaged

5.3 Fan shroud mounting bolt locations

6 Coolant expansion tank - removal and installation

✳✳ WARNING:

Wait until the engine is completely cool before beginning this procedure.

1   Disconnect the cable from the negative battery terminal (see Chapter 5).
2   Raise the vehicle and support it securely on jack stands, then drain the cooling system (see Chapter 1) until the coolant level is lower than that of the tank.
3   Disconnect the hoses from the expansion tank (see illustration).
4   Remove the tank mounting nuts and tank.
5   Installation is the reverse of removal.
6   Refill the cooling system (see Chapter 1).

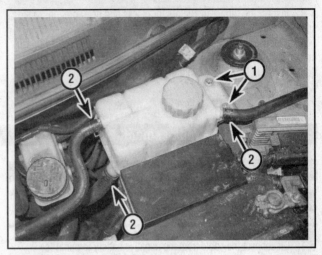

6.3 Coolant expansion tank details

1   *Mounting nuts*   2   *Coolant hoses*

7 Radiator - removal and installation

✳✳ WARNING:

The air conditioning system is under high pressure. DO NOT loosen any fittings or remove any components until after the system has been discharged. Air conditioning refrigerant must be properly discharged into an EPA-approved container at a dealer service department or an automotive air conditioning repair facility. Always wear eye protection when disconnecting air conditioning system fittings.

✳✳ WARNING:

Wait until the engine is completely cool before beginning this procedure.

REMOVAL

1   On 2009 and later models, have the air conditioning system discharged and recovered by a dealer service department or an automotive air conditioning shop before proceeding (see the Warning above).
2   Disconnect the cable from the negative battery terminal (see Chapter 5).
3   Drain the cooling system (see Chapter 1). If the coolant is relatively new and in good condition, save it and reuse it.
4   Remove the engine cooling fan (see Section 5).
5   Disconnect the upper and lower radiator hoses and the expansion tank hose from the radiator. Loosen the hose clamps by squeezing the ends together.
6   On 2009 and later models, disconnect the refrigerant lines from the condenser (see Section 15).

7   Remove the radiator upper mounting bolts and remove the brackets (see illustration).
8   Carefully lift the radiator and condenser (2009 and later models), up and out.
9   On 2009 and later models, once the radiator assembly is removed, remove the condenser mounting bolts and separate the condenser from the radiator.
10   Make sure the rubber radiator insulators that fit on the radiator lower mounting brackets remain in place in the body.
11   Remove bugs and dirt from the radiator with compressed air and a soft brush. Don't bend the cooling fins. Inspect the radiator for leaks and damage. If it requires repair, have a radiator shop do the work.

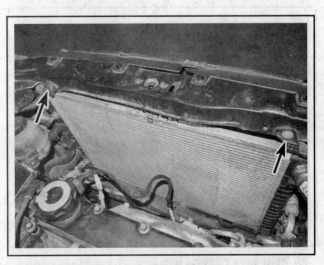

7.7 Radiator upper mounting bracket bolts

INSTALLATION

12 Inspect the rubber insulators for cracks and deterioration. Make sure that they're free of dirt and gravel.

13 Installation is the reverse of removal, making sure the condenser bolts are tightened securely, on 2009 and later models. After installation, fill the cooling system with the correct mixture of antifreeze and water (see Chapter 1).

14 Have the air conditioning system evacuated, recharged and leak tested by the shop that discharged it.

15 Reconnect the battery (see Chapter 5).

16 Start the engine and check for leaks. Allow the engine to reach normal operating temperature, indicated by the upper radiator hose becoming hot. Recheck the coolant level and add more if required.

8 Water pump - replacement

✷✷ WARNING:

The engine must be completely cool before beginning this procedure.

1 Disconnect the cable from the negative battery terminal (see Chapter 5).

2 Remove the air filter housing (see Chapter 4).

3 Loosen the right front wheel lug nuts, raise the front of the vehicle and support it securely on jackstands. Remove the wheel.

4 Drain the cooling system (see Chapter 1).

5 Remove the drivebelt (see Chapter 1).

➡ **Note: If you're working on an LXV engine, loosen the water pump pulley bolts before removing the drivebelt.**

2008 AND EARLIER MODELS (L91 AND LXT ENGINES)

6 Remove the front and rear timing belt covers and timing belt (see Chapter 2A).

7 Remove the water pump bolts (see illustration).

8 Remove the water pump from the cylinder block. be sure the O-ring comes out with the pump. If not, retrieve it from the block.

9 Clean the bolt threads and the threaded holes in the engine and remove any corrosion or sealant.

10 Coat the new O-ring seal with Lubriplate (or equivalent), then install the new O-ring seal onto the water pump and insert the water pump into the block (see illustration). Install the bolts and tighten them to the torque listed in this Chapter's Specifications.

11 Proceed to Step 24.

2009 AND LATER MODELS (LXV ENGINES)

12 Remove the air filter housing (see Chapter 4).

13 Remove the right-side headlight housing (see Chapter 12).

14 Remove the air conditioning line retainer bracket and move the line out of the way, without disconnecting the line.

15 Place a block of wood between the jack head and the oil pan, then carefully raise the engine or transaxle just enough to take the weight off the mounts.

16 Remove the engine mount (see Chapter 2A).

17 Unscrew the water pump pulley bolts and remove the pulley.

18 Unscrew the water pump mounting bolts, then remove the water pump and discard the O-ring.

19 Clean the bolt threads and the threaded holes in the engine and remove any corrosion or sealant. Clean the water pump and engine block mating surfaces.

20 Install a new O-ring into the groove on the water pump.

21 Install the water pump and bolts, tightening the bolts in a criss-cross pattern to the torque listed in this Chapter's Specifications.

22 Install the water pump pulley and tighten the bolts to the torque listed in this Chapter's Specifications.

➡ **Note: It may be necessary to tighten the pulley bolts after the drivebelt is installed (the belt will prevent the pulley from turning).**

23 Proceed to Step 24.

8.7 Water pump mounting bolts

8.10 Install the O-ring onto the water pump and coat it with Lubriplate (or an equivalent lubricant)

ALL MODELS

24 The remainder of installation is the reverse of removal.

25 Refill the cooling system (see Chapter 1).
26 Reconnect the battery (see Chapter 5).
27 Operate the engine to check for leaks.

9 Engine oil cooler (2009 and later models [LXV engines] only) - removal and installation

✱✱ WARNING:

The engine must be completely cool before beginning this procedure.

1 The engine oil cooler is an integral part of the oil filter housing. There is a heat exchanger that is mounted to the backside of the oil filter housing that is serviceable.

REMOVAL

2 Disconnect the cable from the negative battery terminal (see Chapter 5).
3 Drain the engine oil and cooling system (see Chapter 1).
4 Raise the vehicle and support it securely on jackstands.
5 Remove the exhaust manifold/catalytic converter (see Chapter 2A).
6 Remove the coolant pipe-to-coolant housing bolts.
7 Remove the coolant pipe-to-engine front cover bolts.
8 Remove the oil cooler mounting bolts and remove the oil cooler from the side of the cylinder block.

➡ **Note: There are five oil cooler mounting bolts; two in the front and three toward the rear.**

9 Remove the heat exchanger fasteners and exchanger from the oil filter housing. Remove and replace the heat exchanger gaskets.

INSTALLATION

10 Clean the area around the engine block. Remove any debris, deposits or material from the area where the cooler mounts and where the heat exchanger mounts.
11 If removed, install the heat exchanger onto the oil filter/cooler housing with new O-ring gaskets, lubricated with clean engine oil.
12 Tighten the heat exchanger fasteners to the torque listed in this Chapter's Specifications.
13 Install new gaskets into the grooves in the cooler, then install the oil cooler to the oil cooler housing and tighten the bolts to the torque listed in this Chapter's Specifications.
14 Install the coolant pipe with new gaskets and tighten both ends of the pipe to the torque listed in this Chapter's Specifications.
15 The remainder of installation is the reverse of removal.
16 Reconnect the battery (see Chapter 5).
17 Change the engine oil and filter, refill the cooling system (see Chapter 1), run the engine and check for leaks.

10 Coolant temperature sending unit - check and replacement

✱✱ WARNING:

Wait until the engine is completely cool before beginning this procedure.

CHECK

1 The coolant temperature indicator system consists of a warning light or a temperature gauge on the dash and a coolant temperature sending unit mounted on the engine. On the models covered by this manual, the Engine Coolant Temperature (ECT) sensor, which is an information sensor for the Powertrain Control Module (PCM), also functions as the coolant temperature sending unit.
2 If an overheating indication occurs, check the coolant level in the system and then make sure all connectors in the wiring harness between the sending unit and the indicator light or gauge are tight.
3 When the ignition switch is turned to START and the starter motor is turning, the indicator light (if equipped) should come on. This doesn't mean the engine is overheated; it just means that the bulb is good.
4 If the light doesn't come on when the ignition key is turned to START, the bulb might be burned out, the ignition switch might be faulty or the circuit might be open.
5 As soon as the engine starts, the indicator light should go out and remain off, unless the engine overheats. If the light doesn't go out, the wire between the sending unit and the light could be grounded, the sending unit might be defective (have it checked by a dealer service department), or the ignition switch might be faulty (see Chapter 12). Check the coolant to make sure it's correctly mixed. Plain water, with no antifreeze, or coolant that's mainly water, might have too low a boiling point to activate the sending unit (see Chapter 1).

REPLACEMENT

6 See Chapter 6 for the Engine Coolant Temperature (ECT) sensor replacement procedure.

11 Blower motor control module and blower motor - replacement

✳ WARNING:

The models covered by this manual are equipped with a Supplemental Restraint System (SRS), more commonly known as airbags. Always disarm the airbag system before working in the vicinity of any airbag system component to avoid the possibility of accidental deployment of the airbag, which could cause personal injury (see Chapter 12). Do not use a memory saving device to preserve the PCM's memory when working on or near airbag system components.

1   Disconnect the cable from the negative battery terminal (see Chapter 5).
2   Remove the lower insulator panel from below the passenger's side instrument panel (see Chapter 11).

BLOWER MOTOR RESISTOR

➡ Note: The blower motor resistor controls the air conditioning system, heater system and blower motor functions and is powered through the blower motor relay located in the interior fuse/relay panel.

3   Disconnect the electrical connector from the blower motor resistor (see illustration).
4   Remove the mounting screws and pull the resistor out of the housing.
5   Installation is the reverse of removal.
6   Reconnect the battery (see Chapter 5).

BLOWER MOTOR

7   Disconnect the blower motor air cooling hose from the side of the motor.
8   Disconnect the blower motor electrical connector (see illustration).
9   Remove the blower motor fasteners and lower the blower motor assembly from the heater case.
10 Installation is the reverse of removal.
11 Reconnect the battery (see Chapter 5).

11.3 Location of the blower motor resistor electrical connector (1) and mounting screws (2)

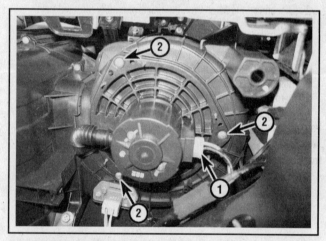

11.8 Blower motor details
1   *Blower motor electrical connector*
2   *Blower motor mounting screws*

12 Heater/air conditioner control assembly - removal and installation

✳ WARNING:

The models covered by this manual are equipped with a Supplemental Restraint System (SRS), more commonly known as airbags. Always disarm the airbag system before working in the vicinity of any airbag system component to avoid the possibility of accidental deployment of the airbag, which could cause personal injury (see Chapter 12). Do not use a memory saving device to preserve the PCM's memory when working on or near airbag system components.

1   Disconnect the cable from the negative battery terminal (see Chapter 5).
2   Remove the ashtray, then remove the dashboard center trim panel (see illustration).
3   Remove the radio trim bezel (see Chapter 12).
4   Remove the heater/air conditioner control mounting screws (see illustration) and pull the control assembly forward.

12.2 Carefully pry out the trim panel below the control assembly

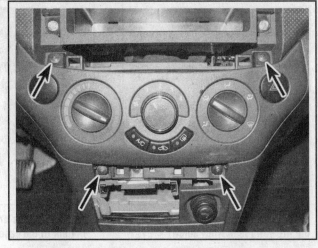

12.4 Heater/air conditioner control screw locations

5   On automatic air conditioning control models, disconnect the electrical connectors to the control assembly, then remove the control assembly.

6   On manual air conditioning control models, unsnap the cables from the retainers, then disconnect the control cables from the control levers (see illustration). Disconnect the electrical connectors, then remove the control assembly.

7   Installation is the reverse of removal.

8   Reconnect the battery (see Chapter 5).

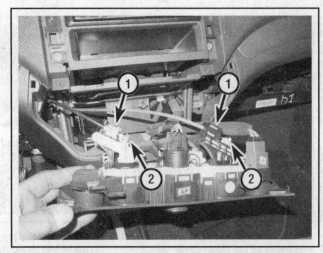

12.6 Unsnap the control cables from the retainers (1) then disconnect the ends of the cables from the control levers (2)

13   Heater core - replacement

※※ WARNING:

The models covered by this manual are equipped with a Supplemental Restraint System (SRS), more commonly known as airbags. Always disarm the airbag system before working in the vicinity of any airbag system component to avoid the possibility of accidental deployment of the airbag, which could cause personal injury (see Chapter 12). Do not use a memory saving device to preserve the PCM's memory when working on or near airbag system components.

※※ WARNING:

The air conditioning system is under high pressure. DO NOT loosen any fittings or remove any components until after the system has been discharged. Air conditioning refrigerant must be properly discharged into an EPA-approved container at a

dealer service department or an automotive air conditioning repair facility. Always wear eye protection when disconnecting air conditioning system fittings.

※※ WARNING:

Wait until the engine is completely cool before beginning this procedure.

➡ Note: For this procedure the instrument panel must be removed. This requires the tagging and disconnection of many electrical connectors and working with hard-to-reach fasteners.

1   Have the air conditioning system discharged and recovered by a dealer service department or an automotive air conditioning shop before proceeding (see the Warning above). Disconnect the cable from the

13.3 Disconnect the heater hoses at the firewall (seen from below)

13.5 Locate the drain hose at the bottom of the case

13.6a Follow the upper cable to the lever on the left side of the case and remove the cable retainer screw, then disconnect the cable from the lever . . .

13.6b . . . then repeat the same procedure on the lower cable

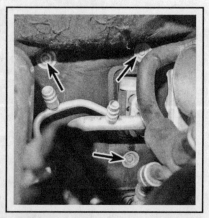

13.7a Remove the screws that secure the heater/evaporator case assembly to the firewall, from the passenger's side . . .

13.7b . . .and the driver's side - 1 of 3 shown

13.9a Remove the instrument panel-to-case screws from the left . . .

negative terminal of the battery (see Chapter 5).

2 Drain the cooling system (see Chapter 1).

3 Disconnect the heater hoses at the firewall (see illustration), then cap the heater core tubes and hoses.

4 Remove the air conditioning refrigerant line block mounting nut and disconnect the block from the thermostatic expansion valve (see illustration 17.2).

5 Working inside the vehicle, rotate the case drain hose, then pull the hose off (see illustration).

6 On manual heater/air conditioning models, remove the cable fasteners, then remove the cables from the levers (see illustrations).

7 Working inside the engine compartment, remove the screws that secure the heater/evaporator case assembly to the firewall (see illustrations).

8 Remove the instrument panel (see Chapter 11).

9 Remove the heater/evaporator case assembly-to-instrument panel screws (see illustrations).

13.9b . . .center . . .

13.9c . . .and end of the case assembly

13.10 Evaporator housing and blower motor case-to-heater core case mounting screw locations

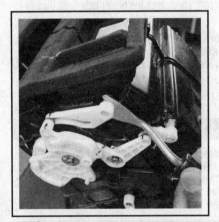

13.11 Remove the lever to the vent door

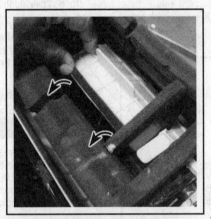

13.12 The vent door must be in the closed position before the case can be separated

13.13a Carefully remove the seal from the heater case halves . . .

10 Remove the evaporator housing and blower motor case mounting screws (see illustration), then separate the cases from the heater core assembly case.

11 Mark the linkage assembly, then disconnect the lever to the vent door (see illustration).

12 Once the vent door lever is removed, place the vent door in the closed position (see illustration).

13 Slowly remove the seals from the heater case (see illustrations).

13.13b . . . and then where the case contacts the firewall

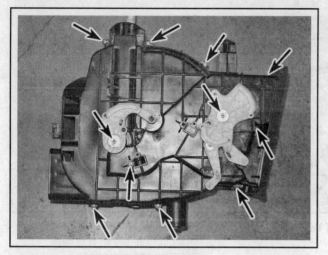

13.14 Case and linkage screw locations

13.15 Remove the heater core cover

14 Remove the linkage screws and levers from the right side of the case (see illustration). Be sure to take notes on how the levers are mounted before you remove them.

15 Remove the heater core cover from the heater case (see illustration).

➡ **Note: The heater core cover has a sealant between the cover and the case that can make the cover difficult to separate. The sealant needs to be saved or replaced when the cover is reinstalled.**

16 Remove the heater core from the case (see illustration).

13.16 Lift the heater core out of the case

✳✳ CAUTION:

There will be a small amount of coolant left in the tubes and heater core. Once the tubes are removed, the coolant will drain out into the vehicle. Make sure to have a small container to catch the fluid and some rags in place to protect the carpet before disconnecting the heater core tubes.

17 Installation is the reverse of removal.
18 Refill the cooling system (see Chapter 1).
19 Have the system evacuated, recharged and leak tested by the shop that discharged it.
20 Reconnect the battery (see Chapter 5).

14 Air conditioning compressor - removal, installation and oil balancing

✳✳ WARNING:

The air conditioning system is under high pressure. DO NOT loosen any fittings or remove any components until after the system has been discharged. Air conditioning refrigerant must be properly discharged into an EPA-approved container at a dealer service department or an automotive air conditioning repair facility. Always wear eye protection when disconnecting air conditioning system fittings.

REMOVAL

1 Have the air conditioning system discharged and recovered by a dealer service department or an automotive air conditioning shop before proceeding (see the Warning above). Disconnect the cable from the negative terminal of the battery (see Chapter 5).

➡ **Note: If you are going to install a new compressor, inform the shop doing the work to record the amount of refrigerant oil recovered when the system is discharged (this measurement will be used when adjusting the compressor oil level during installation.**

2 Loosen the right front wheel lug nuts, raise the vehicle and support it securely on jackstands. Remove the right front wheel.

3 Remove the inner fender splash shield (see Chapter 11).

4 Remove the drivebelt (see Chapter 1).

5 Disconnect the electrical connectors from the compressor (see illustration).

6 Remove the line connector block retaining nut and disconnect the compressor inlet and outlet line assembly from the compressor. Remove and discard the old O-rings.

➥ **Note: Once the compressor is removed, drain and measure the amount of oil from the old compressor.**

7 Remove the compressor mounting bolts and remove the compressor (see illustration).

INSTALLATION

8 If a new compressor is being installed, follow the directions with the compressor regarding the measuring and adding of oil prior to installation.

9 With the old compressor removed, remove the compressor drain plug and allow the oil to drain into a graduated container. Tilt the compressor over to allow both ports to drain into the same container.

10 The clutch may have to be transferred from the original to the new compressor.

11 Before reconnecting the inlet and outlet lines to the compressor, replace the O-rings and lubricate them with refrigerant oil.

12 Once all the oil is drained from the compressor, record the amount that you measured and add the exact amount of oil that you drained from the old compressor to the new one.

13 The remainder of installation is the reverse of removal.

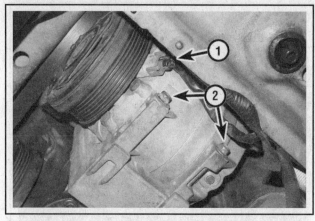

14.5 Compressor mounting details

1 *Field coil electrical connector*
2 *Lower mounting bolts*

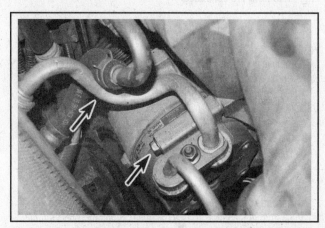

14.7 Remove the upper bolts (the front bolt is not fully visible)

15 Air conditioning condenser - removal and installation

※ WARNING:

The air conditioning system is under high pressure. DO NOT loosen any fittings or remove any components until after the system has been discharged. Air conditioning refrigerant must be properly discharged into an EPA-approved container at a dealer service department or an automotive air conditioning repair facility. Always wear eye protection when disconnecting air conditioning system fittings.

※ WARNING:

Wait until the engine is completely cool before beginning this procedure.

1 Have the air conditioning system discharged by a dealer service department or by an automotive air conditioning shop before proceeding (see Warning above).

2 Disconnect the cable from the negative battery terminal (see Chapter 5).

3 Drain the cooling system (see Chapter 1). If the coolant is relatively new and in good condition, save it and reuse it.

2008 AND EARLIER MODELS

4 Remove the radiator (see Section 7).

5 Remove the front bumper cover (see Chapter 11).

15.6 Remove the condenser line mounting bolts and separate the lines from the condenser

15.8 Condenser mounting bolt locations

6   Disconnect the refrigerant inlet and outlet lines from the condenser (see illustration).

7   Remove the receiver-drier bracket bolt and bracket. Remove the receiver-drier (see Section 18).

8   Remove the condenser mounting bolt/nuts (see illustration), then tilt the top of the condenser inward and lift the condenser out of the vehicle.

2009 AND LATER MODELS

9   Remove the engine cooling fan (see Section 5).

10 Disconnect the upper and lower radiator hoses and the expansion tank hose from the radiator. Loosen the hose clamps by squeezing the ends together.

11 Disconnect the lines to the condenser (see illustration 15.6).

12 Remove the radiator upper mounting bolts and remove the brackets (see illustration 7.7).

13 Carefully lift the radiator and condenser assembly up and out.

14 Once the radiator assembly is removed, remove the condenser mounting bolts and separate the condenser from the radiator.

ALL MODELS

15 On 2008 and earlier models, make sure the rubber mounts are in place and that the bottom of the condenser fits into mounts and the holes in the radiator support.

16 Install the mounting nut or bolts and tighten them to the torque listed in this Chapter's Specifications.

17 Before reconnecting the refrigerant lines to the condenser, coat a pair of new O-rings with refrigerant oil. Install them in the refrigerant line fittings, then tighten the condenser inlet and outlet nuts to the torque listed in this Chapter's Specifications.

18 Installation is otherwise the reverse of removal.

19 Have the system evacuated, recharged and leak tested by the shop that discharged it.

16   Air conditioning pressure sensor - replacement

❊❊ WARNING:

The sensor screws onto a Schrader valve, making it unnecessary to recover the refrigerant to perform this procedure. It is still a good idea to wear safety goggles though, just in case a short spurt of refrigerant escapes when removing the valve.

1   The pressure sensor is located near the right strut tower, mounted to the high-pressure-side refrigerant line. The pressure sensor detects low refrigerant line pressure, switches the compressor off, then back on again to provide higher pressure. If the pressure increases too high, the pressure cut-off switch, located in the high pressure side of the system, shuts the system off.

2   Remove the air filter housing (see Chapter 4).

3   Disconnect the electrical connector from the pressure sensor (see illustration).

16.3 Location of the air conditioning pressure sensor

4   Unscrew the pressure sensor.

➡ **Note: The sensor screws onto a Schrader valve, making it unnecessary to recover the refrigerant.**

5   Lubricate the sensor O-ring with clean refrigerant oil of the correct type.

6   Screw the new sensor into place until hand tight, then tighten it securely.

7   Reconnect the electrical connector.

8   The remainder of installation is the reverse of removal.

17 Air conditioning thermostatic expansion valve (TXV) - general information

❋❋ WARNING:

The air conditioning system is under high pressure. DO NOT loosen any hose fittings or remove any components until the system has been discharged. Air conditioning refrigerant must be properly discharged into an EPA-approved recovery/recycling unit by a dealer service department or an automotive air conditioning repair facility. Always wear eye protection when disconnecting air conditioning system fittings.

1   There are several ways that air conditioning systems convert the high-pressure liquid refrigerant from the compressor to lower-pressure vapor. The conversion takes place at the air conditioning evaporator. The evaporator is chilled as the refrigerant passes through, cooling the airflow through the evaporator for delivery to the vents. The conversion is usually accomplished by a sudden change in the tubing size. Many vehicles have a removable controlled orifice in one of the refrigerant lines at the firewall.

2   The models covered by this manual use a Thermostatic Expansion Valve (TXV) that accomplishes the same thing as a controlled orifice (see illustration). To remove the TXV, have the air conditioning system discharged by a licensed air conditioning technician, then disconnect the refrigerant lines from the TXV at the firewall, remove the two bolts securing the valve, then remove the valve and replace the four O-rings. Installation is the reverse of removal.

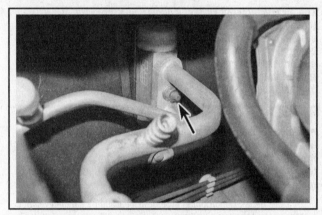

17.2 The Thermostatic Expansion Valve is located on the firewall

18 Air conditioning accumulator (2008 and earlier models) - replacement

❋❋ WARNING:

The air conditioning system is under high pressure. DO NOT loosen any fittings or remove any components until after the system has been discharged. Air conditioning refrigerant must be properly discharged into an EPA-approved container at a dealer service department or an automotive air conditioning repair facility. Always wear eye protection when servicing the air conditioning system.

➡ **Note: 2009 and later models are not equipped with a traditional receiver-drier. Instead, a desiccant cartridge is built into the left side of the condenser. It should be replaced whenever the compressor is replaced or whenever a component has been replaced because of a leak in the system.**

1   Have the air conditioning system discharged by a dealer service department or by an automotive air conditioning shop before proceeding (see Warning above).

2   Remove the cooling fan (see Section 5).

3   Remove the band clamp mounting screw and clamp.

4   Remove the accumulator mounting bolts (see illustration) and remove the accumulator.

➡ **Note: Once the accumulator is removed, drain and measure the amount of oil from the old accumulator.**

5   With the old accumulator removed, allow the oil to drain into a graduated container. Tilt the drier to allow all the oil to drain.

18.4 Accumulator mounting bolts

6 Once all the oil is drained from the accumulator record the amount that you measured and add the exact amount of oil that you drained from the old accumulator into the new one.

7 Installation is the reverse of removal. Be sure to use new O-rings and tighten the mounting bolts to the torque listed in this Chapter's Specifications.

8 Have the system evacuated, recharged and leak tested by the shop that discharged it.

19 Air conditioning refrigerant desiccant (2009 and later models) - replacement

✳✳ WARNING:

The air conditioning system is under high pressure. DO NOT loosen any fittings or remove any components until after the system has been discharged. Air conditioning refrigerant must be properly discharged into an EPA-approved container at a dealer service department or an automotive air conditioning repair facility. Always wear eye protection when servicing the air conditioning system.

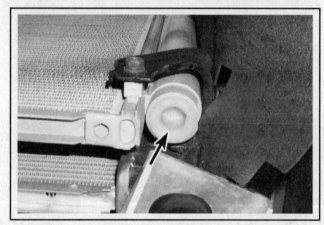

19.4 Typical air conditioning refrigerant desiccant cap (front bumper cover removed for clarity)

➡ Note: 2009 and later models are not equipped with a traditional receiver-drier. Instead, a desiccant cartridge is built into the left side of the condenser. It should be replaced whenever the compressor is replaced or whenever a component has been replaced because of a leak in the system.

1 Have the air conditioning system discharged by a dealer service department or by an automotive air conditioning shop before proceeding (see Warning above).

2 Raise the front of the vehicle and support it securely on jackstands.

3 Remove the splash guard between the bumper cover and the subframe.

4 Using a large Allen wrench or hex bit, unscrew the cap from the desiccant tube on the left side of the condenser (see illustration).

5 Pull the desiccant cartridge from the tube.

6 Installation is the reverse of removal. Be sure to use a new O-ring on the cap.

7 Have the system evacuated, recharged and leak tested by the shop that discharged it.

Specifications

General

Pressure cap rating	Marked on cap
Cooling system capacity	See Chapter 1
HVAC refrigerant type	R-134a
Refrigerant capacity	
2005 and earlier models	21 +/- 1 oz (600 +/- 20 g)
2006 and later models	18 +/- 1 oz (520 +/- 20 g)

Torque specifications	Ft-lbs (unless otherwise indicated)	Nm

➡ **Note: One foot-pound (ft-lb) of torque is equivalent to 12 inch-pounds (in-lbs) of torque. Torque values below approximately 15 ft-lbs are expressed in inch-pounds, since most foot-pound torque wrenches are not accurate at these smaller values.**

	Ft-lbs	Nm
Air conditioning compressor mounting bolts		
2006 and earlier models	26	35
2007 and later models	20	27
Oil cooler/oil filter housing bolts	19	25
Oil cooler pipe bolts	71 in-lbs	8
Oil cooler heat exchanger fasteners	71 in-lbs	8
Low side line-to-condenser bolt	120 in-lbs	14
Refrigerant line manifold-to-condenser bolts	144 in-lbs	16
Refrigerant line manifold-to-compressor nut	24	33
Receiver dryer-to-condenser pipe block nut	89 in-lbs	10
Thermostat housing bolts	15	20
Water pump bolts	89 in-lbs	10

Notes

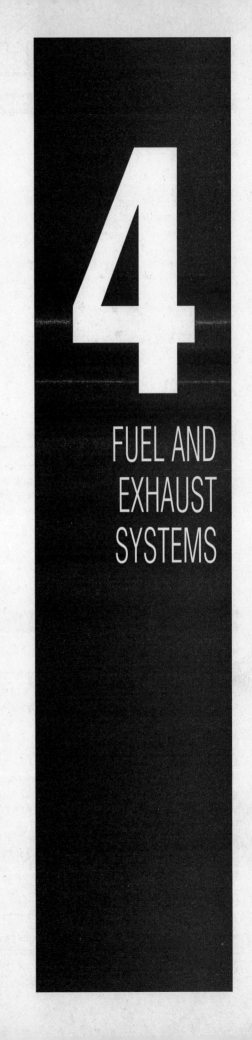

4

FUEL AND
EXHAUST
SYSTEMS

Section

1   General information and precautions

FUEL SYSTEM WARNINGS

1   Gasoline is extremely flammable and repairing fuel system components can be dangerous. Consider your automotive repair knowledge and experience before attempting repairs, which may be better suited for a professional mechanic.

   a) *Don't smoke or allow open flames or bare light bulbs near the work area*
   b) *Don't work in a garage with a gas-type appliance (water heater, clothes dryer)*
   c) *Use fuel-resistant gloves. If any fuel spills on your skin, wash it off immediately with soap and water*
   d) *Clean up spills immediately*
   e) *Do not store fuel-soaked rags where they could ignite*
   f) *Prior to disconnecting any fuel line, you must relieve the fuel pressure (see Section 3)*
   g) *Wear safety glasses*
   h) *Have a proper fire extinguisher on hand*

FUEL SYSTEM

2   This Chapter covers the removal and installation procedures for the important parts of the air intake, fuel and exhaust systems. Because emission control systems are integral parts of the engine management system, there are many cross-references to Chapter 6. Information on the engine management system, information sensors and output actuators is in Chapter 6.

3   The air intake system consists of the air filter housing, the air intake duct, the throttle body, and the intake manifold. Incoming air passes through the air filter element, the Mass Air Flow (MAF) sensor, the air intake duct, the throttle body, the intake manifold plenum and the intake manifold runners before being mixed with fuel sprayed into the intake ports by the fuel injectors.

4   The Sequential Fuel Injection (SFI) system consists of the fuel tank, an electric fuel pump/fuel level sending unit module mounted inside the tank, the fuel pressure regulator (integral with the fuel pump module), the fuel rail, the fuel injectors, and the metal and flexible fuel lines that connect the various components of the SFI system.

5   Fuel is circulated from the fuel pump to the fuel rail through fuel lines running along the underside of the vehicle. Various sections of the fuel line are either rigid metal or nylon, or flexible fuel hose. The various sections of the fuel hose are connected either by quick-connect fittings or threaded metal fittings.

EXHAUST SYSTEM

6   The exhaust system consists of the exhaust manifold, catalytic converter, muffler, tailpipe and all connecting pipes, flanges and clamps. The catalytic converter is an emission control device added to the exhaust system to reduce pollutants.

2   Troubleshooting

FUEL PUMP

1   The fuel pump is located inside the fuel tank. Sit inside the vehicle with the windows closed, turn the ignition key to ON (not START) and listen for the sound of the fuel pump as it's briefly activated. You will only hear the sound for a second or two, but that sound tells you that the pump is working. Alternatively, have an assistant listen at the fuel filler cap.

2   If the pump does not come on, check the fuel pump fuse and ignition main relay (see illustration). If the fuse and relay are okay, check the wiring back to the fuel pump. If the fuse, relay and wiring are okay, the fuel pump is probably defective. If the pump runs continuously with the ignition key in the ON position, the Powertrain Control Module (PCM) is probably defective. Have the PCM checked by a professional mechanic.

FUEL INJECTION SYSTEM

➡ **Note: The following procedure is based on the assumption that the fuel pump is working and the fuel pressure is adequate (see Section 4).**

3   Check all electrical connectors that are related to the system.

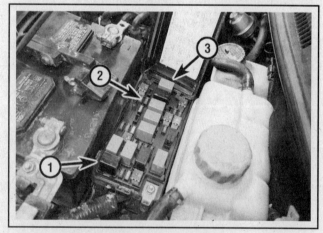

2.2 Fuel system-related underhood fuse/relay box details (2007 model shown - sure to check the underside of the fuse/relay box cover on your model to verify fuse/relay locations)

1   *Ignition main relay (supplies power to the fuel pump fuse)*
2   *Fuel pump fuse (15 amp; receives power from the ignition main relay when the key is in the RUN position)*
3   *Fuel pump relay (activates the fuel pump)*

Check the ground wire connections for tightness.

4   Verify that the battery is fully charged (see Chapter 5).

5   Inspect the air filter element (see Chapter 1).

6   Check all fuses related to the fuel system (see Chapter 12).

7   Check the air induction system between the throttle body and the intake manifold for air leaks. Also inspect the condition of all vacuum hoses connected to the intake manifold and to the throttle body.

8   Remove the air intake duct from the throttle body and look for dirt, carbon, varnish, or other residue in the throttle body, particularly around the throttle plate. If it's dirty, clean it with carb cleaner, a toothbrush and a clean shop towel.

9   With the engine running, place an automotive stethoscope against each injector, one at a time, and listen for a clicking sound that indicates operation (see illustration).

❊❊ WARNING:

Stay clear of the drivebelt and any rotating or hot components.

10   If you can hear the injectors operating, but the engine is misfiring, the electrical circuits are functioning correctly, but the injectors might be dirty or clogged. Try a commercial injector cleaning product (available at auto parts stores). If cleaning the injectors doesn't help, replace the injector(s).

11   If an injector is not operating (it makes no sound), disconnect the injector electrical connector and measure the resistance across the

2.9 An automotive stethoscope is used to listen to the fuel injectors in operation

injector terminals with an ohmmeter. Compare this measurement to the other injectors. If the resistance of the non-operational injector is quite different from the other injectors, replace it.

12   If the injector is not operating, but the resistance reading is within the range of resistance of the other injectors, the PCM or the circuit between the PCM and the injector might be faulty.

3   Fuel pressure relief procedure

1   The fuel system is composed of: the fuel tank and tank-mounted fuel pump/fuel gauge sender unit, the fuel filter, the fuel injectors and the metal pipes and flexible hoses of the fuel lines between these components. All these components contain fuel, which is pressurized as soon as the ignition key is turned to ON, and remains pressurized while the engine is running (and even after the ignition is switched off). Since the pressure remains for some time after the ignition has been switched off, it must be relieved before any fuel lines are disconnected.

2   The fuel pressure is relieved by pulling the fuel pump fuse(s) (see Section 2), then starting the engine, which disables the fuel pump and stalls the engine.

3   Crank the engine an additional 10 seconds after it has stalled,

then disconnect the cable from the negative terminal of the battery (see Chapter 5).

4   Remove the fuel filler cap to relieve any pressure built-up in the fuel tank.

❊❊ WARNING:

This procedure merely relieves the pressure in the system - but remember that fuel is still present in the system components, and take precautions accordingly before disconnecting any of them.

4   Fuel pump/fuel pressure - check

❊❊ WARNING:

Gasoline is extremely flammable, so take extra precautions when you work on any part of the fuel system. See *Fuel system warnings* in Section 1.

FUEL PUMP OPERATION CHECK

1   The fuel pump is located inside the fuel tank, which muffles its sound when the engine is running. But you can actually hear the fuel

pump. Sit inside the vehicle with the windows closed, turn the ignition key to ON (not START) and listen carefully for the sound made by the fuel pump as it's briefly turned on by the PCM to pressurize the fuel system prior to starting the engine. You will only hear the sound for a second or two, but that sound tells you that the pump is working. If you can't hear the pump, remove the fuel filler cap, depress the spring-loaded door inside the fuel filler neck, then have an assistant turn the ignition switch to ON while you listen for the sound of the pump operating for a couple of seconds.

2   If the pump does not come on when the ignition key is turned to ON, check the fuel pump fuse and relay (both of which are located in the engine compartment fuse and relay box). If the fuse and relay are

4.3 Test port on the fuel rail for fuel pressure testing

5 The preferred method to check fuel pressure is to use a scan tool to command the fuel pump On. If a scan tool is not available, turn the ignition key to the On position (but don't start the engine). Note the gauge reading as soon as the pressure stabilizes, and compare it with the pressure listed in this Chapter's Specifications.

6 If the fuel pressure is not within specifications, check the following:

a) *If the pressure is lower than the minimum specified, check for a restriction in the fuel system. If no restrictions are found, replace the fuel pump module (see Section 7).*

b) *If the fuel pressure is higher than the maximum specified, replace the fuel pump module (see Section 7).*

7 Turn the ignition key Off.

8 Verify that the fuel pressure loses no more than 5 psi (34 kPa) in one minute.

a) *If pressure remains constant, go to Step 11.*

b) *If pressure drops more than specified within the allotted time, install a shut-off valve where the fuel line connects to the fuel rail, pressurize the fuel system by turning the ignition key to the On position, then close the shut-off valve and go to Step 10.*

9 Verify that the fuel pressure loses no more than 5 psi (34 kPa) in one minute.

a) *If pressure drops more than specified within the allotted time, there's a leaky injector.*

b) *If pressure remains contant, there's a faulty fuel pump module.*

10 Using the fuel pressure gauge, lower the fuel pressure to 10 psi (69 kPa) and verify that the fuel pressure loses no more than 2 psi (14 kPa) in five minutes.

a) *If pressure remains constant, the system is OK.*

b) *If pressure drops more than specified within the allotted time, there's a faulty fuel pump module.*

11 Relieve the fuel pressure (see Section 3), then disconnect the fuel pressure gauge. Mop up any spilled gasoline.

12 Start the engine and verify that there are no fuel leaks.

okay, check the wiring back to the fuel pump (see Section 7 if you need help locating the fuel pump electrical connector). If the fuse, relay and wiring are okay, the fuel pump is probably defective. If the pump runs continuously with the ignition key in its ON position, the Powertrain Control Module (PCM) is probably defective. Have the PCM checked by a dealer service department or other qualified repair shop.

FUEL PRESSURE CHECK

3 To check the fuel pressure, locate the Schrader valve test port on the fuel rail, unscrew the cap and connect a fuel pressure gauge (see illustration).

4 Relieve the fuel pressure (see Section 3). After you have relieved the fuel pressure, make sure that the bleeder valve on your fuel pressure gauge is CLOSED.

5 Fuel lines and fittings - general information and disconnection

⁕⁕ WARNING:

Gasoline is extremely flammable, so take extra precautions when you work on any part of the fuel system. See *Fuel system warnings* in Section 1.

1 Relieve the fuel pressure before servicing fuel lines or fittings (see Section 3). Disconnect the cable from the negative battery terminal (see Chapter 5) before proceeding.

2 The fuel supply line connects the fuel pump in the fuel tank to the fuel rail on the engine. The Evaporative emissions control (EVAP) system lines connect the fuel tank to the EVAP canister and connect the canister to the intake manifold.

3 Whenever you're working under the vehicle, be sure to inspect all fuel and evaporative emission lines for leaks, kinks, dents and other damage. Always replace a damaged fuel or EVAP line immediately.

4 If you find signs of dirt in the lines during disassembly, disconnect all lines and blow them out with compressed air. Inspect the fuel strainer on the fuel pump pick-up unit for damage and deterioration.

STEEL TUBING

5 It is critical that the fuel lines be replaced with lines of equivalent type and specification.

6 Some steel fuel lines have threaded fittings. When loosening these fittings, hold the stationary fitting with a wrench while turning the tube nut.

PLASTIC TUBING

7 When replacing fuel system plastic tubing, use only original equipment replacement plastic tubing.

⁕⁕ CAUTION:

When removing or installing plastic fuel line tubing, be careful not to bend or twist it too much, which can damage it. Also, plastic fuel tubing is NOT heat resistant, so keep it away from excessive heat.

Disconnecting Fuel Line Fittings

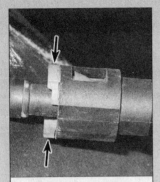

Two-tab type fitting; depress both tabs with your fingers, then pull the fuel line and the fitting apart

On this type of fitting, depress the two buttons on opposite sides of the fitting, then pull it off the fuel line

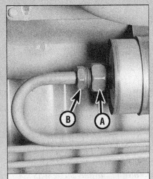

Threaded fuel line fitting; hold the stationary portion of the line or component (A) while loosening the tube nut (B) with a flare-nut wrench

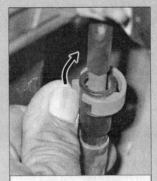

Plastic collar-type fitting; rotate the outer part of the fitting

Metal collar quick-connect fitting; pull the end of the retainer off the fuel line, and disengage the other end from the female side of the fitting . . .

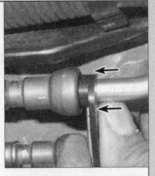

. . . insert a fuel line separator tool into the female side of the fitting, push it into the fitting until it releases the locking tabs inside the fitting, and pull the two halves of the fitting apart

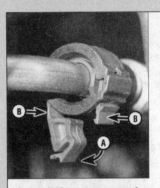

Some fittings are secured by lock tabs. Release the lock tab (A) and rotate it to the fully-opened position, squeeze the two smaller lock tabs (B) . . .

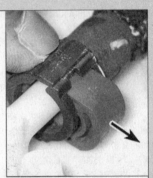

. . . then push the retainer out and pull the fuel line off the pipe

Spring-lock coupling remove the safety cover, install a coupling release tool and close the tool around the coupling . . .

. . . push the tool into the fitting, then pull the two lines apart

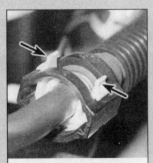

Hairpin clip type fitting: push the legs of the retainer clip together, then push the clip down all the way until it stops and pull the fuel line off the pipe

FLEXIBLE HOSES

8   When replacing fuel system flexible hoses, use only original equipment replacements.

9   Don't route fuel hoses (or metal lines) within four inches of the exhaust system or within ten inches of the catalytic converter. Make sure that no rubber hoses are installed directly against the vehicle, particularly in places where there is any vibration. If allowed to touch some vibrating part of the vehicle, a hose can easily become chafed and it might start leaking. A good rule of thumb is to maintain a minimum of 1/4-inch clearance around a hose (or metal line) to prevent contact with the vehicle underbody.

6   Exhaust system servicing - general information

✳✳ WARNING:

Allow exhaust system components to cool before inspection or repair. Also, when working under the vehicle, make sure it is securely supported on jackstands.

1   The exhaust system consists of the exhaust manifolds, catalytic converter, muffler, tailpipe and all connecting pipes, flanges and clamps. The exhaust system is isolated from the vehicle body and from chassis components by a series of rubber hangers (see illustration). Periodically inspect these hangers for cracks or other signs of deterioration, replacing them as necessary.

2   Conduct regular inspections of the exhaust system to keep it safe and quiet. Look for any damaged or bent parts, open seams, holes, loose connections, excessive corrosion or other defects which could allow exhaust fumes to enter the vehicle. Do not repair deteriorated exhaust system components; replace them with new parts.

3   If the exhaust system components are extremely corroded, or rusted together, a cutting torch is the most convenient tool for removal. Consult a properly-equipped repair shop. If a cutting torch is not available, you can use a hacksaw, or if you have compressed air, there are special pneumatic cutting chisels that can also be used. Wear safety goggles to protect your eyes from metal chips and wear work gloves to protect your hands.

4   Here are some simple guidelines to follow when repairing the exhaust system:

a) *Work from the back to the front when removing exhaust system components.*

6.1 Typical exhaust system hangers. Inspect regularly and replace at the first sign of damage or deterioration

b) *Apply penetrating oil to the exhaust system component fasteners to make them easier to remove.*
c) *Use new nuts, gaskets, hangers and clamps.*
d) *Apply anti-seize compound to the threads of all exhaust system fasteners during reassembly.*
e) *Be sure to allow sufficient clearance between newly installed parts and all points on the underbody to avoid overheating the floor pan and possibly damaging the interior carpet and insulation. Pay particularly close attention to the catalytic converter and heat shield.*

7   Fuel pump module - removal and installation

✳✳ WARNING:

Gasoline is extremely flammable, so take extra precautions when you work on any part of the fuel system. See *Fuel system warnings* in Section 1.

1   Relieve the system fuel pressure (see Section 3).

2   Disconnect the cable from the negative battery terminal (see Chapter 5).

3   Remove the rear seat cushion (see Chapter 11, Section 25).

4   Remove the fuel pump access cover (see illustration).

5   Disconnect the fuel supply line and electrical connectors from the fuel pump/fuel level sending unit module (see illustration). Use a shop rag to soak up any spilled fuel.

6   Loosen the large band clap around the fuel pump module retainer. Remove the band clamp and the retainer (see illustrations).

7   Note the orientation of the fuel pump in relation to the fuel tank to ensure that the fuel pump is correctly realigned when you install it again (see illustration).

8   Remove the fuel pump/fuel level sensor module, taking care not to damage the fuel level sensor float arm and float. You will have to angle it somewhat so the level sensor clears the tank opening (see illustration).

✳✳ WARNING:

There will still be fuel in the bottom of the module and it may spill. Wear gloves and eye protection.

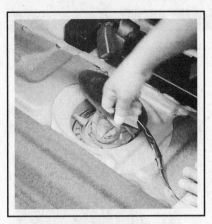

7.4 Remove the fuel pump access cover under the rear seat cushion

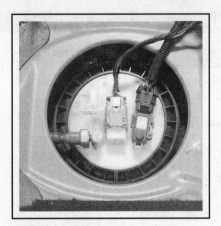

7.5 Disconnect the fuel line and electrical connectors

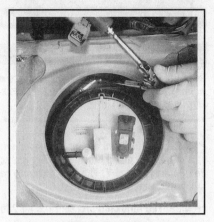

7.6a Loosen the band clamp. . .

7.6b. . . remove the band clamp. . .

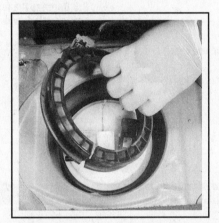

7.6c. . . and remove the fuel pump module retainer

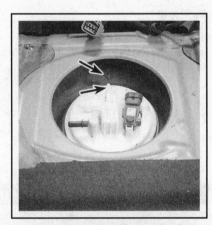

7.7 The raised portion on the fuel pump module must be aligned with the arrow molded into the fuel tank

9   Replace the fuel level sensor if necessary or transfer the float arm to the new module (see Section 8).

10   Before installing the pump, inspect the pump-to-tank seal. It's recommended to replace the seal whenever the module has been removed.

11   Installation is the reverse of removal noting the following items:

a) *Align the fuel pump/fuel level sending unit module with its hole in the tank and carefully insert it into the tank, then align the marks noted in Step 6.*

b) *Make sure that you don't damage the fuel inlet strainer, the float arm or the float during installation. If the float arm is bent, the fuel level that is indicated on the fuel level gauge on the instrument cluster will be incorrect.*

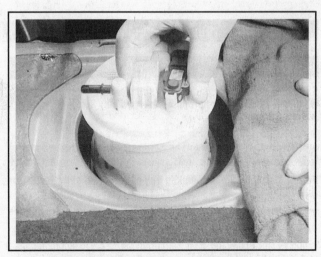

7.8 Carefully remove the fuel pump/fuel level sensor module

8 Fuel level sensor - replacement

✳ WARNING:

Gasoline is extremely flammable, so take extra precautions when you work on any part of the fuel system. See *Fuel system warnings* in Section 1.

➡ **Note:** On 2006 and earlier models, the fuel level sensor is part of the fuel pump module, and is replaced as an assembly. See Sections 4 and 7. The float arm may need to be transferred to the new fuel pump module.

➡ **Note:** The following procedure is for 2007 and later models.

1   Remove the fuel pump module (see Section 7).
2   Place the fuel pump module on a clean workbench surface.
3   Disengage the fuel level sensor electrical connector at the top of the module.
4   Using a terminal tool, remove the fuel level sensor terminal from the connector.
5   Depress the locking tab and slide the fuel level sensor unit from the slots on the module (see illustration).
6   Slide the fuel level sensor unit into place until you hear a click (pull on it to verify that it is locked into place).
7   Insert the fuel level sensor terminal into the connector.
8   The remainder of installation is the reverse of removal.

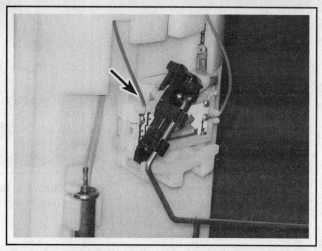

8.5 Depress the locking tab with a pointed tool and slide the sensor unit downward until it's free of its retaining rails

9 Fuel tank pressure sensor - replacement

1   See Chapter 6 for the fuel tank pressure sensor replacement procedure.

10 Fuel tank - removal and installation

✳ WARNING:

Gasoline is extremely flammable, so take extra precautions when you work on any part of the fuel system. See *Fuel system warnings* in Section 1.

✳ WARNING:

Before disconnecting or opening any part of the fuel system, relieve the fuel system pressure (see Section 3).

1   It's easier to remove the fuel tank when it's nearly empty. But there is no fuel tank drain plug, so if that's not possible, try to siphon out the fuel in the tank before removing the tank (see Step 5).
2   Relieve the fuel system pressure (see Section 3).
3   Disconnect the cable from the negative terminal of the battery (see Chapter 5).

4   Loosen the rear wheel lug nuts. Raise the vehicle and support it securely on jackstands. Remove the rear wheels.
5   If there's still a lot of fuel in the tank, insert a small hose into the fill pipe flap and siphon or hand-pump the remaining fuel from the tank now.

✳ WARNING:

Don't start the siphoning action by mouth! Use a siphoning kit (available at most auto parts stores).

➡ **Note:** Depending on the equipment you're using to support the tank, it may be necessary to remove the exhaust pipe and muffler insulators from the hangers and lower the exhaust pipe onto the rear axle for tank removal clearance.

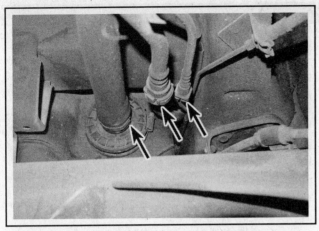

10.6 Disconnect the fuel fill hose and vent lines at the tank

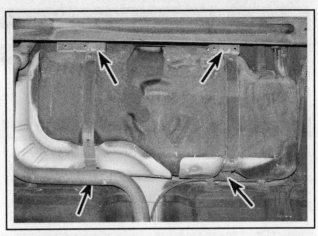

10.12 Fuel tank strap bolts

6   Disconnect the fuel tank filler hose, vent pipe connection and the fuel tank filler vent pipe at the tank (see illustration).

7   Disconnect the parking brake retainer clamps and secure the cable out of the way for tank removal.

8   Disconnect the fuel line at the right front of the tank.

9   Disconnect any wiring harness clips or electrical connectors for the fuel tank.

10   If necessary, remove the exhaust to allow clearance to remove the fuel tank.

11   Support the fuel tank with a transmission jack, if available, or

with a floor jack. If you're going to use a floor jack, put a sturdy piece of plywood between the jack head and the fuel tank to protect the tank. It's also a good idea to have an assistant to help with tank removal.

12   With the tank supported, remove the fuel tank strap bolts (see illustration).

13   Lower the tank enough to have a look at the top of the tank. Disconnect any remaining connectors as necessary.

14   Lower the tank the rest of the way and remove the tank.

15   Installation is the reverse of removal.

11 Air filter housing - removal and installation

1   Loosen the hose clamp and detach the intake duct from the air filter housing (see illustration).

2   Disconnect the breather hose and the Intake Air Temperature (IAT) sensor (2008 and earlier models) or Mass Air Flow /Intake Air Temperature (MAF/IAT) sensor (2009 and later models) electrical connector.

3   Remove the bolts attaching the air filter housing to the vehicle (see illustration).

4   To remove the intake duct, loosen the hose clamp and detach the intake duct from the throttle body.

5   Installation is the reverse of removal.

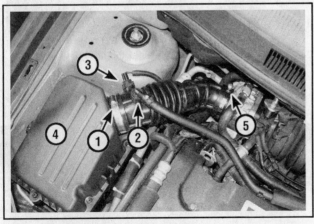

11.1 Air filter housing and duct details

1   Hose clamp
2   Breather hose
3   Intake Air Temperature (IAT) sensor electrical connector
4   Air filter housing
5   Hose clamp

11.3 Air filter housing mounting bolts (housing cover and filter element removed for clarity)

12 Throttle body - removal and installation

Wait until the engine is completely cool before beginning this procedure.

Do not clean the throttle motor with solvent. Also, do not use a metal brush to clean the bore of the throttle body, which is protected by a special coating. Scrubbing the bore with a stiff brush could ruin the coating. Instead, wipe out the bore with a clean shop rag and a little solvent.

Do not use any type of cleaner or solvent that has methyl ethyl ketone (MEK). This type of cleaner or solvent can damage many of the fuel system components. Do not spray solvent or cleaner on any of the gaskets for the throttle body.

1 Disconnect the cable from the negative battery terminal (see Chapter 5).
2 Remove the air filter housing (see Section 11).
3 On 2006 and earlier models, disconnect the throttle cables from the throttle body.
4 Clamp-off the coolant hoses, then disconnect them from the throttle body. (see illustration).
➡ **Note: Be prepared for coolant spillage.**
5 On 2007 and later models, disconnect the throttle actuator motor electrical connector.
➡ **Note: To disconnect the electrical connector, slide out the lock, then depress the release tab.**
➡ **Note: Be prepared for coolant spillage.**
6 On all models, disconnect any vacuum/EVAP hoses or electrical connectors on the throttle body.
7 Remove the throttle body mounting fasteners and remove the throttle body (see illustration).
8 Remove the throttle body gasket or O-ring and inspect it. If the gasket or O-ring isn't cracked, deformed, torn, or otherwise deteriorated, it's okay to reuse it. If it's damaged or worn, replace it.
9 Installation is the reverse of removal. Tighten the throttle body mounting bolts to the torque listed in this Chapter's Specifications.
10 Start the engine and verify that the throttle body operates correctly and that there are no air leaks. Top off the engine coolant as necessary.
11 Whenever the battery has been disconnected, the PCM must relearn its former driveability and performance characteristics (see Chapter 5).

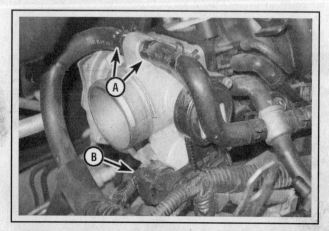

12.4 Disconnect the coolant hoses (A) and, on 2007 and later models, the throttle actuator connector (B)

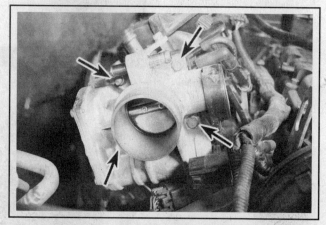

12.7 Remove the throttle body bolts and throttle body

13 Fuel rail and injectors - removal and installation

Gasoline is extremely flammable, so take extra precautions when you work on any part of the fuel system. See *Fuel system warnings* in Section 1.

Wait until the engine is completely cool before beginning this procedure.

1 Relieve the fuel system pressure (see Section 3).
2 Disconnect the cable from the negative battery terminal (see Chapter 5).
3 Remove the engine cover, on models so equipped.
4 Disconnect the following connectors, as applicable, to allow repositioning of the wiring harness:
   a) *Electronic Throttle Control (ETC)*
   b) *Intake Air Temperatore (IAT) sensor*
   c) *Camshaft Position (CMP) sensor*
   d) *Manifold Absolute Pressure (MAP) sensor*
   e) *Fuel injector harness*

13.6 Remove upper intake nuts, bolts and bracket

13.7 Use a special fuel line fitting to disconnect the fuel line at the fuel rail

13.9 Remove the fuel rail mounting bolts

13.10 Pull upward to remove the fuel rail and injectors

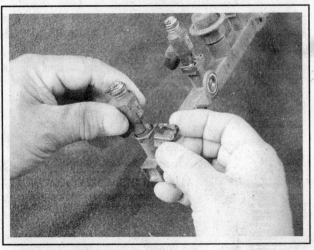

13.11 To release an injector retainer, free it from the small lugs on each side of the injector and pull it off

5   Remove the EVAP purge solenoid-to-intake manifold hose and MAP sensor vacuum hose.

6   On 2008 and earlier models, remove the intake manifold support bracket nuts, bolts and the bracket (see illustration).

7   Disconnect the quick-connect fuel line fitting at the fuel rail (see illustration).

8   On 2008 and earlier models, clamp-off both coolant hoses to the throttle body (see illustration 12.4), then disconnect the throttle body coolant outlet hose to allow removal of the fuel rail.

9   Remove the fuel rail mounting bolts (see illustration).

10   Remove the fuel rail and injectors as a single assembly (see illustration). After removing the fuel rail and injectors, look inside each injector hole and make sure that no O-rings remain in the holes.

FUEL INJECTOR REMOVAL

11   Remove the retainer that secures each fuel injector to the fuel rail and pull out the injector (see illustration).

12   Remove the old O-rings from each injector (see illustration) and discard them. Always install new O-rings on the injectors before reassembling the injectors and the fuel rail.

13.12 Remove and discard the old color-coded O-rings from each injector and install new ones

INSTALLATION

13 Installation is the reverse of removal. To ensure that the new injector O-rings are not damaged when the injectors are installed into the fuel rail and into the intake manifold, lubricate them with clean engine oil. Tighten the fuel rail mounting bolts to the torque listed in this Chapter's Specifications.

14 Before starting the engine, turn the ignition key to the On position to pressurize the fuel system and verify that there are no fuel leaks.

Specifications

Fuel pressure

Key On, engine Off	
2008 and earlier models	55 to 62 psi (380 to 427 kPa)
2009 and later models	53 to 60 psi (365 to 414 kPa)
Pressure drop within one minute of key off	5 psi (34 kPa)

Torque specifications

	Ft-lbs (unless otherwise indicated)	Nm

➡ Note: One foot-pound (ft-lb) of torque is equivalent to 12 inch-pounds (in-lbs) of torque. Torque values below approximately 15 foot-pounds are expressed in inch-pounds, because most foot-pound torque wrenches are not accurate at these smaller values.

	Ft-lbs (unless otherwise indicated)	Nm
Fuel rail mounting bolts		
2008 and earlier models	18	25
2009 and later models	71 in-lbs	8
Throttle body mounting nuts/bolts		
2008 and earlier models	132 in-lbs	15
2009 and later models	71 in-lbs	8
Fuel tank strap bolts	15	20

Section

5

ENGINE
ELECTRICAL
SYSTEMS

1 General information and precautions

GENERAL INFORMATION

Ignition system

1 The ignition system consists of the ignition control module(s), the ignition coil pack/module assembly, the spark plugs, the Camshaft Position (CMP) sensor, the Crankshaft Position (CKP) sensor, the knock sensor and the Powertrain Control Module (PCM).

2 The CKP, CMP and knock sensors are information sensors used by the PCM to control ignition timing and other engine operating parameters. The PCM also uses a number of other information sensors to make decisions regarding the correct ignition timing. These other sensors include the Throttle Position (TP) sensor, the Engine Coolant Temperature (ECT) sensor, the Mass Air Flow (MAF) sensor, the Intake Air Temperature (IAT) sensor, the Vehicle Speed Sensor (VSS) and the transmission gear position sensor or Transmission Range (TR) switch. For more information on these and other sensors, refer to Chapter 6.

Charging system

3 The charging system includes the alternator (with an integral voltage regulator), the Powertrain Control Module (PCM) (2009 and later models with RPO WHB), a charge indicator light on the dash, the battery, a fuse or fusible link and the wiring connecting all of these components. The charging system supplies electrical power for the ignition system, the lights, the radio, etc. The alternator is driven by a drivebelt.

Starting system

4 The starting system consists of the battery, the ignition switch, the starter relay, the Transmission Range (TR) switch, the Powertrain Control Module (2009 and later models with RPO WHB), the starter motor and solenoid assembly, and the wiring connecting all of these components.

PRECAUTIONS

5 Always observe the following precautions when working on the electrical system:

   a) *Be extremely careful when servicing engine electrical components. They are easily damaged if checked, connected or handled improperly.*
   b) *Never leave the ignition switched on for long periods of time when the engine is not running.*
   c) *Never disconnect the battery cables while the engine is running.*
   d) *Maintain correct polarity when connecting battery cables from another vehicle during jump starting - see* Booster battery (jump) starting *in Chapter 0, Section 7.*
   e) *Always disconnect the cable from the negative battery terminal before working on the electrical system, but read the battery disconnection procedure first (see Section 3).*

6 It's also a good idea to review the safety-related information regarding the engine electrical systems located in the *Safety first!* Section at the front of this manual before beginning any operation included in this Chapter.

2 Troubleshooting

IGNITION SYSTEM

1 If a malfunction occurs in the ignition system, do not immediately assume that any particular part is causing the problem. First, check the following items:

   a) *Make sure that the cable clamps at the battery terminals are clean and tight.*
   b) *Test the condition of the battery (see Steps 18 through 21). If it doesn't pass all the tests, replace it.*
   c) *Check the ignition coil pack connections.*
   d) *Check any relevant fuses in the engine compartment fuse and relay box (see Chapter 12). If they're burned, determine the cause and repair the circuit.*

CHECK

⁕⁕ WARNING:

Because of the high voltage generated by the ignition system, use extreme care when performing a procedure involving ignition components.

➡ **Note: The ignition system components on these vehicles are difficult to diagnose. In the event of ignition system failure that you can't diagnose, have the vehicle tested at a dealer service department or other qualified auto repair facility.**

➡ **Note: For the following test, you'll need a spark tester (available at auto parts stores). If you're working on an LXV model, you will also need spark plug wires to connect the coil high-tension terminals to the spark tester and to the other three spark plugs.**

2 If the engine turns over but won't start, verify that there is sufficient secondary ignition voltage to fire the spark plug as follows:

3 On 2009 and later (LXV) models, remove the ignition coil pack (see Section 6), then remove the spark plug boots from the coil pack (to remove the boots, simply pull them off). On 2008 and earlier (L91 and LXT) models, remove the spark plug wire from the spark plug for the coil being tested and install the spark tester (see illustrations).

4 Crank the engine while watching the tester. If the tester flashes, sufficient voltage is reaching the spark plug to fire it.

⁕⁕ CAUTION:

Do NOT crank the engine or allow it to run for more than five seconds; running the engine for more than five seconds may set a Diagnostic Trouble Code (DTC) for a cylinder misfire.

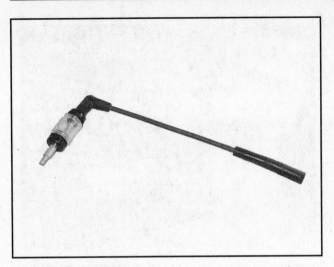

2.3a Spark plug tester

2.3b Here's the setup used for checking to see if the ignition coil(s) is sending power to the spark plug on L91 and LXT models. . .

5   Repeat this test on the remaining cylinders.

6   Proceed on this basis until you have verified that there's a good spark from each coil terminal. If there is, then you have verified that the coils in the coil pack are functioning correctly.

7   If there is no spark from a coil terminal, then either the coil is bad or one or more coil boots is bad. Also inspect the coil pack electrical connector. Make sure that it's clean, tight and in good condition.

8   If all the coils are firing correctly, but the engine misfires when the coil pack is connected to the spark plugs via the boots, then one or more of the plugs might be fouled. Remove and check the spark plugs or install new ones (see Chapter 1).

9   Also inspect the boots carefully for corrosion (high resistance) or deterioration of the insulation (low resistance). If any of the boots look damaged or deteriorated, replace them as a set.

10   No further testing of the ignition system is possible without special tools. If the problem persists, have the ignition system tested by a dealer service department or other qualified repair shop.

CHARGING SYSTEM

11   If a malfunction occurs in the charging system, do not automatically assume the alternator is causing the problem. First check the following items:

   a) *Check the drivebelt tension and condition, as described in Chapter 1. Replace it if it's worn or deteriorated.*

   b) *Make sure the alternator mounting bolts are tight.*

   c) *Inspect the alternator wiring harness and the connectors at the alternator and voltage regulator. They must be in good condition, tight and have no corrosion.*

   d) *Check the fuses in the underhood fuse/relay box. If any are burned, determine the cause, repair the circuit and replace the fuse (the vehicle will not start and/or the accessories will not work if the main fuse is blown).*

   e) *Start the engine and check the alternator for abnormal noises (a shrieking or squealing sound indicates a bad bearing).*

   f) *Check the battery. Make sure it's fully charged and in good condition (one bad cell in a battery can cause overcharging by the alternator).*

2.3c. . . and for the LXV models. If the coil(s) is delivering power to the plug, the tester will flash

   g) *Disconnect the battery cables (negative first, then positive). Inspect the battery posts and the cable clamps for corrosion. Clean them thoroughly if necessary (see Chapter 1). Reconnect the cables (positive first, negative last).*

Alternator - check

12   Use a voltmeter to check the battery voltage with the engine off. It should be at least 12.6 volts (see illustration 2.18).

13   Start the engine and check the battery voltage again. It should now be approximately 13.5 to 15 volts.

14   If the voltage reading is more or less than the specified charging voltage, the voltage regulator is probably defective, which will require replacement of the alternator (the voltage regulator is not replaceable separately). Remove the alternator and have it bench tested (most auto parts stores will do this for you).

15   The charging system (battery) light on the instrument cluster lights up when the ignition key is turned to ON, but it should go out when the engine starts.

2.18 To test the open circuit voltage of the battery, touch the black probe of the voltmeter to the negative terminal and the red probe to the positive terminal of the battery; a fully charged battery should be at least 12.6 volts

2.20 Connect a battery load tester to the battery and check the battery condition under load following the tool manufacturer's instructions

16 If the charging system light stays on after the engine has been started, there is a problem with the charging system. Before replacing the alternator, check the battery condition, alternator belt tension and electrical cable connections.

17 If replacing the alternator doesn't restore voltage to the specified range, have the charging system tested by a dealer service department or other qualified repair shop.

Battery - check

18 Check the battery state of charge. Visually inspect the indicator eye on the top of the battery (if equipped with one); if the indicator eye is black in color, charge the battery as described in Chapter 1. Next perform an open circuit voltage test using a digital voltmeter. With the engine and all accessories Off, touch the negative probe of the voltmeter to the negative terminal of the battery and the positive probe to the positive terminal of the battery (see illustration). The battery voltage should be 12.6 volts or slightly above. If the battery is less than the specified voltage, charge the battery before proceeding to the next test. Do not proceed with the battery load test unless the battery charge is correct.

➡ **Note: The battery's surface charge must be removed before accurate voltage measurements can be made. Turn on the high beams for ten seconds, then turn them off and let the vehicle stand for two minutes.**

19 Disconnect the negative battery cable, then the positive cable from the battery.

20 Perform a battery load test. An accurate check of the battery condition can only be performed with a load tester (see illustration). This test evaluates the ability of the battery to operate the starter and other accessories during periods of high current draw. Connect the load tester to the battery terminals. Load test the battery according to the tool manufacturer's instructions. This tool increases the load demand (current draw) on the battery.

21 Maintain the load on the battery for 15 seconds and observe that the battery voltage does not drop below 9.6 volts. If the battery condition is weak or defective, the tool will indicate this condition immediately.

➡ **Note: Cold temperatures will cause the minimum voltage reading to drop slightly. Follow the chart given in the manufacturer's instructions to compensate for cold climates. Minimum load voltage for freezing temperatures (32 degrees F) should be approximately 9.1 volts.**

STARTING SYSTEM

The starter rotates, but the engine doesn't

22 Remove the starter (see Section 8). Check the overrunning clutch and bench test the starter to make sure the drive mechanism extends fully for proper engagement with the flywheel ring gear. If it doesn't, replace the starter.

23 Check the flywheel ring gear for missing teeth and other damage. With the ignition turned off, rotate the flywheel so you can check the entire ring gear.

The starter is noisy

24 If the solenoid is making a chattering noise, first check the battery (see Steps 18 through 21). If the battery is okay, check the cables and connections.

25 If you hear a grinding, crashing metallic sound when you turn the key to Start, check for loose starter mounting bolts. If they're tight, remove the starter and inspect the teeth on the starter pinion gear and flywheel ring gear. Look for missing or damaged teeth.

26 If the starter sounds fine when you first turn the key to Start, but then stops rotating the engine and emits a zinging sound, the problem is probably a defective starter drive that's not staying engaged with the ring gear. Replace the starter.

The starter rotates slowly

27 Check the battery (see Steps 18 through 21).

28 If the battery is okay, verify all connections (at the battery, the starter solenoid and motor) are clean, corrosion-free and tight. Make sure the cables aren't frayed or damaged.

Check that the starter mounting bolts are tight so it grounds
. Also check the pinion gear and flywheel ring gear for evidence
hanical bind (galling, deformed gear teeth or other damage).

e starter does not rotate at all

30 Check the battery (see Steps 18 through 21).

31 If the battery is okay, verify all connections (at the battery, the
starter solenoid and motor) are clean, corrosion-free and tight. Make
ure the cables aren't frayed or damaged.

32 Check all of the fuses in the underhood fuse/relay box.

33 Check that the starter mounting bolts are tight so it grounds
operly.

34 Check for voltage at the starter solenoid "S" terminal when the
ignition key is turned to the start position. If voltage is present, replace
the starter/solenoid assembly. If no voltage is present, the problem
could be the starter relay, the Transmission Range (TR) switch (see
Chapter 6) or clutch start switch (see Chapter 8), or with an electrical
connector somewhere in the circuit (see the wiring diagrams at the end
of Chapter 12). Also, on many modern vehicles, the Powertrain Control
Module (PCM) and the Body Control Module (BCM) control the voltage
signal to the starter solenoid; on such vehicles a special scan tool is
required for diagnosis.

3   Battery - disconnection and reconnection

✳✳ WARNING:

On models with OnStar, make absolutely sure the ignition key
is in the Off position and Retained Accessory Power (RAP) has
been depleted before disconnecting the cable from the negative
battery terminal. Also, never remove the OnStar fuse with the
ignition key in any position other than Off. If these precautions
are not taken, the OnStar system's back-up battery will be activated, and remain activated, until it goes dead. If this happens,
the OnStar system will not function as it should in the event that
the main vehicle battery power is cut off (as might happen during a collision).

➡ Note: To disconnect the battery for service procedures requir-
ing power to be cut from the vehicle, first open the driver's door
to disable Retained Accessory Power (RAP), then loosen the
cable end bolt and disconnect the cable from the negative battery terminal. Isolate the cable end to prevent it from coming
into accidental contact with the battery terminal.

1   The battery is located in the left side of the engine compartment
on all vehicles covered by this manual. To disconnect the battery for
service procedures that require battery disconnection, simply disconnect the cable from the negative battery terminal (see Section 4). Make
sure that you isolate the cable to prevent it from coming into contact
with the battery negative terminal.

2   Some vehicle systems (radio, alarm system, power door locks, etc.)
require battery power all the time, either to enable their operation or to maintain control unit memory (Powertrain Control Module, automatic transaxle
control module, etc.), which would be lost if the battery were to be disconnected. So before you disconnect the battery, note the following points:

a) *Before connecting or disconnecting the cable from the negative
battery terminal, make sure that you turn the ignition key and the
lighting switch to their OFF positions. Failure to do so could damage semiconductor components.*

b) *On a vehicle with power door locks, it is a wise precaution to
remove the key from the ignition and to keep it with you, so that it
does not get locked inside if the power door locks should engage
accidentally when the battery is reconnected!*

c) *After the battery has been disconnected, then reconnected (or a
new battery has been installed) on vehicles with an automatic
transaxle, the Transaxle Control Module (TCM) will need some
time to relearn its adaptive strategy. As a result, shifting might
feel firmer than usual. This is a normal condition and will not
adversely affect the operation or service life of the transaxle. Even-*

*tually, the TCM will complete its adaptive learning process and
the shift feel of the transaxle will return to normal.*

d) *The engine management system's PCM has some learning capabilities that allow it to adapt or make corrections in response to
minor variations in the fuel system in order to optimize drivability
and idle characteristics. However, the PCM might lose some or
all of this information when the battery is disconnected. The PCM
must go through a relearning process before it can regain its
former drivability and performance characteristics. Until it relearns
this lost data, you might notice a difference in drivability, idle and/
or (if you have an automatic) shift "feel." To facilitate this relearning process, refer to "Enabling the PCM to relearn" below.*

MEMORY SAVERS

3   Devices known as memory savers (typically, small 9-volt batteries) can be used to avoid some of the above problems. A memory
saver is usually plugged into the cigarette lighter, and then you can
disconnect the vehicle battery from the electrical system. The memory
saver will deliver sufficient current to maintain security alarm codes
and - maybe, but don't count on it! - PCM memory. It will also run
unswitched (always on) circuits such as the clock and radio memory,
while isolating the car battery in the event that a short circuit occurs
while the vehicle is being serviced.

✳✳ WARNING:

If you're going to work around any airbag system components,
disconnect the battery and do not use a memory saver. If you
do, the airbag could accidentally deploy and cause personal
injury.

✳✳ CAUTION:

Because memory savers deliver current to operate unswitched
circuits when the battery is disconnected, make sure that the
circuit that you're going to service is actually open before working on it!

ENABLING THE PCM TO RELEARN IDLE

4   After the battery has been reconnected, perform the following

procedure in order to facilitate PCM relearning:

   a) Turn the ignition to the ON position then turn the ignition OFF for fifteen seconds.
   b) Turn the ignition to the ON position for five seconds then turn the ignition OFF for fifteen seconds.
   c) Start the engine and allow it to warm up to its normal operating temperature.
   d) Turn the air conditioning ON for ten seconds, if equipped.
   e) On vehicles equipped with an automatic transaxle, apply the parking brake. Press and hold the brake pedal, while placing the transaxle in drive for ten seconds.
   f) Turn the air conditioning OFF for ten seconds, if equipped.
   g) Drive the vehicle at part-throttle, under moderate acceleration and idle conditions, until normal performance returns.

   h) Park the vehicle and apply the parking brake with the engine running.
   i) On vehicles equipped with a manual transaxle, put the shift lever in NEUTRAL while depressing the brake pedal.
   j) Turn the ignition OFF. Idle learn is complete.

RESETTING POWER WINDOWS AND SUNROOF

15 Power windows: Sit in the vehicle with all of the doors closed. Operate each window (one at a time) to the fully open position, then raise the window until it is closed and hold the switch in the UP position for three seconds.

16 Sunroof: Open the sunroof completely, then close it completely.

4 Battery and battery tray - removal and installation

➡ Note: Battery straps and handlersare available at most auto parts stores for reasonable prices. They make it easier to remove and carry the battery.

1 Remove the battery cover, on models so equipped.

2 Disconnect the cable from the negative terminal of the battery, then loosen the positive cable terminal nut (see illustration).

3 Remove the battery hold-down clamp (see illustration).

4 Lift out the battery. Be careful - it's heavy.

5 To remove the battery tray, unscrew the mounting bolts (see illustration), free any wiring harness retainers, then lift it out.

6 If you are replacing the battery, make sure you get one that's identical, with the same dimensions, amperage rating, cold cranking rating, etc.

7 Installation is the reverse of removal. Connect the positive cable first and the negative cable last.

4.2 Battery details

1   Negative cable terminal   *2   Positive cable terminal*

4.3 Unscrew the wing nuts and remove the battery hold-down clamp

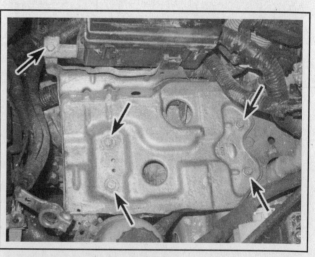

4.5 Battery tray mounting bolts

5   Battery cables - replacement

1   When removing the cables, always disconnect the cable from the negative battery terminal first and hook it up last, or you might accidentally short out the battery with the tool you're using to loosen the cable clamps. Even if you're only replacing the cable for the positive terminal, be sure to disconnect the negative cable from the battery first.

2   Disconnect the old cables from the battery, then trace each of them to their opposite ends and disconnect them. Be sure to note the routing of each cable before disconnecting it to ensure correct installation.

3   If you are replacing any of the old cables, take them with you when buying new cables. It is vitally important that you replace the cables with identical parts.

4   Clean the threads of the solenoid or ground connection with a wire brush to remove rust and corrosion. Apply a light coat of battery terminal corrosion inhibitor or petroleum jelly to the threads to prevent future corrosion.

5   Attach the cable to the solenoid or ground connection and tighten the mounting nut/bolt securely.

6   Before connecting a new cable to the battery, make sure that it reaches the battery post without having to be stretched.

7   Connect the cable to the positive battery terminal first, then connect the ground cable to the negative battery terminal.

6   Ignition coil pack - removal and installation

→ Note: On L91 and LXT engines the ignition coil pack is mounted to the end of the cylinder head. On LXV engines the coil pack is mounted directly over the spark plugs, on top of the cylinder head.

1   Make sure the ignition key is turned Off, then remove the engine cover by pulling it straight up.

2008 AND EARLIER MODELS (L91 AND LXT ENGINES)

2   Remove the oil filler cap, then remove the engine cover mounting bolts and cover (see Chapter 1, Section 25). Temporarily install the oil filler cap.

3   Disconnect the electrical connector from the ignition coil pack (see illustration).

4   Label and disconnect the spark plug wire boots from the coil pack terminals. Grasp the rubber boot, twist the boot half a turn and pull the boot free. Do not pull on the wire itself.

5   Remove the coil pack retaining nuts (see illustration) and detach the coil pack from the end of the cylinder head.

6   Before installing the spark plug wire boots on the ignition coil pack, coat the interior of each boot with silicone dielectric compound.

7   Installation is otherwise the reverse of removal. Tighten the ignition coil pack mounting nuts to the torque listed in this Chapter's Specifications.

2009 AND LATER MODELS (LXV ENGINES)

8   Lift the ignition coil cover up from the top of the valve cover.

9   Disconnect the electrical connector from the ignition coil assembly by sliding the connector lock out, then depress the tab and release the connector.

6.3 Disconnect the electrical connector at the base of the ignition coil pack

6.5 Ignition coil retaining nut locations

6.10 Ignition coil pack bolts

6.11 Grasp the coil pack firmly and pull straight up; the boots should come off with the coil pack - if any of them stay with the spark plugs, pull them off the plugs

10 Remove the two ignition coil pack mounting bolts (see illustration).

11 Pull the ignition coil pack straight up, detaching the spark plug boots (see illustration).

12 If you're replacing the ignition coil pack, remove the four boots from the coil pack and inspect them for cracks, tears and deterioration.

If any of the boots are damaged, replace them.

13 Before installing the boots on the ignition coil pack, coat the interior of each boot with silicone dielectric compound.

14 Installation is otherwise the reverse of removal. Tighten the ignition coil pack mounting bolts to the torque listed in this Chapter's Specifications.

7   Alternator - removal and installation

1 Disconnect the cable from the negative battery terminal (see Section 3).

2 Raise the vehicle and support it securely on jackstands. Remove the under-vehicle splash shield.

3 Remove the drivebelt (see Chapter 1).

4 On L91 and LXT engines, remove the air intake duct (see Chapter 4).

5 Remove the bolt that holds the air conditioning line bracket to the rear of the alternator, if equipped.

6 Disconnect the electrical connectors from the alternator (see illustration).

7 On L91 and LXT models, remove the alternator mounting bolts (see illustration). Lift the alternator up off the mounting bracket, then remove the three bracket mounting bolts and bracket. Guide the alternator out from below (see illustration).

➡ **Note: The third alternator bracket mounting bolt cannot be accessed until the alternator is lifted off the bracket.**

8 On LXV models, remove the alternator mounting bolts and guide the alternator out from below.

9 Installation is the reverse of removal. Tighten the alternator mounting bolts to the torque listed in this Chapter's Specifications.

10 Reconnect the battery (see Section 3).

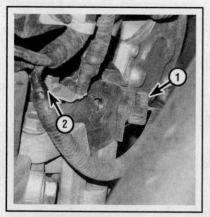

7.6 Disconnect the electrical connector (1) and battery positive cable nut (2)

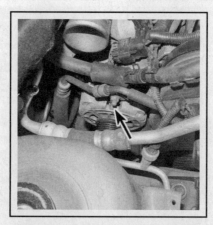

7.7a Remove the upper mounting nut and bolt from above. . .

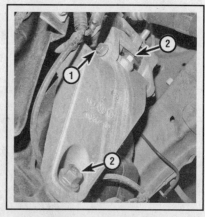

7.7b. . . then remove the lower mounting bolt (1) and nut, lift the alternator up and remove the alternator bracket bolts (2) - two of three shown (L91 nd LXT models)

8   Starter motor - removal and installation

1   Turn the ignition key to OFF, then disconnect the cable from the negative battery terminal (see Section 3).

2   Raise the front of the vehicle and support it securely on jackstands.

3   Disconnect the battery cable (the larger cable) and the starter control wire from the starter motor solenoid terminals (see illustration).

4   Remove the starter motor mounting bolts (see illustrations) and remove the starter motor.

5   Installation is the reverse of removal. Tighten the starter motor mounting bolts to the torque listed in this Chapter's Specifications.

6   Reconnect the battery (see Section 3).

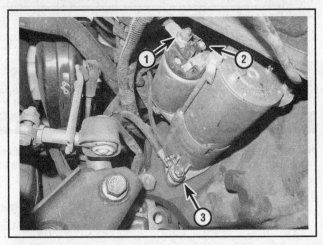

8.3 Starter motor details

1   *Positive cable*
2   *Starter control wire ("S" terminal)*
3   *Ground cable nut (if equipped) and lower mounting bolt*

8.4a The upper mounting bolt can be seen from above. . .

8.4b . . . but is more easily removed with a socket and long extension from below

Specifications

General

Firing order	1-3-4-2
Cylinder numbering	
(from drivebelt end to transaxle end)	1-2-3-4
Ignition timing	Not adjustable

Torque specifications	Ft-lbs (unless otherwise indicated)	Nm

➡ **Note: One foot-pound (ft-lb) of torque is equivalent to 12 inch-pounds (in-lbs) of torque. Torque values below approximately 15 foot-pounds are expressed in inch-pounds, because most foot-pound torque wrenches are not accurate at these smaller values.**

Ignition coil pack mounting bolts		
2008 and earlier models (L91 and LXT engines)	89 in-lbs	10
2009 and later models (LXV engine)	71 in-lbs	8
Alternator mounting bolts	18	25
Starter motor mounting bolts		
2008 and earlier models (L91 and LXT engines)	32	43
2009 and later models (LXV engine)	18	25

6

EMISSIONS AND ENGINE CONTROL SYSTEMS

1 General information

To prevent pollution of the atmosphere from incompletely burned and evaporating gases, and to maintain good driveability and fuel economy, a number of emission control systems are incorporated. They include the:

CATALYTIC CONVERTER

A catalytic converter is an emission control device in the exhaust system that reduces certain pollutants in the exhaust gas stream. There are two types of converters: oxidation converters and reduction converters.

Oxidation converters contain a monolithic substrate (a ceramic honeycomb) coated with the semi-precious metals platinum and palladium. An oxidation catalyst reduces unburned hydrocarbons (HC) and carbon monoxide (CO) by adding oxygen to the exhaust stream as it passes through the substrate, which, in the presence of high temperature and the catalyst materials, converts the HC and CO to water vapor (H_2O) and carbon dioxide (CO_2).

Reduction converters contain a monolithic substrate coated with platinum and rhodium. A reduction catalyst reduces oxides of nitrogen (NOx) by removing oxygen, which in the presence of high temperature and the catalyst material produces nitrogen (N) and carbon dioxide (CO_2).

Catalytic converters that combine both types of catalysts in one assembly are known as "three-way catalysts" or TWCs. A TWC can reduce all three pollutants.

EVAPORATIVE EMISSIONS CONTROL (EVAP) SYSTEM

The Evaporative Emissions Control (EVAP) system prevents fuel system vapors (which contain unburned hydrocarbons) from escaping into the atmosphere. On warm days, vapors trapped inside the fuel tank expand until the pressure reaches a certain threshold. Then the fuel vapors are routed from the fuel tank through the fuel vapor vent valve and the fuel vapor control valve to the EVAP canister, where they're stored temporarily until the next time the vehicle is operated. When the conditions are right (engine warmed up, vehicle up to speed, moderate or heavy load on the engine, etc.) the PCM opens the canister purge valve, which allows fuel vapors to be drawn from the canister into the intake manifold. Once in the intake manifold, the fuel vapors mix with incoming air before being drawn through the intake ports into the combustion chambers where they're burned up with the rest of the air/fuel mixture. The EVAP system is complex and virtually impossible to troubleshoot without the right tools and training.

EXHAUST GAS RECIRCULATION (EGR) SYSTEM

The EGR system reduces oxides of nitrogen by recirculating exhaust gases from the exhaust manifold, through the EGR valve and intake manifold, then back to the combustion chambers, where it mixes with the incoming air/fuel mixture before being consumed. These recirculated exhaust gases dilute the incoming air/fuel mixture, which cools the combustion chambers, thereby reducing NOx emissions.

The EGR system consists of the Powertrain Control Module (PCM), the EGR valve, the EGR valve position sensor and various other information sensors that the PCM uses to determine when to open the EGR valve. The degree to which the EGR valve is opened is referred to as "EGR valve lift." The PCM is programmed to produce the ideal EGR valve lift for varying operating conditions. The EGR valve position sensor, which is an integral part of the EGR valve, detects the amount of EGR valve lift and sends this information to the PCM. The PCM then compares it with the appropriate EGR valve lift for the operating conditions. The PCM increases current flow to the EGR valve to increase valve lift and reduces the current to reduce the amount of lift. If EGR flow is inappropriate to the operating conditions (idle, cold engine, etc.) the PCM simply cuts the current to the EGR valve and the valve closes.

SECONDARY AIR INJECTION (AIR) SYSTEM

Some models are equipped with a secondary air injection (AIR) system. The secondary air injection system is used to reduce tailpipe emissions on initial engine start-up. The system uses an electric motor/pump assembly, relay, vacuum valve/solenoid, air shut-off valve, check valves and tubing to inject fresh air directly into the exhaust manifolds. The fresh air (oxygen) reacts with the exhaust gas in the catalytic converter to reduce HC and CO levels. The air pump and solenoid are controlled by the PCM through the AIR relay. During initial start-up, the PCM energizes the AIR relay, the relay supplies battery voltage to the air pump and the vacuum valve/solenoid, engine vacuum is applied to the air shut-off valve which opens and allows air to flow through the tubing into the exhaust manifolds. The PCM will operate the air pump until closed loop operation is reached (approximately four minutes). During normal operation, the check valves prevent exhaust backflow into the system.

POWERTRAIN CONTROL MODULE (PCM)

The Powertrain Control Module (PCM) is the brain of the engine management system. It also controls a wide variety of other vehicle systems. In order to program the new PCM, the dealer needs the vehicle as well as the new PCM. If you're planning to replace the PCM with a new one, there is no point in trying to do so at home because you won't be able to program it yourself.

POSITIVE CRANKCASE VENTILATION (PCV) SYSTEM

The Positive Crankcase Ventilation (PCV) system reduces hydrocarbon emissions by scavenging crankcase vapors, which are rich in unburned hydrocarbons. A PCV valve or orifice regulates the flow of gases into the intake manifold in proportion to the amount of intake vacuum available.

The PCV system generally consists of the fresh air inlet hose, the PCV valve or orifice and the crankcase ventilation hose (or PCV hose). The fresh air inlet hose connects the air intake duct to a pipe on the valve cover. The crankcase ventilation hose (or PCV hose) connects the PCV valve or orifice in the valve cover to the intake manifold.

Information Sensors

Accelerator Pedal Position (APP) sensor - as you press the accelerator pedal, the APP sensor alters its voltage signal to the PCM in proportion to the angle of the pedal, and the PCM commands a motor inside the throttle body to open or close the throttle plate accordingly

Camshaft Position (CMP) sensor - produces a signal that the PCM uses to identify the number 1 cylinder and to time the firing sequence of the fuel injectors

Crankshaft Position (CKP) sensor - produces a signal that the PCM uses to calculate engine speed and crankshaft position, which enables it to synchronize ignition timing with fuel injector timing, and to detect misfires

Engine Coolant Temperature (ECT) sensor - a thermistor (temperature-sensitive variable resistor) that sends a voltage signal to the PCM, which uses this data to determine the temperature of the engine coolant

Fuel tank pressure sensor - measures the fuel tank pressure and controls fuel tank pressure by signaling the EVAP system to purge the fuel tank vapors when the pressure becomes excessive

Intake Air Temperature (IAT) sensor - monitors the temperature of the air entering the engine and sends a signal to the PCM to determine injector pulse-width (the duration of each injector's on-time) and to adjust spark timing (to prevent spark knock)

Knock sensor - a piezoelectric crystal that oscillates in proportion to engine vibration which produces a voltage output that is monitored by the PCM. This retards the ignition timing when the oscillation exceeds a certain threshold

Manifold Absolute Pressure (MAP) sensor - monitors the pressure or vacuum inside the intake manifold. The PCM uses this data to determine engine load so that it can alter the ignition advance and fuel enrichment

Mass Air Flow (MAF) sensor - measures the amount of intake air drawn into the engine. It uses a hot-wire sensing element to measure the amount of air entering the engine

Oxygen sensors - generates a small variable voltage signal in proportion to the difference between the oxygen content in the exhaust stream and the oxygen content in the ambient air. The PCM uses this information to maintain the proper air/fuel ratio. A second oxygen sensor monitors the efficiency of the catalytic converter

Throttle Position (TP) sensor - a potentiometer that generates a voltage signal that varies in relation to the opening angle of the throttle plate inside the throttle body. Works with the PCM and other sensors to calculate injector pulse width (the duration of each injector's on-time)

Photos courtesy of Wells Manufacturing, except APP and MAF sensors.

2   On Board Diagnosis (OBD) system

GENERAL DESCRIPTION

1   All models are equipped with the second generation OBD-II system. This system consists of an on-board computer known as the Powertrain Control Module (PCM), and information sensors, which monitor various functions of the engine and send data to the PCM. This system incorporates a series of diagnostic monitors that detect and identify fuel injection and emissions control system faults and store the information in the computer memory. This system also tests sensors and output actuators, diagnoses drive cycles, freezes data and clears codes.

2   The PCM is the brain of the electronically controlled fuel and emissions system. It receives data from a number of sensors and other electronic components (switches, relays, etc.). Based on the information it receives, the PCM generates output signals to control various relays, solenoids (fuel injectors) and other actuators. The PCM is specifically calibrated to optimize the emissions, fuel economy and driveability of the vehicle.

3   It isn't a good idea to attempt diagnosis or replacement of the PCM or emission control components at home while the vehicle is under warranty. Because of a federally-mandated warranty which covers the emissions system components and because any owner-induced damage to the PCM, the sensors and/or the control devices may void this warranty, take the vehicle to a dealer service department if the PCM or a system component malfunctions.

SCAN TOOL INFORMATION

4   Because extracting the Diagnostic Trouble Codes (DTCs) from an engine management system is now the first step in troubleshooting many computer-controlled systems and components, a code reader, at the very least, will be required (see illustration). More powerful scan tools can also perform many of the diagnostics once associated with expensive factory scan tools (see illustration). If you're planning to obtain a generic scan tool for your vehicle, make sure that it's compatible with OBD-II systems. If you don't plan to purchase a code reader or scan tool and don't have access to one, you can have the codes extracted by a dealer service department or an independent repair shop.

➡ **Note: Some auto parts stores even provide this service.**

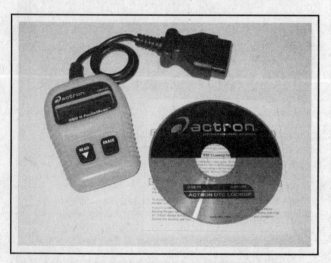

2.4a Simple code readers are an economical way to extract trouble codes when the CHECK ENGINE light comes on

2.4b Hand-held scan tools like these can extract computer codes and also perform diagnostics

3   Obtaining and clearing Diagnostic Trouble Codes (DTCs)

All models covered by this manual are equipped with on-board diagnostics. When the PCM recognizes a malfunction in a monitored emission or engine control system, component or circuit, it turns on the Malfunction Indicator Light (MIL) on the dash. The PCM will continue to display the MIL until the problem is fixed and the Diagnostic Trouble Code (DTC) is cleared from the PCM's memory. You'll need a scan tool to access any DTCs stored in the PCM.

Before outputting any DTCs stored in the PCM, thoroughly inspect ALL electrical connectors and hoses. Make sure that all electri-cal connections are tight, clean and free of corrosion. And make sure that all hoses are correctly connected, fit tightly and are in good condition (no cracks or tears).

ACCESSING THE DTCS

1   The Diagnostic Trouble Codes (DTCs) can only be accessed with a code reader or scan tool. Professional scan tools are expensive, but relatively inexpensive generic code readers or scan tools (see illustra-

tions 2.4a and 2.4b) are available at most auto parts stores. Simply plug the connector of the scan tool into the diagnostic connector (see illustration). Then follow the instructions included with the scan tool to extract the DTCs.

2   Once you have outputted all of the stored DTCs, look them up on the accompanying DTC chart.

3   After troubleshooting the source of each DTC, make any necessary repairs or replace the defective component(s).

Clearing the DTCs

4   Clear the DTCs with the code reader or scan tool in accordance with the instructions provided by the tool's manufacturer.

DIAGNOSTIC TROUBLE CODES

5   The accompanying tables are a list of the Diagnostic Trouble Codes (DTCs) that can be accessed by a do-it-yourselfer working at home (there are many, many more DTCs available to professional mechanics with proprietary scan tools and software, but those codes cannot be accessed by a generic scan tool). If, after you have checked and repaired the connectors, wire harness and vacuum hoses (if applicable) for an emission-related system, component or circuit, the problem persists, have the vehicle checked by a dealer service department or other qualified repair shop.

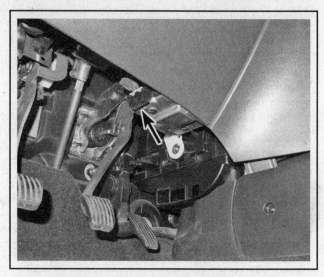

3.1 The Data Link Connector (DLC) is located at the lower edge of the dash, below the steering column

OBD-II TROUBLE CODES

➡ **Note: Not all trouble codes apply to all models.**

Code	Code identification
P0010	Intake cam CMP, actuator circuit
P0011	Intake cam CMP, performance problem
P0013	Exhaust cam CMP, actuator circuit
P0014	Exhaust cam CMP, performance problem
P0016	CKP-to-Intake CMP, correlation problem
P0017	CKP-to-exhaust CMP, correlation problem
P0030	O2 heater control circuit (sensor 1)
P0031	O2 heater control circuit, low voltage (sensor 1)
P0032	O2 heater control circuit, high voltage (sensor 1)
P0036	O2 heater control circuit (sensor 2)
P0037	O2 heater control circuit, low voltage (sensor 2)
P0038	O2 heater control circuit, high voltage (sensor 2)
P0053	O2 heater resistance (sensor 1)
P0054	O2 heater resistance (sensor 2)
P0068	Throttle body airflow performance problem

OBD-II TROUBLE CODES (CONTINUED)

➡ **Note: Not all trouble codes apply to all models.**

Code	Code identification
P0101	Mass air flow or volume problem, IAT, MAF, or MAP
P0102	Mass air flow or volume air flow circuit, low input
P0103	Mass air flow or volume air flow circuit, high input
P0106	Manifold absolute pressure or barometric pressure circuit, range or performance problem
P0107	Manifold absolute pressure or barometric pressure circuit, low input
P0108	Manifold absolute pressure or barometric pressure circuit, high input
P0110	Intake Air temperature (IAT) sensor circuit
P0111	Intake Air temperature (IAT) sensor, performance problem
P0112	Intake air temperature circuit, low input
P0113	Intake air temperature circuit, high input
P0114	Intake Air temperature (IAT) sensor circuit, intermittent
P0115	Engine coolant temperature sensor, circuit problem
P0116	Engine coolant temperature sensor, performance problem
P0117	Engine coolant temperature circuit, low input
P0118	Engine coolant temperature circuit, high input
P0119	Engine coolant temperature circuit, intermittent
P0120	Throttle position or pedal position sensor/switch circuit malfunction
P0121	Throttle position or pedal position sensor/switch circuit, range or performance problem
P0122	Throttle position or pedal position sensor/switch circuit, low input
P0123	Throttle position or pedal position sensor/switch circuit, high input
P0125	Insufficient coolant temperature for closed loop fuel control
P0126	Engine coolant temperature (ECT) insufficient for closed loop
P0128	Coolant thermostat (coolant temperature below thermostat regulating temperature)
P0130	O2 sensor circuit malfunction (sensor 1)
P0131	O2 sensor circuit, low voltage (sensor 1)
P0132	O2 sensor circuit, high voltage (sensor 1)
P0133	O2 sensor circuit, slow response (sensor 1)
P013A	O2 sensor circuit, slow response, rich to lean (sensor 2)

Code	Code identification
P013B	O2 sensor circuit, slow response, lean to rich (sensor 2)
P013E	O2 sensor circuit, delayed response, rich to lean (sensor 2)
P013F	O2 sensor circuit, delayed response, lean to rich (sensor 2)
P015A	O2 sensor circuit, delayed response, rich to lean (sensor 1)
P015B	O2 sensor circuit, delayed response, lean to rich (sensor 1)
P0134	O2 sensor circuit - no activity detected (sensor 1)
P0135	O2 sensor heater circuit malfunction (sensor 1)
P0136	O2 sensor circuit malfunction (sensor 2)
P0137	O2 sensor circuit, low voltage (sensor 2)
P0138	O2 sensor circuit, high voltage (sensor 2)
P0139	O2 sensor - slow response (sensor 2)
P0140	O2 sensor circuit - no activity detected (sensor 2)
P0141	O2 sensor heater circuit malfunction (sensor 2)
P0171	System too lean
P0172	System too rich
P018B	Fuel system sensor performance problem
P018C	Fuel system sensor circuit, low voltage
P018D	Fuel system sensor circuit, high voltage
P0201	Injector circuit malfunction - cylinder no. 1
P0202	Injector circuit malfunction - cylinder no. 2
P0203	Injector circuit malfunction - cylinder no. 3
P0204	Injector circuit malfunction - cylinder no. 4
P0217	Engine coolant overtemperature
P0218	Transmission overheating condition
P0220	Throttle position or pedal position sensor/switch B circuit malfunction
P0222	Throttle position or pedal position sensor/switch B circuit, low input
P0223	Throttle position or pedal position sensor/switch B circuit, high input
P0230	Fuel pump primary circuit malfunction
P0231	Fuel pump control circuit, low voltage
P0232	Fuel pump control circuit, high voltage

OBD-II TROUBLE CODES (CONTINUED)

→ Note: Not all trouble codes apply to all models.

Code	Code identification
P023F	Fuel pump control circuit
P0234	Turbocharger over-boost
P0236	Turbocharger boost system performance problem
P0237	Turbocharger boost sensor circuit, low voltage
P0238	Turbocharger boost sensor circuit, high voltage
P0243	Turbocharger wastegate solenoid control circuits
P0245	Turbocharger wastegate solenoid valve control circuit, low voltage
P0246	Turbocharger wastegate solenoid valve control circuit, high voltage
P025A	Fuel pump control module enable circuit
P0261	Injector 1 control circuit, low voltage
P0262	Injector 1 control circuit, high voltage
P0264	Injector 2 control circuit, low voltage
P0265	Injector 2 control circuit, high voltage
P0267	Injector 3 control circuit, low voltage
P0268	Injector 3 control circuit, high voltage
P0270	Injector 4 control circuit, low voltage
P0271	Injector 4 control circuit, high voltage
P0299	Turbocharger under-boost
P0300	Random/multiple cylinder misfire detected
P0301	Cylinder 1 misfire
P0302	Cylinder 2 misfire
P0303	Cylinder 3 misfire
P0304	Cylinder 4 misfire
P0313	Misfire detected with low fuel level
P0314	Single cylinder engine misfire detected
P0315	Crankshaft position system - variation not learned
P0317	Rough road sensor signal not detected
P0324	Knock sensor no. 1 circuit malfunction

Code	Code identification
P0325	Knock sensor no. 1 circuit malfunction
P0326	Knock sensor no. 1 circuit, range or performance problem
P06B6	Control module knock sensor processor performance problem
P0327	Knock sensor no. 1 circuit, low input
P0328	Knock sensor no. 1 circuit, low input
P0331	Knock sensor 2 performance problem
P0335	Crankshaft position sensor A circuit malfunction
P0336	Crankshaft position sensor A circuit - range or performance problem
P0337	Crankshaft position (CKP) sensor, circuit low duty cycle
P0340	Intake camshaft position sensor, circuit problem
P0341	Intake camshaft position sensor, performance problem
P0351	Ignition coil 1, control circuit
P0352	Ignition coil 2, control circuit
P0353	Ignition coil 3, control circuit
P0354	Ignition coil 4, control circuit
P0365	Exhaust camshaft position sensor, circuit problem
P0366	Exhaust camshaft position sensor, performance problem
P0401	Exhaust gas recirculation (EGR) flow insufficient
P0402	Exhaust gas recirculation (EGR) flow excessive
P0403	Exhaust gas recirculation (EGR), solenoid control circuit problem
P0404	Exhaust gas recirculation (EGR), open position performance
P0405	Exhaust gas recirculation (EGR), position sensor circuit - low voltage
P0406	Exhaust gas recirculation (EGR), position sensor circuit - high voltage
P042E	Exhaust gas recirculation (EGR), closed position performance
P0420	Catalyst system efficiency below threshold
P0441	Evaporative emissions (EVAP) system, continuous purge flow
P0442	Evaporative emission control system, small leak detected
P0443	Evaporative emission control system, purge control valve circuit malfunction
P0446	Evaporative emission control system, vent control circuit malfunction
P0449	Evaporative emission control system, vent valve/solenoid circuit malfunction

OBD-II TROUBLE CODES (CONTINUED)

➡ Note: Not all trouble codes apply to all models.

Code	Code identification
P0451	Fuel tank pressure sensor range or performance problem
P0452	Fuel tank pressure sensor low input
P0453	Fuel tank pressure sensor high input
P0454	Fuel tank pressure sensor, circuit intermittent
P0455	Evaporative emission (EVAP) control system leak detected (large leak or no purge flow)
P0456	Evaporative emission (EVAP) system, very small leak detected
P0458	Evaporative emission (EVAP) purge solenoid, control circuit open
P0459	Evaporative emission (EVAP) purge solenoid, control circuit shorted
P0461	Fuel level sensor, performance problem
P0462	Fuel level sensor, low voltage
P0463	Fuel level sensor, high voltage
P0464	Fuel level sensor, circuit intermittent
P0488	Exhaust gas recirculation (EGR), closed position performance problem
P0496	Evaporative emission system - high purge flow
P0498	Evaporative emission (EVAP) vent solenoid valve, control circuit open
P0499	Evaporative emission (EVAP) vent solenoid valve, control circuit shorted
P0502	Vehicle speed sensor circuit, low input
P0503	Vehicle speed sensor circuit, Intermittent, erratic or high input
P0506	Idle control system, rpm lower than expected
P0507	Idle control system, rpm higher than expected
P050B	Ignition timing performance
P050D	Cold start rough idle
P0562	System voltage low
P0563	System voltage high
P0564	Cruise control system, multi-function input signal
P0575	Cruise control circuit, switch signal
P0601	Control module read only memory performance problem (ECM)
P0602	(ECM) control module, not programmed

Code	Code identification
P0603	(ECM) control module, long term memory reset
P0604	(ECM) control module, random access memory (RAM) performance problem
P0606	ECM processor performance problem
P061B	Control module, torque calculation performance problem
P062F	Control module, long term memory performance problem
P0607	Control module performance problem
P0627	Fuel pump enable circuit problem
P0628	Fuel pump enable circuit, low voltage
P0629	Fuel pump enable circuit, high voltage
P0630	VIN is not programmed or mismatched with engine control module (ECM)
P0641	Sensor 5-volt reference 1, circuit performance problem
P06A6	Sensor 5-volt reference 1, performance problem
P0645	AC clutch relay, control circuit
P0646	AC clutch relay 1, low voltage
P0647	AC clutch relay 1, high voltage
P0650	Malfunction indicator lamp (MIL), control circuit malfunction
P0651	Sensor 5-volt reference 2, circuit performance problem
P0660	Intake manifold tuning control valve control circuit, performance problem
P0661	Intake manifold tuning control valve control circuit, low voltage
P0662	Intake manifold tuning control valve control circuit, high voltage
P0685	Ignition relay, control circuit
P0686	Ignition relay, control circuit, low voltage
P0687	Ignition relay, control circuit, high voltage
P0689	Ignition relay, feedback circuit, low voltage
P0690	Ignition relay, feedback circuit, high voltage
P0691	Cooling fan output circuit, low voltage
P069E	Fuel pump control module, requested MIL illumination
P0697	Sensor 5-volt reference 3, circuit performance problem
P06A3	Sensor 5-volt reference 4, circuit performance problem
P0705	Transmission range sensor, circuit malfunction (PRNDL input)

OBD-II TROUBLE CODES (CONTINUED)

➥ **Note: Not all trouble codes apply to all models.**

Code	Code identification
P0711	Transmission fluid temperature sensor circuit, range or performance problem
P0712	Transmission fluid temperature sensor circuit, low input
P0713	Transmission fluid temperature sensor circuit, high input
P0717	Input speed sensor circuit, low voltage
P0723	Output speed sensor, circuit intermittent
P0724	Torque converter/brake switch B circuit, high
P0741	Torque converter clutch, circuit performance problem or stuck in off position
P0742	Torque converter clutch circuit, stuck in on position
P0751	Shift solenoid A, performance problem or stuck in off position
P0752	Shift solenoid A, stuck in on position
P0756	Shift solenoid B, performance problem or stuck in off position
P0757	Shift solenoid B, stuck in on position

4 Accelerator Pedal Position (APP) sensor - replacement

1   Turn the ignition key to OFF.
2   Disconnect the electrical connector from the APP sensor (see illustration).
3   Remove the APP sensor mounting fasteners and detach the APP sensor assembly.
4   Installation is the reverse of removal.

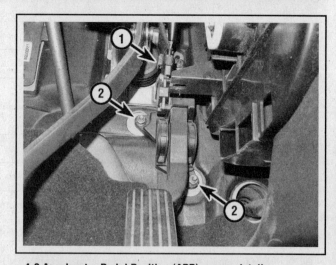

4.2 Accelerator Pedal Position (APP) sensor details
1   *APP sensor electrical connector*
2   *Mounting nuts*

5 Camshaft Position (CMP) sensor(s) - replacement

1 Disconnect the cable from the negative terminal of the battery (see Chapter 5).

2008 AND EARLIER MODELS (L91 AND LXT ENGINES)

➡ **Note: The camshaft position sensor is located under the timing belt cover between the camshaft sprockets.**

2 Remove the engine cover (see Chapter 1, Section 25).

3 Disconnect the sensor electrical connector at the top of the timing belt cover (see illustration).

4 Remove the timing belt cover (see Chapter 2A).

5 Remove the sensor mounting bolts (see illustration), then remove the sensor from behind the sprockets.

6 Installation is the reverse of removal.

2009 AND LATER MODELS (LXV ENGINE)

➡ **Note: The camshaft position sensors are located at the rear (left end) of the cylinder head. The intake CMP sensor is closest to the firewall side. The exhaust CMP sensor is closest to radiator side of the engine.**

7 Unplug the electrical connector from the CMP sensor(s) from the end of the cylinder head (see illustration).

8 Remove the CMP sensor retaining bolt and remove the CMP sensor.

9 Installation is the reverse of removal. Lubricate the O-ring with clean engine oil and tighten the CMP sensor bolt securely.

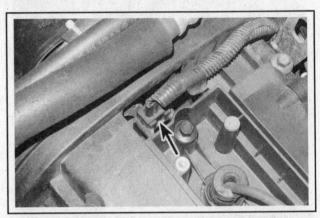

5.3 Disconnect the connector from the top of the sensor

5.5 CMP sensor mounting bolts - L91 and LXT engines

5.7 Exhaust CMP sensor (A) and intake CMP sensor (B) - LXV engines

6 Crankshaft Position (CKP) sensor - replacement

➡ **Note: After replacing the sensor, follow the relearn idle procedure in Chapter 5, Section 3. If this is not done, a diagnostic code P0315 will be set.**

1 Turn the ignition key to OFF.

2 Raise the vehicle and support it securely on jackstands.

2008 AND EARLIER MODELS (L91 AND LXT ENGINES)

➡ **Note: The crankshaft position sensor is located on the front side of the engine block, just below the oil filter housing.**

3 Disconnect the crankshaft sensor electrical connector at the top of the engine, near the oil dipstick.

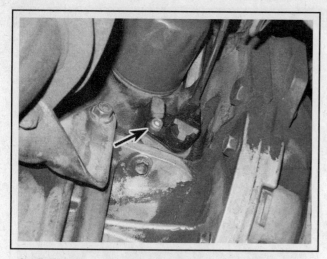

6.4 Follow the sensor wire up to the connector and disconnect the connector, then remove the sensor retaining bolt

4   Remove the sensor retaining bolt (see illustration).
5   Remove the sensor and O-ring.
6   Installation is the reverse of removal. Lubricate the O-ring with clean engine oil prior to installing. Check for oil leaks immediately after starting the engine.

2009 AND LATER MODELS (LXV ENGINE)

➡ **Note: The crankshaft position sensor is located on the rear side of the engine block, directly behind the starter motor.**

7   Remove the starter motor (see Chapter 5).
8   Disconnect the electrical connector from the CKP sensor.
9   Unscrew the CKP sensor mounting bolt and remove the sensor.
10 Even if you're planning to reuse the old CKP sensor, remove the old O-ring and discard it. Always install a new O-ring when installing the CKP sensor.
11 Installation is the reverse of removal. Tighten the CKP sensor mounting bolt securely.

---

7   Engine Coolant Temperature (ECT) sensor(s) - replacement

※ WARNING:

Wait until the engine is completely cool before beginning this procedure.

➡ **Note: On L91 and LXT engines, the coolant temperature sensor is located on the rear side of the cylinder head just below the intake manifold. On LXV engines there are two engine coolant temperature sensors used: an upper one, located on the thermostat housing and a lower one, mounted in the lower right side of the radiator.**

1   Turn the ignition key to OFF.
2   Drain the cooling system (see Chapter 1).

ENGINE-MOUNTED ECT SENSOR

2008 and earlier models (L91 and LXT engines)

3   Raise the vehicle and support it securely on jackstands.
4   Locate the sensor from under the vehicle at the rear of the cylinder head just below the intake manifold.

➡ **Note: The sensor can be accessed through the large opening in the intake manifold support bracket.**

5   Disconnect the electrical connector from the ECT sensor (see illustration).
6   Unscrew the ECT sensor from the cylinder head.
7   Don't seal the threads of the new sensor with Teflon tape, as this will interfere with the grounding of the sensor. Apply a small amount of liquid sealant to the threads before installation.
8   Installation is the reverse of removal. Tighten the ECT sensor to the torque listed in this Chapter's Specifications. Refill the cooling system (see Chapter 1).

LXV engines

9   Disconnect the electrical connector from the ECT sensor, which is located on the thermostat housing.
10 Pull out the retaining clip, then twist and pull the sensor from its bore.
11 Installation is the reverse of removal.

➡ **Note: Make sure the retaining clip is fully seated.**

12 Refill the cooling system (see Chapter 1).

RADIATOR-MOUNTED ECT SENSOR

13 Locate the sensor on the right rear side of the radiator, at the bottom.
14 Disconnect the sensor electrical connector, then remove the sensor from the radiator.
15 Installation is the reverse of removal.
16 Refill the cooling system (see Chapter 1).

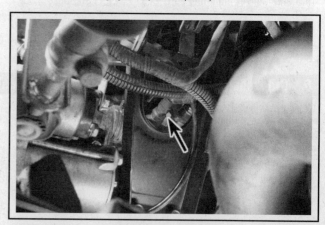

7.5 Location of the engine-mounted coolant temperature sensor (L91 and LXT engines)

8   Knock sensor - replacement

➡ **Note: The knock sensor is located on the rear side of the engine block to the rear of the starter motor.**

1   Make sure the ignition key is turned to the OFF position.

2   Raise the front of the vehicle and support it securely on jackstands.

3   On L91 and LXT models, remove the intake manifold support bracket (see Chapter 2A).

4   Disconnect the knock sensor electrical connector (see illustration).

5   Remove the knock sensor retaining bolt.

6   Remove the knock sensor.

7   Installation is the reverse of removal. Tighten the knock sensor retaining bolt to the torque listed in this Chapter's Specifications.

8.4 Knock sensor details

1   *Electrical connector*   2   *Mounting bolt*

9   Manifold Absolute Pressure (MAP) sensor - replacement

➡ **Note: After the repair, the vehicle may not perform normally as the system goes through its "idle learn process" or "variation learn." If this is not done, a diagnostic code P0315 will be set.**

1   Turn the ignition key to OFF.

2   Disconnect the MAP sensor electrical connector (see illustration).

3   On L91 and LXT models, remove the mounting bolt and sensor, then disconnect the vacuum line from the bottom of the sensor.

4   On LXV models, remove the mounting bolt and pull the sensor from the intake manifold.

5   Installation is the reverse of removal.

9.2 MAP sensor location - L91 engine shown

10   Mass Air Flow/Intake Air Temperature (MAF/IAT) sensor - replacement

➡ **Note: The MAF/IAT sensor is only used on LXV models and is located in the duct between the air filter housing and the throttle body.**

➡ **Note: After the repair, the vehicle may not perform normally as the system goes through its "idle learn process" after a new sensor is replaced.**

1   Turn the ignition key to OFF.

2   Disconnect the electrical connector from the sensor.

3   Remove the clamps from each side of the sensor, then remove the sensor from the ducts.

4   Installation is the reverse of removal.

11 Intake Air Temperature (IAT) sensor - replacement

→ Note: The IAT sensor is used on L91 and LXT models and is mounted on the air intake duct.

→ Note: After the repair, the vehicle may not perform normally as the system goes through its "idle learn process" after a new sensor is replaced.

1 Turn the ignition key to OFF.
2 Disconnect the electrical connector from the sensor (see illustration).
3 Pull the sensor from the grommet in the air intake tube.
4 Installation is the reverse of removal.

11.2 Intake Air Temperature (IAT) sensor location

12 Rough road sensor - replacement

→ Note: The rough road sensor is only used on 2008 and earlier models and is located on the left side of the engine compartment attached to the body just forward of the firewall.

→ Note: After the repair, the vehicle may not perform normally as the system goes through its "idle learn process."

1 Turn the ignition key to OFF. Remove the coolant expansion tank and position it aside without disconnecting the hoses (see Chapter 3).
2 Disconnect the electrical connector from the sensor (see illustration).
3 Unscrew the sensor from the body.
4 Installation is the reverse of removal.

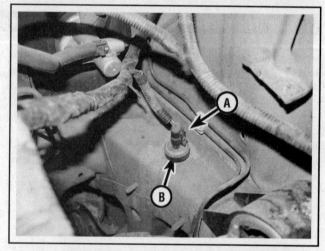

12.2 Disconnect the elevctrical connector (A), then slide a wrench between the sensor and the body (B) and unscrew the sensor

13 Vehicle Speed Sensor(s) (VSS) - replacement

AUTOMATIC TRANSAXLE

Input speed sensor (ISS)

→ Note: The input (ISS) is located on the top of the transaxle, toward the cylinder head.

1 Turn the ignition key to OFF.
2 Disconnect the electrical connector from the input speed sensor.
3 Remove the input speed sensor bolt and remove the sensor from the top of the transaxle.
4 Remove the old O-ring from the VSS sensor and discard it (even

if you're planning to reuse the old VSS sensor). Coat the new O-ring with Dexron III transmission fluid and install it onto the sensor.

5 Installation is the reverse of removal.

Output speed sensor (OSS)

→ Note: The output speed sensor (OSS) is located on the top of the transaxle, toward the body and just in front of the transaxle mount.

6 Disconnect the output shaft speed (OSS) sensor electrical connector.

7   Remove the output speed sensor bolt and remove the sensor from the transaxle.

8   Remove the old O-ring from the OSS sensor and discard it (even if you're planning to reuse the old sensor). Coat the new O-ring with T-IV transmission fluid and install it onto the sensor.

9   Installation is the reverse of removal.

MANUAL TRANSAXLE

➡ **Note: The VSS is located on the top of the transaxle and is part of the speedometer driven gear. If necessary, remove the coolant expansion tank for access (see Chapter 3).**

10   Turn the ignition key to OFF.

11   Disconnect the electrical connector from the VSS sensor (see illustration).

12   Remove the hold-down bolt and pull the sensor/speedometer driven gear from the top of the transaxle.

13   Installation is the reverse of removal.

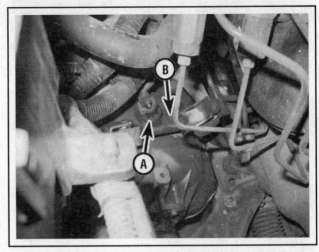

13.11 Vehicle Speed Sensor (VSS) (A) and hold-down bolt (B)

14 Oxygen sensors - replacement

❄ CAUTION:

Because it is installed in the exhaust manifold or pipe, both of which contract when cool, an oxygen sensor might be very difficult to loosen when the engine is cold. Rather than risk damage to the sensor or its mounting threads, start and run the engine for a minute or two, then shut it off. Be careful not to burn yourself during the following procedure.

1   Be particularly careful when servicing an oxygen sensor:

  a) Oxygen sensors have a permanently attached pigtail and an electrical connector that cannot be removed. Damaging or removing the pigtail or electrical connector will render the sensor useless.

  b) Keep grease, dirt and other contaminants away from the electrical connector and the louvered end of the sensor.

  c) Do not use cleaning solvents of any kind on an oxygen sensor.

  d) Oxygen sensors are extremely delicate. Do not drop a sensor or handle it roughly.

  e) Make sure that the silicone boot on the sensor is installed in the correct position. Otherwise, the boot might melt and it might prevent the sensor from operating correctly.

REPLACEMENT

➡ **Note: After the repair the vehicle may not perform normally as the system goes through its "idle learn process." It may be necessary to use the GM's TECH-2 scan tool to speed up the "learn process."**

Upstream oxygen sensor (Sensor 1)

➡ **Note: The upstream oxygen sensor is located in the exhaust manifold.**

2   Turn the ignition key to the OFF position.

3   Disconnect the upstream oxygen sensor electrical connector, which is located on a bracket near the left end of the cylinder head. The connectors will have a CPA (connector position assurance) clip that must be pulled to disconnect the connector.

4   Using an oxygen sensor socket (available at most auto parts stores), unscrew the upstream oxygen sensor (see illustrations). If the sensor is difficult to loosen, spray some penetrant onto the sensor threads and allow it to soak in for awhile.

14.4a Follow the harness from the oxygen sensor (A) to the electrical connector (B) and unplug it. . .

14.4b. . . then use an oxygen sensor socket to unscrew it (L91 engine shown)

14.7 Detach the downstream O2 sensor electrical connector from the bracket, then unplug it

14.8 Use an oxygen sensor socket to unscrew the downstream oxygen sensor (Sensor 2)

Downstream oxygen sensor (Sensor 2)

5   Turn the ignition key to OFF.

6   Raise the vehicle and support it securely on jackstands.

7   Disconnect the oxygen sensor electrical connector, which is located on a bracket attached to the rear of the engine block (see illustration). On some models, the connector will have a CPA (connector position assurance) clip that must be pulled to disconnect the connector.

8   Unscrew the downstream oxygen sensor (see illustration), which is located below the catalytic converter. If the sensor is difficult to loosen, spray some penetrant onto the sensor threads and allow it to soak in for awhile.

Either sensor

9   If you're going to install the old sensor, apply anti-seize compound to the threads of the sensor to facilitate future removal. If you're going to install a new oxygen sensor, it's not necessary to apply anti-seize compound to the threads. The threads on new sensors already have anti-seize compound on them.

10   Installation is otherwise the reverse of removal. Tighten the sensor to the torque listed in this Chapter's Specifications.

15 Transmission Range (TR) switch - replacement and adjustment

➡ **Note: The TR switch is located on the left side of the transmission.**

1   Apply the parking brake and put the shift lever in NEUTRAL.

2   Disconnect the cable from the negative terminal of the battery (see Chapter 5).

3   Raise the vehicle and place it securely on jackstands.

4   Disconnect the electrical connector from the TR switch.

5   Remove the E-clip and disconnect the shift cable from the manual lever.

6   Remove the manual lever nut and remove the manual lever.

7   Use a punch and unstake the lock washer, then remove the nut.

8   Remove the TR switch mounting bolts and remove the TR switch.

9   Install the TR switch and hand tighten the mounting bolts.

10   Install a new lock washer and nut and tighten the nut to 106 in-lbs (12 Nm).

11   Temporarily install the shift lever, then turn the lever coun-terclockwise until it stops, then rotate it clockwise for two clicks or notches.

12   Align the groove on the sensor with the neutral line, then tighten the bolts to the torque listed in this Chapter's Specifications.

13   Using a punch or screwdriver, fold the lock washer over and stake it against the nut.

14   If you're installing the old unit, simply align the groove with the line of the TR switch and install the switch.

15   Installation is the reverse of removal. After installing the TR switch, verify that the engine will start only in PARK and NEUTRAL. If it starts in any other gear, readjust the switch.

16   To adjust the TR switch, loosen the switch mounting bolts and turn it slightly one way or the other until the engine starts only in PARK and NEUTRAL, then tighten the mounting bolts securely.

17   If the switch was replaced it may be necessary to adjust the control cable (see Chapter 7B).

16 Powertrain Control Module (PCM) - removal and installation

※ CAUTION:

To avoid electrostatic discharge damage to the PCM, handle the PCM only by its case. Do not touch the electrical terminals during removal and installation. If available, ground yourself to the vehicle with an anti-static ground strap, available at computer supply stores.

➡ Note: The procedures in this section apply only to removing and installing the PCM that is already installed in your vehicle. If you need a new PCM, it must be programmed with new software and calibrations. This procedure requires the use of GM's TECH-2 scan tool and GM's latest PCM-programming software, so you WILL NOT BE ABLE TO REPLACE THE PCM AT HOME.

➡ Note: The PCM is a highly reliable component and rarely requires replacement. Since the PCM is the most expensive part of the engine management system, you should be absolutely positive that it has failed before replacing it. If in doubt, have

the system tested by an experienced drivability technician at a dealer service department or other qualified repair shop.

➡ Note: The PCM is located in the engine compartment mounted to the inside of the left front fender, on the strut tower.

1   Disconnect the cable from the negative terminal of the battery (see Chapter 5).

2   Noting their orientation to the PCM, disconnect the two electrical connectors from the PCM (see illustrations).

3   On L91 and LXT models, remove the PCM mounting nuts and remove the PCM from the mounting bracket (see illustration).

4   On LXV models, remove the PCM bracket mounting bolts and remove the PCM and bracket assembly, then remove the PCM from the bracket.

5   Installation is the reverse of removal.

6   When the battery has been reconnected, the PCM must relearn its former drivability and performance problem characteristics (see Chapter 5, Section 3).

16.2a Depress the tab (1) to unlock the release lever (2). . .

16.2b. . . then flip the release lever open and unplug the connector

16.3 PCM mounting nuts (L91 model shown)

17 Catalytic converter - replacement

L91 AND LXT ENGINES

1   Raise the vehicle and support it securely on jackstands.

2   Remove the exhaust manifold heat shield (see Chapter 2A, Section 6).

3   Remove the exhaust manifold-to-converter nuts (see illustration) and support bracket bolt.

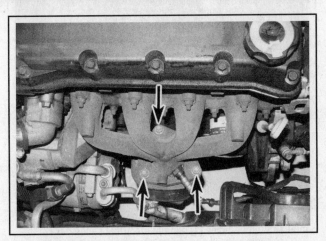

17.3 Remove the exhaust manifold-to-converter nuts

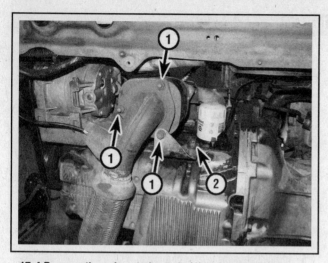

17.4 Remove the exhaust pipe nuts (1) and support bracket bolt (2)

4 Support the catalytic converter, then remove the exhaust pipe-to-converter nuts (see illustration) and support bracket bolt.

5 Remove the exhaust pipe and bracket, then lower the converter out of the vehicle.

6 Installation is the reverse of removal. Tighten the mounting nuts to the torque listed in this Chapter's Specifications.

LXV ENGINES

7 On LXV models, the catalytic converter is integrated into the exhaust manifold and cannot be serviced separately. To remove or replace the catalytic converter, see Chapter 2A.

18 Evaporative Emissions Control (EVAP) system - component replacement

☀ WARNING:

Fuel and fuel vapors are extremely flammable. See the *Fuel system warnings* in Chapter 4, Section 1.

EVAP CANISTER PURGE SOLENOID

1 Turn the ignition key to OFF.

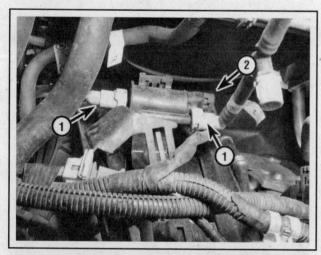

18.3 To remove the EVAP purge solenoid, disconnect the inlet and outlet hoses (1) and the electrical connector (2)

2 Locate the EVAP canister purge solenoid. On L91 and LXT models it's mounted to the intake manifold support bracket; and on LXV models it's located on the intake manifold.

3 Disconnect the canister purge solenoid electrical connector (see illustration).

4 Disconnect the inlet and outlet purge hoses from the canister purge solenoid. Cap the lines to prevent dirt, dust and moisture from entering the EVAP system while the lines are open.

5 On 2006 and earlier L91 models, remove the mounting bracket bolt and solenoid with the bracket, then unclip the solenoid from its bracket.

6 On 2007 L91 and 2008 LXT models, raise the vehicle and support it on jackstands, then pull the canister purge solenoid from its mounting bracket.

7 On LXV models, slide the canister purge solenoid from its mounting tab.

8 Installation is the reverse of removal.

EVAP CANISTER VENT SOLENOID

➡ **Note: The canister vent solenoid is located in the fenderwell behind the right rear wheel.**

9 Raise the rear of the vehicle and support it securely on jackstands.

L91 and LXT models

10 Remove the EVAP canister vent solenoid bracket bolt and lower the solenoid and bracket down.

18.11 Disconnect this connector at the canister vent solenoid

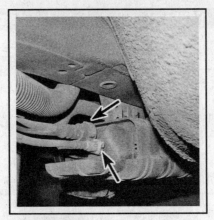

18.20 Disconnect the quick-connect hose fittings from the EVAP canister

18.21 Canister bracket tab retaining bolt

11 Disconnect the electrical connector at the EVAP canister vent solenoid (see illustration).

12 Disconnect the vent hose and unclip the vent solenoid from the valve.

13 Installation is the reverse of removal.

LXV models

14 Disconnect the electrical connector at the EVAP canister vent solenoid.

15 Disconnect the vent hoses.

16 Unclip the vent solenoid from the EVAP canister bracket by pushing it to the left away from the body.

17 Installation is the reverse of removal.

EVAP CANISTER

➡ **Note: The canister is located in the fenderwell behind the right rear wheel.**

18 Raise the rear of the vehicle and support it securely on jackstands.

19 On LXV models, remove the EVAP canister vent solenoid (see Steps 14 through 16).

20 Disconnect the hoses from the EVAP canister (see illustration).

➡ **Note: For information on how to disconnect the quick-connect fittings, refer to Chapter 4.**

21 On L91 and LXT models, remove the bolt(s) that secures the canister bracket tab (see illustration) to the vehicle. Slide the canister out of the holder and remove the canister.

➡ **Note: On 2006 and earlier L91 models, once the canister is removed, remove the canister cover fasteners and separate the cover from the canister.**

22 On LXV models, remove the canister bracket mounting bolts and

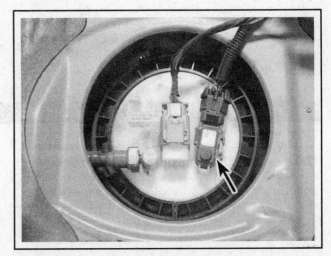

18.26 Location of the fuel tank pressure sensor

lower the canister from the vehicle, then unclip the canister from its mounting bracket.

23 Installation is the reverse of removal.

FUEL TANK PRESSURE SENSOR

24 Remove the rear seat (see Chapter 11).

25 Remove the fuel pump access cover (see Chapter 4).

26 Disconnect the electrical connector from the fuel tank pressure sensor (see illustration).

27 The sensor is mounted to the fuel pump module by rubber grommets. Rock it out of the module cover using two screwdrivers to pry under the sensor.

28 Installation is the reverse of removal.

19 Positive Crankcase Ventilation (PCV) system - component replacement

PCV VALVE (L91 AND LXT MODELS)

1   Remove the engine cover, if equipped.

2   Disconnect the hose from the valve cover.

3   Unscrew the PCV valve from the valve cover (see illustration) and remove the valve.

4   Installation is the reverse of removal.

CRANKCASE VENT HOUSING (LXV) MODELS

5   Remove the valve cover (see Chapter 2A). The vent housing is an integral component of the valve cover and it cannot be replaced separately.

6   Installation is the reverse of removal.

19.3 Unscrew the PCV valve from the valve cover

20 Exhaust Gas Recirculation (EGR) system

1   The Exhaust Gas Recirculation (EGR) system is used to lower NOx (oxides of nitrogen) emission levels caused by high combustion temperatures. The EGR valve recirculates a small amount of exhaust gases into the intake manifold. The additional mixture lowers the temperature of combustion thereby reducing the formation of NOx compounds.

2   The EGR system consists of an electronic EGR valve and the PCM. The PCM controls the EGR flow rate by energizing the EGR valve solenoid coil, opening or closing the EGR passage in small increments. The PCM monitors the EGR valve pintle position with an EGR position sensor that is built into the EGR valve. This system allows for precise control of EGR flow, achieving optimum EGR flow depending on engine operating conditions.

CHECK

3   A scan tool is required for complete testing of the EGR valve, control system and circuits. However, there are several tests the home mechanic can perform on the system to verify operation but they are limited and are useful only in the case of definite system failure.

4   Disconnect the electrical connector from the EGR valve. Connect the negative lead of a voltmeter to a good engine ground point and probe terminal E of the EGR valve electrical connector (harness side) with the positive lead (see illustration). Turn the ignition key On - the battery voltage should be indicated on the meter. If battery voltage is not indicated, check the circuits from the PCM to the EGR valve. If the circuits are good, have the PCM diagnosed by a dealer service department or other qualified repair shop.

5   Check the voltage supply and ground circuits to the EGR valve position sensor. Disconnect the electrical connector from the EGR valve. Connect the positive lead of a voltmeter to terminal D of the EGR valve electrical connector (harness side). Connect the negative lead to ground. Turn the ignition key On - approximately 5.0 volts should be indicated on the meter. If the 5.0 volt supply voltage is not present, check the circuits from the PCM to the EGR valve. If the circuits are good, have the PCM diagnosed by a dealer service department or other qualified repair shop.

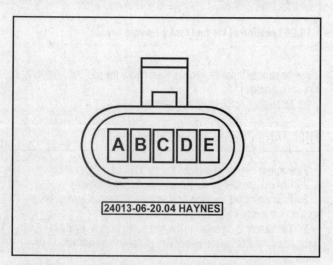

24013-06-20.04 HAYNES

20.4 EGR valve harness connector terminal identification

A   EGR valve control
B   Low reference voltage
C   Pintle position
    sensor signal
D   5-volt reference voltage
E   Ignition 12-volt supply

20.7 EGR valve mounting bolts

20.13 Remove the EGR pipe mounting bracket bolt, then lower the pipe from the vehicle

EGR VALVE REPLACEMENT

6   Disconnect the electrical connector from the EGR valve.
7   Remove the EGR valve mounting bolts (see illustration). Remove the EGR valve and gasket, if equipped. Discard the gasket if equipped.
8   Using a gasket scraper, clean the EGR valve surfaces.
9   Installation is the reverse of removal.

EGR VALVE PIPE REPLACEMENT

10   Raise the vehicle and support it securely on jackstands.

11   Remove the EGR pipe mounting bolts and separate the pipe from the intake manifold.
12   Remove the EGR pipe mounting bolts and separate the pipe from the side of EGR valve.
13   Remove the EGR pipe bracket mounting bolt (see illustration), then remove the EGR pipe.
14   Installation is the reverse of removal. Tighten the pipe mounting bolts to the torque listed in this Chapter's Specifications.

21   Fuel tank pressure sensor - replacement

❊ WARNING:

Fuel and fuel vapors are extremely flammable. See the *Fuel system warnings* in Chapter 4, Section 1.

1   Remove the rear seat (see Chapter 11).
2   Remove the fuel pump module access cover (see Chapter 4).
3   Disconnect the electrical connector from the fuel tank pressure sensor (see illustration).
4   Pull the sensor out of the grommet in the fuel pump module.
5   Installation is the reverse of removal.

21.3 Fuel tank pressure sensor location

22 Camshaft Position (CMP) Actuator system (2009 and later models) - description and component replacement

DESCRIPTION

1   These models are equipped with the Camshaft Position (CMP) Actuator System. By changing camshaft timing (angle) in relation to the crankshaft, this electro-hydraulic system opens the valves earlier or later depending on operating conditions, improving engine performance, fuel economy, and lowering emissions.

2   The CMP Actuator system consists of the CMP sensors, the Powertrain Control Module (PCM), the CMP actuator solenoids and the CMP actuators. The actuators are specially designed camshaft sprockets with oil passages inside them.

3   In response to signals from the CMP sensors, the PCM signals the CMP actuator solenoids that control the amount of engine oil flow to the CMP actuators. The pressurized engine oil unseats a locking pin inside each actuator, then flows through a vane and rotor assembly. Each actuator has two oil passages: one to advance the camshaft and one to retard it. If the oil is directed through the advance passage, the vane and rotor assembly advances that camshaft in relation to the crankshaft position; if the oil is directed through the retard passage, the assembly retards the cam.

COMPONENT REPLACEMENT

CMP sensor(s)

4   See Section 5 for this procedure.

CMP actuator solenoid valves

➡ **Note: There are two CMP actuator solenoids, one for each camshaft, located in the sides of the cylinder head toward the front; this procedure applies to both.**

5   Remove the engine cover, if equipped.
6   Disconnect the electrical connector from the CMP actuator solenoid valve(s).
7   Remove the solenoid valve mounting bolt.
8   Remove the solenoid(s) from the cylinder head.
9   Inspect the CMP actuator solenoid O-ring(s) and replace if necessary.
10 Installation is the reverse of removal. Tighten the CMP actuator solenoid(s) mounting bolt(s) to the torque listed in this Chapter's Specifications.

CMP actuators

11 See Chapter 2A, Section 7 for this procedure.

Torque specifications	Ft-lbs (unless otherwise indicated)	Nm

➡ **Note: One foot-pound (ft-lb) of torque is equivalent to 12 inch-pounds (in-lbs) of torque. Torque values below approximately 15 foot-pounds are expressed in inch-pounds, because most foot-pound torque wrenches are not accurate at these smaller values.**

Catalytic converter-to-manifold nuts		
2008 and earlier models (L91 and LXT engines)	37	50
2009 and later models (LXV engine)	37	50
Pipe-to-muffler nuts	22	30
Exhaust pipe bracket nuts		
2008 and earlier models (L91 and LXT engines)	37	50
2009 and later models (LXV engine)	30	40
Coolant temperature sensor	15	20
CKP sensor bolt		
2008 and earlier models		
(L91 and LXT engines)	58 in-lbs	6.5
2009 and later models (LXV engine)	40 in-lbs	4.5
CMP sensor bolt		
2008 and earlier models		
(L91 and LXT engines)	62 in-lbs	7
2009 and later models (LXV engine)	40 in-lbs	4.5
CMP actuator solenoid valve mounting bolts	53 in-lbs	6
Knock sensor retaining bolt	15	20
Oxygen sensors		
2008 and earlier models		
(L91 and LXT engines)	31	42
2009 and later models (LXV engine)	30	40
EGR valve mounting bolts	22	30
EGR valve pipe mounting bolts		
EGR pipe-to-EGR valve bolts	89 in-lbs	10
EGR pipe-to-intake manifold bolts	106 in-lbs	12

Notes

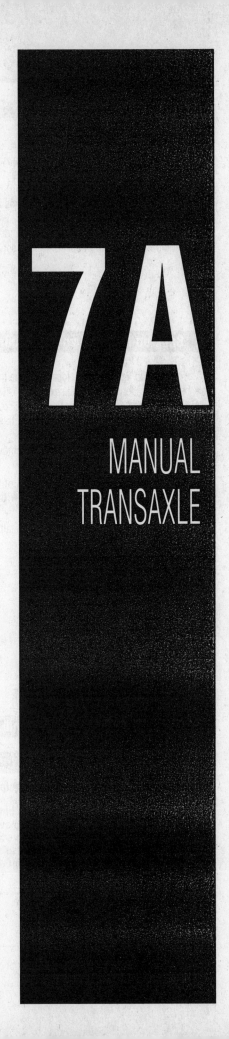

7A

MANUAL
TRANSAXLE

Section

1   General Information

1   The vehicles covered by this manual are equipped with either a 5-speed manual or a 4-speed automatic transaxle. This Part of Chapter 7 contains information on the manual transaxle. All models use either the D16 (hydraulic clutch actuation) or Y4M (mechanical clutch actuation) transaxle. Service procedures for the automatic transaxle are contained in Chapter 7B.

2   Because of the complexity of the manual transaxle and the specialized equipment necessary to perform most service operations, this Chapter contains only those procedures related to general diagnosis, adjustment and removal and installation procedures.

3   If the transaxle requires major repair work, it should be left to a dealer service department or an automotive or transmission repair shop. Once properly diagnosed, however, you can remove and install the transaxle yourself and save the expense, and have the repair work done by a transmission shop.

2   Back-up light switch - replacement

1   The back-up light switch is located on the front of the transaxle case, below the battery on D16 transaxles; On Y4M transaxles it's located on the top of the case, near the left end cover.

2   Disconnect the electrical connector from the back-up light switch (see illustration).

3   Unscrew the switch from the case and remove the gasket. Discard the gasket.

➡ **Note: To avoid rounding off the corners of the switch, use a socket or box-end wrench to remove the switch, not an open-end wrench.**

4   Clean the threads, apply sealant, then install a new gasket and screw in the switch, tightening it securely.

5   Reconnect the electrical connector.

6   Check the operation of the back-up lights.

2.2 Disconnect the electrical connector and unscrew the back-up light switch (D16 transaxle shown)

3   Shifter assembly, linkage and cables - removal, installation and adjustment

✳✳ WARNING:

The models covered by this manual are equipped with a Supplemental Restraint System (SRS), more commonly known as airbags. Always disarm the airbag system before working in the vicinity of any airbag system component to avoid the possibility of accidental deployment of the airbag, which could cause personal injury (see Chapter 12). Do not use a memory saving device to preserve the PCM's memory when working on or near airbag system components.

SHIFT KNOB

1   The shift knob is not serviceable and is not designed to be removed from the shifter assembly.

D16 TRANSAXLE

Shifter assembly

2   Disconnect the negative battery cable (see Chapter 5, Section 3).

3   Working inside the vehicle, remove the shifter boot (see illustration) to access the shifter mechanism (see Chapter 11, Section 21).

4   Rotate the shifter lever stop clamp counterclockwise (see illustration).

5   Slide the retainer pin outwards and remove the shifter from the shift rod (see illustration).

6   Disconnect the shift rod by loosening the shift rod clamp (see illustration).

7   Remove the bolts attaching the shifter assembly to the vehicle (see illustration) and remove the shift rod and shifter assembly from the vehicle together.

8   Installation is reverse of removal.

3.3 Pry up the shifter boot

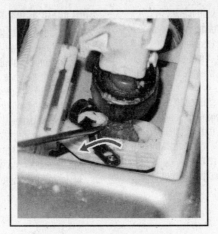

3.4 Rotate the shifter lever clamp

3.5 Slide the retainer pin outwards (A) and remove the shifter from the shift rod (B)

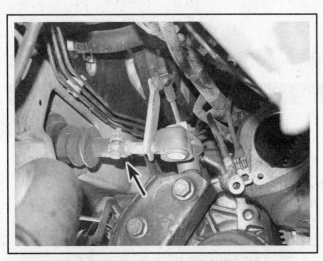

3.6 Disconnect the shift rod by loosening the clamp

3.7 Remove the bolts and the shifter assembly with the shift rod

Shift linkage adjustment

9 Disconnect the negative battery cable (see Chapter 5, Section 3).

10 Working at the transaxle end of the shift rod, loosen the shift rod clamp bolt (see illustration 3.6), allowing the shift rod and gear selector lever to move independently from each other.

11 Remove the plug from the shift lever hole. Rotate the shift rod/ lever until a 5mm Allen wrench or drill bit can be inserted through the hole to lock the shift lever in place.

12 Working inside the vehicle, remove the shifter boot to access the shifter mechanism (see Chapter 11, Section 21).

13 Place the gearshift lever close to the left side of the NEUTRAL position. Insert a 5mm Allen wrench or drill bit through the hole to lock the shifter in place with the housing.

14 Working at the transaxle, tighten the shift rod clamp bolt.

15 Remove the 5mm Allen wrenches or drill bits. Check for proper shifting of the transaxle.

16 Install the shifter boot and connect the negative battery cable.

Y4M TRANSAXLE

Shifter assembly

17 Working inside the vehicle, remove the floor center console (see Chapter 11, Section 21). Position the carpet to allow access to the shift cable at the shifter.

18 Remove the clips and washers attaching the shift cables to the shift levers at the shifter and remove the clips attaching the cables to the cable bracket. Disconnect the shift cables from the shift levers.

19 Remove the four bolts attaching the shifter assembly to the vehicle and remove the shifter assembly.

20 Installation is reverse of removal. Adjust the shift cables as necessary.

Shift cables

21 Remove the battery (see Chapter 5).

22 Remove the air intake hose between the air filter and throttle body.

23 Remove the clips and washers attaching the shift cables to the shift levers at the transaxle and remove the clips attaching the cables to the cable bracket. Disconnect the shift cables from the shift levers.

24 Working inside the vehicle, remove the floor center console (see Chapter 11, Section 21). Position the carpet to allow access to the shift cable at the shifter.

25 Remove the clips and washers attaching the shift cables to the shift levers at the shifter and remove the clips attaching the cables to the cable bracket. Disconnect the shift cables from the shift levers.

26 Remove the nuts attaching the cable grommet to the firewall and pull the cables into the passenger compartment to remove.

27 Installation is the reverse of the removal procedure. Adjust the cable as necessary.

Shift cable adjustment

28 Remove the battery (see Chapter 5).

29 Remove the air intake hose between the air filter and throttle body.

30 Loosen the shift cable adjustment bolt at the shift levers.

31 Working inside the vehicle, remove the shift boot at the shifter assembly (see Chapter 11, Section 21).

32 With the shifter assembly in neutral, install a screwdriver in the select arm adjustment hole to lock the shifter in place.

33 Working in the engine compartment, tighten the shift cable adjustment bolt to the torque listed in this Chapter's Specifications. Check for proper shifting of the transaxle.

34 Install the shifter boot, battery and air intake hose.

4   Driveaxle oil seals - replacement

1   Lubricant leaks occasionally occur due to wear of the driveaxle oil seals. Replacement of these seals is relatively easy, since the repairs can be performed without removing the transaxle from the vehicle.

2   The driveaxle oil seals are located in either side of the transaxle, where the inner Constant Velocity (CV) joints are splined into the differential. If leakage at the seal is suspected, raise the vehicle and support it securely on jackstands. If the seal is leaking, fluid will be found on the side of the transaxle.

3   Remove the driveaxle (see Chapter 8). If you're replacing the right side driveaxle seal, also remove the intermediate shaft.

4   Carefully pry the oil seal out of the transaxle bore with a screwdriver or prybar (see illustration).

5   If the oil seal cannot be removed with a screwdriver or prybar, a special oil seal removal tool (available at auto parts stores) will be required.

6   To install the new oil seal, use a seal driver or a large deep socket as a drift. Drive it into the bore squarely until it is flush with the transaxle case or carrier flange (see illustration). Lubricate the lip of the new seal with multi-purpose grease.

7   Install the driveaxle (see Chapter 8). Be careful not to damage the lip of the new seal.

8   Top off the transaxle with the proper lubricant as necessary (see Chapter 1).

4.4 Pry the oil seal out of the transaxle bore

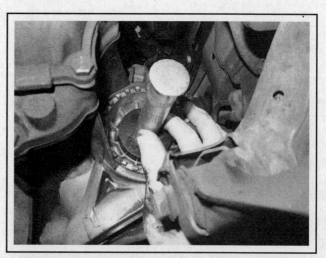

4.6 Use a seal driver or a large deep socket to drive the seal into the bore squarely

5   Manual transaxle - removal and installation

➡ **Note: The vehicle must be raised and safely supported so that it is high enough to allow the transaxle to come out the bottom of the engine compartment.**

➡ **Note: With all the work done to remove the transaxle, this is the best time to inspect and/or replace the clutch assembly (see Chapter 8).**

REMOVAL

1   Disconnect the negative battery cable (see Chapter 5).
2   Remove the battery and battery tray (see Chapter 5).
3   Loosen the front wheel lug nuts. Raise the vehicle and support it securely on jackstands placed under the unibody frame rails. Drain the transaxle lubricant (see Chapter 1, Section 24).
4   Remove the wheels, then unstake both driveaxle/hub nuts.
5   Disconnect the electrical connector for the back-up light switch, then disconnect the wire harness from the transaxle (see Section 2).
6   Remove both driveaxles (see Chapter 8, Section 10).

D16 transaxle

7   Support the engine using an engine support or engine hoist.
8   Disconnect the Vehicle Speed Sensor (VSS) connector (see Chapter 6, Section 13).
9   Disconnect the shift rod from the shift linkage (see Section 3).
10 Remove the bolts attaching the clutch release cylinder to the transaxle and remove the release cylinder (see Chapter 8, Section 6).

✳✳ CAUTION:

Do not depress the clutch pedal while the release cylinder is detached or the release cylinder will be damaged.

11 Remove the two bolts attaching the damping block to the crossmember.
12 Disconnect the upper transaxle mount by removing the mount-to-transaxle bolts (see illustration).
13 Remove the three upper transaxle-to-engine bolts.
14 Support the transaxle with a transmission jack. Secure the transaxle to the jack with straps or chains so it doesn't fall off during removal.
15 Remove the seven lower transaxle-to-engine bolts.
16 Make a final check that all wires, hoses, brackets and mounts have been disconnected from the transaxle, then slide the transaxle jack toward the side of the vehicle until the transaxle input shaft is clear of the engine. Make sure you keep the transaxle level as you do this.
17 Move the transaxle away from the engine until the input shaft clears the clutch. Slowly lower the transaxle and remove from the vehicle.

Y4M transaxle

✳✳ WARNING:

Wait until the engine is completely cool before beginning this procedure.

18 Remove the air filter housing (see Chapter 4, Section 11).
19 Remove the clips and washers attaching the shift cables to the shift levers at the transaxle and remove the clips attaching the cables to the cable bracket. Disconnect the shift cables from the shift levers.
20 Disconnect the electrical harness strap and remove the ground cable bolt and ground cable.
21 Drain the cooling system (see Chapter 1). Disconnect the lower radiator hose pipe bracket bolt and disconnect the lower radiator hose at the pipe.
22 Remove the Crankshaft Position Sensor (CKP) (see Chapter 6, Section 6).
23 Remove the Vehicle Speed Sensor (VSS) (see Chapter 6, Section 13).
24 Remove the starter motor (see Chapter 5).
25 Support the engine using an engine support or engine hoist.
26 Remove the two upper transaxle-to-engine bolts.
27 Remove the clutch cable adjustment nut and disconnect the clutch cable from the bracket.
28 Remove the stabilizer bar (see Chapter 10, Section 4).
29 Remove the clutch cover plate from the transaxle.
30 Remove the three nuts for the exhaust and two bolts for the bracket and disconnect the exhaust pipe from the exhaust manifold.
31 Remove the upper transaxle mount from the vehicle.
32 Support the transaxle with a transmission jack. Secure the transaxle to the jack with straps or chains so it doesn't fall off during removal.
33 Remove the damping block nut and bolt and the four rear mount bracket bolts and the bracket.
34 Remove the two bolts attaching the damping block to the crossmember.
35 Remove the two lower transaxle-to-engine bolts.
36 Make a final check that all wires, hoses, brackets and mounts have been disconnected from the transaxle, then slide the transaxle jack toward the side of the vehicle until the transaxle input shaft is clear of the engine. Make sure you keep the transaxle level as you do this.
37 Move the transaxle away from the engine until the input shaft clears the clutch. Slowly lower the transaxle and remove from the vehicle.

5.12 Remove the transaxle mount-to-transaxle bolts

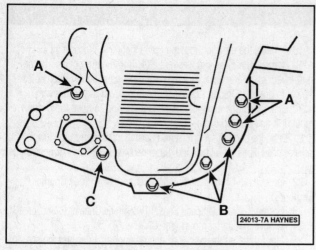

5.38 Tighten the transaxle-to-engine bolts to the proper torque for the corresponding bolts (D16 transaxle)

INSTALLATION

38 Installation of the transaxle is a reversal of the removal procedure, but note the following points:

a) Apply a thin film of high-temperature grease to the splines of the transaxle input shaft.

b) Tighten the transaxle-to-engine mounting bolts to the torque listed in this Chapter's Specifications. If you're working on a D16 transaxle, be sure to note the different torque values for the indicated fasteners (see illustration).

c) Tighten the driveaxle/hub nuts to the torque value listed in the Chapter 8 Specifications.

d) Tighten the wheel lug nuts to the torque listed in the Chapter 1 Specifications.

e) Fill the transaxle with the correct type and amount of manual transmission lubricant as described in Chapter 1.

6   Manual transaxle overhaul - general information

1 Overhauling a manual transaxle is a difficult job for the do-it-yourselfer. It involves the disassembly and reassembly of many small parts. Numerous clearances must be precisely measured and, if necessary, changed with select-fit spacers and snap-rings. As a result, if transaxle problems arise, it can be removed and installed by a competent do-it-yourselfer, but overhaul should be left to a transmission repair shop. Rebuilt transaxles may be available - check with your dealer parts department and auto parts stores. At any rate, the time and money involved in an overhaul is almost sure to exceed the cost of a rebuilt unit.

2 Nevertheless, it's not impossible for an inexperienced mechanic to rebuild a transaxle if the special tools are available and the job is done in a deliberate step-by-step manner so nothing is overlooked.

3 The tools necessary for an overhaul include internal and external snap-ring pliers, a bearing puller, a slide hammer, a set of pin punches, a dial indicator and possibly a hydraulic press. In addition, a large, sturdy workbench and a vise or transaxle stand will be required.

4 During disassembly of the transaxle, make careful notes of how each piece comes off, where it fits in relation to other pieces and what holds it in place.

5 Before taking the transaxle apart for repair, it will help if you have some idea what area of the transaxle is malfunctioning. Certain problems can be closely tied to specific areas in the transaxle, which can make component examination and replacement easier. Refer to the *Troubleshooting* section at the front of this manual for information regarding possible sources of trouble.

Specifications

General

Transaxle lubricant type	See Chapter 1
Transaxle lubricant capacity	See Chapter 1

Torque specifications	Ft-lbs (unless otherwise indicated)	Nm

➡ **Note: One foot-pound (ft-lb) of torque is equivalent to 12 inch-pounds (in-lbs) of torque. Torque values below approximately 15 foot-pounds are expressed in inch-pounds, because most foot-pound torque wrenches are not accurate at these smaller values.**

Rear mount bracket bolts	44	60
Dampening block nut/bolt	59	80
Damping block-to-subframe bolts	41	55
D16		
Shift rod clamp bolt	124 in-lbs	14
Transaxle-to-engine bolts		
Upper	54	73
Lower		
Bolts A	54	73
Bolts B	15	23
Bolt C	23	31
Shifter housing-to-floor bolts	62 in-lbs	7
Upper transaxle mount bolts	44	60
Y4M		
Transaxle-to-engine bolts	44	60
Ground wire bolt	10	13
Shift cable adjustment bolt	106 in-lbs	71
Upper transaxle mount bolts	37	50

Notes

7B

AUTOMATIC
TRANSAXLE

Section

1   General information

1   All information on the 81-40LE automatic transaxle is included in this Part of Chapter 7. Information for the manual transaxle can be found in Chapter 7A.

2   Because of the complexity of the automatic transaxles and the specialized equipment necessary to perform most service operations, this Chapter contains only those procedures related to general diagno-sis, adjustment and removal and installation procedures.

3   If the transaxle requires major repair work, it should be left to a dealer service department or an automotive or transmission repair shop. Once properly diagnosed, however, you can remove and install the transaxle yourself and save the expense, and have the repair work done by a transmission shop.

2   Diagnosis - general

1   Automatic transaxle malfunctions may be caused by five general conditions:

   a) *Poor engine performance*
   b) *Improper adjustments*
   c) *Hydraulic malfunctions*
   d) *Mechanical malfunctions*
   e) *Malfunctions in the computer or its signal network*

2   Diagnosis of these problems should always begin with a check of the easily repaired items: fluid level and condition (see Chapter 1), shift cable adjustment and shift lever installation. Next, perform a road test to determine if the problem has been corrected or if more diagnosis is necessary. If the problem persists after the preliminary tests and cor-rections are complete, additional diagnosis should be performed by a dealer service department or other qualified transmission repair shop. Refer to the *Troubleshooting* section at the front of this manual for infor-mation on symptoms of transaxle problems.

PRELIMINARY CHECKS

3   Drive the vehicle to warm the transaxle to normal operating tem-perature.

4   Check the fluid level as described in Chapter 1:

   a) *If the fluid level is unusually low, add enough fluid to bring it up to the proper level, then check for external leaks (see following).*
   b) *If the fluid level is abnormally high, drain off the excess, and then check the drained fluid for contamination by coolant. The presence of engine coolant in the automatic transmission fluid indicates that a failure has occurred in the internal radiator oil cooler walls that separate the coolant from the transmission fluid (see Chapter 3).*
   c) *If the fluid is foaming, drain it and refill the transaxle, then check for coolant in the fluid, or a high fluid level.*

5   Check for the presence of Diagnostic Trouble Codes (see Chap-ter 6).

➡ **Note: If the engine is malfunctioning, do not proceed with the preliminary checks until repairs have been made and the engine runs normally.**

6   Check and adjust the shift cable, if necessary (see Section 4).

7   If hard shifting is experienced, inspect the shift cable under the center console and at the shift lever on the transaxle (see Section 4).

FLUID LEAK DIAGNOSIS

8   Most fluid leaks are easy to locate visually. Repair usually con-sists of replacing a seal or gasket. If a leak is difficult to find, the follow-ing procedure may help.

9   Identify the fluid. Make sure it's transmission fluid and not engine oil or brake fluid (automatic transmission fluid in these vehicles is a deep red color).

10 Try to pinpoint the source of the leak. Drive the vehicle several miles, then park it over a large sheet of cardboard. After a minute or two, you should be able to locate the leak by determining the source of the fluid dripping onto the cardboard.

11 Make a careful visual inspection of the suspected component and the area immediately around it. Pay particular attention to gasket mating surfaces. A mirror is often helpful for finding leaks in areas that are hard to see.

12 If the leak still cannot be found, clean the suspected area thor-oughly with a degreaser or solvent, then dry it thoroughly.

13 Drive the vehicle for several miles at normal operating tempera-ture and varying speeds. After driving the vehicle, visually inspect the suspected component again.

14 Once the leak has been located, the cause must be determined before it can be properly repaired. If a gasket is replaced but the sealing flange is bent, the new gasket will not stop the leak. The bent flange must be straightened.

15 Before attempting to repair a leak, check to make sure that the fol-lowing conditions are corrected or they may cause another leak.

➡ **Note: Some of the following conditions cannot be fixed with-out highly specialized tools and expertise. Such problems must be referred to a qualified transmission shop or a dealer service department.**

Seal leaks

16 If a transaxle seal is leaking, the fluid level may be too high, the vent may be plugged, the seal bore may be damaged, the seal itself may be damaged or improperly installed, the surface of the shaft protruding through the seal may be damaged or a loose bearing may be causing excessive shaft movement.

17 Periodically check the area around the sensors for leakage. If transmission fluid is evident, check the seals for damage.

Case leaks

18 If the case itself appears to be leaking, the casting is porous and will have to be repaired or replaced.

19 Make sure the oil cooler hose fittings are tight and in good con-dition.

3 Driveaxle oil seals - replacement

➡ **Note: This procedure requires special tools. Read through the entire procedure before beginning. If the special tools can't be obtained (or suitable equivalents can't be fabricated), have the procedure performed at a dealer service department or other qualified repair shop.**

1   Oil leaks can occur due to wear of the driveaxle oil seals. Replacement of these seals is relatively easy, since the repairs can be performed without removing the transaxle from the vehicle.

2   The driveaxle oil seals are located in the sides of the transaxle, where the driveaxles are attached. If leakage at the seal is suspected, raise the vehicle and support it securely on jackstands. If the seal is leaking, fluid will be found on the sides of the transaxle.

3   Remove the driveaxle (see Chapter 8).

4   Use a screwdriver or seal removal tool to carefully pry the oil seal out of the transaxle bore (see illustration).

5   Coat the outside and inside diameters of the new seal with a small amount of transmission fluid.

6   Using a seal installation tool or a socket the same diameter as the oil seal, install the new oil seal. Drive it into the bore squarely and make sure it's seated to the original depth (see illustration).

7   Install the driveaxle (see Chapter 8).

✳ CAUTION:

The seal can be easily damaged by the splines of the driveaxle or intermediate shaft.

8   The remainder of installation is the reverse of removal. Check the transaxle fluid level, adding as necessary (see Chapter 1).

3.4 Pry the oil seal out of the transaxle bore

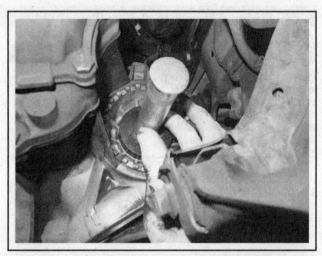

3.6 Use a seal driver or a large deep socket to drive the seal into the bore squarely

4 Shift cable - removal, installation and adjustment

✳ WARNING:

The models covered by this manual are equipped with a Supplemental Restraint System (SRS), more commonly known as airbags. Always disarm the airbag system before working in the vicinity of any airbag system component to avoid the possibility of accidental deployment of the airbag, which could cause personal injury (see Chapter 12).

REMOVAL

1   In the event of hard shifting, disconnect the cable at the transaxle and operate the shifter from the driver's seat. If the shift lever moves smoothly through all positions with the cable disconnected, then the cable should be adjusted as described at the end of this Section. To remove and install the shift cable, perform the following:

2   Remove the center console (see Chapter 11).

3   Remove the cable adjusting nut and disconnect the cable from the shift lever assembly.

4   Remove the clip attaching the cable housing to the shift lever assembly bracket and disconnect the shift cable.

5   Working in the engine compartment, disconnect the shift cable end from the shift lever on the transaxle.

6   Remove the clip attaching the cable housing to the bracket and disconnect the shift cable.

7   Trace the shift cable to where it passes through the vehicle's body, then pry the large rubber cable grommet from the vehicle.

8   Carefully remove the shift cable by pulling it through the hole in the vehicle from the engine compartment side.

INSTALLATION

9   Installation is the reverse of removal, noting the following points:

 a) *Install the shift cable to its original path within the engine compartment and passenger cabin.*

 b) *The cable end fittings must be firmly snapped back into place onto their respective levers.*

ADJUSTMENT

10 Remove the shift lever trim from the center console (see Chapter 11, Section 21).

11 Place the shift lever inside the car in Park. Loosen the cable adjustment nut.

12 Rotate the Park Neutral Position (PNP) switch counterclockwise until the lever stops.

13 Pull on the shift cable and tighten the cable adjustment nut to the torque listed in this Chapter's Specifications.

14 Make sure the engine will start in the Park and Neutral positions only, and all of the gear ranges can be selected.

15 If the engine can be started in any position other than Park or Neutral, check the adjustment of the Transmission Range Switch (see Chapter 6), then adjust and check the shift cable again.

5   Shift lever - removal and installation

✳ WARNING:

The models covered by this manual are equipped with a Supplemental Restraint System (SRS), more commonly known as airbags. Always disarm the airbag system before working in the vicinity of any airbag system component to avoid the possibility of accidental deployment of the airbag, which could cause personal injury (see Chapter 12).

1   Disconnect the cable from the negative terminal of the battery (see Chapter 5).

2   Remove the center console (see Chapter 11).

3   Disconnect any electrical connectors to the shift lever assembly.

4   Remove the cable adjusting nut and disconnect the cable from the shift lever assembly.

5   Remove the four shift lever assembly mounting bolts and lift the assembly out.

6   Transfer any parts as necessary if the assembly is being replaced.

7   Installation is reverse of removal. Make sure to adjust the shift cable once the shift lever has been reinstalled (see Section 4).

6   Transaxle Control Module (TCM) - removal and installation

1   The Transaxle Control Module (TCM) is located next to the brake pedal under the driver's side of the instrument panel. Diagnosis requires detailed knowledge of the transaxle's operation and construction as well as access to specialized test equipment. Because of these factors, diagnosis and repair of the Transaxle Control Module (TCM) itself are beyond the scope of this manual. It is therefore essential that problems with the Transaxle Control Module (TCM) are referred to a dealer service department or other qualified repair facility for assessment and repair.

7   Automatic transaxle - removal and installation

➡ **Note: The vehicle must be raised and supported so that it is high enough to allow the transaxle to come out the bottom of the engine compartment.**

REMOVAL

1   Place the vehicle in PARK with the parking brake engaged.

2   Disconnect the negative battery cable, then remove the battery and battery tray (see Chapter 5).

3   Raise and support the vehicle on jack stands or a hoist.

4   Remove the under-vehicle splash shield if equipped.

5   Drain the transaxle fluid (see Chapter 1, Section 22), then remove both driveaxles (see Chapter 8, Section 10).

6   Disconnect the transaxle cooling lines from the transaxle.

7   Disconnect the shift cable from the shift lever at the transaxle (see Section 4).

8   Support the engine (from above only) using an engine hoist or engine support fixture.

9   Disconnect the input and output shaft speed sensor connectors. Disconnect the transmission range sensor connector at the transaxle shift lever. Disconnect the main transaxle electrical connector.

10 Mark the relationship of the torque converter to the driveplate so they can be installed in the same relative position, then remove the torque converter-to-driveplate bolts. Turn the crankshaft 120-degrees at a time for access to each bolt.

11 Push the torque converter into the bellhousing so it doesn't stay with the engine when the transaxle is removed.

12 Remove the damping block and rear mounting bracket.

13 Remove the three bolts attaching the upper transaxle mount to the vehicle.

14 Remove the three upper engine-to-transaxle mounting bolts.

15 Support the transaxle with a transmission jack. Secure the transaxle to the jack with straps or chains so it doesn't fall off during removal.

16 Remove the seven lower engine-to-transaxle mounting bolts.

17 Make a final check that all wires, hoses, brackets and mounts have been disconnected from the transaxle. Slide the transaxle jack toward the side of the vehicle until the transaxle is clear of the engine locating dowels, then lower it. Keep the transaxle level as you do this.

INSTALLATION

18 Installation is the reverse of removal, noting the following points:
 a) *As the torque converter is reinstalled, ensure that the drive tangs at the center of the torque converter hub engage with the recesses in the automatic transaxle fluid pump inner gear. This can be confirmed by turning the torque converter while pushing it toward the transaxle. If it isn't fully engaged, it will clunk into place.*
 b) *When installing the transaxle, make sure the match-marks you made on the torque converter and driveplate line up.*
 c) *Install all of the driveplate-to-torque converter bolts before tightening any of them.*

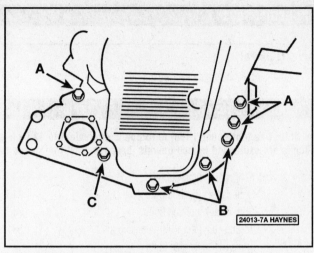

7.18 Tighten the transaxle-to-engine mounting bolts to the proper torque for the corresponding bolt

 d) *Tighten the driveplate-to-torque converter bolts to the torque listed in this Chapter's Specifications.*
 e) *Tighten the transaxle-to-engine mounting bolts (see illustration) to the torque listed in this Chapter's Specifications.*
 f) *Tighten the driveaxle/hub nuts to the torque value listed in the Chapter 8 Specifications.*
 g) *Tighten the wheel lug nuts to the torque listed in the Chapter 1 Specifications.*
 h) *Fill the transaxle with the correct type and amount of automatic transmission fluid as described in Chapter 1.*
 i) *Shift transaxle into all gear positions to confirm shift cable adjustment. Readjust if necessary (see Section 4).*

8   Automatic transaxle overhaul - general information

1   In the event of a problem occurring, it will be necessary to establish whether the fault is electrical, mechanical or hydraulic in nature, before any repair work can be considered. Diagnosis requires detailed knowledge of the transaxle's operation and construction as well as access to specialized test equipment. Because of these factors, diagnosis and repair of the transaxle itself are beyond the scope of this manual. It is therefore essential that problems with the automatic transaxle are referred to a dealer service department or other qualified repair facility for assessment.

2   Note that a faulty transaxle should not be removed before the vehicle has been diagnosed by a knowledgeable technician equipped with the proper tools, as troubleshooting must be performed with the transaxle installed in the vehicle.

Specifications

General

Lubricant type and capacity   See Chapter 1

Torque specifications	Ft-lbs (unless otherwise indicated)	Nm

➡ **Note: One foot-pound (ft-lb) of torque is equivalent to 12 inch-pounds (in-lbs) of torque. Torque values below approximately 15 foot-pounds are expressed in inch-pounds, because most foot-pound torque wrenches are not accurate at these smaller values.**

	Ft-lbs	Nm
Rear mount bracket bolts	44	60
Shift cable adjusting nut	71 in-lbs	8
Shift lever mounting bolts	71 in-lbs	8
Torque converter-to-driveplate bolts	33	45
Transaxle-to-engine bolts		
A bolts	54	73
B bolts	15	21
C bolt	23	31
Upper transaxle mount bolts	54	73

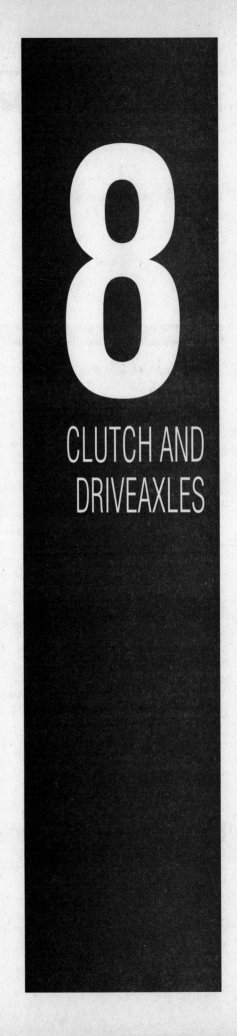

8

CLUTCH AND
DRIVEAXLES

Section

1 General Information

1 The information in this Chapter deals with the components that transmit power to the front wheels, except for the transaxle, which is dealt with in Chapters 7A and 7B. For the purposes of this Chapter, these components are grouped into two categories: clutch and driveaxles. Separate Sections within this Chapter offer general descrip-tions and checking procedures for both groups.

2 Since nearly all the procedures covered in this Chapter involve working under the vehicle, make sure it's securely supported on sturdy jackstands or on a hoist where the vehicle can be easily raised and low-ered.

2 Clutch - description and check

1 All vehicles with a manual transaxle have a single dry plate, diaphragm-spring type clutch. The clutch disc has a splined hub that allows it to slide along the splines of the transaxle input shaft. The clutch and pressure plate are held in contact by spring pressure exerted by the diaphragm in the pressure plate.

2 The clutch release system is operated by either hydraulic pres-sure or a cable (depending on installed transmission).

3 The D16 manual transaxle is equipped with a hydraulic clutch release system. The hydraulic release system consists of the clutch pedal, a master cylinder and a shared common reservoir with the brake master cylinder, a release (or slave) cylinder, the hydraulic line con-necting the two components, a release lever, and release bearing. The release cylinder is installed concentric to the input shaft. When the clutch pedal is depressed, a pushrod pushes against brake fluid inside the master cylinder, applying hydraulic pressure to the release cylinder, which pushes the release lever and release bearing against the dia-phragm fingers of the clutch pressure plate.

4 The Y4M manual transaxle is equipped with a mechanical clutch release system. The mechanical release system consists of the clutch pedal, a cable, a release lever, and release bearing. The release bear-ing is installed concentric to the input shaft and attached to the release lever. When the clutch pedal is depressed, the cable pulls on the release lever, which pushes the release bearing against the diaphragm fingers of the clutch pressure plate.

5 Unless you're replacing components with obvious damage, do these preliminary checks to diagnose clutch problems:

a) *The first check should be of the fluid level in the master cylinder. If the fluid level is low, add fluid as necessary and inspect the hydraulic system for leaks. If the master cylinder reservoir is dry, bleed the system as described in Section 7 and recheck the clutch operation.*

b) *Check the clutch cable for damage, bent brackets, or excessive play. Adjust or replace as necessary.*

c) *To check clutch spin-down time, run the engine at normal idle speed with the transaxle in Neutral (clutch pedal up - engaged). Disengage the clutch (pedal down), wait several seconds and shift the transaxle into Reverse. No grinding noise should be heard. A grinding noise would most likely indicate a bad pressure plate or clutch disc.*

d) *To check for complete clutch release, run the engine (with the parking brake applied to prevent vehicle movement) and hold the clutch pedal approximately 1/2-inch from the floor. Shift the transaxle between first gear and Reverse several times. If the shift is rough, component failure is indicated.*

e) *Visually inspect the pivot bushing at the top of the clutch pedal to make sure there's no binding or excessive play.*

3 Clutch cable - replacement

➡ **Note: This procedure applies to models with a Y4M transaxle only.**

1 Remove the battery (see Chapter 5, Section 3).

2 Working in the engine compartment, remove the clutch cable adjustment nut from the end of the cable at the transaxle clutch lever and remove the cable from the mounting bracket.

3 Remove the clutch cable-to-firewall mounting nuts.

4 Working inside the vehicle, disconnect the clutch cable from the clutch pedal assembly and remove the cable from the vehicle through the engine compartment.

5 Installation is reverse of removal. Adjust the clutch cable as nec-essary. See Section 4.

4   Clutch cable - adjustment

➡ **Note: This procedure applies to models with a Y4M transaxle only.**

➡ **Note: Clutch cable adjustment is performed by adjusting the clutch pedal freeplay.**

1   Check the clutch pedal freeplay and compare against the Specifications in this Chapter's Specifications.

2   If the clutch pedal freeplay is out of specification, adjust using the adjustment nut at the end of the clutch cable in the engine compartment.

3   If the clutch pedal freeplay cannot be adjusted to specification, check the items listed in Section 2.

5   Clutch master cylinder - removal and installation

REMOVAL

1   Under the dash on the driver's side, pull the clip near the top of the clutch pedal that secures the clutch master cylinder pushrod pin to the pedal (see illustration). Remove the pin and pull the clutch pedal upward to disengage it.

2   Working inside the engine compartment, remove as much fluid as you can from the brake master cylinder reservoir with a syringe, such as an old turkey baster (the clutch master cylinder is supplied with fluid from the brake fluid reservoir).

⚹⚹ **WARNING:**

If a baster is used, never again use it for the preparation of food.

⚹⚹ **WARNING:**

Don't depress the brake pedal until the reservoir has been refilled, otherwise air may be introduced into the brake hydraulic system.

3   Place rags under the fluid fittings and prepare caps or plastic bags to cover the ends of lines or fittings once they are disconnected.

⚹⚹ **CAUTION:**

Brake fluid will damage paint. Cover all body parts and be careful not to spill fluid during this procedure.

4   Disconnect the fluid feed hose from the clutch master cylinder (see illustration), plugging it to prevent spilling brake fluid.

5   Detach the hydraulic line from the clutch master cylinder. If available, use a flare-nut wrench to avoid rounding-off the corners of the fitting.

6   Remove the clutch master cylinder mounting nuts and detach the cylinder from the firewall.

INSTALLATION

7   Place the master cylinder pushrod through the firewall and tighten the mounting nuts to the torque listed in this Chapter's Specifications.

8   Insert the clutch master cylinder pushrod into the retainer on the clutch pedal until there is an audible click heard. Verify the pushrod is locked into the pedal retainer by trying to pull the pushrod back out.

9   Connect the hydraulic line to the clutch master cylinder.

10 Attach the fluid feed hose to the clutch master cylinder.

11 Fill the reservoir with brake fluid conforming to DOT 3 specifications and bleed the clutch system as outlined in Section 7.

12 Check the feel of the brake pedal. If it feels spongy when depressed, bleed the brake hydraulic system (see Chapter 9).

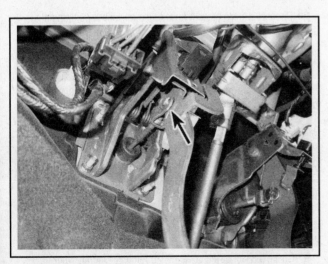

5.1 Pull the clip that secures the clutch master cylinder pushrod pin to the pedal

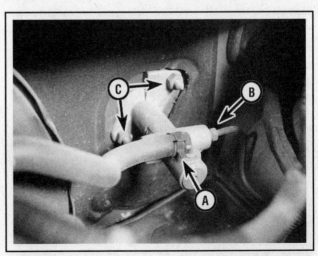

5.4 Disconnect the fluid feed hose (A), the hydraulic line (B), and remove the clutch master cylinder mounting nuts (C)

6 Clutch release cylinder - replacement

1   Remove the banjo bolt and disconnect the hydraulic line from the release cylinder (see illustration).

➡ **Note: Discard the sealing washers - new ones should be obtained for installation.**

2   Unscrew the fasteners securing the release cylinder to the transaxl and remove the release cylinder.

3   Installation is the reverse of removal, noting the following points:

a) *Lubricate the contact point with the clutch lever with a light film of high-temperature grease.*

b) *Apply a thread locking compound to the release cylinder mounting fasteners and tighten them to the torque listed in this Chapter's Specifications.*

c) *Connect the hydraulic fitting. Be sure to use new sealing washers on either side of the fitting.*

d) *Check the fluid level in the brake fluid reservoir, adding brake fluid conforming to DOT 3 specifications until the level is correct.*

e) *Bleed the system (see Section 7).*

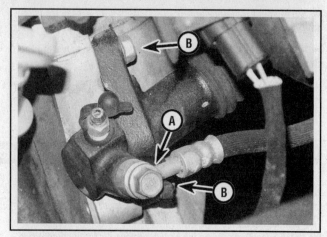

6.1 Remove the banjo bolt (A) and the fasteners securing the release cylinder to the transaxle (B)

7 Clutch hydraulic system - bleeding

➡ **Note: Bleed the hydraulic system whenever any part of the system has been removed or the fluid level has fallen so low that air has been drawn into the master cylinder. The bleeding procedure is very similar to bleeding a brake system.**

1   Fill the brake master cylinder reservoir with new brake fluid conforming to DOT 3 specifications.

7.2 Clutch release cylinder bleeder valve fitting

✳✳ CAUTION:

Do not re-use any of the fluid coming from the system during the bleeding operation or use fluid which has been inside an open container for an extended period of time.

2   Connect a brake bleeder hose to the bleeder valve fitting at the clutch release cylinder (see illustration).

3   Have an assistant fully depress and release the clutch pedal several times.

4   With the clutch pedal depressed, open the bleeder valve.

5   Continue to have your assistant depress the clutch pedal. Close the bleeder valve when fluid stops coming out of the release cylinder.

6   Have your assistant release the clutch pedal only after the bleeder valve is closed.

7   Continue this process until all air is removed from the system, indicated by no air bubbles.

➡ **Note: Wash the area with water to remove any spilled brake fluid.**

8   Check the brake fluid level again, and add some, if necessary, to bring it to the appropriate level. Check carefully for proper operation before placing the vehicle into normal service.

9   Check the feel of the brake pedal. If it feels spongy when depressed, bleed the brake hydraulic system (see Chapter 9).

8 Clutch components - removal, inspection and installation

✳ WARNING:

Dust produced by clutch wear is hazardous to your health. DO NOT blow it out with compressed air and DO NOT inhale it. DO NOT use gasoline or petroleum-based solvents to remove the dust. Brake system cleaner should be used to flush the dust into a drain pan. After the clutch components are wiped clean with a rag, dispose of the contaminated rags and cleaner in a covered, marked container.

REMOVAL

1 Access to the clutch components is normally accomplished by removing the transaxle, leaving the engine in the vehicle. If the engine is being removed for major overhaul, check the clutch for wear and replace worn components as necessary. However, the relatively low cost of the clutch components compared to the time and trouble spent gaining access to them warrants their replacement anytime the engine or transaxle is removed, unless they are new or in near-perfect condition. The following procedures are based on the assumption the engine will stay in place.

2 Remove the transaxle (see Chapter 7A). Support the engine while the transaxle is out. Preferably, an engine support fixture or a hoist should be used to support it from above.

3 To support the clutch disc during removal, install a clutch alignment tool through the clutch disc hub. The tool is available at most auto parts stores.

4 Carefully inspect the flywheel and pressure plate for indexing marks. The marks are usually an X, an O or a black mark. If they cannot

be found, scribe or paint marks yourself so the pressure plate and the flywheel will be in the same alignment during installation (see illustration).

5 Turning each bolt a little at a time, loosen the pressure plate-to-flywheel bolts. Work in a criss-cross pattern until all spring pressure is relieved evenly. Then hold the pressure plate securely and completely remove the bolts, followed by the pressure plate and clutch disc.

6 To remove the clutch release bearing, detach it from the release arm and slide it off the transaxle input shaft.

7 To remove the pilot bearing, use a slide hammer with an appropriate adapter or a suitable tool.

INSPECTION

8 Ordinarily, when a problem occurs in the clutch, it can be attributed to wear of the clutch driven plate assembly (clutch disc). However, all components should be inspected at this time.

9 Inspect the flywheel for cracks, heat checking, grooves and other obvious defects. If the imperfections are slight, a machine shop can machine the surface flat and smooth, which is highly recommended regardless of the surface appearance. Refer to Chapter 2A for the flywheel removal and installation procedure.

10 Inspect the lining on the clutch disc. There should be at least 1/16-inch of lining above the rivet heads. Check for loose rivets, distortion, cracks, broken springs/dampers and other obvious damage (see illustration). As mentioned above, ordinarily the clutch disc is routinely replaced, so if in doubt about the condition, replace it with a new one.

11 The clutch release bearing and pilot bearing should also be replaced along with the clutch disc.

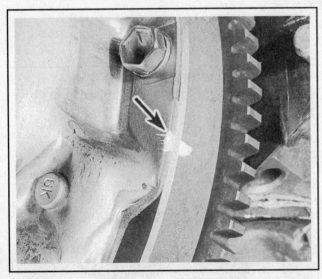

8.4 Mark the relationship of the pressure plate to the flywheel (if you're planning to re-use the old pressure plate)

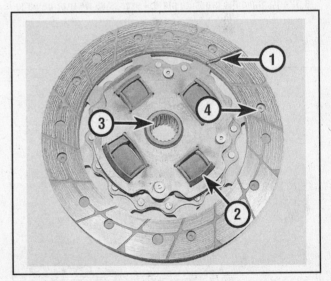

8.10 The clutch disc

1 *Lining - this will wear down in use*
2 *Springs or dampers - check for cracking and deformation*
3 *Splined hub - the splines must not be worn and should slide smoothly on the transmission input shaft splines*
4 *Rivets - these secure the lining and will damage the flywheel or pressure plate if allowed to contact the surfaces*

12 Check the machined surfaces and the diaphragm spring fingers of the pressure plate (see illustrations). If the surface is grooved or otherwise damaged, replace the pressure plate. Also check for obvious damage, distortion, cracking, etc. Light glazing can be removed with emery cloth or sandpaper. If a new pressure plate is required, new and remanufactured units are available.

INSTALLATION

13 Install the pilot bearing into the end of the crankshaft carefully using a brass drift or a socket of the same diameter as the pilot bearing. Lubricate the transaxle input shaft tip with a light film of high-temperature grease before installation.

14 Clean the flywheel and pressure plate machined surfaces with brake system cleaner. It's important that no oil or grease is on these surfaces or the lining of the clutch disc. Handle the parts only with clean hands.

15 Position the clutch disc and pressure plate against the flywheel with the clutch held in place with an alignment tool (see illustration). Make sure the disc is installed properly (most replacement clutch discs will be marked "flywheel side" or something similar - if not marked, install the clutch disc with the damper springs toward the transaxle).

16 Tighten the pressure plate-to-flywheel bolts only finger tight, working around the pressure plate.

17 Center the clutch disc by ensuring the alignment tool extends through the splined hub and into the pilot bearing in the crankshaft. Wiggle the tool up, down or side-to-side as needed to center the disc. Install and tighten the pressure plate-to-flywheel bolts a little at a time, working in a criss-cross pattern to prevent distorting the cover. After all of the bolts are snug, tighten them to the torque listed in this Chapter's Specifications. Remove the alignment tool.

18 Before installing the clutch release bearing, lubricate the input shaft and clutch release lever contact points with a light film of high-temperature grease. Install the clutch release bearing by sliding onto the transaxle input shaft and engaging with the clutch release lever.

19 Install the transaxle and all components removed previously.

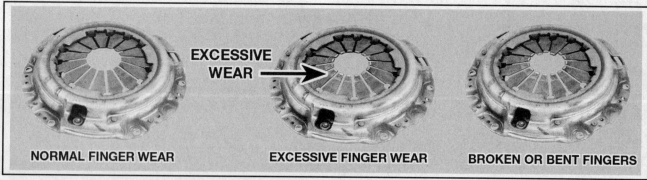

NORMAL FINGER WEAR   EXCESSIVE FINGER WEAR   BROKEN OR BENT FINGERS

EXCESSIVE WEAR

8.12a Replace the pressure plate if excessive wear or damage is noted

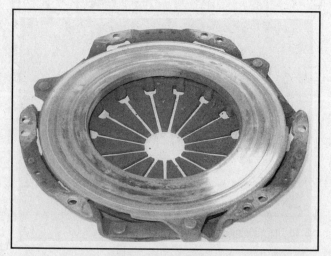

8.12b Inspect the pressure plate surface for excessive score marks, cracks and signs of overheating

8.15 Center the clutch disc in the pressure plate with a clutch alignment tool

9 Clutch pedal position sensor - check and replacement

1   In the passenger compartment, remove the driver's side lower trim panel, if equipped (see Chapter 11).

CHECK

2   Verify that the engine will not start when the clutch pedal is released. Now, depress the clutch pedal - the engine should start.

3   Locate the sensor on the clutch pedal bracket and unplug the electrical connector.

4   Using an ohmmeter, verify that there is continuity between the terminals of the sensor when the pedal is depressed. There should be no continuity when the pedal is released.

5   If the sensor does not work as described, replace it.

REPLACEMENT

6   Unplug the electrical connector from the sensor (see illustration).

7   Turn the sensor 90-degrees and pull it from its bracket.

8   Installation is the reverse of removal. The sensor is self-adjusting, so there's no need for adjustment.

9   Verify that the engine doesn't start when the clutch pedal is released, and does start when the pedal is depressed.

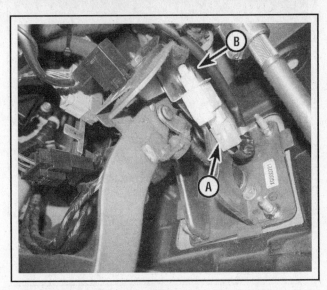

9.6 Unplug the electrical connector and twist the sensor 90-degrees to free it from the bracket

10 Driveaxles - removal and installation

✱✱ WARNING:

The manufacturer recommends replacing the driveaxle/hub nuts with new ones whenever they are removed.

REMOVAL

1   Set the parking brake. Remove the wheel cover or hubcap.

2   If you're working on a model with a manual transaxle, drain the transaxle lubricant (see Chapter 1).

3   Loosen the front wheel lug nuts, raise the vehicle and suapport it securely on jackstands. Remove the wheel.

4   Unstake the driveaxle/hub nut (see illustration).

5   Remove the driveaxle/hub nut (see illustration).

✱✱ CAUTION:

Discard the nut and obtain a new one for installation.

10.4 Use a hammer and chisel to unstake the driveaxle/hub nut

10.5 Insert a large punch or screwdriver into the disc cooling vanes and allow it to rest against the caliper, then unscrew the driveaxle/hub nut

10.8 If the driveaxle sticks in the hub splines, a puller like this can be used to push it out

10.10 Remove the damping block bolts (rear transaxle mount) and the bracket

10.12 Using a large prybar, carefully pry the inner end of the driveaxle from the transaxle

6 Disconnect the tie-rod end from the steering knuckle (see Chapter 10).

7 Disconnect the ABS wheel speed sensor (see Chapter 9). Separate the control arm balljoint from the steering knuckle (see Chapter 10).

8 To loosen the driveaxle from the hub splines, tap the end of the driveaxle with a soft-faced hammer. If the driveaxle is stuck in the hub splines and won't move, it may be necessary to push it from the hub with a puller (see illustration).

9 Pull out on the steering knuckle and detach the driveaxle from the hub. Suspend the outer end of the driveaxle on a bungee cord or piece of wire.

10 If you're removing the right-side driveaxle, remove the damping block nut and bolt and the four rear mount bracket bolts and the bracket (see illustration).

➡ Note: This step isn't absolutely necessary, but makes prying out the driveaxle easier.

11 Before you remove the driveaxle, look for lubricant leakage in the area around the differential seal. If there's evidence of a leak, you'll want to replace the seal after removing the driveaxle (see Chapter 7A or 7B).

⁂ CAUTION:

The seal is easily damaged by the splines on the driveaxle, which can cut the seal and cause a fluid leak.

12 Position a prybar against the inner joint and carefully pry the joint out of the transaxle (see illustration). Do not use the driveaxle to pull on the inner joint. Doing so might damage the inner joint components. Remove the driveaxle assembly, being careful not to over-extend the inner joint or damage the axleshaft boots.

13 Should it become necessary to move the vehicle while the driveaxle is out, place a large bolt with two large washers (one on each side of the hub) through the hub and tighten the nut securely.

INSTALLATION

14 Installation is the reverse of removal, noting the following points:

a) Apply a film of multi-purpose grease around the splines of the joints.

b) When installing the driveaxle, push it in sharply to seat the driveaxle set-ring. To make sure the set-ring is properly seated, attempt to pull the inner CV joint housing out of the transaxle by hand. If the set-ring is properly seated the inner joint will not move out.

c) Clean all foreign matter from the driveaxle outer CV joint threads and coat the splines with multi-purpose grease. Guide the driveaxle into the hub splines and install the NEW driveaxle/hub nut. Tighten the nut securely but not to the specified torque at this time.

d) Reconnect the control arm and tie-rod end, then tighten the suspension fasteners to the torque listed in the Chapter 10 Specifications.

e) Insert a punch into the disc cooling vanes and tighten the driveaxle/hub nut to the torque listed in this Chapter's Specifications, then stake the collar of the nut into the groove in the driveaxle.

f) Install the wheel and lug nuts, then lower the vehicle.

g) Tighten the wheel lug nuts to the torque listed in the Chapter 10 Specifications.

h) Add transaxle lubricant if it was drained or if any fluid spilled out (see Chapter 1).

Specifications

Clutch fluid type	See Chapter 1	

Clutch cable adjustment specifications	**Inches**	**mm**
Clutch pedal travel for disengaging clutch	4.5 to 5.1	120 to 130
Clutch pedal-to-floor clearance at clutch engagement	1.9 to 2.3	50 to 60

Torque specifications

	Ft-lbs (unless otherwise indicated)	**Nm**

➡ **Note: One foot-pound (ft-lb) of torque is equivalent to 12 inch-pounds (in-lbs) of torque. Torque values below approximately 15 foot-pounds are expressed in inch-pounds, because most foot-pound torque wrenches are not accurate at these smaller values.**

	Ft-lbs (unless otherwise indicated)	Nm
Clutch pressure plate-to-flywheel bolts		
D16 transaxle	132 in-lbs	15
Y4M transaxle	156 in-lbs	18
Clutch master cylinder nuts	16	22
Clutch release cylinder bolts	15	20
Dampening block nut/bolt	59	80
Driveaxle/hub nut	221	300
Rear mount bracket bolts	44	60
Wheel lug nuts	See Chapter 1	

Notes

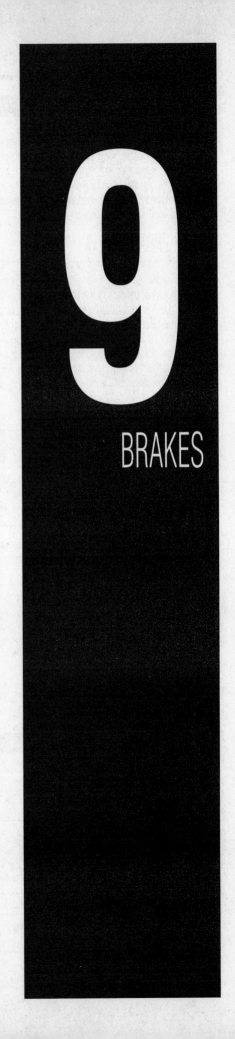

9

BRAKES

Section

1 General Information

1 The vehicles covered by this manual are equipped with hydraulically operated front and rear brake systems. The front brakes are disc type and the rear brakes are drum type. Both the front and rear brakes are self adjusting. The disc brakes automatically compensate for pad wear, while the drum brakes incorporate an adjustment mechanism that is activated as the brake is applied.

HYDRAULIC SYSTEM

2 The hydraulic system consists of two separate circuits. The master cylinder has separate reservoir chambers for the two circuits, and, in the event of a leak or failure in one hydraulic circuit, the other circuit will remain operative. On models without ABS, the master cylinder incorporates proportioning valves to limit pressure to the rear brakes past a certain point to prevent rear-wheel lockup. On models with ABS, a dynamic proportioning valve, integral with the ABS hydraulic unit, provides brake balance to each individual wheel.

POWER BRAKE BOOSTER

3 The power brake booster, utilizing engine manifold vacuum, and atmospheric pressure to provide assistance to the hydraulically operated brakes, is mounted on the firewall in the engine compartment.

PARKING BRAKE

4 The parking brake operates the rear brakes only, through cable actuation. It's activated by a lever mounted in the center console.

SERVICE

5 After completing any operation involving disassembly of any part of the brake system, always test drive the vehicle to check for proper braking performance before resuming normal driving. When testing the brakes, perform the tests on a clean, dry, flat surface. Conditions other than these can lead to inaccurate test results.

6 Test the brakes at various speeds with both light and heavy pedal pressure. The vehicle should stop evenly without pulling to one side or the other. Avoid locking the brakes, because this slides the tires and diminishes braking efficiency and control of the vehicle.

7 Tires, vehicle load and wheel alignment are factors which also affect braking performance.

PRECAUTIONS

8 There are some general cautions and warnings involving the brake system on this vehicle:

a) *Use only brake fluid conforming to DOT 3 specifications.*

b) *The brake pads and linings contain fibers that are hazardous to your health if inhaled. Whenever you work on brake system components, clean all parts with brake system cleaner. Do not allow the fine dust to become airborne. Also, wear an approved filtering mask.*

c) *Safety should be paramount whenever any servicing of the brake components is performed. Do not use parts or fasteners that are not in perfect condition, and be sure that all clearances and torque specifications are adhered to. If you are at all unsure about a certain procedure, seek professional advice. Upon completion of any brake system work, test the brakes carefully in a controlled area before putting the vehicle into normal service. If a problem is suspected in the brake system, don't drive the vehicle until it's fixed.*

2 Troubleshooting

PROBABLE CAUSE — **CORRECTIVE ACTION**

No brakes - pedal travels to floor

PROBABLE CAUSE	CORRECTIVE ACTION
1 Low fluid level 2 Air in system	1 and 2 Low fluid level and air in the system are symptoms of another problem - a leak somewhere in the hydraulic system. Locate and repair the leak
3 Defective seals in master cylinder	3 Replace master cylinder
4 Fluid overheated and vaporized due to heavy braking	4 Bleed hydraulic system (temporary fix). Replace brake fluid (proper fix)

PROBABLE CAUSE   **CORRECTIVE ACTION**

Brake pedal slowly travels to floor under braking or at a stop

1 Defective seals in master cylinder	1 Replace master cylinder
2 Leak in a hose, line, caliper or wheel cylinder	2 Locate and repair leak
3 Air in hydraulic system	3 Bleed the system, inspect system for a leak

Brake pedal feels spongy when depressed

1 Air in hydraulic system	1 Bleed the system, inspect system for a leak
2 Master cylinder or power booster loose	2 Tighten fasteners
3 Brake fluid overheated (beginning to boil)	3 Bleed the system (temporary fix). Replace the brake fluid (proper fix)
4 Deteriorated brake hoses (ballooning under pressure)	4 Inspect hoses, replace as necessary (it's a good idea to replace all of them if one hose shows signs of deterioration)

Brake pedal feels hard when depressed and/or excessive effort required to stop vehicle

1 Power booster faulty	1 Replace booster
2 Engine not producing sufficient vacuum, or hose to booster clogged, collapsed or cracked	2 Check vacuum to booster with a vacuum gauge. Replace hose if cracked or clogged, repair engine if vacuum is extremely low
3 Brake linings contaminated by grease or brake fluid	3 Locate and repair source of contamination, replace brake pads or shoes
4 Brake linings glazed	4 Replace brake pads or shoes, check discs and drums for glazing, service as necessary
5 Caliper piston(s) or wheel cylinder(s) binding or frozen	5 Replace calipers or wheel cylinders
6 Brakes wet	6 Apply pedal to boil-off water (this should only be a momentary problem)
7 Kinked, clogged or internally split brake hose or line	7 Inspect lines and hoses, replace as necessary

Excessive brake pedal travel (but will pump up)

1 Drum brakes out of adjustment	1 Adjust brakes
2 Air in hydraulic system	2 Bleed system, inspect system for a leak

Troubleshooting (continued)

PROBABLE CAUSE	CORRECTIVE ACTION

Excessive brake pedal travel (but will not pump up)

PROBABLE CAUSE	CORRECTIVE ACTION
1 Master cylinder pushrod misadjusted	1 Adjust pushrod
2 Master cylinder seals defective	2 Replace master cylinder
3 Brake linings worn out	3 Inspect brakes, replace pads and/or shoes
4 Hydraulic system leak	4 Locate and repair leak

Brake pedal doesn't return

PROBABLE CAUSE	CORRECTIVE ACTION
1 Brake pedal binding	1 Inspect pivot bushing and pushrod, repair or lubricate
2 Defective master cylinder	2 Replace master cylinder

Brake pedal pulsates during brake application

PROBABLE CAUSE	CORRECTIVE ACTION
1 Brake drums out-of-round	1 Have drums machined by an automotive machine shop
2 Excessive brake disc runout or disc surfaces out-of-parallel	2 Have discs machined by an automotive machine shop
3 Loose or worn wheel bearings	3 Adjust or replace wheel bearings
4 Loose lug nuts	4 Tighten lug nuts

Brakes slow to release

PROBABLE CAUSE	CORRECTIVE ACTION
1 Malfunctioning power booster	1 Replace booster
2 Pedal linkage binding	2 Inspect pedal pivot bushing and pushrod, repair/lubricate
3 Malfunctioning proportioning valve	3 Replace proportioning valve
4 Sticking caliper or wheel cylinder	4 Repair or replace calipers or wheel cylinders
5 Kinked or internally split brake hose	5 Locate and replace faulty brake hose

Brakes grab (one or more wheels)

PROBABLE CAUSE	CORRECTIVE ACTION
1 Grease or brake fluid on brake lining	1 Locate and repair cause of contamination, replace lining
2 Brake lining glazed	2 Replace lining, deglaze disc or drum

Troubleshooting (continued)

PROBABLE CAUSE | **CORRECTIVE ACTION**

Vehicle pulls to one side during braking

PROBABLE CAUSE	CORRECTIVE ACTION
1 Grease or brake fluid on brake lining	1 Locate and repair cause of contamination, replace lining
2 Brake lining glazed	2 Deglaze or replace lining, deglaze disc or drum
3 Restricted brake line or hose	3 Repair line or replace hose
4 Tire pressures incorrect	4 Adjust tire pressures
5 Caliper or wheel cylinder sticking	5 Repair or replace calipers or wheel cylinders
6 Wheels out of alignment	6 Have wheels aligned
7 Weak suspension spring	7 Replace springs
8 Weak or broken shock absorber	8 Replace shock absorbers

Brakes drag (indicated by sluggish engine performance or wheels being very hot after driving)

PROBABLE CAUSE	CORRECTIVE ACTION
1 Brake pedal pushrod incorrectly adjusted	1 Adjust pushrod
2 Master cylinder pushrod (between booster and master cylinder) incorrectly adjusted	2 Adjust pushrod
3 Obstructed compensating port in master cylinder	3 Replace master cylinder
4 Master cylinder piston seized in bore	4 Replace master cylinder
5 Contaminated fluid causing swollen seals throughout system	5 Flush system, replace all hydraulic components
6 Clogged brake lines or internally split brake hose(s)	6 Flush hydraulic system, replace defective hose(s)
7 Sticking caliper(s) or wheel cylinder(s)	7 Replace calipers or wheel cylinders
8 Parking brake not releasing	8 Inspect parking brake linkage and parking brake mechanism, repair as required
9 Improper shoe-to-drum clearance	9 Adjust brake shoes
10 Faulty proportioning valve	10 Replace proportioning valve

Brakes fade (due to excessive heat)

PROBABLE CAUSE	CORRECTIVE ACTION
1 Brake linings excessively worn or glazed	1 Deglaze or replace brake pads and/or shoes
2 Excessive use of brakes	2 Downshift into a lower gear, maintain a constant slower speed (going down hills)
3 Vehicle overloaded	3 Reduce load
4 Brake drums or discs worn too thin	4 Measure drum diameter and disc thickness, replace drums or discs as required
5 Contaminated brake fluid	5 Flush system, replace fluid
6 Brakes drag	6 Repair cause of dragging brakes
7 Driver resting left foot on brake pedal	7 Don't ride the brakes

PROBABLE CAUSE	CORRECTIVE ACTION

Brakes noisy (high-pitched squeal)

PROBABLE CAUSE	CORRECTIVE ACTION
1 Glazed lining	1 Deglaze or replace lining
2 Contaminated lining (brake fluid, grease, etc.)	2 Repair source of contamination, replace linings
3 Weak or broken brake shoe hold-down or return spring	3 Replace springs
4 Rivets securing lining to shoe or backing plate loose	4 Replace shoes or pads
5 Excessive dust buildup on brake linings	5 Wash brakes off with brake system cleaner
6 Brake drums worn too thin	6 Measure diameter of drums, replace if necessary
7 Wear indicator on disc brake pads contacting disc	7 Replace brake pads
8 Anti-squeal shims missing or installed improperly	8 Install shims correctly

Brakes noisy (scraping sound)

PROBABLE CAUSE	CORRECTIVE ACTION
1 Brake pads or shoes worn out; rivets, backing plate or brake shoe metal contacting disc or drum	1 Replace linings, have discs and/or drums machined (or replace)

Brakes chatter

PROBABLE CAUSE	CORRECTIVE ACTION
1 Worn brake lining	1 Inspect brakes, replace shoes or pads as necessary
2 Glazed or scored discs or drums	2 Deglaze discs or drums with sandpaper (if glazing is severe, machining will be required)
3 Drums or discs heat checked	3 Check discs and/or drums for hard spots, heat checking, etc. Have discs/ drums machined or replace them
4 Disc runout or drum out-of-round excessive	4 Measure disc runout and/or drum out-of-round, have discs or drums machined or replace them
5 Loose or worn wheel bearings	5 Adjust or replace wheel bearings
6 Loose or bent brake backing plate (drum brakes)	6 Tighten or replace backing plate
7 Grooves worn in discs or drums	7 Have discs or drums machined, if within limits (if not, replace them)
8 Brake linings contaminated (brake fluid, grease, etc.)	8 Locate and repair source of contamination, replace pads or shoes
9 Excessive dust buildup on linings	9 Wash brakes with brake system cleaner

PROBABLE CAUSE | **CORRECTIVE ACTION**

Brakes chatter (continued)

Probable Cause	Corrective Action
10 Surface finish on discs or drums too rough after machining (especially on vehicles with sliding calipers)	10 Have discs or drums properly machined
11 Brake pads or shoes glazed	11 Deglaze or replace brake pads or shoes

Brake pads or shoes click

Probable Cause	Corrective Action
1 Shoe support pads on brake backing plate grooved or excessively worn	1 Replace brake backing plate
2 Brake pads loose in caliper	2 Loose pad retainers or anti-rattle clips
3 Also see items listed under Brakes chatter	

Brakes make groaning noise at end of stop

Probable Cause	Corrective Action
1 Brake pads and/or shoes worn out	1 Replace pads and/or shoes
2 Brake linings contaminated (brake fluid, grease, etc.)	2 Locate and repair cause of contamination, replace brake pads or shoes
3 Brake linings glazed	3 Deglaze or replace brake pads or shoes
4 Excessive dust buildup on linings	4 Wash brakes with brake system cleaner
5 Scored or heat-checked discs or drums	5 Inspect discs/drums, have machined if within limits (if not, replace discs or drums)
6 Broken or missing brake shoe attaching hardware	6 Inspect drum brakes, replace missing hardware

Rear brakes lock up under light brake application

Probable Cause	Corrective Action
1 Tire pressures too high	1 Adjust tire pressures
2 Tires excessively worn	2 Replace tires
3 Defective proportioning valve	3 Replace proportioning valve

Brake warning light on instrument panel comes on (or stays on)

Probable Cause	Corrective Action
1 Low fluid level in master cylinder reservoir (reservoirs with fluid level sensor)	1 Add fluid, inspect system for leak, check the thickness of the brake pads and shoes
2 Failure in one half of the hydraulic system	2 Inspect hydraulic system for a leak

Troubleshooting (continued)

PROBABLE CAUSE	CORRECTIVE ACTION

Brake warning light on instrument panel comes on (or stays on) (continued)

PROBABLE CAUSE	CORRECTIVE ACTION
3 Piston in pressure differential warning valve not centered	3 Center piston by bleeding one circuit or the other (close bleeder valve as soon as the light goes out)
4 Defective pressure differential valve or warning switch	4 Replace valve or switch
5 Air in the hydraulic system	5 Bleed the system, check for leaks
6 Brake pads worn out (vehicles with electric wear sensors - small probes that fit into the brake pads and ground out on the disc when the pads get thin)	6 Replace brake pads (and sensors)

Brakes do not self adjust

Disc brakes

PROBABLE CAUSE	CORRECTIVE ACTION
1 Defective caliper piston seals	1 Replace calipers. Also, possible contaminated fluid causing soft or swollen seals (flush system and fill with new fluid if in doubt)
2 Corroded caliper piston(s)	2 Same as above

Drum brakes

PROBABLE CAUSE	CORRECTIVE ACTION
1 Adjuster screw frozen	1 Remove adjuster, disassemble, clean and lubricate with high-temperature grease
2 Adjuster lever does not contact star wheel or is binding	2 Inspect drum brakes, assemble correctly or clean or replace parts as required
3 Adjusters mixed up (installed on wrong wheels after brake job)	3 Reassemble correctly
4 Adjuster cable broken or installed incorrectly (cable-type adjusters)	4 Install new cable or assemble correctly

Rapid brake lining wear

PROBABLE CAUSE	CORRECTIVE ACTION
1 Driver resting left foot on brake pedal	1 Don't ride the brakes
2 Surface finish on discs or drums too rough	2 Have discs or drums properly machined
3 Also see Brakes drag	

3 Anti-lock Brake System (ABS) - general information

GENERAL INFORMATION

1   The anti-lock brake system is designed to maintain vehicle steerability, directional stability and optimum deceleration under severe braking conditions on most road surfaces. It does so by monitoring the rotational speed of each wheel and controlling the brake line pressure to each wheel during braking. This prevents the wheels from locking up.

2   The ABS system has three main components - the wheel speed sensors, the electronic control unit (ECU) and hydraulic unit (which are combined into one assembly). Four wheel speed sensors - one at each wheel - send a variable voltage signal to the control unit, which monitors these signals, compares them to its program and determines whether a wheel is about to lock up. When a wheel is about to lock up, the control unit signals the hydraulic unit to reduce hydraulic pressure (or not increase it further) at that wheel's brake. Pressure modulation is handled by electrically operated solenoid valves.

3   If a problem develops within the system, an "ABS" warning light will glow on the dashboard. Sometimes, a visual inspection of the ABS system can help you locate the problem. Carefully inspect the ABS wiring harness. Pay particularly close attention to the harness and connections near each wheel. Look for signs of chafing and other damage caused by incorrectly routed wires. If a wheel sensor harness is damaged, the sensor must be replaced.

✲✲ WARNING:

Do NOT try to repair an ABS wiring harness. The ABS system is sensitive to even the smallest changes in resistance. Repairing the harness could alter resistance values and cause the system to malfunction. If the ABS wiring harness is damaged in any way, the damaged portion must be replaced.

✲✲ CAUTION:

Make sure the ignition is turned off before unplugging or reattaching any electrical connections.

DIAGNOSIS AND REPAIR

4   On models equipped with ABS, if a dashboard warning light comes on and stays on while the vehicle is in operation, the ABS system requires attention. Although special electronic ABS diagnostic testing tools are necessary to properly diagnose the system, you can perform a few preliminary checks before taking the vehicle to a dealer service department.

 a) *Check the brake fluid level in the reservoir.*
 b) *Verify that the computer electrical connectors are securely connected.*
 c) *Check the electrical connectors at the hydraulic control unit.*
 d) *Check the fuses.*
 e) *Follow the wiring harness to each wheel and verify that all connections are secure and that the wiring is undamaged.*

5   If the above preliminary checks do not rectify the problem, the vehicle should be diagnosed by a dealer service department or other qualified repair shop. Due to the complex nature of this system, all actual repair work must be done by a qualified automotive technician.

WHEEL SPEED SENSOR - REPLACEMENT

6   Make sure the ignition key is turned to the Off position. Loosen the wheel lug nuts, raise the vehicle and support it securely on jackstands, then remove the wheel.

7   Trace the wiring harness back from the sensor, detaching it from all brackets and clips, then disconnect the electrical connector.

8   Remove the mounting bolt then pull the sensor out from the steering knuckle or the rear axle trailing arm flange/brake backing plate.

9   Installation is the reverse of removal. Tighten the sensor to the torque listed in this Chapter's Specifications.

10 Install the wheel and lug nuts, tightening them securely. Lower the vehicle and tighten the lug nuts to the torque listed in the Chapter 1 Specifications.

4 Disc brake pads - replacement

✲✲ WARNING:

Disc brake pads must be replaced on both front or both rear wheels at the same time - never replace the pads on only one wheel. Also, the dust created by the brake system is harmful to your health. Never blow it out with compressed air and don't inhale any of it. An approved filtering mask should be worn when working on the brakes. Do not, under any circumstances, use petroleum-based solvents to clean brake parts. Use brake system cleaner only!

➡ **Note: Disc brake pad replacement for rear disc brakes is similar to the Steps outlined below for the front pads. See Section 5 for details of rear caliper mounting.**

ALL MODELS

1   Remove the cap from the brake fluid reservoir.

2   Loosen the wheel lug nuts, raise the front of the vehicle and support it securely on jackstands. Block the wheels at the opposite end.

3   Remove the wheels. Work on one brake assembly at a time, using

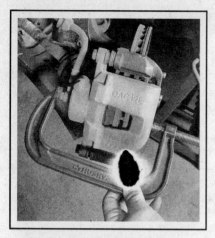

4.5 Before removing the caliper, depress the piston into the bottom of its bore in the caliper with a large C-clamp to make room for the new pads

4.6a Always wash the brakes with brake cleaner before disassembling anything

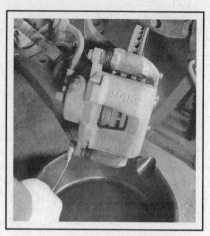

4.6b Remove the caliper lower guide pin bolt. . .

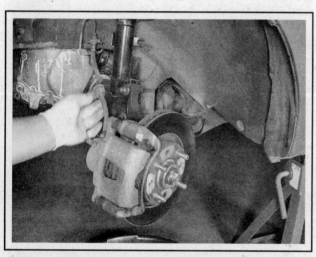

4.6c. . . pull the brake hose out of the bracket. . .

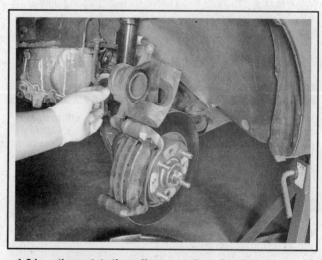

4.6d. . . then rotate the caliper away from the disc and support it with a length of wire

4.6e Pull the inner pad from the support plates in the caliper mount

the assembled brake for reference if necessary.

4   Inspect the brake disc carefully as outlined in Section 6. If machining is necessary, follow the information in that Section to remove the disc, at which time the pads can be removed as well.

5   Push the piston back into its bore to provide room for the new brake pads. A C-clamp can be used to accomplish this (see illustration). As the piston is depressed to the bottom of the caliper bore, the fluid in the master cylinder will rise. Make sure that it doesn't overflow. If necessary, siphon off some of the fluid.

6   Follow the accompanying photos (illustrations 4.6a through 4.6l), for the actual pad replacement procedure. Be sure to stay in order and read the caption under each illustration.

7   After the job has been completed, firmly depress the brake pedal a few times to bring the pads into contact with the disc. Check the level of the brake fluid, adding some if necessary. Check the operation of the brakes carefully before placing the vehicle into normal service.

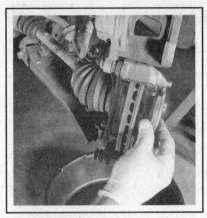

4.6f Pull the outer pad out of the caliper mount

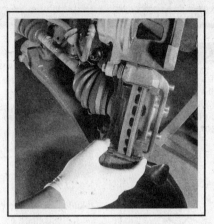

4.6g Remove and inspect the support plates - if they're damaged or fit loosely, replace them. Before installing the support plates, lightly lubricate the contact areas on the mounting bracket with silicone brake lubricant

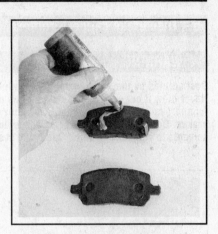

4.6h Apply some anti-squeal compound to the backs of the new brake pads

4.6i Clean the caliper guide pins of dirt and grease, then coat them with caliper lube

4.6j With the support plates installed, install the outer pad

4.6k Install the new outer pad - the inner pad has a brake wear sensor, which should be positioned at the bottom

4.6l Install the guide pins and caliper, then install the guide pin bolts and tighten them to the torque listed in this Chapter's Specifications

5 Disc brake caliper - removal and installation

✳✳ WARNING:

Dust created by the brake system is harmful to your health. Never blow it out with compressed air and don't inhale any of it. An approved filtering mask should be worn when working on the brakes. Do not, under any circumstances, use petroleum-based solvents to clean brake parts. Use brake system cleaner only.

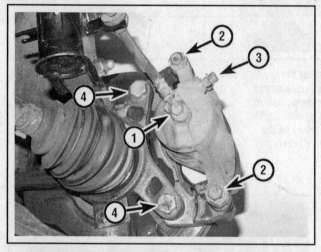

5.2 Front brake caliper details:

1   Brake hose banjo bolt
2   Caliper guide pin bolts
3   Bleeder screw
4   Caliper mounting bracket bolts

➡ Note: If replacement is indicated (usually because of fluid leakage), it is recommended that the calipers be replaced, not overhauled. New and factory rebuilt units are available on an exchange basis, which makes this job quite easy. Always replace the calipers in pairs - never replace just one of them.

REMOVAL

1   Loosen - but don't remove - the lug nuts on the front wheels. Raise the front of the vehicle and support it securely on jackstands. Remove the front wheels.
2   Disconnect the brake line from the caliper and plug it to keep contaminants out of the brake system and to prevent losing any more brake fluid than is necessary (see illustration).

➡ Note: If you're only removing the caliper for access to other components, don't disconnect the hose.

3   Remove the caliper guide pin bolts. Detach the caliper from its mounting bracket.

INSTALLATION

4   Install the caliper by reversing the removal procedure. Remember to replace the copper sealing washers on either side of the brake line fitting with new ones. Tighten the caliper guide pin bolts and the brake line banjo fitting bolt to the torque listed in this Chapter's Specifications.
5   Bleed the brake system (see Section 11).
6   Install the wheels and lug nuts and lower the vehicle. Tighten the wheel lug nuts to the torque listed in the Chapter 1 Specifications.

6 Brake disc - inspection, removal and installation

✳✳ WARNING:

The dust created by the brake system is harmful to your health. Never blow it out with compressed air and don't inhale any of it. An approved filtering mask should be worn when working on the brakes. Do not, under any circumstances, use petroleum-based solvents to clean brake parts. Use brake system cleaner only!

INSPECTION

1   Loosen the wheel lug nuts, raise the vehicle and support it securely on jackstands. Remove the wheel and install the lug nuts to hold the disc in place against the hub flange.

➡ Note: If the lug nuts don't contact the disc when screwed on all the way, install washers under them. If you're checking the rear disc, release the parking brake.

2   Remove the two caliper mounting bracket-to-steering knuckle bolts (see illustration 5.2) and remove the caliper and bracket as a unit. It isn't necessary to disconnect the brake hose. Suspend the caliper/bracket out of the way with a piece of wire.
3   Visually inspect the disc surface for score marks and other dam-

age. Light scratches and shallow grooves are normal after use and may not always be detrimental to brake operation, but deep scoring requires disc refinishing by an automotive machine shop. Be sure to check both sides of the disc (see illustration). If pulsating has been noticed during application of the brakes, suspect disc runout.

6.3 The brake pads on this vehicle were obviously neglected, as they wore down completely and cut deep grooves into the disc - wear this severe means the disc must be replaced

6.4a To check disc runout, mount a dial indicator as shown and rotate the disc

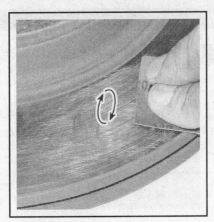

6.4b Using a swirling motion, remove the glaze from the disc surface with sandpaper or emery cloth

6.5 Use a micrometer to measure disc thickness

4   To check disc runout, install the lug nuts to secure the disc to the hub, using washers if necessary. Place a dial indicator at a point about 1/2-inch from the outer edge of the disc (see illustration). Set the indicator to zero and turn the disc. The indicator reading should not exceed the specified allowable runout limit. If it does, the disc should be refinished by an automotive machine shop. If you elect not to have the discs resurfaced, remove the glaze from the surface with emery cloth or sandpaper, using a swirling motion (see illustration).

➡ Note: Some professionals recommend resurfacing the discs when replacing brake pads regardless of the dial indicator reading, as this will impart a smooth finish and ensure a perfectly flat surface, eliminating any brake pedal pulsation or other undesirable symptoms.

5   It's absolutely critical that the disc not be machined to a thickness under the specified minimum thickness. The minimum (or discard) thickness is cast or stamped into the disc. The disc thickness can be checked with a micrometer (see illustration).

REMOVAL

6   Remove the disc mounting screws, then remove the disc (see illustration). If the disc has never been removed, there may be wave washers on the wheel studs securing it to the hub flange. Simply cut them off and discard them. If the disc is stuck to the hub, use a mallet to knock it loose. Penetrating oil applied around the disc's hub will also help (but don't let any oil get onto the disc friction surface). Clean the disc with brake cleaner after you're done.

INSTALLATION

7   Clean the inner opening in the disc, and the area of the hub on which it seats. Remove any rust with fine emery paper before reinstalling the disc.

6.6 Remove the disc mounting screws

8   Place the disc in position over the threaded studs, aligning the hole for the disc mounting screw, then install the screw and tighten the screw securely.

9   Install the caliper mounting bracket and caliper, tightening the bolts to the torque values listed in this Chapter's Specifications.

➡ Note: The caliper mounting bracket bolts are of a special self-locking design; do not attempt to clean the threaded holes with a tap, or the threads of the bolt with a die.

10 Install the wheel and lug nuts, then lower the vehicle to the ground. Tighten the lug nuts to the torque listed in the Chapter 1 Specifications. Depress the brake pedal a few times to bring the brake pads into contact with the disc. Bleeding won't be necessary unless the brake hose was disconnected from the caliper. Check the operation of the brakes carefully before driving the vehicle.

7 Drum brake shoes - replacement

✳ WARNING:

Drum brake shoes must be replaced on both wheels at the same time - never replace the shoes on only one wheel. Also, the dust created by the brake system is harmful to your health. Never blow it out with compressed air and don't inhale any of it. An approved filtering mask should be worn when working on the brakes. Do not, under any circumstances, use petroleum-based solvents to clean brake parts. Use brake system cleaner only!

1   Loosen the wheel lug nuts, raise the rear of the vehicle and support it securely on jackstands. Block the front wheels to keep the vehicle from rolling. Release the parking brake.

2   Remove the wheels.

3   If you're working on a 2004 model or a 2005 model up to VIN no. 5B4426447, remove the brake drum by referring to Chapter 10, Section 12.

➡ **Note: All four rear brake shoes must be replaced at the same time, but to avoid mixing up parts, work on only one brake assembly at a time.**

4   Follow the accompanying illustrations for the brake shoe replacement procedure (see illustrations 7.4a through 7.4t). Be sure to stay in order and read the caption under each illustration.

➡ **Note: If the brake drum cannot be easily removed, make sure the parking brake is completely released. If the drum still cannot be pulled off, the brake shoes will have to be retracted. This is done by first removing the plug from the backing plate. With the plug removed, push the lever off the adjuster star wheel with a narrow screwdriver while turning the adjuster wheel with another screwdriver, moving the shoes away from the drum. The drum should now come off.**

5   Before reinstalling the drum, it should be checked for cracks, score marks, deep scratches and hard spots, which will appear as small discolored areas. If the hard spots cannot be removed with fine emery cloth or if any of the other conditions listed above exist, the drum must be taken to an automotive machine shop to have it resurfaced.

➡ **Note: Professionals recommend resurfacing the drums each time a brake job is done. Resurfacing will eliminate the possibility of out-of-round drums. If the drums are worn so much that they can't be resurfaced without exceeding the maximum allowable diameter (stamped into the drum), then new drums will be required. At the very least, if you elect not to have the drums resurfaced, remove the glaze from the surface with emery cloth using a swirling motion.**

6   Install the brake drum on the axle flange (be sure to line-up the retaining screw holes). Pump the brake pedal a couple of times, then turn the adjuster star wheel until the shoes rub on the drum when you turn it. Back off the star wheel adjustment a couple of clicks, pump the brake pedal a couple of times, then turn the drum and listen for the sound of the shoes rubbing. If they are, turn the adjuster star wheel until the shoes stop rubbing.

7   Install the wheel and lug nuts, then lower the vehicle. Tighten the lug nuts to the torque listed in the Chapter 1 Specifications.

8   Make a number of forward and reverse stops and operate the parking brake to adjust the brakes until satisfactory pedal action is obtained.

9   Check the operation of the brakes carefully before driving the vehicle.

7.4a Remove the drum retaining screws from the face of the drum (except 2004 and early 2005 models). If they're stuck, the use of an impact driver will be necessary

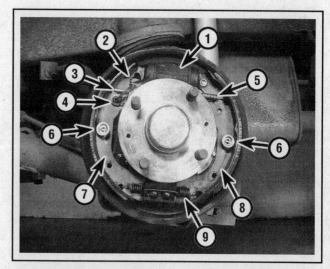

7.4b Rear drum brake details

1	Wheel cylinder	6	Hold-down spring and pin
2	Upper return spring link	7	Leading brake shoe
3	Adjuster screw assembly	8	Trailing brake shoe
4	Adjuster pawl	9	Brake shoe lower
5	Brake shoe upper return spring		return spring

7.4c Always wash the brakes with brake cleaner before disassembling anything

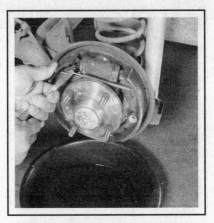

7.4d Using locking pliers, disconnect the end of the upper return spring from the spring link

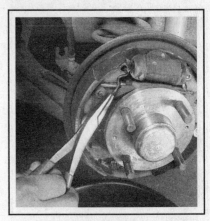

7.4e Remove the upper return spring link from the leading brake shoe and adjuster pawl

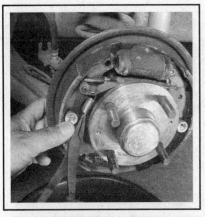

7.4f Remove the adjuster pawl return spring

7.4g Remove the adjuster pawl

7.4h Remove the retainer and hold-down spring from the leading shoe

7.4i Remove the leading shoe and lower return spring

7.4j Remove the adjuster

7.4k Remove the retainer and hold-down spring from the trailing shoe

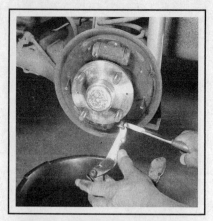

7.4l Use pliers to pull on the cable end and disconnect the parking brake cable from the lever

7.4m Clean and lube the pads on the backing plates with high-temperature brake grease

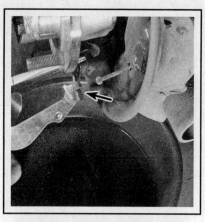

7.4n Using needle nose pliers pull the parking brake cable spring back and hold it, then connect the cable to the parking brake lever

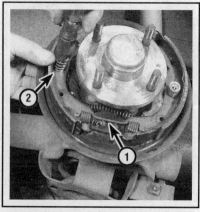

7.4o Install the trailing shoe and hold-down spring, then connect the lower return spring (1), to both shoes and install the leading shoe and hold-down spring (2)

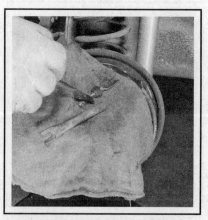

7.4p Clean and lube the threads of the adjuster and reinstall the adjuster in between the shoes (the long end faces toward the rear)

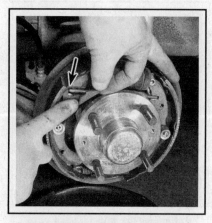

7.4q Install the adjuster pawl onto the pin

7.4r Connect the pawl return spring to the pawl and the back side of the shoe

7.4s Install the upper return spring link

7.4t Connect the upper return spring to the trailing shoe, then use pliers to pull the spring until it can be connected to the spring link

8 Wheel cylinder - removal and installation

➡ **Note: If replacement is indicated (usually because of fluid leakage or sticky operation), it is recommended that the wheel cylinders be replaced, not overhauled. Always replace the wheel cylinders in pairs - never replace just one of them.**

REMOVAL

1 Block the front wheels to keep the vehicle from rolling. Loosen the rear wheel lug nuts, raise the rear of the vehicle and support it securely on jackstands.

2 Remove the wheel.

3 Release the parking brake and remove the brake drum as described in Section 7.

4 Remove the brake shoes (see Section 7).

5 Remove all dirt and foreign material from around the wheel cylinder.

6 At the rear of the backing plate, unscrew the brake line fitting, using a flare-nut wrench, if available (see illustration). Don't pull the brake line away from the wheel cylinder (it could become kinked).

7 Remove the wheel cylinder mounting bolt and detach the wheel cylinder from the backing plate.

INSTALLATION

8 Place the wheel cylinder in position and connect the brake line fitting finger tight. Install the wheel cylinder mounting bolt and tighten them to the torque listed in this Chapter's Specifications. Tighten the brake line fitting securely. Install the bleeder screw and cap.

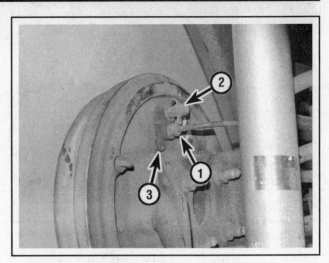

8.6 Rear wheel cylinder details

1	Fluid line fitting	3	Mounting bolt
2	Bleed screw		

9 Install the brake shoes (see Section 7).

10 Install the brake drum on the hub flange, then install the wheel and lug nuts.

11 Bleed the brake system as outlined in Section 11.

12 Lower the vehicle to the ground, then tighten the lug nuts to the torque listed in the Chapter 1 Specifications. Check the operation of the brakes carefully before driving the vehicle in traffic.

9 Master cylinder - removal and installation

REMOVAL

1 The master cylinder is located in left rear corner of the engine compartment, mounted to the power brake booster.

2 Disconnect the negative battery cable (see Chapter 5).

3 Remove as much fluid as you can from the reservoir with a suction gun or an old turkey baster.

✳✳ WARNING:

If a baster is used, never again use it for the preparation of food.

✳✳ WARNING:

Don't depress the brake pedal until the reservoir has been refilled, otherwise air may be introduced into the brake hydraulic system.

4 On models with a manual transaxle, disconnect the clutch fluid hose from the brake master cylinder reservoir (see illustration 9.6). Plug the line or wrap it with a plastic bag.

✳✳ CAUTION:

Brake fluid will damage paint. Cover all painted surfaces around the work area and be careful not to spill fluid during this procedure.

5 Place rags under the fluid fittings and prepare caps or plastic bags to cover the ends of the lines once they are disconnected. Loosen the fittings at the ends of the brake lines where they enter the master cylinder. To prevent rounding off the corners on these nuts, the use of a flare-nut wrench, which wraps around the nut, is preferred. Pull the brake lines slightly away from the master cylinder and plug the ends to prevent contamination.

6 Disconnect the electrical connector at the brake fluid level switch on the master cylinder reservoir, then remove the nuts attaching the master cylinder to the power booster (see illustration). Pull the master cylinder off the studs and out of the engine compartment. Again, be careful not to spill the fluid as this is done.

7 If a new master cylinder is being installed, drive out the two retaining pins that hold the reservoir to the master cylinder body. Transfer the reservoir to the new master cylinder. If the same master cylinder is to be installed, check the condition of the master cylinder-to-booster seal for damage or hardness, replacing it if necessary.

➡ **Note: Install new seals when transferring the reservoir.**

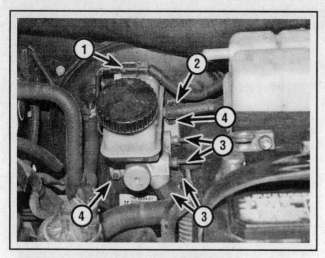

9.6 Brake master cylinder mounting details

1   Brake fluid level sensor connector
2   Clutch fluid hose
3   Brake line fittings
4   Mounting nuts

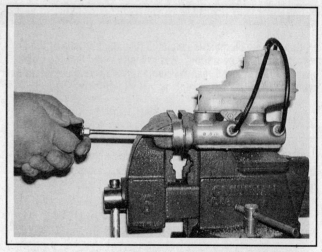

9.9 The best way to bleed air from the master cylinder before installing it on the vehicle is with a pair of bleeder tubes that direct brake fluid into the reservoir during bleeding (typical)

INSTALLATION

8   Bench bleed the new master cylinder before installing it. Mount the master cylinder in a vise, with the jaws of the vise clamping on the mounting flange.

9   Attach a pair of master cylinder bleeder tubes to the outlet ports of the master cylinder (see illustration).

10   If equipped, plug the clutch hose fitting. Fill the reservoir with brake fluid of the recommended type (see Chapter 1).

11   Slowly push the pistons into the master cylinder (a large Phillips screwdriver can be used for this) - air will be expelled from the pressure chambers and into the reservoir. Because the tubes are submerged in fluid, air can't be drawn back into the master cylinder when you release the pistons.

12   Repeat the procedure until no more air bubbles are present.

13   Remove the bleed tubes, one at a time, and install plugs in the open ports to prevent fluid leakage and air from entering. Install the reservoir cap.

14   Install the master cylinder over the studs on the power brake booster and tighten the new attaching nuts only finger tight at this time.

➡ **Note: Install a new O-ring onto the sleeve of the master cylinder.**

15   Thread the brake line fittings into the master cylinder by hand until you know they are started straight. Since the master cylinder is still a bit loose, it can be moved slightly in order for the fittings to thread in easily. Do not strip the threads as the fittings are tightened.

16   Tighten the mounting nuts to the torque listed in this Chapter's Specifications, then tighten the brake line fittings securely.

17   Connect the brake fluid switch electrical connector.

18   On models with manual transaxles, connect the fluid hose from the clutch master cylinder.

➡ **Note: On manual transaxle models, the clutch hydraulic system will have to be bled (see Chapter 8).**

19   Fill the master cylinder reservoir with fluid, then bleed the master cylinder and the brake system as described in Section 11. To bleed the cylinder on the vehicle, have an assistant depress the brake pedal and hold the pedal to the floor. Loosen the fitting to allow air and fluid to escape, then close the fitting. Repeat this procedure on both fittings until the fluid is clear of air bubbles.

✳✳ CAUTION:

Have plenty of rags on hand to catch the fluid - brake fluid will ruin painted surfaces. After the bleeding procedure is completed, rinse the area under the master cylinder with clean water.

20   Test the operation of the brake system carefully before placing the vehicle into normal service.

✳✳ WARNING:

Do not operate the vehicle if you are in doubt about the effectiveness of the brake system. It is possible for air to become trapped in the anti-lock brake system hydraulic control unit. If the pedal continues to feel spongy after repeated bleedings or the BRAKE or ANTI-LOCK light stays on, have the vehicle towed to a dealer service department or other qualified shop to be bled with the aid of a scan tool.

10 Brake hoses and lines - inspection and replacement

1 About every six months, with the vehicle raised and placed securely on jackstands, the flexible hoses which connect the steel brake lines with the front and rear brake assemblies should be inspected for cracks, chafing of the outer cover, leaks, blisters and other damage. These are important and vulnerable parts of the brake system and inspection should be complete. A light and mirror will be needed for a thorough check. If a hose exhibits any of the above defects, replace it with a new one.

FLEXIBLE HOSES

2 Clean all dirt away from the ends of the hose.

3 To disconnect a brake hose from the brake line, unscrew the tube nut with a flare-nut wrench, then remove the U-clip from the female fitting at the bracket and remove the hose from the bracket (see illustration).

4 Disconnect the hose from the caliper, discarding the sealing washers on either side of the fitting.

5 Using new sealing washers, attach the new brake hose to the caliper.

6 To reattach a brake hose to the metal line, insert the end of the hose through the frame bracket, make sure the hose isn't twisted, then attach the metal line by tightening the tube nut fitting securely. Install the U-clip at the frame bracket.

7 Carefully check to make sure the suspension or steering components don't make contact with the hose.

8 Bleed the brake system (see Section 11).

METAL BRAKE LINES

9 When replacing brake lines, be sure to use the correct parts.

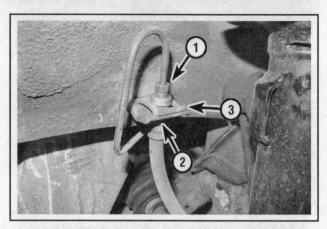

10.3 Using a flare-nut wrench, unscrew the threaded fitting on the brake line (1) while holding the hose end (2) with an open-end wrench, then pry the U-clip (3) off the end of the hose and separate the hose from the bracket

Don't use copper tubing for any brake system components. Purchase steel brake lines from a dealer parts department or auto parts store.

10 Prefabricated brake line, with the tube ends already flared and fittings installed, is available at auto parts stores and dealer parts departments. These lines can be bent to the proper shapes using a tubing bender.

11 When installing the new line, make sure it's well supported in the brackets and has plenty of clearance between moving or hot components.

12 After installation, check the master cylinder fluid level and add fluid as necessary. Bleed the brake system (see Section 11) and test the brakes carefully before placing the vehicle into normal operation.

11 Brake hydraulic system - bleeding

✳✳ WARNING:

If air has found its way into the hydraulic control unit, the system must be bled with the use of a scan tool. If the brake pedal feels spongy even after bleeding the brakes, or the ABS light on the instrument panel does not go off, or if you have any doubts whatsoever about the effectiveness of the brake system, have the vehicle towed to a dealer service department or other repair shop equipped with the necessary tools for bleeding the system.

✳✳ WARNING:

Wear eye protection when bleeding the brake system. If the fluid comes in contact with your eyes, immediately rinse them with water and seek medical attention.

✳✳ CAUTION:

Brake fluid will damage paint. Cover all painted surfaces around the work area and be careful not to spill fluid during this procedure.

➥ **Note:** Bleeding the brake system is necessary to remove any air that's trapped in the system when it's opened during removal and installation of a hose, line, caliper, wheel cylinder or master cylinder.

1 It will probably be necessary to bleed the system at all four brakes if air has entered the system due to a low fluid level, or if the brake lines have been disconnected at the master cylinder.

2 If a brake line was disconnected only at a wheel, then only that caliper or wheel cylinder must be bled.

3 If a brake line is disconnected at a fitting located between the master cylinder and any of the brakes, that part of the system served by the disconnected line must be bled, beginning with the fitting closest to the master cylinder and then working downstream.

➥ **Note: This would include the ABS EBCM/EBTCM module.**

4 Remove any residual vacuum (or hydraulic pressure) from the power brake booster by applying the brake several times with the engine off.

5 Remove the master cylinder reservoir cap and fill the reservoir with brake fluid. Reinstall the cap.

➥ **Note: Check the fluid level often during the bleeding operation and add fluid as necessary to prevent the fluid level from falling low enough to allow air bubbles into the master cylinder.**

11.8 When bleeding the brakes, a hose is connected to the bleed screw at the caliper or wheel cylinder and submerged in brake fluid - air will be seen as bubbles in the tube and container (all air must be expelled before moving to the next wheel)

6   Have an assistant on hand, as well as a supply of new brake fluid, an empty clear plastic container, a length of plastic, rubber or vinyl tubing to fit over the bleeder valve and a wrench to open and close the bleeder valve.

7   Working at the right-rear wheel, loosen the bleeder screw slightly, then tighten it to a point where it's snug but can still be loosened quickly and easily.

8   Place one end of the tubing over the bleeder screw fitting and submerge the other end in brake fluid in the container (see illustration).

9   Have the assistant slowly depress the brake pedal and hold it in the depressed position.

10   While the pedal is held depressed, open the bleeder screw just enough to allow a flow of fluid to leave the valve. Watch for air bubbles to exit the submerged end of the tube. When the fluid flow slows after a couple of seconds, tighten the screw and have your assistant release the pedal.

11   Repeat Steps 9 and 10 until no more air is seen leaving the tube, then tighten the bleeder screw and proceed to the left front wheel, the left rear wheel and the right front wheel, in that order, and perform the same procedure. Check the fluid in the master cylinder reservoir frequently.

12   Never use old brake fluid. It contains moisture that can boil, rendering the brake system inoperative.

13   Refill the master cylinder with fluid at the end of the operation.

14   Check the operation of the brakes. The pedal should feel solid when depressed, with no sponginess. If necessary, repeat the entire process.

✳✳ WARNING:

Do not operate the vehicle if you are in doubt about the effectiveness of the brake system. It is possible for air to become trapped in the anti-lock brake system hydraulic control unit, so, if the pedal continues to feel spongy after repeated bleedings or the BRAKE or ANTI-LOCK light stays on, have the vehicle towed to a dealer service department or other qualified shop to be bled with the aid of a scan tool.

12 Power brake booster - removal and installation

OPERATING CHECK

1   Depress the brake pedal several times with the engine off and make sure that there is no change in the pedal reserve distance.

2   Depress the pedal and start the engine. If the pedal goes down slightly, operation is normal.

AIRTIGHTNESS CHECK

3   Start the engine and turn it off after one or two minutes. Depress the brake pedal several times slowly. If the pedal goes down farther the first time but gradually rises after the second or third depression, the booster is airtight.

4   Depress the brake pedal while the engine is running, then stop the engine with the pedal depressed. If there is no change in the pedal reserve travel after holding the pedal for 30 seconds, the booster is airtight.

REMOVAL AND INSTALLATION

✳✳ CAUTION:

Brake fluid will damage paint. Cover all painted surfaces around the work area and be careful not to spill fluid during this procedure.

5   The power brake booster is not rebuildable. If a problem develops, it must be replaced with a new one.

6   Disconnect the cable from the negative terminal of the battery (see Chapter 5). Remove the master cylinder (see Section 9), but don't disconnect the brake lines.

➡ **Note: If equipped with a manual transaxle, disconnect and plug the clutch fluid hose and reservoir port.**

7   Disconnect the vacuum hose check valve from the power brake booster.

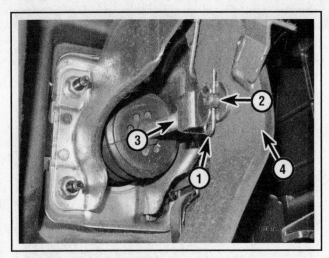

12.11 Brake booster details

1   *Retaining clip*   3   *Booster pushrod*
2   *Clevis pin*   4   *Brake pedal arm*

12.12 Brake booster mounting nuts - 3 of 4 shown

8   In the passenger compartment, remove the driver's side under-dash panel, if equipped.

9   Disconnect the brake light switch (see Section 14).

10   Unhook the brake pedal return spring from the brake pedal and bracket.

11   Using needle-nose pliers, pull out the retaining clip and clevis pin, then disconnect the pushrod from the brake pedal arm (see illustration).

12   Remove the booster-to-firewall mounting nuts (see illustration).

13   Guide the booster unit away from the firewall and out of the engine compartment. Retrieve the gasket if it isn't stuck to the booster.

14   Remove the rubber boot and pushrod-to-adjustment sleeve retaining clip from the end of the booster and pushrod.

15   Place a wrench on the flat spots of the pushrod, then use another wrench to loosen the lock nut and remove the pushrod.

16   Remove the adjustment sleeve from the pushrod, then remove the lock nut.

17   Install the jamb nut and adjustment sleeve on to the booster, then tighten the lock nut and adjustment sleeve to the torque listed in this Chapter's Specifications.

18   Insert the pushrod into the adjustment sleeve and temporarily install the retaining clip.

19   To install the booster, place it into position (using a new gasket) and tighten the nuts to the torque listed in this Chapter's Specifications.

20   Measure the distance between the power brake booster spacer block and the hole in the pushrod (see illustration) and compare it to the dimension listed in this Chapter's Specifications. If necessary, loosen the locknut and turn the adjusting sleeve in or out to the specified length, then tighten the nut.

21   Install the rubber boot over the pushrod.

22   Install the booster into the firewall and tighten the mounting nuts to the torque listed in this Chapter's Specifications.

23   Lubricate the pushrod clevis pin with multi-purpose grease and install the pin through the booster pushod clevis and brake pedal arm. Install the retaining clip through the clevis pin.

24   Reconnect the vacuum hose.

25   Install the master cylinder.

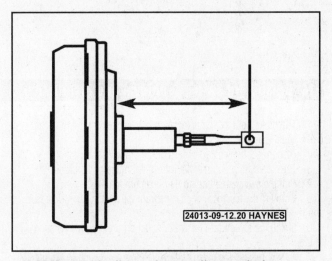

12.20 Measure the distance between the power brake booster body and the hole in the pushrod. Compare your measurement to the dimension listed in this Chapter's Specifications. If necessary, loosen the lock nut and tighten or loosen the adjustment sleeve. Then tighten the lock nut before installing the booster

26   Reconnect the battery.

27   Carefully test the operation of the brakes before placing the vehicle in normal service.

⁂ WARNING:

Do not operate the vehicle if you are in doubt about the effectiveness of the brake system. It is possible for air to become trapped in the anti-lock brake system hydraulic control unit. If the pedal continues to feel spongy after repeated bleedings or the BRAKE or ANTI-LOCK light stays on, have the vehicle towed to a dealer service department or other qualified shop to be bled with the aid of a scan tool.

13 Parking brake - adjustment

1   Release the parking brake, then raise the rear of the vehicle and support it securely on jackstands.

2   Adjust the rear brake shoes (see Section 7).

3   Check the parking brake cables under the vehicle and make sure they have free movement.

4   Remove the center console (see Chapter 12).

5   Locate the parking brake cable adjusting nut (see illustration).

6   Turn the adjustment nut until the rear wheels become hard to turn.

7   Back the adjustment nut off until the rear wheels have little or no drag. Apply the parking brake lever, then release it and verify that the wheels turn freely. If the wheels do not turn freely, back the adjustment nut off until the wheels turn freely when the parking brake lever is released.

8   Reinstall the center console.

13.5 Parking brake cable adjusting nut

14 Brake light switch - removal and installation

1   The brake light switch is located on a bracket at the top of the brake pedal (see illustration).

2   Disconnect the wiring harness at the brake light switch.

3   Turn the switch and remove it from the brake pedal bracket.

4   Pull the switch shaft out to its maximum length.

5   Connect the electrical connector from the switch, then depress and hold the brake pedal down.

6   Install the switch into the brake pedal bracket using a twisting motion.

7   Slowly release the brake pedal and allow the switch to be forced inward until the pedal stops.

8   Make sure the brake lights come on when the brake pedal is depressed and go off when the pedal is released. If not, repeat Steps 4 through 7 until the brake lights function properly.

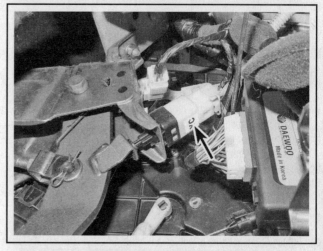

14.1 The brake light switch is located on a bracket near the top of the brake pedal

Specifications

General

Brake fluid type	See Chapter 1
Brake booster pushrod length	10 inches (278.5 mm)

Disc brakes

Brake pad minimum thickness	See Chapter 1
Disc lateral runout limit	0.002 inch (0.06 mm)
Disc minimum thickness	Cast into disc
Parallelism (thickness variation) limit	0.001 inch (0.025 mm)

Drum brakes

Maximum drum diameter	Cast into drum
Shoe lining minimum thickness	See Chapter 1

Torque specifications

➡ **Note: One foot-pound (ft-lb) of torque is equivalent to 12 inch-pounds (in-lbs) of torque. Torque values below approximately 15 foot-pounds are expressed in inch-pounds, because most foot-pound torque wrenches are not accurate at these smaller values.**

	Ft-lbs (unless otherwise noted)	Nm
Brake disc retaining screws	35 to 40 in-lbs	4 to 4.5
Brake hose and brake hose banjo fitting bolt	30	40
Caliper guide pin bolts	20	27
Caliper mounting bracket bolts	70	95
Caliper bleeder valve	53 in-lbs	6
Brake drum backing plate-to-rear axle nuts/bolts	21	28
Brake drum-to-hub screws	35 in-lbs	4
Hub nut (caulking nut)	140	190
Master cylinder mounting nuts	168 in-lbs	18
Power brake booster mounting nuts	108 in-lbs	12
Power brake booster sleeve and lock nut	144 in-lbs	16
Wheel cylinder mounting bolts	71 in-lbs	8
Wheel cylinder bleeder screw	80 in-lbs	9
ABS wheel speed sensor bolt	80 in-lbs	9
Wheel lug nuts	See Chapter 1	

Notes

10

SUSPENSION AND STEERING SYSTEMS

1   General Information

1   The front suspension is a MacPherson strut design. The upper end of each strut is attached to the vehicle's body strut support. The lower end of the strut is connected to the upper end of the steering knuckle. The steering knuckle is attached to a balljoint mounted on the outer end of the suspension control arm. A stabilizer bar connected to each strut and mounted to the suspension crossmember reduces body roll during cornering (see illustration).

2   The rear suspension employs two trailing arms that pivot on bushings on the underbody, connected by a stamped steel axle beam, with two coil springs and two shock absorbers (see illustration).

3   The power-assisted rack-and-pinion steering gear is attached to the front suspension subframe. The steering gear actuates the tie-rods,

which are attached to the steering knuckles. The steering column is designed to collapse in the event of an accident. The power steering system uses hydraulic fluid circulated by an engine-driven accessory pump.

4   Frequently, when working on the suspension or steering system components, you may come across fasteners that seem impossible to loosen. These fasteners on the underside of the vehicle are continually subjected to water, road grime, mud, etc., and can become rusted or frozen in place, making them extremely difficult to remove. In order to unscrew these stubborn fasteners without damaging them (or other components), use lots of penetrating oil and allow it to soak in for a while. Using a wire brush to clean exposed threads will also

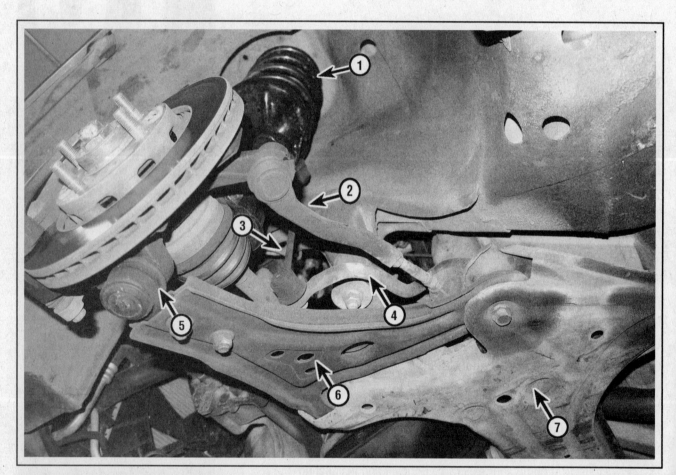

1.1 Front suspension and steering components

1	*Strut/coil spring assembly*	*4*	*Stabilizer bar*	*6*	*Control arm*
2	*Tie-rod end*	*5*	*Balljoint*	*7*	*Subframe*
3	*Stabilizer bar link*				

ease removal of the nut or bolt and prevent damage to the threads. Sometimes a sharp blow with a hammer and punch will break the bond between a nut and bolt threads, but care must be taken to prevent the punch from slipping off the fastener and ruining the threads. Heating the stuck fastener and surrounding area with a torch sometimes helps too, but isn't recommended because of the obvious dangers associated with fire. Long breaker bars and extension, or cheater, pipes will increase leverage, but never use an extension pipe on a ratchet - the ratcheting mechanism could be damaged. Sometimes tightening the nut or bolt first will help to break it loose. Fasteners that require drastic measures to remove should always be replaced with new ones.

5   Since most of the procedures dealt with in this Chapter involve jacking up the vehicle and working underneath it, a good pair of jackstands will be needed. A hydraulic floor jack is the preferred type of jack to lift the vehicle, and it can also be used to support certain components during various operations.

✳✳ WARNING:

Never, under any circumstances, rely on a jack to support the vehicle while working on it. Whenever any of the suspension or steering fasteners are loosened or removed, they must be inspected and, if necessary, replaced with new ones of the same part number or of original equipment quality and design. Torque specifications must be followed for proper reassembly and component retention. Never attempt to heat or straighten any suspension or steering components. Instead, replace any bent or damaged part with a new one.

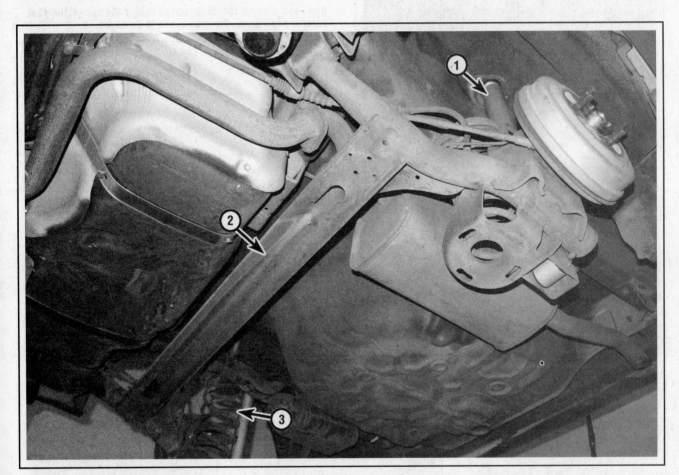

1.2 Rear suspension components

1   Shock absorber

2   Rear axle beam

3   Coil spring

2 Strut assembly (front) - removal, inspection and installation

⁂ WARNING:

Always replace the struts and/or coil springs in pairs - never replace just one strut or one coil spring (this could cause dangerous handling peculiarities).

REMOVAL

1 Loosen the wheel lug nuts, raise the vehicle and support it securely on jackstands. Remove the wheel.
2 Disconnect the stabilizer bar link from the strut (see illustration).

2.2 Separate the stabilizer bar link and brake hose from the strut assembly

3 Detach the brake hose from the bracket on the strut. Also, if equipped, detach the ABS wheel speed sensor harness from the strut.
4 Remove the strut-to-knuckle nuts (see illustration) and knock the bolts out with a hammer and punch.
5 Separate the strut from the steering knuckle. Be careful not to overextend the inner CV joint. Also, don't let the steering knuckle fall outward, as the brake hose could be damaged.
6 If equipped, remove the strut nut protective cap.
7 Remove the strut-to-body nut using a J-42468 GM front strut mount nut wrench or equivalent tool. Use a ratchet and socket on the strut damper shaft to keep it from turning (see illustrations).
8 Remove the strut from the vehicle.

⁂ CAUTION:

Don't use a power tool to loosen or tighten the nut - if the strut damper shaft spins, the strut could be damaged.

INSPECTION

9 Check the strut body for leaking fluid, dents, cracks and other obvious damage that would warrant repair or replacement.
10 Check the coil spring for chips or cracks in the spring coating (this can cause premature spring failure due to corrosion). Inspect the spring seat for cuts, hardness and general deterioration.
11 Check the coil spring ends are in their respective locations on the top and bottom supports.
12 If any undesirable conditions exist, proceed to the strut disassembly procedure (see Section 3).

2.4 Strut-to-steering knuckle nuts and bolts

2.7a Hold the strut damper shaft from turning while unscrewing the strut-to-body nut

2.7b You can fabricate your own tool out of a crow's foot and a 7/8-inch (or 22 mm) socket if you can't find the correct GM tool. This is the one we made. The square drive of the socket was bored out to allow a 1/4-inch drive 9 mm socket to pass through

INSTALLATION

13 Guide the strut assembly up into the fenderwell and align the assembly in the strut tower. Once the assembly is in the strut tower, install the bushing, washer and mounting nut so the strut won't fall back through.

14 Slide the steering knuckle into the strut flange and insert the two bolts. Install the nuts and tighten them to the torque listed in this Chapter's Specifications.

15 Reattach the brake hose (and ABS harness, if equipped) to the strut bracket and reconnect the stabilizer bar link.

16 Install the wheel and lug nuts, then lower the vehicle and tighten the lug nuts to the torque listed in the Chapter 1 Specifications.

17 Tighten the upper mounting nut to the torque listed in this Chapter's Specifications.

18 Have the front wheel alignment checked and, if necessary, adjusted.

3 Strut/coil spring - replacement

❋❋ WARNING:

The manufacturer recommends replacing the damper shaft nut with a new one whenever it is removed.

➡ Note: You'll need a spring compressor for this procedure. Spring compressors are available on a daily rental basis at most auto parts stores or equipment yards.

1 If the struts or coil springs exhibit the telltale signs of wear (leaking fluid, loss of damping capability, chipped, sagging or cracked coil springs) explore all options before beginning any work. The strut/coil spring assemblies are not serviceable and must be replaced if a problem develops. However, strut assemblies complete with springs may be available on an exchange basis, which eliminates much time and work. Whichever route you choose to take, check on the cost and availability of parts before disassembling your vehicle.

❋❋ WARNING:

Disassembling a strut is potentially dangerous and utmost attention must be directed to the job, or serious injury may result. Use only a high-quality spring compressor and carefully follow the manufacturer's instructions furnished with the tool. After removing the coil spring from the strut assembly, set it aside in a safe, isolated area.

DISASSEMBLY

2 Remove the strut and spring assembly (see Section 2). Mount the strut clevis bracket portion of the strut assembly in a vise and unbolt the upper strut cap cover, exposing the damper shaft nut.

❋❋ CAUTION:

Do not clamp any other portion of the strut assembly in the vise as it will be damaged. Line the vise jaws with wood or rags to prevent damage to the unit and don't tighten the vise excessively.

3 Following the tool manufacturer's instructions, install the spring compressor (which can be obtained at most auto parts stores or equipment yards on a daily rental basis) on the spring and compress it sufficiently to relieve all the spring pressure from the upper spring seat (see illustration). This can be verified by wiggling the spring or the upper support mount.

4 While holding the strut rod from turning with a wrench, unscrew the damper shaft nut (the same tool that was used to remove the strut-to-body nut can be used).

5 Remove the nut and the upper mount and bearing. Lay the parts out in the exact order in which they are removed. Check the rubber portion of the upper mount for cracking and general deterioration. If there is any separation of the rubber, replace it.

6 Remove the upper spring seat from the damper shaft. Check the lower rubber cushion of the spring seat for cracking and hardness; replace it if necessary. Inspect the bearing in the spring seat for smooth operation. If it doesn't turn smoothly, replace it.

7 Slide the rubber bump stop off the damper shaft. Check the bump stop for cracking and general deterioration. If there is any deterioration of the rubber, replace it.

3.3 Install the spring compressor following the tool manufacturer's instructions; compress the spring until all pressure is relieved from the upper spring seat (you can verify this by wiggling the spring)

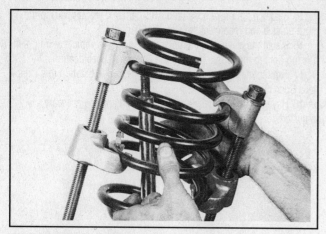

3.8 Carefully remove the compressed spring from the strut

3.10 When installing the spring, make sure the end rests against the raised stop

8   Carefully lift the compressed spring from the assembly (see illustration) and set it in a safe place.

※ WARNING:

When removing the compressed spring, lift it off carefully and set it in a safe place. Keep the ends of the spring away from your body.

➡ Note: If you are disassembling both struts at the same time, mark the springs LEFT and RIGHT so you don't mix them up (they're different).

REASSEMBLY

9   Extend the damper shaft to its full length and install the rubber bump stop.

10 Carefully place the compressed coil spring onto the lower seat of the damper, with the end of the spring resting against the raised stop (see illustration).

11 Install the bearing and upper insulator/spring seat.

12 Install the upper mount and damper shaft nut, then tighten it to the torque listed in this Chapter's Specifications. Remove the spring compressor tool.

13 Install the strut/spring assembly (see Section 2).

4   Stabilizer bar, bushings and links (front) - removal and installation

BUSHINGS AND LINKS

1   Loosen the front wheel lug nuts, raise the front of the vehicle, support it securely on jackstands and remove the front wheels.

2   Remove and discard the nuts that attach the upper and lower ends of the stabilizer bar links to the strut/coil spring assembly and to the stabilizer bar (see illustrations). Detach the links.

3   Lower and support the subframe (see Section 20) enough to access the stabilizer bar mounting bracket fasteners.

4.2a Remove the nut and detach the upper end of the link from the strut. . .

4.2b. . . and the lower end from the bar

4   Remove the bolts and nuts from the stabilizer bar bushing brackets (see illustration).

5   Inspect the retainer bushings for cracks and tears. If either bushing is broken, damaged, distorted or worn, replace the stabilizer bar and bushings as a set. If the ballstuds on the links are loose or otherwise worn, replace the links.

6   Install the bushings and brackets on the stabilizer bar, then install the bushing bracket fasteners, tightening them to the torque listed in this Chapter's Specifications.

➡ **Note: Vegetable oil can be used on the bushings to ease installation.**

7   Install the links, tightening the link nuts to the torque listed in this Chapter's Specifications.

STABILIZER BAR

8   Detach the links from the bar and remove the bushing bracket bolts (see Steps 1 through 4).

9   Lower the subframe (see Section 20) far enough to allow you to maneuver the stabilizer bar out by twisting it out through the right wheel opening.

10 Installation is the reverse of the removal procedure.

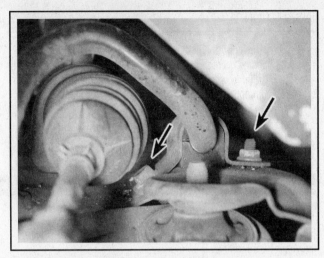

4.4 Remove the stabilizer bar bracket fasteners

---

5   Control arm - removal, inspection and installation

REMOVAL

1   Loosen the wheel lug nuts on the side to be disassembled. Apply the parking brake, raise the front of the vehicle, support it securely on jackstands and remove the wheel.

2   Loosen, but don't remove, the balljoint-to-steering knuckle nut, then use a balljoint separator to pop the tapered shaft of the balljoint from the steering knuckle (see illustration). Remove the nut and detach the balljoint from the steering knuckle (see illustration).

✳ CAUTION:

Be careful not to damage the balljoint boot.

3   Remove the bolts that attach the control arm to the subframe (see illustration).

4   Remove the control arm.

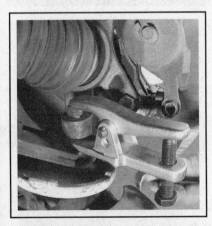

5.2a Use a balljoint separator to pop the balljoint free from the steering knuckle. . .

5.2b. . . then remove the nut and pull the balljoint from the steering knuckle

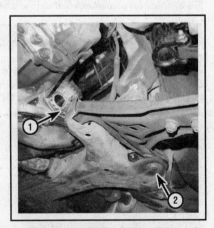

5.3 Control arm-to-subframe bolts

1   *Front pivot bolt*
2   *Rear bushing bolt*

INSPECTION

5   Check the control arm for distortion and the bushings for wear, replacing parts as necessary. Do not attempt to straighten a bent control arm. If a bushing is cracked or shows signs of wear, take the control arm to an automotive machine shop and have the bushing replaced.

INSTALLATION

6   Installation is the reverse of removal; tighten all of the fasteners to the torque values listed in this Chapter's Specifications.

7   Install the wheel and lug nuts, lower the vehicle and tighten the lug nuts to the torque listed in the Chapter 1 Specifications.

➡ **Note: It's a good idea to have the front wheel alignment checked and, if necessary, adjusted.**

6   Balljoints - check and replacement

1   Raise the front of the vehicle and support it securely on jackstands. Apply the parking brake and block the rear wheels to keep the vehicle from rolling off the jackstands.

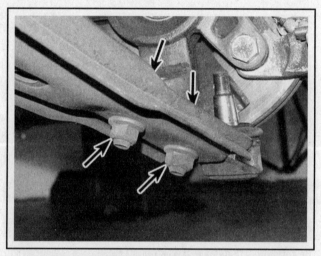

6.6 Balljoint-to-control arm nuts/bolts

CHECK

2   Place a large prybar under the balljoint and resting on the wheel, then try to pry the balljoint up while feeling for movement between the balljoint and steering knuckle. Now, pry between the control arm and the steering knuckle and try to lever the control arm down while feeling for movement between the balljoint and steering knuckle. If any movement is evident in either check, the balljoint is worn.

3   Have an assistant grasp the tire at the top and bottom and move the top of the tire in-and-out. Touch the balljoint stud nut. If any looseness is felt, suspect a worn balljoint stud or a widened hole in the steering knuckle boss. If the latter problem exists, the steering knuckle should be replaced as well as the balljoint.

4   Separate the control arm from the steering knuckle (see Section 5). Using your fingers (don't use pliers), try to twist the stud in the socket. If the stud turns, the balljoint must be replaced.

REPLACEMENT

5   Separate the balljoint from the steering knuckle (see Section 5).

6   Remove the balljoint-to-control arm nuts and bolts and slide the balljoint out of the end of the control arm (see illustration).

7   Installation is the reverse of removal. Be sure to tighten all fasteners to the torque values listed in this Chapter's Specifications.

7   Steering knuckle - removal and installation

✳✳ WARNING:

Dust created by the brake system is harmful to your health. Never blow it out with compressed air and don't inhale any of it. Do not, under any circumstances, use petroleum-based solvents to clean brake parts. Use brake system cleaner only.

REMOVAL

1   Loosen the wheel lug nuts, raise the vehicle and support it securely on jackstands. Remove the wheel, then loosen the driveaxle/ hub nut (see Chapter 8).

2   Remove the brake caliper with its bracket and support them with a piece of wire as described in Chapter 9. Remove the brake disc from the hub. Also remove the ABS wheel speed sensor, if equipped.

3   Loosen, but do not remove the strut-to-steering knuckle bolt/ nuts.

4   Separate the tie-rod end from the steering knuckle arm (see Section 15).

5   Separate the balljoint from the steering knuckle (see Section 5).

6   Remove the driveaxle/hub nut and push the driveaxle from the hub as described in Chapter 8. Support the end of the driveaxle with a piece of wire.

7   The strut-to-knuckle bolts can now be removed.

8   Separate the steering knuckle from the strut.

INSTALLATION

9   Guide the knuckle and hub assembly into position, inserting the driveaxle into the hub.

10 Push the knuckle into the strut flange and install the bolts and

nuts, but don't tighten them yet.

11 Connect the balljoint to the knuckle and tighten the nut to the torque listed in this Chapter's Specifications.

12 Attach the tie-rod end to the steering knuckle arm (see Section 15). Tighten the strut bolts/nuts and the tie-rod end nut to the torque values listed in this Chapter's Specifications.

13 Install the ABS wheel speed sensor, if equipped.

14 Place the brake disc on the hub and install the caliper mounting bracket and caliper as outlined in Chapter 9.

15 Install the driveaxle/hub nut and tighten it to the torque listed in the Chapter 8 Specifications, then stake the nut.

16 Install the wheel and lug nuts.

17 Lower the vehicle and tighten the lug nuts to the torque listed in the Chapter 1 Specifications.

18 Have the front-end alignment checked and, if necessary, adjusted.

8   Hub and bearing assembly (front) - replacement

✸✸ WARNING:

Dust created by the brake system is harmful to your health. Never blow it out with compressed air and don't inhale any of it. Do not, under any circumstances, use petroleum-based solvents to clean brake parts. Use brake system cleaner only.

✸✸ WARNING:

Working with hydraulic presses or large gear pullers can be dangerous. If you are not confident in tackling this task we suggest you take this to a professional repair shop.

1 Remove the steering knuckle (see Section 7).

2 Press the wheel hub out of the steering knuckle with a hydraulic press or use a large puller with the proper adapter to push the hub out of the bearing.

3 Locate the snap-ring in the steering knuckle securing the wheel bearing in the hub. Remove the snap-ring and place the knuckle back into the press or equivalent puller.

4 Press the wheel bearing out of the steering knuckle, from the back to the front.

5 Clean the bore in the knuckle.

6 Reverse the removal procedure to install the new bearing.

➡ **Note: Do not forget to reinstall the snap-ring before installing the hub. The hub and bearing must be fully seated back in the knuckle before installing the steering knuckle.**

7 Install the steering knuckle (see Section 7).

9   Rear shock absorbers - removal and installation

✸✸ WARNING:

Always replace the shock absorbers in pairs - never replace just one of them.

1 Loosen the rear wheel lug nuts. Chock the front wheels to keep the vehicle from rolling, then raise the rear of the vehicle and support it securely on jackstands. Remove the rear wheels.

2 Use a floor jack to support the rear axle on the side you are working on. Position the jack head under the coil spring pocket.

3 Remove the shock absorber upper and lower mounting bolts (see illustrations).

4 Installation is the reverse of removal. Be sure to tighten the bolts to the torque listed in this Chapter's Specifications.

✸✸ CAUTION:

Before tightening the lower mounting bolt, raise the suspension with the floor jack to simulate normal ride height.

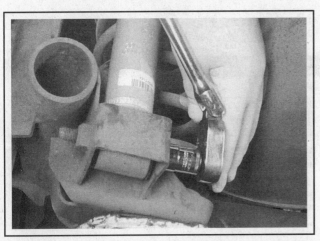

9.3a Location of the rear shock absorber lower mounting bolt. . .

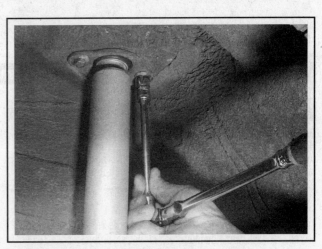

9.3b. . . and the upper mounting bolts

10 Rear coil springs - replacement

1   Loosen the rear wheel lug nuts. Chock the front wheels to keep the vehicle from rolling, then raise the rear of the vehicle and support it securely on jackstands. Remove the rear wheels.

2   Use floor jacks to support the rear axle on each side. Place the jack heads under the coil spring pockets.

3   Mark each spring to make sure they are installed into their original locations.

4   Remove the shock absorber lower mounting bolt on each side (see Section 9).

5   A little at a time, carefully lower both sides of the rear axle assembly, allowing it to pivot down until the coil spring tension is released.

6   The coil springs can be lifted off the pads on the rear axle assembly.

7   If the springs are being replaced, transfer the upper and lower spring pads to the new springs.

8   Installation is the reverse of removal. Before tightening the shock absorber lower mounting bolts, raise the rear axle with the floor jacks to simulate normal ride height.

11 Rear axle assembly - removal and installation

1   Loosen the rear wheel lug nuts. Chock the front wheels to keep the vehicle from rolling, then raise the rear of the vehicle and support it securely on jackstands. Remove the rear wheels.

2   Disconnect the brake pipes from the hoses at the trailing arms and plug the fittings to prevent entry of dirt or excessive fluid loss (see Chapter 9).

3   Disconnect the ABS electrical connectors at the rear axle, if equipped.

4   Release the ends of the parking brake cables from the rear brakes (see Chapter 9). Also free the cables from any brackets on the rear axle.

5   Remove the coil springs (see Section 10).

6   Support the rear axle with a pair of floor jacks and have an assistant on hand, or use a transmission jack on which you can chain the axle securely.

7   Remove the mounting bolts securing the axle bushing brackets to the body on each side, at the front of the trailing arms.

➡ **Note: If the rear axle through-bolts are removed, the final tightening must be with the vehicle at normal ride height.**

8   Carefully lower the rear axle assembly to the floor.

9   Inspect the trailing arm pivot bushings for signs of deterioration. If they are in need of replacement, take the axle assembly to an automotive machine shop to have the bushings replaced.

10 Installation is the reverse of removal, noting the following points:

a) *Raise the rear axle assembly to approximate ride height before tightening the through-bolts (if they were removed for bushing replacement).*

b) *Align the axle bushing brackets to the body on each side by inserting a 12 mm pin in the frontmost bolt hole on each side, through the bracket and into the body, then install and tighten the bolts.*

c) *Tighten the fasteners to the torque listed in this Chapter's Specifications.*

d) *Bleed the brake system (see Chapter 9).*

e) *Tighten the wheel lug nuts to the torque listed in the Chapter 1 Specifications.*

f) *Have the rear wheel alignment checked and, if necessary, adjusted.*

12 Hub and bearing assembly (rear) - replacement

❋❋ **WARNING:**

Dust created by the brake system is harmful to your health. Never blow it out with compressed air and don't inhale any of it. Do not, under any circumstances, use petroleum-based solvents to clean brake parts. Use brake system cleaner only.

1   Loosen the rear wheel lug nuts. Chock the front wheels to keep the vehicle from rolling, then raise the rear of the vehicle and support it securely on jackstands. Remove the rear wheels and release the parking brake.

2004 MODELS AND 2005 MODELS UP TO VIN NO. 5B426447

❋❋ **WARNING:**

Working with hydraulic presses or large gear pullers can be dangerous. If you are not confident in tackling this task we suggest you take this to a professional repair shop.

2   The rear hub and brake drum is held on by a large nut that has a bent (staked) end that wedges into the spindle shaft. Unstake the nut

and unscrew it from the spindle.

3 Remove the brake drum and hub/bearing assembly from the spindle.

4 Lay the drum on a workbench with the wheel studs pointing up. Using snap-ring pliers, remove the snap-ring from the hub of the drum.

5 Press the bearings out of the drum with a hydraulic press or use a drawbolt-type puller with the proper adapter to pull the bearing out of the drum's hub, from the inside of the drum to the outside (wheel stud side).

6 Clean the bore in the brake drum.

7 Reverse the removal procedure to install the new bearing.

8 Install the brake drum and hub nut, tightening the nut to the torque listed in this Chapter's Specifications, then stake the collar of the nut into the spindle groove.

2005 MODELS (FROM VIN NO. 5B426447) AND LATER MODELS

9 Remove the brake drum (see Chapter 9). If equipped, also remove the ABS wheel speed sensor.

10 The rear hub is held on by a large nut that has a bent (staked) end that wedges into the spindle shaft. Unstake the nut and unscrew it from the spindle.

11 Pull the hub and bearing off of the spindle.

➡ **Tip: Depending on the condition of the bearing when you're removing it, part of the bearing can seize onto the spindle. Heat, penetrating oils, and a bit of hammer and chisel work will break it free. Always wear eye protection.**

12 Check the hub bearing for wear or damage. Spin it with your fingers and check for rough, loose or noisy rotation. The bearing can't be replaced separately, so if the bearing is bad or any other problems are found, replace the hub as an assembly.

13 Installation is the reverse of removal. Clean the brake surfaces and the axle flange before installing the hub/bearing assembly. Tighten the spindle nut to the torque listed in this Chapter's Specifications, then stake the collar of the nut into the spindle groove.

14 Install the wheel and lug nuts, lower the vehicle and tighten the lug nuts to the torque listed in the Chapter 1 Specifications.

13 Steering wheel - removal and installation

✳✳ WARNING:

These models are equipped with a Supplemental Restraint System (SRS), more commonly known as airbags. Always disable the airbag system before working in the vicinity of any airbag system component to avoid the possibility of accidental deployment of the airbag(s), which could cause personal injury (see Chapter 12).

✳✳ WARNING:

Do not use a memory saving device to preserve the PCM or radio memory when working on or near airbag system components.

✳✳ WARNING:

The manufacturer recommends replacing the steering wheel retaining nut with a new one whenever it is removed.

REMOVAL

1 Park the vehicle with the wheels pointing straight ahead.

2 Disable the airbag system (see Chapter 12, Section 25).

3 Disconnect the cable from the negative terminal of the battery (see Chapter 5).

4 Remove the switches from either side of the steering wheel, then remove the two bolts on either side of the steering wheel that secure the airbag (see illustrations).

13.4a Remove these two screws from the left side of the steering wheel

13.4b Remove these two screws from the right side of the steering wheel

13.4c Disconnect the electrical connection to remove the switch (same on the opposite side)

13.4d Remove the airbag Torx screw from the right side. . .

13.4e. . . and the left side of the steering wheel

13.5 Squeeze the tabs on the side of the electrical connectors, then unplug them

13.6 Steering wheel hub and steering shaft index marks

13.11 Remove the screws from the clockspring

5   Pull the airbag off the steering wheel, then disconnect the electrical connectors (see illustration).

⁑ WARNING:

When carrying the airbag module, keep the driver's side of it away from your body, and when you set it down (in an isolated area), have the driver's side facing up and away from your face.

6   Remove the steering wheel nut, then mark the relationship of the steering wheel to the shaft (if no marks exist) (see illustration).

7   Remove the steering wheel from the steering column shaft, feeding the wiring harness through the hole in the wheel.

⁑ CAUTION:

While the steering wheel is removed, DO NOT turn the steering shaft. If you do so, the airbag clockspring could be damaged.

Clockspring removal

8   Remove the steering column covers (see Chapter 11, Section 24).

9   Remove the knee bolster side lower instrument panel trim (see Chapter 11).

10 Disconnect the clockspring and horn electrical connections at the bottom portion of the steering column.

➡ **Note: It is helpful to apply a piece of masking tape across the clockspring face to keep it centered while it is off the vehicle.**

11 Remove the screws retaining the clockspring to the steering column (see illustration).

⁑ WARNING:

Obtain new clockspring screws for installation.

12 Detach the clockspring from the steering column.

INSTALLATION

13 Make absolutely sure that the clockspring is centered with the arrows aligned on the clockspring face in alignment. This shouldn't be a problem as long as you have not turned the steering shaft while the wheel was removed, or the hub of the clockspring. If necessary, center

the clockspring as follows:

   a) Turn the hub of the clockspring clockwise until it reaches the end of its travel (don't apply too much force).

   b) Turn the hub counterclockwise about three turns and align the arrow on the hub with the arrow on the clockspring housing.

   c) Prevent the clockspring hub from moving by applying a strip of tape across the clockspring body and hub. Remove the tape after the clockspring has been installed on the steering column.

14 Installation is the reverse of removal, noting the following points:

   a) Make sure the airbag clockspring is centered before installing the steering wheel.

   b) When installing the steering wheel, align the marks on the shaft and the steering wheel hub.

   c) Install, then tighten a NEW steering wheel nut to the torque listed in this Chapter's Specifications.

   d) Install the airbag module on the steering wheel and tighten the bolts to the torque listed in this Chapter's Specifications.

   e) Enable the airbag system (see Chapter 12).

14 Steering column - removal and installation

※※ WARNING:

These models are equipped with airbags. Always disable the airbag system before working in the vicinity of any airbag system component to avoid the possibility of accidental deployment of the airbag(s), which could cause personal injury (see Chapter 12).

※※ WARNING:

Do not use a memory saving device to preserve the PCM's memory when working on or near airbag system components.

REMOVAL

1 Park the vehicle with the wheels in the straight-ahead position. Disconnect the cable from the negative terminal of the battery (see Chapter 5). Disable the airbag system (see Chapter 12).

2 Remove the steering wheel (see Section 13) and the steering column covers (see Chapter 11).

3 Remove the clockspring (see Section 13).

4 Remove the knee bolster (see Chapter 11).

5 Disconnect the electrical connector for the shift interlock solenoid from the ignition lock cylinder.

6 Disconnect any other electrical connectors that may interfere with removal.

7 Mark the relationship of the steering column shaft to the intermediate shaft, then remove the pinch bolt (see illustration).

8 Remove the steering column mounting fasteners (see illustration), then guide the column out from the instrument panel.

※※ WARNING:

The steering column tie strap bolts located on top of the steering column are torque sensitive and have been tightened while the vehicle was being produced. Do not try to loosen or tighten the tie strap bolts at any time or the column may be damaged. If the column is damaged the vehicle may not perform properly, resulting in a crash or personal injury.

INSTALLATION

9 Guide the column into position, connecting the steering shaft with the intermediate shaft. Align the marks made in Step 7.

10 Install the mounting fasteners, tightening them to the torque listed in this Chapter's Specifications.

11 Install the pinch bolt and tighten it to the torque listed in this Chapter's Specifications.

12 The remainder of installation is the reverse of removal. Refer to Section 13 for the clockspring, steering wheel and airbag module installation details.

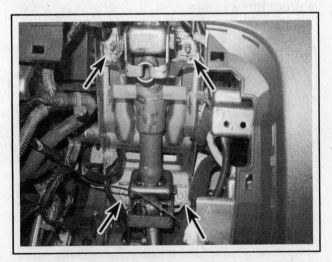

14.7 Mark the relationship of the two shafts, then remove the pinch bolt

14.8 Steering column mounting fasteners

15 Tie-rod ends - removal and installation

REMOVAL

1 Loosen the wheel lug nuts, raise the front of the vehicle and support it securely on jackstands. Apply the parking brake and block the rear wheels to keep the vehicle from rolling off the jackstands. Remove the wheel.

2 Loosen the tie-rod end jam nut (see illustration).

3 Mark the relationship of the tie-rod end to the threaded portion of the tie-rod. This will ensure the toe-in setting is restored when reassembled (see illustration).

4 Loosen the nut from the tie-rod end ballstud a few turns. Disconnect the tie-rod end ballstud from the steering knuckle arm with a puller (see illustration).

5 Remove the nut from the ballstud and discard it (use a new one during installation). Separate the tie-rod end from the steering knuckle, then unscrew the tie-rod end from the tie-rod.

INSTALLATION

6 Thread the tie-rod end onto the tie-rod to the marked position and connect the tie-rod end to the steering arm. Install the nut on the ballstud and tighten it to the torque listed in this Chapter's Specifications.

7 Tighten the jam nut securely and install the wheel and lug nuts. Lower the vehicle and tighten the lug nuts to the torque listed in the Chapter 1 Specifications.

8 Have the front end alignment checked and, if necessary, adjusted.

15.2 Using two wrenches, loosen the jam nut

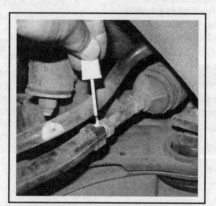

15.3 Mark the position of the tie-rod end in relation to the threads

15.4 Disconnect the tie-rod end from the steering knuckle arm with a puller

16 Steering gear boots - removal and installation

1 Loosen the lug nuts, raise the vehicle and support it securely on jackstands. Remove the wheel.

2 Remove the tie-rod end and jam nut (see Section 15).

3 Remove the outer steering gear boot clamp with a pair of pliers (see illustrations). Cut off the inner boot clamp with a pair of diagonal cutters. Slide off the boot.

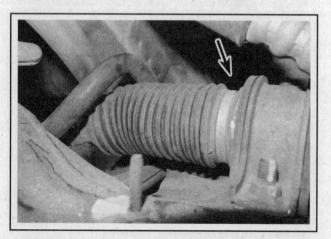

16.3a Cut the inner boot clamp off to remove it

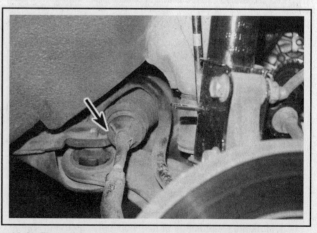

16.3b The smaller clamp can be removed with a pair of pliers

4   Before installing the new boot, wrap the threads and serrations on the end of the steering rod with a layer of tape so the small end of the new boot isn't damaged.

5   Slide the new boot into position on the steering gear until it seats in the groove of the steering rod and install new clamps.

6   Remove the tape and install the tie-rod end (see Section 15).

7   Install the wheel and lug nuts. Lower the vehicle and tighten the lug nuts to the torque listed in the Chapter 1 Specifications.

8   Have the front end alignment checked and, if necessary, adjusted.

17 Steering gear - removal and installation

❈❈ WARNING:

Make sure the steering shaft is not turned while the steering gear is removed or you could damage the airbag system clockspring. To prevent the shaft from turning, place the ignition key in the LOCK position or thread the seat belt through the steering wheel and clip it into place.

❈❈ WARNING:

Do not place any part of your body under the transaxle assembly, engine or subframe when it's supported only by a hoist or other lifting device.

REMOVAL

1   Disconnect the cable from the negative battery terminal (see Chapter 5). Position the wheels straight ahead and remove the ignition key.

2   Inside the vehicle, mark the relationship of the U-joint to the steering gear input shaft, then remove the pinch-bolt securing the U-joint to the steering gear input shaft (see illustration).

3   Loosen the front wheel lug nuts, raise the front of the vehicle and support it securely on jackstands. Remove both front wheels.

4   Detach the tie-rod ends from the steering knuckles (see Section 15).

5   Detach the stabilizer bar links from the stabilizer bar (see Section 4).

6   Separate the control arm balljoints from the steering knuckles (see Section 5).

7   Disconnect the power steering pressure and return lines from the steering gear.

➡ **Note: Don't disconnect the other two pressure lines that run from the control valve (where the input shaft enters the steering gear) and the steering gear housing.**

8   Remove the transaxle rear mount through-bolt.

9   Support the subframe with a floor jack. Remove the subframe mounting nuts (see Section 20) and lower it.

10 Remove the fasteners from the steering gear clamps (see illustration) and remove the steering gear.

11 Installation is the reverse of removal, noting the following points:

a) Tighten all fasteners to the torque values listed in this Chapter's Specifications.

b) Reconnect the negative battery cable (see Chapter 5).

c) Add fluid (see Chapter 1), then bleed the power steering system (see Section 19).

d) Have the front end alignment checked and, if necessary, adjusted.

17.2 Mark the relationship of the universal joint to the steering gear input shaft, then remove the U-joint pinch bolt

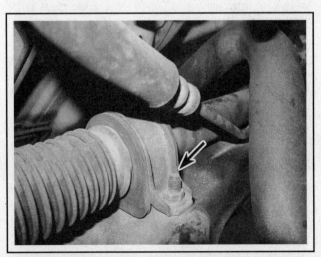

17.10 The steering gear is mounted to the subframe with a clamp on each side (right side shown, left side similar)

18 Power steering pump and reservoir - removal and installation

RESERVOIR

1 Using a suction gun, remove as much fluid from the reservoir as you can.

2 Detach the hoses from the reservoir by first squeezing the clamps and sliding them back, then pulling the hoses off. Cover the exposed ends of the hoses to prevent any debris from getting into the hoses.

3 Remove the reservoir mounting nuts.

4 Installation is the reverse of removal. Fill the reservoir with the recommended fluid (see Chapter 1), then bleed the power steering system.

POWER STEERING PUMP

2008 and earlier models

5 Remove the air filter housing (see Chapter 4).

6 Remove the drivebelt (see Chapter 1).

7 Drain the fluid by disconnecting the pressure and return lines from the pump.

8 Unbolt the air conditioning compressor and position it aside (see Chapter 3).

✳ WARNING:

Don't disconnect the refrigerant lines from the compressor.

9 Loosen the right-front wheel lug nuts, then raise the front of the vehicle and support it securely on jackstands. Remove the wheel.

10 Remove the air conditioning compressor mounting bracket.

11 Unbolt the power steering pump from the air conditioning compressor mounting bracket.

12 Installation is the reverse of removal. Fill the power steering system with the proper fluid (see Chapter 1), then bleed the system (see Section 19).

2009 and later models

13 Remove the drivebelt (see Chapter 1).

14 Drain the fluid by disconnecting the pressure and return lines from the pump.

15 Remove the two mounting bolts from the back side of the pump and detach the pump from the bracket.

16 Installation is the reverse of removal. Fill the power steering system with the proper fluid (see Chapter 1), then bleed the system (see Section 19).

19 Power steering system - bleeding

1 The power steering system must be bled whenever a line is disconnected. Bubbles can be seen in power steering fluid that has air in it and the fluid will often have a tan or milky appearance. Low fluid level can cause air to mix with the fluid, resulting in a noisy pump as well as foaming of the fluid.

2 Check the fluid level in the reservoir, adding the specified fluid necessary to bring it to the MIN mark (see Chapter 1).

3 Start the engine and slowly turn the steering wheel several times from left-to-right and back again. Do not turn the wheel completely from lock-to-lock. Check the fluid level, topping it up as necessary until it remains at the MAX mark and no more bubbles are visible.

20 Subframe - removal and installation

1   Disconnect the cable from the negative battery terminal (see Chapter 5).

2   Loosen the front wheel lug nuts, raise the front of the vehicle and support it securely on jackstands (see illustration). Remove both front wheels.

➡ **Note: The jackstands must be placed behind the subframe, on the unibody frame rails.**

3   Remove the lower intermediate shaft pinch bolt and detach the intermediate shaft from the steering gear (see Section 17).

4   Detach the control arm balljoints from the steering knuckles (see Section 5).

5   Detach the stabilizer bar links from the stabilizer bar (see Section 4).

6   Detach the tie-rod ends from the steering knuckles (see Section 15).

7   Unbolt the transaxle rear mount from the subframe.

8   Place a drain pan under the steering gear, then detach the power steering presssure and return lines from the gear.

9   Support the subframe with a floor jack, then remove the subframe mounting bolts and nuts (see illustration).

10 Lower the subframe slowly, making sure nothing is still connected.

11 Installation is the reverse of removal, noting the following points:

a) *Reconnect the negative battery cable (see Chapter 5).*
b) *Tighten all fasteners to the proper torque values.*
c) *Bleed the power steering system (see Section 19).*
d) *Have the front end alignment checked and, if necessary, adjusted.*

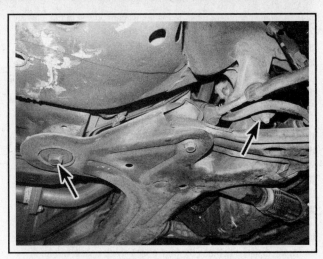

20.9 Remove the subframe-to-chassis mounting bolts and nuts (right side shown, left side identical)

21 Wheels and tires - general information

1   All vehicles covered by this manual are equipped with metric-sized fiberglass or steel belted radial tires (see illustration). Use of other size or type of tires may affect the ride and handling of the vehicle. Don't mix different types of tires, such as radials and bias belted, on the same vehicle as handling may be seriously affected. It's recommended that tires be replaced in pairs on the same axle, but if only one tire is being replaced, be sure it's the same size, structure and tread design as the other.

2   Because tire pressure has a substantial effect on handling and wear, the pressure on all tires should be checked at least once a month or before any extended trips (see Chapter 1).

3   Wheels must be replaced if they are bent, dented, leak air, have elongated bolt holes, are heavily rusted, out of vertical symmetry or if the lug nuts won't stay tight. Wheel repairs that use welding or peening are not recommended.

4   Tire and wheel balance is important in the overall handling, braking and performance of the vehicle. Unbalanced wheels can adversely affect handling and ride characteristics as well as tire life. Whenever a tire is installed on a wheel, the tire and wheel should be balanced by a shop with the proper equipment.

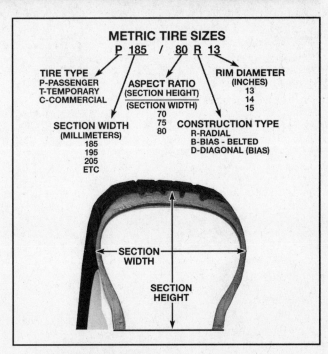

21.1 Metric tire size code

22 Wheel alignment - general information

1   A wheel alignment refers to the adjustments made to the wheels so they are in proper angular relationship to the suspension and the ground. Wheels that are out of proper alignment not only affect vehicle control, but also increase tire wear. The front end angles normally measured are camber, caster and toe-in (see illustration). Toe-in on the front end are adjustable; if the camber and/or caster is not correct, check for bent components. Rear wheel alignment is not adjustable.

2   Getting the proper wheel alignment is a very exacting process, one in which complicated and expensive machines are necessary to perform the job properly. Because of this, you should have a technician with the proper equipment perform these tasks. We will, however, use this space to give you a basic idea of what is involved with a wheel alignment so you can better understand the process and deal intelligently with the shop that does the work.

3   Toe-in is the turning in of the wheels. The purpose of a toe specification is to ensure parallel rolling of the wheels. In a vehicle with zero toe-in, the distance between the front edges of the wheels will be the same as the distance between the rear edges of the wheels. The actual amount of toe-in is normally only a fraction of an inch. Toe-in is controlled by the tie-rod end position on the tie-rod. Incorrect toe-in will cause the tires to wear improperly by making them scrub against the road surface.

4   Camber is the tilting of the wheels from vertical when viewed from one end of the vehicle. When the wheels tilt out at the top, the camber is said to be positive (+). When the wheels tilt in at the top the camber is negative (-). The amount of tilt is measured in degrees from vertical and this measurement is called the camber angle. This angle affects the amount of tire tread which contacts the road and compensates for changes in the suspension geometry when the vehicle is cornering or traveling over an undulating surface.

5 . Caster is the tilting of the front steering axis from the vertical. A tilt toward the rear is positive caster and a tilt toward the front is negative caster. Caster is not adjustable on these vehicles.

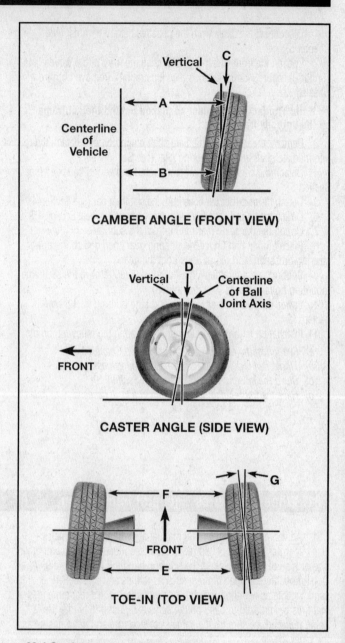

CAMBER ANGLE (FRONT VIEW)

CASTER ANGLE (SIDE VIEW)

TOE-IN (TOP VIEW)

22.1 Camber, caster and toe-in angles

A minus B = C (degrees camber)
D = degrees caster
E minus F = toe-in (measured in inches)
G = toe-in (expressed in degrees)

Specifications

General

Torque specifications	Ft-lbs (unless otherwise indicated)	Nm

➡ **Note: One foot-pound (ft-lb) of torque is equivalent to 12 inch-pounds (in-lbs) of torque. Torque values below approximately 15 foot-pounds are expressed in inch-pounds, because most foot-pound torque wrenches are not accurate at these smaller values.**

Front suspension

	Ft-lbs	Nm
Strut		
Damper shaft nut	44	60
Strut-to-body nut	44	60
Strut-to-steering knuckle bolts/nuts	74	100
Stabilizer bar		
Stabilizer bar link nuts	37	50
Stabilizer bar bracket bolts/nuts	18	25
Control arm-to-subframe bolts (front and rear)	81	110
Balljoint-to-steering knuckle nut	41	55
Balljoint-to-control arm nuts	111	150
Subframe-to-body nuts	111	150
Driveaxle/hub nut	See Chapter 8	

Rear suspension

	Ft-lbs	Nm
Rear axle trailing arm		
Bracket-to-body bolts	85	115
Axle-to-bracket through-bolt/nut	52	70
Rear hub/bearing nut		
2004 models	148	200
2005 and later models	140	190
Shock absorber		
Lower mounting bolt/nut	53	72
Upper mounting bolts	37	50

Steering system

	Ft-lbs	Nm
Airbag module-to-steering wheel bolts	71 in-lbs	8
Intermediate shaft-to-steering column pinch bolt	16	22
Intermediate shaft-to-steering gear pinch bolt	16	22
Steering column mounting fasteners	16	22
Steering gear mounting bolts	37	50
Steering wheel nut	28	38
Tie-rod end-to-steering knuckle nut	33	45

Notes

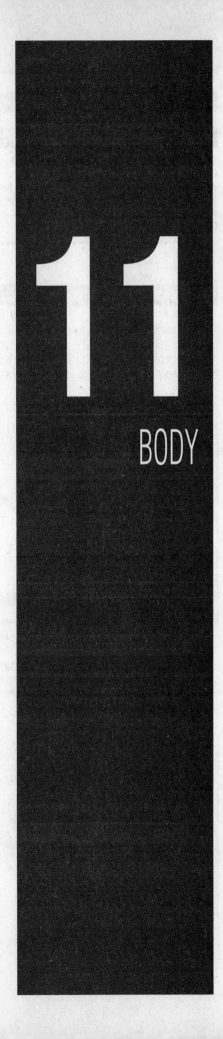

11

BODY

Section

1 General information

Certain body components are particularly vulnerable to accident damage and can be unbolted and repaired or replaced. Among these parts are the hood, doors, tailgate, liftgate, bumpers and front fenders.

Only general body maintenance practices and body panel repair procedures within the scope of the do-it-yourselfer are included in this Chapter.

2 Repair minor paint scratches

No matter how hard you try to keep your vehicle looking like new, it will inevitably be scratched, chipped or dented at some point. If the metal is actually dented, seek the advice of a professional. But you can fix minor scratches and chips yourself. Buy a touch-up paint kit from a dealer service department or an auto parts store. To ensure that you get the right color, you'll need to have the specific make, model and year of your vehicle and, ideally, the paint code, which is located on a special metal plate under the hood or in the door jamb.

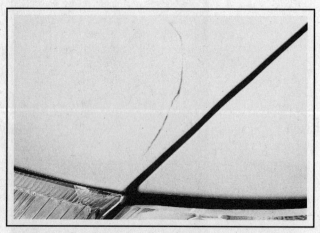

Make sure the damaged area is perfectly clean and rust free. If the touch-up kit has a wire brush, use it to clean the scratch or chip. Or use fine steel wool wrapped around the end of a pencil. Clean the scratched or chipped surface only, not the good paint surrounding it. Rinse the area with water and allow it to dry thoroughly

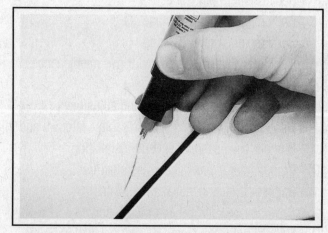

Thoroughly mix the paint, then apply a small amount with the touch-up kit brush or a very fine artist's brush. Brush in one direction as you fill the scratch area. Do not build up the paint higher than the surrounding paint

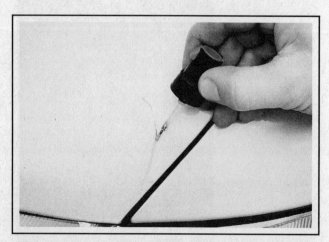

If the vehicle has a two-coat finish, apply the clear coat after the color coat has dried

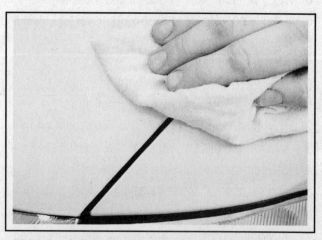

Wait a few days for the paint to dry thoroughly, then rub out the repainted area with a polishing compound to blend the new paint with the surrounding area. When you're happy with your work, wash and polish the area

3   Body repair - minor damage

PLASTIC BODY PANELS

1   The following repair procedures are for minor scratches and gouges. Repair of more serious damage should be left to a dealer service department or qualified auto body shop. Below is a list of the equipment and materials necessary to perform the following repair procedures on plastic body panels.

Wax, grease and silicone removing solvent
Cloth-backed body tape
Sanding discs
Drill motor with three-inch disc holder
Hand sanding block
Rubber squeegees
Sandpaper
Non-porous mixing palette
Wood paddle or putty knife
Curved-tooth body file
Flexible parts repair material

FLEXIBLE PANELS (BUMPER TRIM)

2   Remove the damaged panel, if necessary or desirable. In most cases, repairs can be carried out with the panel installed.

3   Clean the area(s) to be repaired with a wax, grease and silicone removing solvent applied with a water-dampened cloth.

4   If the damage is structural, that is, if it extends through the panel, clean the backside of the panel area to be repaired as well. Wipe dry.

5   Sand the rear surface about 1-1/2 inches beyond the break.

6   Cut two pieces of fiberglass cloth large enough to overlap the break by about 1-1/2 inches. Cut only to the required length.

7   Mix the adhesive from the repair kit according to the instructions included with the kit, and apply a layer of the mixture approximately 1/8-inch thick on the backside of the panel. Overlap the break by at least 1-1/2 inches.

8   Apply one piece of fiberglass cloth to the adhesive and cover the cloth with additional adhesive. Apply a second piece of fiberglass cloth to the adhesive and immediately cover the cloth with additional adhesive in sufficient quantity to fill the weave.

9   Allow the repair to cure for 20 to 30 minutes at 60-degrees to 80-degrees F.

10   If necessary, trim the excess repair material at the edge.

11   Remove all of the paint film over and around the area(s) to be repaired. The repair material should not overlap the painted surface.

12   With a drill motor and a sanding disc (or a rotary file), cut a "V" along the break line approximately 1/2-inch wide. Remove all dust and loose particles from the repair area.

13   Mix and apply the repair material. Apply a light coat first over the damaged area; then continue applying material until it reaches a level slightly higher than the surrounding finish.

14   Cure the mixture for 20 to 30 minutes at 60-degrees to 80-degrees F.

15   Roughly establish the contour of the area being repaired with a body file. If low areas or pits remain, mix and apply additional adhesive.

16   Block sand the damaged area with sandpaper to establish the actual contour of the surrounding surface.

17   If desired, the repaired area can be temporarily protected with several light coats of primer. Because of the special paints and techniques required for flexible body panels, it is recommended that the vehicle be taken to a paint shop for completion of the body repair.

STEEL BODY PANELS

♦ **See photo sequence**

Repairing simple dents

➡ **Note: These photos illustrate a method of repairing simple dents. They are intended to supplement Body repair - minor damage in this Chapter and should not be used as the sole instructions for body repair on these vehicles.**

18   When repairing dents, the first job is to pull the dent out until the affected area is as close as possible to its original shape. There is no point in trying to restore the original shape completely as the metal in the damaged area will have stretched on impact and cannot be restored to its original contours. It is better to bring the level of the dent up to a point that is about 1/8-inch below the level of the surrounding metal. In cases where the dent is very shallow, it is not worth trying to pull it out at all.

19   If the backside of the dent is accessible, it can be hammered out gently from behind using a soft-face hammer. While doing this, hold a block of wood firmly against the opposite side of the metal to absorb the hammer blows and prevent the metal from being stretched.

20   If the dent is in a section of the body which has double layers, or some other factor makes it inaccessible from behind, a different technique is required. Drill several small holes through the metal inside the damaged area, particularly in the deeper sections. Screw long, self-tapping screws into the holes just enough for them to get a good grip in the metal. Now pulling on the protruding heads of the screws with locking pliers can pull out the dent.

21   The next stage of repair is the removal of paint from the damaged area and from an inch or so of the surrounding metal. This is easily done with a wire brush or sanding disk in a drill motor, although it can be done just as effectively by hand with sandpaper. To complete the preparation for filling, score the surface of the bare metal with a screwdriver or the tang of a file or drill small holes in the affected area. This will provide a good grip for the filler material. To complete the repair, see the Section on filling and painting.

Repair of rust holes or gashes

22   Remove all paint from the affected area and from an inch or so of the surrounding metal using a sanding disk or wire brush mounted in a drill motor. If these are not available, a few sheets of sandpaper will do the job just as effectively.

23   With the paint removed, you will be able to determine the severity of the corrosion and decide whether to replace the whole panel, if possible, or repair the affected area. New body panels are not as expensive as most people think and it is often quicker to install a new panel than to repair large areas of rust.

24   Remove all trim pieces from the affected area except those which will act as a guide to the original shape of the damaged body, such as headlight shells, etc. Using metal snips or a hacksaw blade, remove all loose metal and any other metal that is badly affected by rust. Hammer the edges of the hole in to create a slight depression for the filler material.

25   Wire-brush the affected area to remove the powdery rust from the surface of the metal. If the back of the rusted area is accessible, treat it with rust inhibiting paint.

26   Before filling is done, block the hole in some way. This can be done with sheet metal riveted or screwed into place, or by stuffing the hole with wire mesh.

These photos illustrate a method of repairing simple dents. They are intended to supplement Body repair - minor damage in this Chapter and should not be used as the sole instructions for body repair on these vehicles.

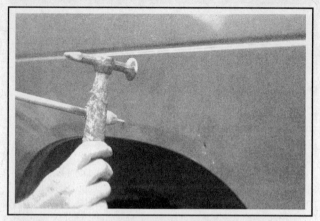

1 If you can't access the backside of the body panel to hammer out the dent, pull it out with a slide-hammer-type dent puller. Tap with a hammer near the edge of the dent to help 'pop' the metal back to its original shape, about 1/8-inch below the surface of the surrounding metal

2 Using coarse-grit sandpaper, remove the paint down to the bare metal. Clean the repair area with wax/silicone remover.

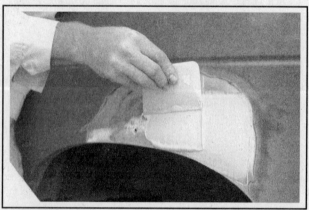

3 Following label instructions, mix up a batch of plastic filler and hardener, then quickly press it into the metal with a plastic applicator. Work the filler until it matches the original contour and is slightly above the surrounding metal

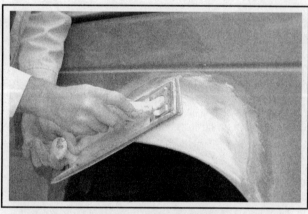

4 Let the filler harden until you can just dent it with your fingernail. File, then sand the filler down until it's smooth and even. Work down to finer grits of sandpaper - always using a board or block - ending up with 360 or 400 grit

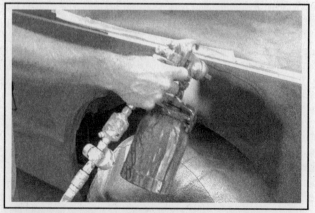

5 When the area is smooth to the touch, clean the area and mask around it. Apply several layers of primer to the area. A professional-type spray gun is being used here, but aerosol spray primer works fine

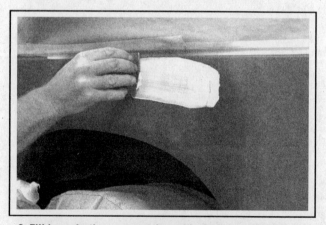

6 Fill imperfections or scratches with glazing compound. Sand with 360 or 400-grit and re-spray. Finish sand the primer with 600 grit, clean thoroughly, then apply the finish coat. Don't attempt to rub out or wax the repair area until the paint has dried completely (at least two weeks)

27 Once the hole is blocked off, the affected area can be filled and painted. See the following subsection on filling and painting.

Filling and painting

28 Many types of body fillers are available, but generally speaking, body repair kits which contain filler paste and a tube of resin hardener are best for this type of repair work. A wide, flexible plastic or nylon applicator will be necessary for imparting a smooth and contoured finish to the surface of the filler material. Mix up a small amount of filler on a clean piece of wood or cardboard (use the hardener sparingly). Follow the manufacturer's instructions on the package, otherwise the filler will set incorrectly.

29 Using the applicator, apply the filler paste to the prepared area. Draw the applicator across the surface of the filler to achieve the desired contour and to level the filler surface. As soon as a contour that approximates the original one is achieved, stop working the paste. If you continue, the paste will begin to stick to the applicator. Continue to add thin layers of paste at 20-minute intervals until the level of the filler is just above the surrounding metal.

30 Once the filler has hardened, the excess can be removed with a body file. From then on, progressively finer grades of sandpaper should be used, starting with a 180-grit paper and finishing with 600-grit wet-or-dry paper. Always wrap the sandpaper around a flat rubber or wooden block, otherwise the surface of the filler will not be completely flat. During the sanding of the filler surface, the wet-or-dry paper should be periodically rinsed in water. This will ensure that a very smooth finish is produced in the final stage.

31 At this point, the repair area should be surrounded by a ring of bare metal, which in turn should be encircled by the finely feathered edge of good paint. Rinse the repair area with clean water until all of the dust produced by the sanding operation is gone.

32 Spray the entire area with a light coat of primer. This will reveal any imperfections in the surface of the filler. Repair the imperfections with fresh filler paste or glaze filler and once more smooth the surface with sandpaper. Repeat this spray-and-repair procedure until you are satisfied that the surface of the filler and the feathered edge of the paint are perfect. Rinse the area with clean water and allow it to dry completely.

33 The repair area is now ready for painting. Spray painting must be carried out in a warm, dry, windless and dust free atmosphere. These conditions can be created if you have access to a large indoor work area, but if you are forced to work in the open, you will have to pick the day very carefully. If you are working indoors, dousing the floor in the work area with water will help settle the dust that would otherwise be in the air. If the repair area is confined to one body panel, mask off the surrounding panels. This will help minimize the effects of a slight mismatch in paint color. Trim pieces such as chrome strips, door handles, etc., will also need to be masked off or removed. Use masking tape and several thickness of newspaper for the masking operations.

34 Before spraying, shake the paint can thoroughly, then spray a test area until the spray painting technique is mastered. Cover the repair area with a thick coat of primer. The thickness should be built up using several thin layers of primer rather than one thick one. Using 600-grit wet-or-dry sandpaper, rub down the surface of the primer until it is very smooth. While doing this, the work area should be thoroughly rinsed with water and the wet-or-dry sandpaper periodically rinsed as well. Allow the primer to dry before spraying additional coats.

35 Spray on the top coat, again building up the thickness by using several thin layers of paint. Begin spraying in the center of the repair area and then, using a circular motion, work out until the whole repair area and about two inches of the surrounding original paint is covered. Remove all masking material 10 to 15 minutes after spraying on the final coat of paint. Allow the new paint at least two weeks to harden, then use a very fine rubbing compound to blend the edges of the new paint into the existing paint. Finally, apply a coat of wax

4   Body repair - major damage

1   Major damage must be repaired by an auto body shop specifically equipped to perform body and frame repairs. These shops have the specialized equipment required to do the job properly.

2   If the damage is extensive, the frame must be checked for proper alignment or the vehicle's handling characteristics may be adversely affected and other components may wear at an accelerated rate.

3   Due to the fact that all of the major body components (hood, fenders, etc.) are separate and replaceable units, any seriously damaged components should be replaced rather than repaired. Sometimes the components can be found in a wrecking yard that specializes in used vehicle components, often at considerable savings over the cost of new parts.

5   Upholstery, carpets and vinyl trim - maintenance

UPHOLSTERY AND CARPETS

1   Every three months remove the floormats and clean the interior of the vehicle (more frequently if necessary). Use a stiff whiskbroom to brush the carpeting and loosen dirt and dust, then vacuum the upholstery and carpets thoroughly, especially along seams and crevices.

2   Dirt and stains can be removed from carpeting with basic household or automotive carpet shampoos available in spray cans. Follow the directions and vacuum again, then use a stiff brush to bring back the "nap" of the carpet.

3   Most interiors have cloth or vinyl upholstery, either of which can be cleaned and maintained with a number of material-specific cleaners or shampoos available in auto supply stores. Follow the directions on the product for usage, and always spot-test any upholstery cleaner on an inconspicuous area (bottom edge of a backseat cushion) to ensure that it doesn't cause a color shift in the material.

4   After cleaning, vinyl upholstery should be treated with a protectant.

➡ **Note: Make sure the protectant container indicates the product can be used on seats - some products may make a seat too slippery.**

❊❊ **CAUTION:**

Do not use protectant on vinyl-covered steering wheels.

5   Leather upholstery requires special care. It should be cleaned regularly with saddlesoap or leather cleaner. Never use alcohol, gasoline, nail polish remover or thinner to clean leather upholstery.

6   After cleaning, regularly treat leather upholstery with a leather conditioner, rubbed in with a soft cotton cloth. Never use car wax on leather upholstery.

7   In areas where the interior of the vehicle is subject to bright sunlight, cover leather seating areas of the seats with a sheet if the vehicle is to be left out for any length of time.

VINYL TRIM

8   Don't clean vinyl trim with detergents, caustic soap or petroleum-based cleaners. Plain soap and water works just fine, with a soft brush to clean dirt that may be ingrained. Wash the vinyl as frequently as the rest of the vehicle.

9   After cleaning, application of a high-quality rubber and vinyl protectant will help prevent oxidation and cracks. The protectant can also be applied to weather-stripping, vacuum lines and rubber hoses, which often fail as a result of chemical degradation, and to the tires.

6   Fastener and trim removal

1   There is a variety of plastic fasteners used to hold trim panels, splash shields and other parts in place in addition to typical screws, nuts and bolts. Once you are familiar with them, they can usually be removed without too much difficulty.

2   The proper tools and approach can prevent added time and expense to a project by minimizing the number of broken fasteners and/or parts.

3   The following illustration shows various types of fasteners that are typically used on most vehicles and how to remove and install them (see illustration). Replacement fasteners are commonly found at most auto parts stores, if necessary.

Fasteners

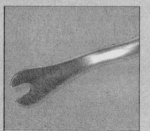

This tool is designed to remove special fasteners. A small pry tool used for removing nails will also work well in place of this tool

A Phillips head screwdriver can be used to release the center portion, but light pressure must be used because the plastic is easily damaged. Once the center is up, the fastener can easily be pried from its hole

Here is a view with the center portion fully released. Install the fastener as shown, then press the center in to set it

This fastener is used for exterior panels and shields. The center portion must be pried up to release the fastener. Install the fastener with the center up, then press the center in to set it

This type of fastener is used commonly for interior panels. Use a small blunt tool to press the small pin at the center in to release it . . .

. . . the pin will stay with the fastener in the released position

Reset the fastener for installation by moving the pin out. Install the fastener, then press the pin flush with the fastener to set it

This fastener is used for exterior and interior panels. It has no moving parts. Simply pry the fastener from its hole like the claw of a hammer removes a nail. Without a tool that can get under the top of the fastener, it can be very difficult to remove

4   Trim panels are typically made of plastic and their flexibility can help during removal. The key to their removal is to use a tool to pry the panel near its retainers to release it without damaging surrounding areas or breaking-off any retainers. The retainers will usually snap out of their designated slot or hole after force is applied to them. Stiff plastic tools designed for prying on trim panels are available at most auto parts stores (see illustration). Tools that are tapered and wrapped in protective tape, such as a screwdriver or small pry tool, are also very effective when used with care.

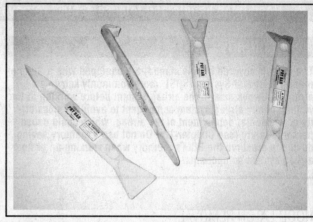

6.4 These small plastic pry tools are ideal for prying off trim panels

7   Hood - removal, installation and adjustment

➡ **Note: The hood is somewhat awkward to remove and install; at least two people should perform this procedure.**

REMOVAL AND INSTALLATION

1   Open the hood, then place blankets or pads over the fenders and cowl area of the body. This will protect the body and paint as the hood is lifted off.
2   Disconnect the windshield wiper washer hose and any cables or wires that will interfere with removal.
3   Make marks around the hood hinges to ensure proper alignment during installation (see illustration).
4   Have an assistant support the weight of the hood while you remove the hinge-to-hood nuts and lift off the hood.
5   Installation is the reverse of removal. Align the hinges with the marks made in Step 3, then tighten the nuts securely.

ADJUSTMENT

6   Fore-and-aft and side-to-side adjustment of the hood is done by moving the hood after loosening the hinge-to-body bolts. Up-and-down adjustments at the rear of the hood are made by loosening the hinge-to-hood bolts.
7   Mark around the entire hinge so you can determine the amount of movement.
8   Loosen the bolts and move the hood into correct alignment. Move it only a little at a time. Tighten the hinge bolts and carefully lower the hood to check the position.
9   Adjust the hood latch (see Section 8) and the hood bumpers on the fenders so the front of the hood, when closed, is flush with the fenders (see illustration).
10   The hood latch assembly, as well as the hinges, should be periodically lubricated with white lithium-base grease to prevent binding and wear.

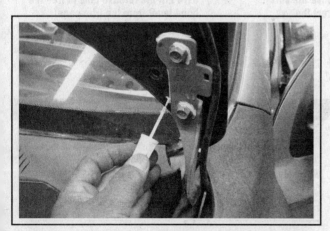

7.3 Draw alignment marks around the hood hinges to ensure proper alignment of the hood when it's reinstalled

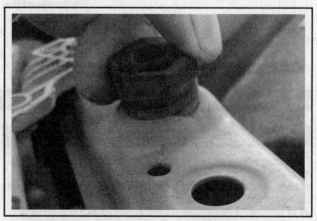

7.9 To adjust the vertical height of the leading edge of the hood so that it's flush with the fenders, turn each hood bumper clockwise (to lower the hood) or counterclockwise (to raise the hood)

8   Hood latch handle and release cable - removal and installation

❊❊ WARNING:

The models covered by this manual are equipped with a Supplemental Restraint System (SRS), more commonly known as airbags. Always disarm the airbag system before working in the vicinity of any airbag system component to avoid the possibility of accidental deployment of the airbag, which could cause personal injury (see Chapter 12). Do not use a memory saving device to preserve the PCM's memory when working on or near airbag system components.

HOOD LATCH REMOVAL

1 Open the hood.
2 Remove the radiator grille (see Section 11).
3 Mark the location of the hood latch with a scribe, paint, or marker.
4 Remove the bolts securing the latch to the core support (see illustration).
5 Disconnect the release cable by pressing in on the plastic tabs (see illustration).
6 Remove the latch.
7 Installation is the reverse of removal.

HOOD RELEASE CABLE AND INSIDE HANDLE REMOVAL

8 Open the hood.
9 Remove the radiator grille (see Section 11).
10 Loosen the lug nuts to the left front wheel.
11 Raise and support the vehicle on a flat surface with jackstands. Check to be sure it is stable and well supported.
12 Remove the left front tire and fender liner.
13 Pull the inside release handle to gain access to the screws securing it to the panel.
14 Disconnect the cable from the inside handle by applying pressure to the plastic tabs (see illustration).
15 Remove the hood latch and remove the cable from the latch.
16 Pull the grommet loose at the firewall with a flat bladed screwdriver.
17 Pull the cable out through the fender opening.
18 Disconnect any cable stays that secure the cable to the inner section of the fender.
19 Fish the cable through the front of the fender area by pulling on the cable from the under hood latch.
20 Installation is the reverse of removal.

8.4 Hood latch mounting fasteners

8.5 Pull the latch above the core support and disconnect the release cable

8.14 Lift the release tabs to free the hood lever from the trim panel

9   Bumper covers - removal and installation

❊❊ WARNING:

The models covered by this manual are equipped with a Supplemental Restraint System (SRS), more commonly known as airbags. Always disarm the airbag system before working in the vicinity of any airbag system component to avoid the possibility of accidental deployment of the airbag, which could cause personal injury (see Chapter 12). Do not use a memory saving device to preserve the PCM's memory when working on or near airbag system components.

1 Apply the parking brake, raise the vehicle and support it securely on jackstands. Use masking tape to protect the paint on adjacent panels while removing either front or rear bumper covers.

FRONT BUMPER COVER

2 Remove both front tires.
3 Remove the fasteners securing the under vehicle splash shield, then remove the splash shield.

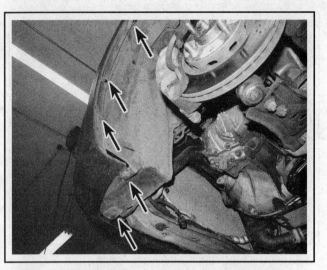

9.4 Remove the fasteners on the front edge of the inner fender splash shields

9.5 Remove these mounting fasteners from both sides of the bumper cover

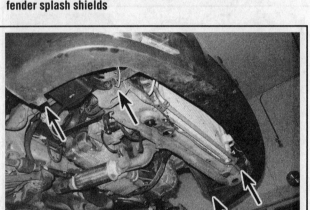

9.6 Bumper cover lower mounting fasteners

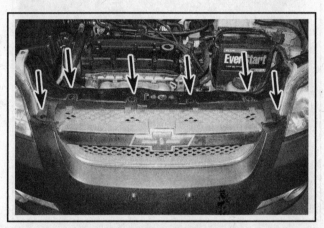

9.7 Bumper cover upper mounting fasteners

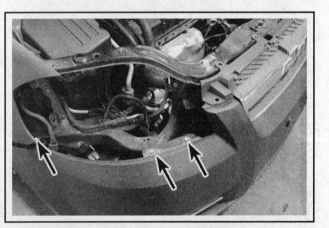

9.9a Remove the fasteners from the right side. . .

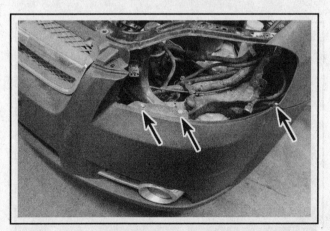

9.9b. . . and left side headlight housing opening

4   Remove the fasteners securing the front of the inner fender splash shields (see illustration). Then pull back the splash shield.

5   Inside the inner fender, remove the fasteners securing the upper part of the bumper cover to the fender (see illustration).

6   Remove the fasteners securing the bottom of the bumper cover (see illustration).

7   Remove the bumper cover upper mounting fasteners (see illustration).

8   Remove both headlight housings (see Chapter 12, Section 17).

9   Remove the fasteners from the headlight housing openings (see illustrations).

10 With the aid of a helper, carefully remove the bumper cover

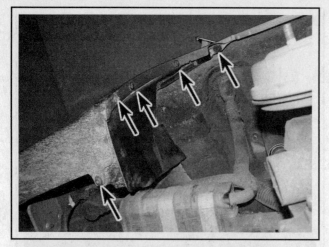

9.15 Rear fender well splash shield mounting fasteners

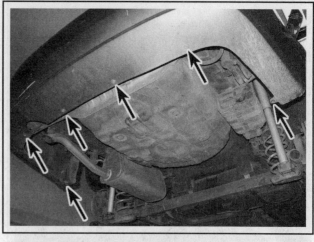

9.16 Bumper cover lower mounting fasteners

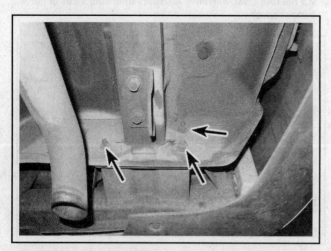

9.17 Remove these fasteners

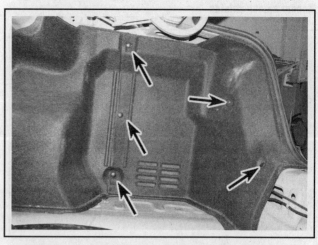

9.18 Remove the fasteners securing the inside trunk panels

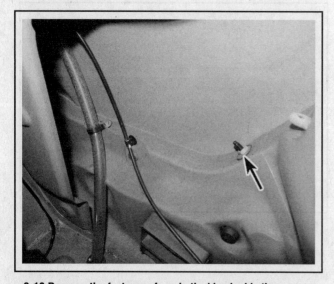

9.19 Remove the fasteners from both sides inside the rear compartment

observing any fasteners or electrical connections you might have missed.

11 Lay the bumper cover in a safe place with as many points of contact as possible. This will help avoid any stress on the painted surface and help prevent the paint finish from cracking.

12 Installation is the reverse of removal.

REAR BUMPER COVER

13 Open the trunk or rear hatch lid, whichever is applicable.

14 Disconnect the electrical connectors from the taillights, side marker lights and license plate light, then remove the taillights (see Chapter 12).

15 Remove the fasteners from the rear fender well splash shields and pull the shield back (see illustration).

16 Remove the fasteners securing the bottom of the bumper cover (see illustration).

17 Remove the fasteners securing the bumper cover to the energy absorbing shock from the underside of the vehicle (see illustration).

18 Remove the rear trim covers inside the trunk/rear hatch area (see illustration).

19 Remove the bumper cover fasteners from the inside of the rear compartment area (see illustration).

9.20a Remove the mounting fasteners. . .

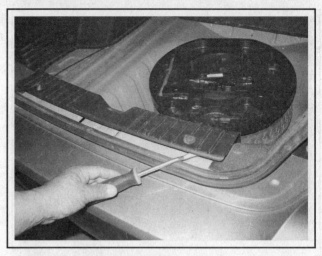

9.20b. . . then carefully pry the panel off

20 Remove the rear compartment bumper cover trim panel (see illustrations).

21 Remove the fasteners across the top of the rear bumper cover (see illustration).

☀ CAUTION:

It is possible to damage the rear bumper cover if all of the tabs are not disengaged before trying to remove it.

22 With the aid of a helper, carefully remove the fascia, observing any bolts or electrical connections you might have missed.

23 Lay the bumper cover in a safe place with as many points of contact as possible. This will help avoid any stress on the painted surface and help prevent the paint finish from cracking.

24 Installation is the reverse of removal.

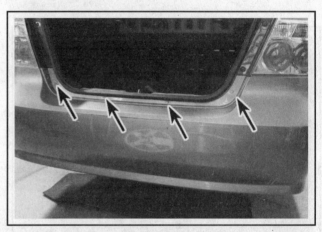

9.21 Bumper cover upper mounting fasteners

10 Front fender - removal and installation

1 Loosen the front wheel lug nuts. Raise the vehicle, support it securely on jackstands and remove the front wheel. Use masking tape on adjacent body panels to prevent scratching the paint while removing the fender.

2 Remove the inner fender splash shield fasteners and remove the shield (see illustration).

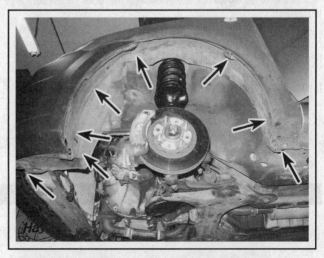

10.2 You can reuse the plastic retainers and screws for reinstalling the splash shield

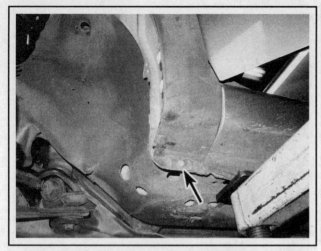

10.3 Remove the bolt, but save it for reinstalling

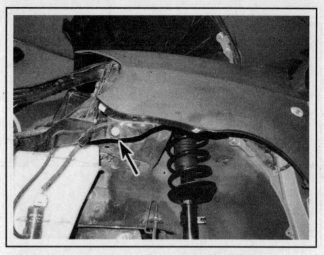

10.4 This bolt is only accessible after the front fascia is removed

10.6 With the door open, remove this fastener

10.7 You can reach up inside the fender and disconnect the side marker light. Then remove the side marker light fixture

3   Remove the fender bolt at the bottom of the rocker panel (see illustration).

4   Remove the front bumper cover (see Section 9) then, remove the bolt securing the front of the fender bracket to the body (see illustration).

5   You can carefully pull the bumper away far enough to get to the hidden bolt or remove the entire front fascia.

6   With the door open, remove the fastener from the rear of the fender (see illustration).

7   Disconnect the side marker light fixture (see illustration).

8   Remove the upper fender bolts and lift off the fender. It's a good idea to have an assistant support the fender while it's being moved away from the vehicle to prevent damage to the surrounding body panels.

9   Installation is the reverse of removal. Check the alignment of the fender to the hood and front edge of the door before final tightening of the fender fasteners.

11 Radiator grille - removal and installation

1   Radiator grille is part of the front bumper cover and is replaced as one piece (see Section 9).

12 Cowl cover - removal and installation

1 Open the hood.
2 Remove the wiper arms (see Chapter 12).
3 Remove the cowl weather strip seal (see illustration).
4 Remove the screws securing the covers to the cowl (see illustrations), then remove the covers.
5 Installation is the reverse of removal.

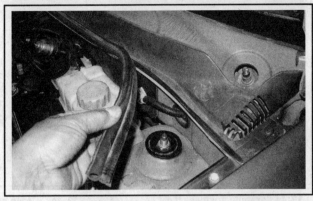

12.3 Pull the cowl seal off and set it aside for reinstalling

12.4a Remove the fasteners securing the cowl cover on the left side. . .

12.4b. . . then the right side cowl comes off after the left side has been removed

13 Door trim panels - removal and installation

✳✳ WARNING:

The models covered by this manual are equipped with a Supplemental Restraint System (SRS), more commonly known as airbags. Always disarm the airbag system before working in the vicinity of any airbag system component to avoid the possibility of accidental deployment of the airbag, which could cause personal injury (see Chapter 12). Do not use a memory saving device to preserve the PCM's memory when working on or near airbag system components.

REMOVAL

➡ Note: Procedures for the rear doors are similar to the front doors.

1 Lower the window.
2 Disconnect the cable from the negative terminal of the battery (see Chapter 5).

3 Carefully pry off the sail panel. Driver's side has the manual mirror controls in it and will need to be removed or laid off to the side (see illustration).

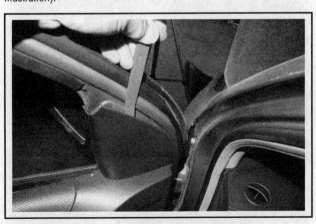

13.3 Disengage the clips and remove the sail panel

13.4a Carefully pry loose the trim panel. . .

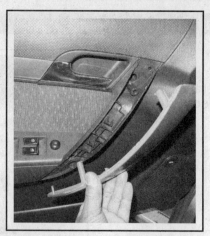

13.4b. . . then carefully pull the trim straight off

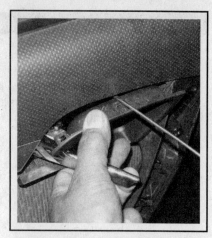

13.5 Carefully pry off the trim behind the door handle and remove it

13.6 Remove the trim panel mounting fasteners

13.10 Use a trim tool to release the fasteners around the door panel

4 Remove the trim panel from the door pull handle (see illustrations).

5 Remove the trim piece from behind the door handle (see illustration).

6 Remove the fasteners securing the door pull handle (see illustration).

7 If you're working on a hatchback model, remove the screw securing the inside handle and pry the handle free from the door panel. Remove the actuating rods from the inside handle.

8 If you're working on a hatchback model, remove the fasteners along the bottom of the door panel.

9 Remove the actuating rods from the inside handle.

10 Remove the door trim panel using a trim panel removal tool (see illustration). Start from the bottom of the trim panel and work around the perimeter until all the fasteners have been released from the door.

11 Lift the trim panel up to disengage the panel from the upper door ridge. (A slight rap with the palm of your hand while lifting will free any clips or fasteners along the top edge.) Unplug any electrical connectors, and remove the panel.

12 For access to components inside the door, reconnect the battery negative terminal and re-attach the window switch. Then raise the window fully. Carefully peel back the plastic watershield. Set the watershield aside for reinstalling.

INSTALLATION

13 Prior to installation of the door trim panels, reinstall any clips in the panel which may have come out during removal.

14 Position the wire harness connectors for the power door lock switch and the power window switch (if equipped) on the back of the panel, then place the panel in position in the door. Press the door panel into place until the clips are seated.

15 The remainder of installation is the reverse of removal.

14 Door - removal, installation and adjustment

⁕⁕⁕ WARNING:

The models covered by this manual are equipped with a Supplemental Restraint System (SRS), more commonly known as airbags. Always disarm the airbag system before working in the vicinity of any airbag system component to avoid the possibility of accidental deployment of the airbag, which could cause personal injury (see Chapter 12). Do not use a memory saving device to preserve the PCM's memory when working on or near airbag system components.

→ Note: The door is heavy and somewhat awkward to remove and install - at least two people should perform this procedure.

REMOVAL AND INSTALLATION

1 Raise the window completely in the door. Open the door all the way and support it on jacks or blocks covered with rags to prevent damaging the paint.

2 Remove the door trim panel and watershield as described in Section 13.

3 Remove the kick panel and disconnect the electrical connectors leading to the door.

4 Detach the rubber grommet from the car side of the jam and feed the wiring harness through the opening that is connected to the door.

5 Mark around the door hinge reinforcement plates with a pen or a scribe to facilitate realignment during reassembly.

6 With an assistant holding the door, remove the hinge bolts and lift the door off (see illustration).

7 Installation is the reverse of removal.

ADJUSTMENT

8 Having proper door-to-body alignment is a critical part of a well-functioning door assembly. First check the door hinge pins for excessive play. Fully open the door and lift up and down on the door without lifting the body. If a door has 1/16-inch or more excessive play, the hinges should be replaced.

9 Door-to-body alignment adjustments are made by loosening the hinge-to-body bolts or hinge-to-door bolts and moving the door. Proper body alignment is achieved when the top of the doors are parallel with the roof section, the front door is flush with the fender, the rear door is flush with the rear quarter panel and the bottom of the doors are aligned with the lower rocker panel. If these goals can't be reached by adjusting the hinge-to-body or hinge-to-door bolts, body alignment shims may have to be purchased and inserted behind the hinges to achieve correct alignment.

10 To adjust the door-closed position, mark around the striker plate to provide a reference point, then check that the door latch is contacting the center of the latch striker. If not, adjust the up and down position first (see illustration).

11 Finally, adjust the latch striker sideways position so that the door outer panel is flush with the center pillar or rear quarter panel and provides positive engagement with the latch mechanism.

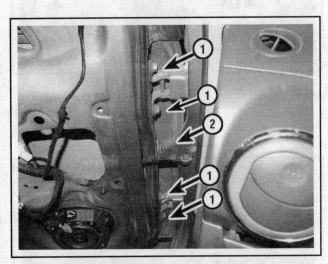

14.6 Push the wire connector into the door, then remove the bolts securing the hinges

1 Hinge mounting fasteners
2 Wire harness

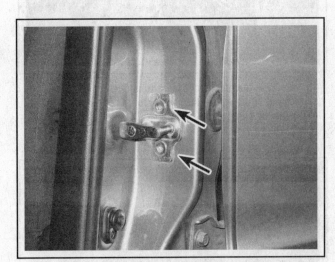

14.10 Adjust the door lock striker by loosening the mounting screws and gently tapping the striker in the desired direction

15 Door latch, lock cylinder and handles - removal and installation

✳ WARNING:

The models covered by this manual are equipped with a Supplemental Restraint System (SRS), more commonly known as airbags. Always disarm the airbag system before working in the vicinity of any airbag system component to avoid the possibility of accidental deployment of the airbag, which could cause personal injury (see Chapter 12). Do not use a memory saving device to preserve the PCM's memory when working on or near airbag system components.

✳ CAUTION:

Wear gloves when working inside the door openings to protect against cuts from sharp metal edges.

FRONT AND REAR DOORS

1   Remove the door trim panel (see Section 13).
2   Carefully remove the watershield. The watershield will need to be reinstalled.

Outside door handle

3   Reconnect the negative battery cable and the window switch. Raise the window until it is fully closed.
4   Working from inside the door, disconnect the outside latch rod (see illustration).
5   Remove the end cap from the door (see illustration).
6   Reaching through the hole, unscrew the lock housing. Then, pull back on the door handle to remove (see illustrations).
7   Installation is the reverse of removal.

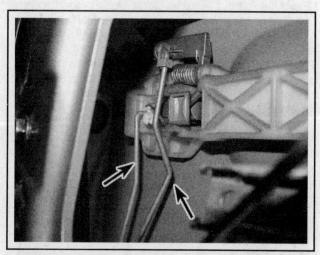

15.4 Release the plastic clip by rotating the clip bottom section out of the way of the control rod, then pull the rod out of the plastic clip

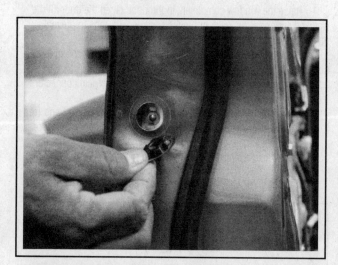

15.5 Save the plastic clip for reinstalling

15.6a Using the hole in the end of the door, unscrew the lock housing

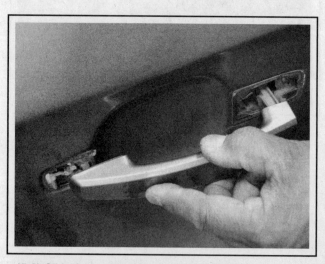

15.6b Slide the handle rearward, then pull it off

Inside door handle

8   Remove the screw securing the handle to the door.

9   Pull back to release the tab and disconnect the actuator rods.

10   Installation is the reverse of removal.

Door latch removal

➡ **Note: The door latch also contains the electric door lock as part of its assembly.**

11   Disconnect the outside door handle (see Steps 4 thru 6).

12   Disconnect the electrical connections from the door latch (see illustration).

13   Remove the three screws securing the latch to the door edge (see illustration).

14   Remove the latch from the inside of the door (see illustrations).

15   Installation is the reverse of removal.

Door lock cylinder

16   Remove the outside door handle, (see Section 15 and Section 13).

17   With the outside latch removed, release the retaining clip securing the lock cylinder in the latch housing.

18   Installation is otherwise the reverse of removal.

15.12 Lift the tab and pull off the connector

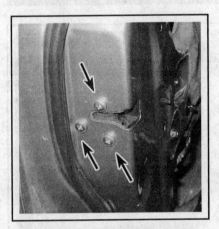

15.13 A hand impact with the proper bit works best to remove them if they are stuck.

15.14a With the actuator rods still attached to the latch, lift the latch out of the door

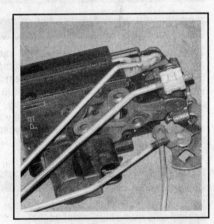

15.14b Reference back to this picture to reinstall the actuator rods correctly

16   Door window glass - removal and installation

✳✳ WARNING:

The models covered by this manual are equipped with a Supplemental Restraint System (SRS), more commonly known as airbags. Always disarm the airbag system before working in the vicinity of any airbag system component to avoid the possibility of accidental deployment of the airbag, which could cause personal injury (see Chapter 12). Do not use a memory saving device to preserve the PCM's memory when working on or near airbag system components.

✳✳ CAUTION:

Wear gloves when working inside the door openings to protect against cuts from sharp metal edges.

1   Remove the door trim panel and the plastic watershield (see Section 13).

2   Remove the outside window scraper seal.

3   Lower the window half-way down to expose the window mounting fasteners.

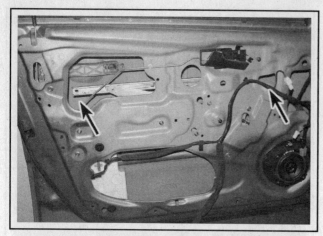

16.4 Front door glass-to-regulator bolt locations (door glass has already been removed)

4   From inside the door, remove the fasteners securing the window glass to the window regulator. (see illustration).
5   Remove the bolts to the guide rail and remove it.
6   Slide the glass up and toward the inside of the door to remove it.
7   Installation is the reverse of removal.

17 Door window glass regulator - removal and installation

✳✳ WARNING:

The models covered by this manual are equipped with a Supplemental Restraint System (SRS), more commonly known as airbags. Always disarm the airbag system before working in the vicinity of any airbag system component to avoid the possibility of accidental deployment of the airbag, which could cause personal injury (see Chapter 12). Do not use a memory saving device to preserve the PCM's memory when working on or near airbag system components.

✳✳ CAUTION:

Wear gloves when working inside the door openings to protect against cuts from sharp metal edges.

17.2 Tape the window up out of the way, or remove the window glass entirely

WINDOW REGULATOR - ELECTRIC OR MANUAL WINDOW

1   Remove the door trim panel and the plastic watershield (see Section 13).
2   Remove the window glass (see Section 16). Or, unbolt the window and tape it up out of the way (see illustration).
3   Disconnect the electrical connector from the window regulator motor (if applicable).
4   Remove the fasteners securing the window regulator to the door (see illustration).
5   Remove the regulator assembly through the largest door opening.

➡ Note: It will sometimes take a bit of fiddling around to get the large gear positioned just right to get it to come through the opening. Be sure to follow the same orientation when reinstalling the assembly.

6   Lubricate the rollers and wear points on the regulator with white grease before installation.
7   Installation is the reverse of removal.

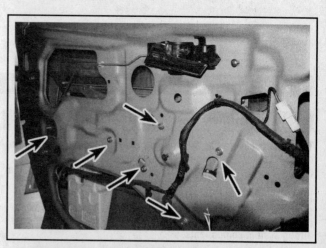

17.4 Remove the fasteners securing the window track and regulator assembly

18 Mirrors - removal and installation

⁕⁕ WARNING:

The models covered by this manual are equipped with a Supplemental Restraint System (SRS), more commonly known as airbags. Always disarm the airbag system before working in the vicinity of any airbag system component to avoid the possibility of accidental deployment of the airbag, which could cause personal injury (see Chapter 12). Do not use a memory saving device to preserve the PCM's memory when working on or near airbag system components.

OUTSIDE MIRRORS

1   Both electric and manual outside mirrors are removed in the same manner, except for the electrical connection on the electric mirror assembly.

2   Remove the sail trim from the inside of the door (Section 13).

3   Disconnect the electrical connector (if applicable), then remove the fasteners securing the mirror assembly to the door frame (see illustration).

4   Disconnect the electrical connector (if applicable) then, remove the mirror assembly.

5   Installation is the reverse of removal.

Mirror glass

6   Push the face of the mirror in at the bottom until the mirror reaches the stop.

7   Insert a trim removal tool behind the glass until it reaches the first support rib, then pry outward carefully until the mirror glass is free.

8   Install the mirror glass and align the mirror face to the backing plate.

9   Carefully apply pressure to the glass, using a thick pad across the glass until the mirror glass clicks into place.

INSIDE MIRROR

10   Carefully pry the mirror base from the trim panel and pull back to remove (see illustration).

19 Trunk lid - removal

➡ **Note: The trunk lid is heavy and somewhat awkward to remove and install - at least two people should perform this procedure.**

1   Open the trunk, then remove the trunk lid liner (see illustration).

2   Disconnect any electrical connectors, ground wires and harness retaining clips.

11   Installation is the reverse of removal.

➡ **Note: If the mount plate itself has come off the windshield, adhesive kits are available at auto parts stores to re-secure it. Follow the instructions included with the kit.**

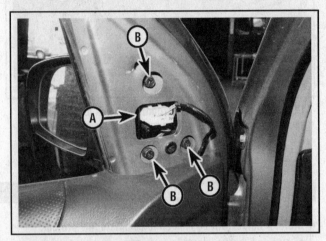

18.3 Disconnect the electrical connector (A), then remove the mounting fasteners (B)

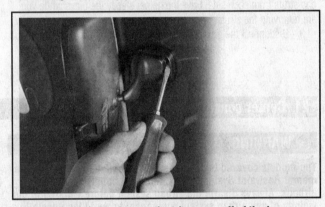

18.10 Use a trim tool to pry the trim cover off of the base

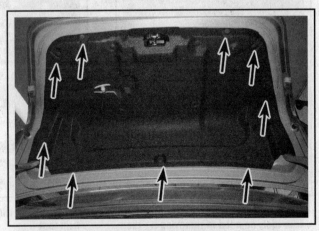

19.1 Remove the fasteners securing the liner

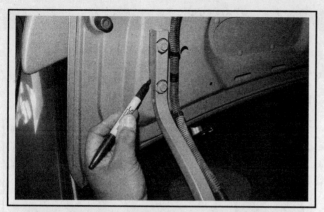

19.3 Draw alignment marks around the trunk hinges to ensure proper alignment, then remove the trunk fasteners

3   Mark the position of the trunk lid to the trunk hinges with a marker or a scribe (see illustration).

4   With an assistant holding the trunk lid, remove the lid-to-hinge bolts and remove the trunk lid.

➡ **Note: When reinstalling the trunk lid, align the lid-to-hinge fasteners with the marks made during removal.**

5   Installation is the reverse of removal.

20   Rear hatch - removal

➡ **Note: A helper will be needed to complete this project.**

1   Raise the hatch to its full open position.

2   Support the hatch with a suitable support while you remove the gas struts from each side. Have the helper steady the glass while you are removing the struts.

3   Disconnect the grommet between the hatch and the roof line. Pull the leads out and disconnect them.

4   Disconnect the rear wiper washer hose, if equipped.

5   Mark the bolt and hinge locations with paint, marker or scribe.

6   Remove the bolts.

7   With the aid of your helper, lift the hatch off of the car and set in a safe place for re-installation.

8   Installation is the reverse of removal.

21   Center console - removal and installation

✳✳ **WARNING:**

The models covered by this manual are equipped with a Supplemental Restraint System (SRS), more commonly known as airbags. Always disarm the airbag system before working in the vicinity of any airbag system component to avoid the possibility of accidental deployment of the airbag, which could cause personal injury (see Chapter 12). Do not use a memory saving device to preserve the PCM's memory when working on or near airbag system components.

1   Disconnect the cable from the negative battery terminal (see Chapter 5).

2   Remove the manual gear shift boot, if applicable, by applying inward pressure to the base, releasing the tabs (see illustration).

3   Remove the trim from the parking brake lever (see illustrations).

4   Remove the screws securing the center console (two in the front on either side and one inside the cup holder) (see illustrations).

5   Remove the console front trim panel (see illustration).

6   Remove the screw inside the cup holder (see illustration).

21.2 Pry the shift boot trim with a flat trim tool, no need in removing it - the console will slide over it

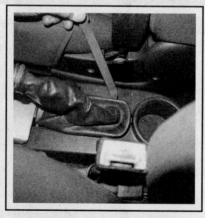

21.3a Pry the trim up with a flat trim tool

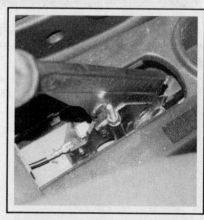

21.3b Pull trim boot over the parking brake handle (it will end up inside out) to expose the inside of the console

21.4a Left side forward screw securing the console

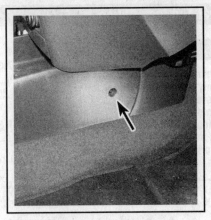

21.4b Right side forward screw securing the console

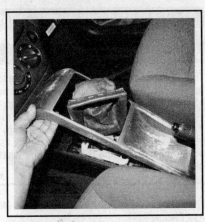

21.5 Pry up from the outside edges to free the trim panel

21.6 Remove the rubber protector to get to the screw hidden underneath it

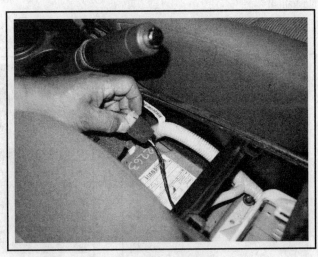

21.7 Disconnect the electrical connections

7   Disconnect the electrical connections under the center console (see illustration).

8   Check for any additional connectors or fasteners that may have been added that need to be removed.

9   Remove the center console by lifting the back first then slide it backwards then up and out of the car (see illustration).

10 Installation is the reverse of removal.

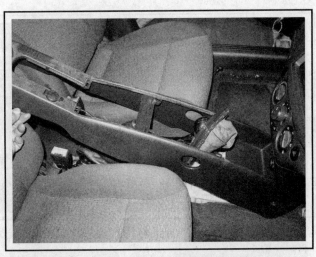

21.9 Carefully lift the console out from between the seats

22 Dashboard trim panels - removal and installation

1 Disconnect the cable from the negative terminal of the battery (see Chapter 5).

INSTRUMENT CLUSTER TRIM PANEL

2 Remove the two screws securing the trim to the instrument cluster. Located on the under side (top section) of the trim panel (see illustration).

3 Gently pry the trim loose on each side, then tilt it out and remove the trim as well as the upper trim section (see illustrations).
4 Remove the trim panel.
5 Installation is the reverse of removal.

INSTRUMENT PANEL CENTER TRIM PANEL

6 Carefully pry the edges of the center trim panel loose (see illustration).
7 Lift the trim off of the center panel (see illustration).
8 Installation is the reverse of removal.

KNEE BOLSTER

9 Remove the knee bolster trim panel by gently prying around the corners to release the pressure clips (see illustration).
10 Installation is the reverse of removal. Make sure the clips are engaged properly before pushing the knee bolster firmly into place.

22.2 Remove these two screws

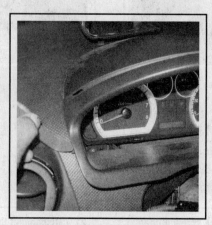

22.3a Pry the edges loose. . .

22.3b. . . then remove the upper and lower trim pieces

22.6 Using a flat trim tool, carefully pry the trim loose

22.7 Lift the trim panel off

22.9 Pry at each corner with a flat trim tool to release the clips

GLOVE BOX

11 Open the glove box and press in on the sides to release the door stops, then allow the glove box to lower past the door stops (see illustration). Lift the glove box off of the hinge connection.

12 Installation is the reverse of removal.

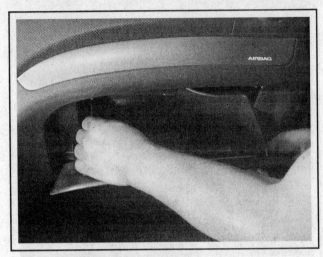

22.11 Press in the sides of the door

23   Interior trim panels - removal and installation

✳✳ WARNING:

The models covered by this manual are equipped with a Supplemental Restraint System (SRS), more commonly known as airbags. Always disarm the airbag system before working in the vicinity of any airbag system component to avoid the possibility of accidental deployment of the airbag, which could cause personal injury (see Chapter 12). Do not use a memory saving device to preserve the PCM's memory when working on or near airbag system components.

➡ **Note: The support sections above the plane of the hood are known as pillars. These pillars are lettered from the front to the back of the car with a letter corresponding to their location."A" being the windshield to the front door opening."B" obviously would be the next support area. Knowing this will aid in ordering parts, talking with a professional body man or mechanic as well as increase your knowledge of automotive terms.**

1 Disconnect the cable from the negative battery terminal (see Chapter 5).

A PILLAR TRIM REMOVAL

2 Grasp the A pillar trim by the edges and pull it away from the A pillar support.

3 Lift the trim out of the bottom corner of the dash and remove (see illustration).

4 Installation is the reverse of removal.

B PILLAR TRIM REMOVAL

Lower B pillar trim removal

5 Remove the rocker panel trim plates (see Steps 27 thru 29).

6 Remove the lower B pillar trim panel by grasping the edges and pull toward the center of the car.

7 Check to see that all the friction clips have remained on the trim panel before reinstalling. Otherwise pry the friction clip out of the slots in the B pillar area and reattach them onto the plastic tabs corresponding to the slots.

8 Installation is the reverse of removal.

Upper B pillar trim removal

9 Remove the lower B pillar trim panel.

10 Remove the screws hidden by the lower B pillar on the bottom section of the upper B pillar.

11 Remove the seat belt bracket.

12 Grasp the edges of the upper B pillar trim panel and pull toward the center of the car to release the friction clips.

23.3 A flat trim tool can help loosen the A pillar in order to grab hold of the edges and then pull it free

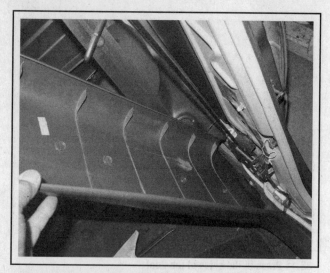

23.19 Tilt the top edge of the C pillar inward, then lift to remove it

23.35 Remove the package tray fasteners

13 Remove the upper B pillar trim panel.

14 Check to see that all the friction clips have remained on the trim panel before reinstalling. Otherwise pry the friction clip out of the slots in the B pillar area and reattach them onto the plastic tabs corresponding to the slots.

15 Installation is the reverse of removal.

C PILLAR TRIM REMOVAL (ALSO KNOWN AS THE QUARTER PANEL TRIM)

Lower quarter panel trim removal

16 Remove the rear rocker panel trim plates.

17 Remove the rear seat cushion and seat back (not necessary but it will give you a bit more room).

18 Remove the screws securing the lower quarter panel trim to the quarter panel.

19 Grasp the edges of the lower quarter panel and pull toward the center of the car to remove (see illustration).

20 Remove the lower quarter panel trim.

21 Installation is the reverse of removal.

Upper quarter panel trim removal

22 Remove the lower quarter panel trim (see Steps 6 thru 10).

23 Remove the seat belt bolt connecting it to the trim panel.

24 Grasp the upper quarter panel trim by the edges and pull toward the center of the car.

25 Remove the panel.

26 Installation is the reverse of removal.

ROCKER PANEL TRIM PLATE REMOVAL (OR SILL PLATE)

27 Remove the screws securing the rocker panel trim to the rocker panel.

28 Pry up the panel with a flat trim tool.

29 Remove the rocker panel trim plate.

30 Installation is the reverse of removal.

REAR WINDOW SHELF REMOVAL

31 Remove the right and left side C pillar trim (see previous Sections).

32 Remove the high mounted brake light fixture.

33 Remove the child seat anchors.

34 Remove the back panel trim plate.

35 Remove the plastic retaining clips securing the package tray (see illustration).

36 Slide the shelf out toward the center of the car.

37 Remove the shelf.

38 Installation is the reverse of removal.

SUN VISOR REMOVAL

39 Remove the screw securing the visor to the roof.

40 Pull down and disconnect the electrical connector, if applicable.

41 Installation is the reverse of removal.

PASSENGER GRAB HANDLES AND COAT HOOK REMOVAL

42 Remove the screw securing the handle or coat hook to the roof line.

43 Pull the handle/coat hook away from the headliner.

44 Installation is the reverse of removal.

24 Steering column covers - removal and installation

1 Turn the steering wheel and remove the fasteners securing the upper cover (see illustration).
2 Separate the top cover from the bottom (see illustration).
3 Remove the fasteners securing the lower cover to the steering column (see illustration).
5 Remove the lower covers.
6 Installation is the reverse of removal.

24.1 Remove the fasteners securing the upper cover (left side shown, right side similar)

24.2 Separate the covers

24.3 Lower cover screw locations

25 Seats - removal and installation

FRONT SEAT

1 Move the seat forward and remove the seat mounting bolts (see illustration).

25.1 Front seat rear mounting bolts

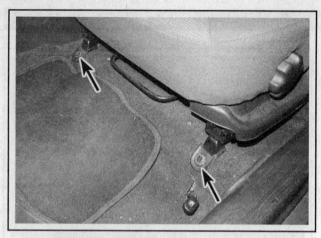

25.2 Front seat front mounting bolts

2 Move the seat rearward as far as possible and remove the two mounting bolts (see illustration).

3 Tilt seat back and disconnect the seatbelt wiring and any other electrical connectors under the seat.

4 Lift the seat cushion area and tilt toward the outside of the car. Start by guiding the seat cushion area out of the door followed by the back rest section.

5 Installation is the reverse of removal.

REAR SEAT

Seat cushion removal

6 Lift corners of the rear seat cushion up to disengage the fasteners.

➡ **Note: The rear seat cushion corners must be lifted up with force to disengage the fasteners.**

7 When reinstalling, line up the rear tabs, and the front pins. Then, push down on the front corners to snap them back into place.

Seat back removal

8 Remove the bolts securing the seat back to the support frame. Four per side.

9 Pull the bottom out slightly and lift up on the entire seat back to free it from the upper clips.

10 Installation is the reverse of removal.

26 Sun roof removal

1 Remove the headliner (Section 23).

2 Disconnect the electrical connections to the sun roof module and sun roof motor.

3 Unstrap the sun roof module and remove it.

4 Remove the bolts securing the sun roof drive motor. Remove the motor.

5 Disconnect the four drain tubes on each corner of the sun roof assembly.

➡ **Tip: From this step on you will need an assistant to help hold the sun roof assembly.**

6 Remove the screws securing the sun roof to the roof bracket.

7 Lower the sun roof and guide it out of a rear door.

8 Installation is the reverse of removal.

27 Instrument panel - removal and installation

✳ **WARNING:**

The models covered by this manual are equipped with a Supplemental Restraint System (SRS), more commonly known as airbags. Always disable the airbag system before working in the vicinity of any airbag system components to avoid the possibility of accidental deployment of the airbags, which could cause personal injury (see Chapter 12). Do not use a memory saving device to preserve the PCM's memory when working on or near airbag system components.

➡ **Note: This is a difficult procedure for the home mechanic. There are many hidden fasteners, difficult angles to work in and many electrical connectors to tag and disconnect/connect. We recommend that this procedure be done only by an experienced do-it-yourselfer.**

1 During removal of the instrument panel, make careful notes of how each piece comes off, where it fits in relation to other pieces and what holds it in place. If you note how each part is installed before removing it, getting the instrument panel back together again will be much easier.

27.11 Carefully pry off the cover (right side shown, left side similar)

27.14 Remove the pinch bolt, then disconnect the shaft

27.15a Carefully pry up the door sill trim. . .

27.15b. . . then remove the fastener securing the panel, then remove the panel

2   It is not necessary, but it is suggested to remove both front seats to allow additional working space and lessen the chance of damage to the seats during this procedure.

3   Turn the front wheels to the straight-ahead position and secure the steering column with the ignition lock.

4   Disconnect the cable from the negative battery terminal (see Chapter 5).

5   Wait at least two minutes to allow the airbag system back-up power supply to become depleted (see Chapter 12).

6   Remove the front seats (see Section 25).

7   Remove the steering wheel (see Chapter 10).

8   Remove the steering column covers (see Section 24).

9   Remove all of the dashboard trim panels as described in Section 22.

10 Remove the instrument cluster (see Section 24).

11 Remove the instrument panel side covers (see illustration).

12 Remove the radio and heater control assembly (see Chapter 3).

13 Remove the center console, if equipped (see Section 21).

14 Disconnect the steering shaft (at the end of the steering column) from the intermediate shaft (see illustration).

15 Remove the door sill trim panels from each side of the vehicle (see illustrations).

16 Remove the front pillar trim from each side of the vehicle (see Section 23).

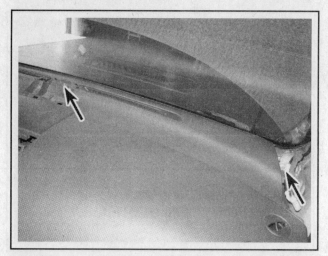

27.18a Remove the fasteners from the top of the instrument panel (fastener on the left side not shown in photo)

27.18b Remove the fastener at the center of the instrument panel

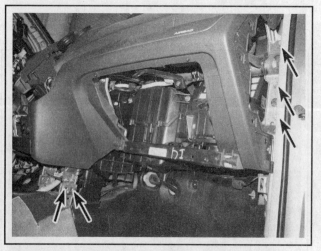

27.18c Remove the fasteners at the right side and the fasteners at the bottom of the panel

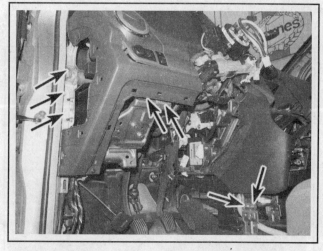

27.18d Remove the fasteners on the left side of the instrument panel

27.19 With the help of an assistant, carefully remove the instrument panel

17 Disconnect the instrument panel electrical connectors.

➡ **Note: A number of electrical connectors must be disconnected in order to remove the instrument panel. Most are designed so that they will only fit on the matching connector (male or female), but if there is any doubt, mark the connectors with masking tape and a marking pen before disconnecting them.**

18 Remove the instrument panel mounting fasteners (see illustrations).

19 With the help of an assistant, slowly and carefully move the instrument panel away from the firewall. Make certain that any electrical connectors or components that hinder removal are detached to avoid damage to them while moving the instrument panel outwards (see illustration).

20 Installation is the reverse of removal. Be certain to reconnect all electrical connectors and secure their wiring harnesses during installation.

12

CHASSIS
ELECTRICAL
SYSTEM

1 General Information

1   The electrical system is a 12-volt, negative ground type. Power for the lights and all electrical accessories is supplied by a lead/acid battery, which is charged by the alternator.

2   This Chapter covers repair and service procedures for the various electrical components not associated with the engine. Information on the battery, alternator and starter motor can be found in Chapter 5.

3   It should be noted that when portions of the electrical system are serviced, the negative battery cable should be disconnected from the battery to prevent electrical shorts and/or fires.

2 Electrical troubleshooting - general information

1   A typical electrical circuit consists of an electrical component, any switches, relays, motors, fuses, fusible links or circuit breakers related to that component and the wiring and connectors that link the component to both the battery and the chassis. To help you pinpoint an electrical circuit problem, wiring diagrams are included at the end of this Chapter.

2   Before tackling any troublesome electrical circuit, first study the appropriate wiring diagrams to get a complete understanding of what makes up that individual circuit. Trouble spots, for instance, can often be narrowed down by noting if other components related to the circuit are operating properly. If several components or circuits fail at one time, chances are the problem is in a fuse or ground connection, because several circuits are often routed through the same fuse and ground connections.

3   Electrical problems usually stem from simple causes, such as loose or corroded connections, a blown fuse, a melted fusible link or a failed relay. Visually inspect the condition of all fuses, wires and connections in a problem circuit before troubleshooting the circuit.

4   If test equipment and instruments are going to be utilized, use the diagrams to plan ahead of time where you will make the necessary connections in order to accurately pinpoint the trouble spot.

5   The basic tools needed for electrical troubleshooting include a circuit tester or voltmeter (a 12-volt bulb with a set of test leads can also be used), a continuity tester, which includes a bulb, battery and set of test leads, and a jumper wire, preferably with a circuit breaker incorporated, which can be used to bypass electrical components (see illustrations). Before attempting to locate a problem with test instruments, use the wiring diagram(s) to decide where to make the connections.

VOLTAGE CHECKS

6   Voltage checks should be performed if a circuit is not functioning properly. Connect one lead of a circuit tester to either the negative battery terminal or a known good ground. Connect the other lead to a connector in the circuit being tested, preferably nearest to the battery or fuse (see illustration). If the bulb of the tester lights, voltage is present, which means that the part of the circuit between the connector and the battery is problem free. Continue checking the rest of the circuit in the same fashion. When you reach a point at which no voltage is present, the problem lies between that point and the last test point with voltage. Most of the time the problem can be traced to a loose connection.

➡ **Note: Keep in mind that some circuits receive voltage only when the ignition key is in the Accessory or Run position.**

FINDING A SHORT

7   One method of finding shorts in a circuit is to remove the fuse and connect a test light or voltmeter in place of the fuse terminals. There should be no voltage present in the circuit. Move the wiring harness from side-to-side while watching the test light. If the bulb goes on, there is a short to ground somewhere in that area, probably where the insulation has rubbed through. The same test can be performed on each component in the circuit, even a switch.

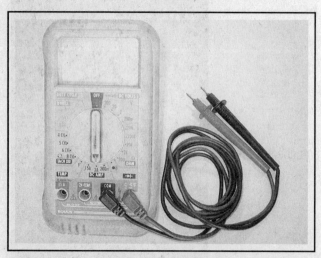

2.5a The most useful tool for electrical troubleshooting is a digital multimeter that can check volts, amps, and test continuity

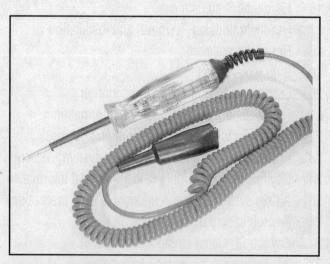

2.5b A test light is a very handy tool for checking voltage

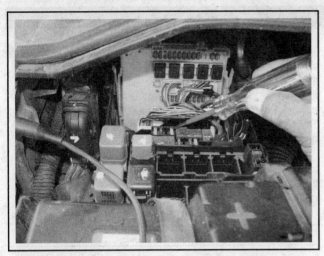

2.6 In use, a basic test light's lead is clipped to a known good ground, then the pointed probe can test connectors, wires or electrical sockets - if the bulb lights, the part being tested has battery voltage

2.9 With a multimeter set to the ohms scale, resistance can be checked across two terminals - when checking for continuity, a low reading indicates continuity, a high reading indicates lack of continuity

GROUND CHECK

8   Perform a ground test to check whether a component is properly grounded. Disconnect the battery and connect one lead of a continuity tester or multimeter (set to the ohms scale), to a known good ground. Connect the other lead to the wire or ground connection being tested. If the resistance is low (less than 5 ohms), the ground is good. If the bulb on a self-powered test light does not go on, the ground is not good.

CONTINUITY CHECK

9   A continuity check is done to determine if there are any breaks in a circuit - if it is passing electricity properly. With the circuit off (no power in the circuit), a self-powered continuity tester or multimeter can be used to check the circuit. Connect the test leads to both ends of the circuit (or to the power end and a good ground), and if the test light comes on the circuit is passing current properly (see illustration). If the resistance is low (less than 5 ohms), there is continuity; if the reading is 10,000 ohms or higher, there is a break somewhere in the circuit. The same procedure can be used to test a switch, by connecting the continuity tester to the switch terminals. With the switch turned On, the test light should come on (or low resistance should be indicated on a meter).

FINDING AN OPEN CIRCUIT

10 When diagnosing for possible open circuits, it is often difficult to locate them by sight because the connectors hide oxidation or terminal misalignment. Merely wiggling a connector on a sensor or in the wiring harness may correct the open circuit condition. Remember this when an open circuit is indicated when troubleshooting a circuit. Intermittent problems may also be caused by oxidized or loose connections.

11 Electrical troubleshooting is simple if you keep in mind that all electrical circuits are basically electricity running from the battery, through the wires, switches, relays, fuses and fusible links to each electrical component (light bulb, motor, etc.) and to ground, from which it is passed back to the battery. Any electrical problem is an interruption in the flow of electricity to and from the battery.

ELECTRICAL BACKFEED CHECKING

12 Back feed in a electrical circuit happens when one electrical system crosses over onto another electrical system, or in some cases when something internally in a processor sends out the wrong signal at the wrong time to a component. Some electrical checks can be obvious once you understand the fundamentals of electrical current flow.

13 One of the most common back feeds is from a tail light bulb that has two filaments in the bulb. Such as a 1157 bulb or a 3157 bulb. If the bulb is in backwards or someone installs the wrong kind of bulb say, a 1156 (single element-single post bulb) in a 1157 socket the two contact points inside the socket will cause the backfeed. (You can't put the 3157 in backwards, the power and ground leads are always on opposite sides and opposite ends of each other, but the ground lead is common to both circuits, but you can have a loss of the ground circuit.)

14 An example of this would be someone changing out a brake lamp and installs the wrong bulb type. Then, when you push on the brake pedal you'll notice the turn signal indicators or the park lights and dash lights come on. Conversely, if you turned on the parking lights and you see the turn signal indicators on in the dash, this would be an example of backfeed in action. There are many other ways a backfeed can happen too. For example, when you see or hear something that is acting peculiar especially after reconnecting numerous electrical connections. Go back to what you did last, disconnect it and check that the wire colors on each side of the connection are a match. You might have connected the wrong leads together or installed the wrong type of electrical component for your car.

15 Always, recheck your work.

3 Fuses and fusible links - general information

FUSES

1 The electrical circuits of the vehicle are protected by a combination of fuses, circuit breakers and fusible links. The main fuse/relay panel is in the engine compartment (see illustration), while the interior fuse/relay panel is located inside the passenger compartment (see illustration). Each of the fuses is designed to protect a specific circuit, and the various circuits are identified on the fuse panel itself.

2 Several sizes of fuses are employed in the fuse blocks. There are small, medium and large sizes of the same design, all with the same blade terminal design. The medium and large fuses can be removed with your fingers, but the small fuses require the use of pliers or the small plastic fuse-puller tool found in most fuse boxes.

3 If an electrical component fails, always check the fuse first. The best way to check the fuses is with a test light. Check for power at the exposed terminal tips of each fuse. If power is present at one side of the fuse but not the other, the fuse is blown. A blown fuse can also be identified by visually inspecting it (see illustration).

4 Be sure to replace blown fuses with the correct type. Fuses (of the same physical size) of different ratings may be physically interchangeable, but only fuses of the proper rating should be used. Replacing a fuse with one of a higher or lower value than specified is not recommended. Each electrical circuit needs a specific amount of protection. The amperage value of each fuse is molded into the top of the fuse body.

5 If the replacement fuse immediately fails, don't replace it again until the cause of the problem is isolated and corrected. In most cases, this will be a short circuit in the wiring caused by a broken or deteriorated wire.

FUSIBLE LINKS

6 On these models, large, high-amperage fuses are used instead of traditional fusible links. They are located in the underhood fuse/relay box (see illustration 3.1a).

3.1a The engine compartment fuse/relay box is mounted next to the battery in the engine compartment. All the fuses and relays are listed by location and function on the underside of the fuse/relay box cover

3.1b The interior fuse/relay box is on the driver's side on the end of the dash panel. Open the driver's door and remove the access panel. The fuses are marked on the back of the access panel

3.3 When a fuse blows, the element between the terminals melts

4 Circuit breakers - general information

1 Circuit breakers protect certain circuits, such as the power windows or heated seats. Depending on the vehicle's accessories, there may be one or two circuit breakers, located in the fuse/relay box in the engine compartment.

2 Because the circuit breakers reset automatically, an electrical overload in a circuit breaker-protected system will cause the circuit to fail momentarily, then come back on. If the circuit does not come back on, check it immediately.

3 For a basic check, pull the circuit breaker up out of its socket on the fuse panel, but just far enough to probe with a voltmeter. The breaker should still contact the sockets. With the voltmeter negative lead on a good chassis ground, touch each end prong of the circuit breaker with the positive meter probe. There should be battery voltage at each end. If there is battery voltage only at one end, the circuit breaker must be replaced.

4 Some circuit breakers must be reset manually.

5   Relays - general information

1   Several electrical accessories in the vehicle, such as the fuel injection system, horns, starter, and fog lamps use relays to transmit the electrical signal to the component. Relays use a low-current circuit (the control circuit) to open and close a high-current circuit (the power cir- cuit). If the relay is defective, that component will not operate properly. Most relays are mounted in the engine compartment fuse/relay box (see illustration 3.1a).

6   Electrical connectors - general information

1   Most electrical connections on these vehicles are made with multiwire plastic connectors. The mating halves of many connectors are secured with locking clips molded into the plastic connector shells. The mating halves of some large connectors, such as some of those under the instrument panel, are held together by a bolt through the center of the connector.

2   To separate a connector with locking clips, use a small screw- driver to pry the clips apart carefully, then separate the connector halves. Pull only on the shell, never pull on the wiring harness, as you may damage the individual wires and terminals inside the connectors. Look at the connector closely before trying to separate the halves. Often the locking clips are engaged in a way that is not immediately clear.

Electrical connectors

Most electrical connectors have a single release tab that you depress to release the connector

Some electrical connectors have a retaining tab which must be pried up to free the connector

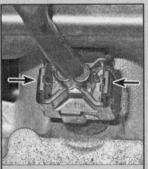

Some connectors have two release tabs that you must squeeze to release the connector

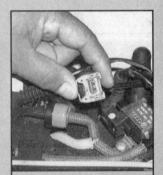

Some connectors use wire retainers that you squeeze to release the connector

Critical connectors often employ a sliding lock (1) that you must pull out before you can depress the release tab (2)

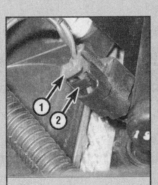

Here's another sliding-lock style connector, with the lock (1) and the release tab (2) on the side of the connector

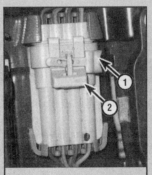

On some connectors the lock (1) must be pulled out to the side and removed before you can lift the release tab (2)

Some critical connectors, like the multi-pin connectors at the Powertrain Control Module employ pivoting locks that must be flipped open

Additionally, many connectors have more than one set of clips.

3   Each pair of connector terminals has a male half and a female half. When you look at the end view of a connector in a diagram, be sure to understand whether the view shows the harness side or the component side of the connector. Connector halves are mirror images of each other, and a terminal shown on the right side end-view of one half will be on the left side end-view of the other half.

4   It is often necessary to take circuit voltage measurements with a connector connected. Whenever possible, carefully insert a small straight pin (not your meter probe) into the rear of the connector shell to contact the terminal inside, then clip your meter lead to the pin. This kind of connection is called "backprobing." When inserting a test probe into a terminal, be careful not to distort the terminal opening. Doing so can lead to a poor connection and corrosion at that terminal later. Using the small straight pin instead of a meter probe results in less chance of deforming the terminal connector.

7   Steering column switches - replacement

❉❉ WARNING:

The models covered by this manual are equipped with a Supplemental Restraint System (SRS), more commonly known as airbags. Always disarm the airbag system before working in the vicinity of any airbag system component to avoid the possibility of accidental deployment of the airbag, which could cause personal injury (see Section 25).

1   Disconnect the cable from the negative terminal of the battery (see Chapter 5).

2   Remove the steering column covers (see Chapter 11).

➡ **Note: Both the wiper switch and the turn signal switch (multi-function switch) are removed using this same procedure.**

3   Disconnect the electrical connectors, then depress the locking tabs and remove either of the two switches from the steering column (see illustrations).

4   Installation is the reverse of removal.

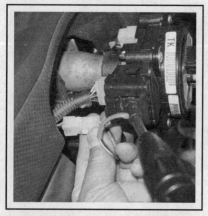

7.3a Disconnect the cruise control connector (if equipped)

7.3b Press the tabs inward and pull the switch out

7.3c The wiper switch is removed the same way

8   Brake light switch, fog lamp switch, power outlet, dash mounted switches, DRL and lighting module replacement

1   Disconnect the cable from the negative terminal of the battery (see Chapter 5).

OUTSIDE MIRROR AND DASH DIMMER CONTROL (DASH MOUNTED SWITCHES)

2   Using a flat bladed trim tool or equivalent, slide it under the edge of the trim and pry the trim away from the dash (see illustrations).

3   Both switches are held in by plastic prongs on either side of the switch. Using a small flat screwdriver, carefully release the clips and pull the switch from the trim panel.

4   Disconnect the electrical connectors.

5   Installation is reverse of removal.

BRAKE LIGHT SWITCH REMOVAL

6   Locate the brake light switch mounted on the support bracket under the dash.

7   Disconnect the electrical connector to the brake switch. (For referencing, check the wiring diagram for the correct colored leads so that you know you are disconnecting the correct switch leads.)

8   Twist the switch housing counterclockwise and remove.

9   Installation is the reverse of removal.

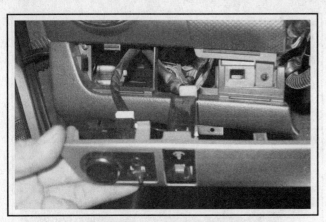

8.2a Pull the trim with the switches out far enough to gain access to the connectors

8.2b Disconnect the electrical connectors

BRAKE LIGHT SWITCH INSTALLATION

10 Pull the brake switch shaft out to its maximum length.

11 While depressing the brake pedal down as far as possible, insert the brake switch into its mounting area and turn the switch clockwise.

12 Slowly release the brake pedal. The force of the pedal will automatically adjust the brake switch shaft to its proper position.

13 Reconnect the electrical connector to the brake switch.

14 Reconnect the negative battery cable and check that the brake lights are working correctly.

FOG LAMP SWITCH

15 The fog lamp switch is mounted on the instrument panel to the right of the steering column.

16 Pry the switch out of the dash using a small flat bladed screwdriver or equivalent trim removal tool.

17 Disconnect the electrical connector.

18 Installation is the reverse of removal.

POWER OUTLET/CIGARETTE LIGHTER REMOVAL

19 Remove the cigarette lighter element.

20 Remove the center console (see Chapter 11).

21 Disconnect the electrical connections to the cigarette/power outlet.

22 Hold the outside portion of the outlet with one finger inserted in the outlet while turning the rear portion counterclockwise.

23 Remove the two parts of the outlet.

24 Installation is the reverse of removal.

DRL MODULE REPLACEMENT

➡ **Note: DRL (Daytime Running Light) module is located below the driver's dash area near the center console. Use the wiring diagrams provided to check the wire colors at the connection to insure you are disconnecting the correct module. There are similar size and shape modules in the same general area.**

25 Remove the driver's side knee bolster (see Chapter 11).

26 Unbolt the DRL module, disconnect the electrical connections and remove the module.

27 Installation is the reverse of removal.

LIGHTING MODULE REPLACEMENT

➡ **Note: The lighting module (if equipped) is located below the driver's knee bolster area. Use the wiring diagrams provided to be sure of which unit you are disconnecting. Some modules are identical in size and are in the same area.**

28 Remove the two screws securing the lighting module to the support bracket. Disconnect the electrical connection and remove the module.

29 Installation is the reverse of removal.

| **9** | **Ignition switch, key lock cylinder and key - replacement** |

❋❋ WARNING:

The models covered by this manual are equipped with a Supplemental Restraint System (SRS), more commonly known as airbags. Always disarm the airbag system before working in the vicinity of any airbag system component to avoid the possibility of accidental deployment of the airbag, which could cause personal injury (see Section 25).

1 Disconnect the cable from the negative terminal of the battery (see Chapter 5).

2 Remove the steering column covers (see Chapter 11).

IGNITION SWITCH HOUSING REMOVAL

3 Insert the ignition key into the lock cylinder and rotate the key lock cylinder to the RUN position.

9.4 Remove the fastener securing the ignition switch

9.8 Remove the fasteners securing the switch (one fastener not visible in photo)

4   Remove the mounting fastener from the ignition switch (see illustration).

5   Remove the ignition switch.

6   Installation is the reverse of removal.

KEY LOCK CYLINDER

7   Remove the steering wheel (see Chapter 10).

8   Remove the KEY REMINDER switch (see illustration), then disconnect the electrical connector.

9   Insert the ignition key into the lock cylinder and rotate the key lock cylinder to the ACC position. Press the detent clip in with a 2.5mm Allen wrench or equivalent tool of that size. With a slight wiggle of the key and the detent depressed, draw the lock cylinder out of the ignition switch body by pulling the key outward.

10 Installation is the reverse of removal.

10   Instrument cluster - removal and installation

✳ WARNING:

The models covered by this manual are equipped with a Supplemental Restraint System (SRS), more commonly known as airbags. Always disarm the airbag system before working in the vicinity of any airbag system component to avoid the possibility of accidental deployment of the airbag, which could cause personal injury (see Section 25).

1   Disconnect the cable from the negative terminal of the battery (see Chapter 5).

2   Remove the instrument cluster trim panel (see Chapter 11).

3   Remove the instrument cluster retaining screws, then remove the cluster (see illustration).

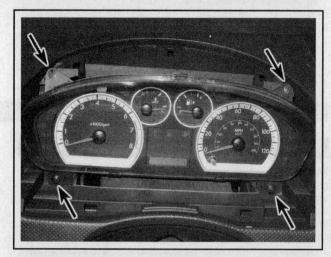

10.3 Instrument cluster screw locations

4   Disconnect the electrical connector(s) from the cluster (see illustration).

5   Installation is the reverse of removal.

10.4 Disconnect the electrical connector(s).

11 Wiper motor - removal and installation

1   Disconnect the cable from the negative terminal of the battery (see Chapter 5).

2   Remove the wiper arm weather cap and retaining nut (see illustrations).

3   Remove the left portion of the cowl cover (see Chapter 12).

4   Disconnect the electrical connector to the wiper motor.

5   Remove the fasteners securing the wiper assembly to the cowl support area (see illustration).

6   Remove the wiper assembly from the vehicle.

7   Installation is the reverse of removal.

11.2a Pry the weather cap off

11.2b Remove the retaining nut, then (using a wiper arm puller) remove the wiper arm

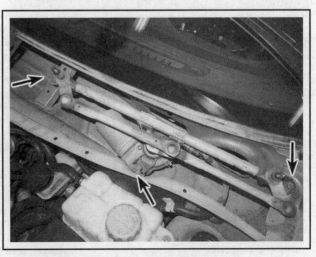

11.5 Wiper assembly mounting fasteners

WIPER WASHER RESERVOIR REPLACEMENT

8 Disconnect the cable from the negative terminal of the battery (see Chapter 5).

9 Remove the left front wheel well (see Chapter 11).

10 Locate and disconnect the electrical connections to the wiper washer pump.

11 Remove the fasteners securing the washer reservoir to the inner fender support area.

12 Remove the washer reservoir.

13 Installation is the reverse of removal.

12 Radio and speakers - removal and installation

✳✳ WARNING:

The models covered by this manual are equipped with a Supplemental Restraint System (SRS), more commonly known as airbags. Always disarm the airbag system before working in the vicinity of any airbag system component to avoid the possibility of accidental deployment of the airbag, which could cause personal injury (see Section 25).

RADIO

1 Disconnect the cable from the negative terminal of the battery (see Chapter 5).

2 Remove the center trim panel (see Chapter 11).

3 Remove the radio control assembly mounting screws and pull the controller out of the dash.

4 Disconnect the antenna cable, the electrical connectors and the ground strap from the back of the radio.

5 Installation is the reverse of removal.

SPEAKERS

A-pillar speakers (tweeters)

6 Remove the A-pillar trim panel (see Chapter 11).

7 Disconnect the electrical connector from the tweeter (see illustration).

8 Carefully pry the speaker out of the mounting bracket, and remove the speaker.

9 Installation is the reverse of removal.

Door speakers

10 Remove the door trim panel (see Chapter 11).

11 Remove the speaker mounting fasteners (see illustration).

12 Pull out the speaker and disconnect the electrical connector.

13 Installation is the reverse of removal.

Rear speakers - Sedan models

14 Remove the rear package tray (see Chapter 11).

15 Remove the mounting screws and pull the speaker housing out (see illustration).

16 Disconnect the electrical connector from the speaker.

17 Installation is the reverse of removal.

Rear speakers - Hatchback

18 Remove the rear cargo area side trim panel (see Chapter 11).

19 Disconnect the electrical connector from the speaker.

20 Remove the screws retaining the speaker to the trim panel.

21 Remove the speaker.

22 Installation is the reverse of removal.

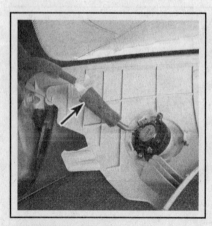

12.7 Disconnect the electrical connector

12.11 Remove the mounting fasteners, then pull up the speaker and disconnect the electrical connector

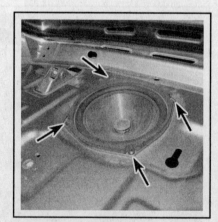

12.15 Remove the speaker mounting fasteners

13 Antenna - removal and installation

1   Disconnect the cable from the negative terminal of the battery (see Chapter 5).
2   Remove the interior overhead dome light fixture (see Chapter 11).
3   Unscrew the antenna mounting base.

4   Remove the antenna base and disconnect the electrical connectors.
5   Installation is the reverse of removal.

14 Rear window defogger - check and repair

1   The rear window defogger consists of a number of horizontal elements baked onto the glass surface.
2   Small breaks in the element can be repaired without removing the rear window.

CHECK

3   Turn the ignition switch and defogger system switches to the ON position. Using a voltmeter, place the positive probe against the defogger grid positive terminal and the negative probe against the ground terminal. If battery voltage is not indicated, check the fuse, defogger switch and related wiring. If voltage is indicated, but all or part of the defogger doesn't heat, proceed with the following tests.

4   When measuring voltage during the next two tests, wrap a piece of aluminum foil around the tip of the voltmeter positive probe and press the foil against the heating element with your finger (see illustration). Place the negative probe on the defogger grid ground terminal.
5   Check the voltage at the center of each heating element (see illustration). If the voltage is 5 or 6-volts, the element is okay (there is no break). If the voltage is zero, the element is broken between the center of the element and the positive end. If the voltage is 10 to 12-volts the element is broken between the center of the element and ground. Check each heating element.
6   Connect the negative lead to a good body ground. The reading should stay the same. If it doesn't, the ground connection is bad.

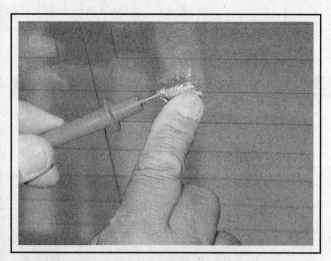

14.4 When measuring the voltage at the rear window defogger grid, wrap a piece of aluminum foil around the positive probe of the voltmeter and press the foil against the wire with your finger

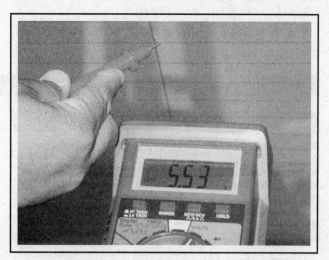

14.5 To determine if a heating element has broken, check the voltage at the center of each element; if the voltage is 5 or 6-volts, the element is unbroken, but if the voltage is 10 or 12-volts, the element is broken between the center and the ground side. If there is no voltage, the element is broken between the center and the positive side

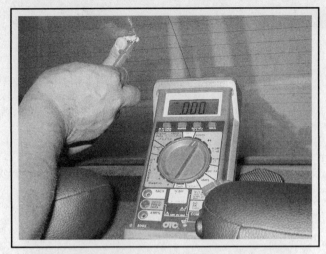

14.7 To find the break, place the voltmeter negative lead against the defogger ground terminal, place the voltmeter positive lead with the foil strip against the heating element at the positive terminal end and slide it toward the negative terminal end. The point at which the voltmeter reading changes abruptly is the point at which the element is broken

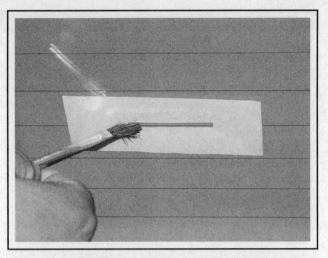

14.13 To use a defogger repair kit, apply masking tape to the inside of the window at the damaged area, then brush on the special conductive coating

7   To find the break, place the voltmeter negative probe against the defogger ground terminal. Place the voltmeter positive probe with the foil strip against the heating element at the positive terminal end and slide it toward the negative terminal end. The point at which the voltmeter deflects from several volts to zero is the point at which the heating element is broken (see illustration).

REPAIR

8   Repair the break in the element using a repair kit specifically recommended for this purpose, available at most auto parts stores. Included in this kit is plastic conductive epoxy.

9   Prior to repairing a break, turn off the system and allow it to cool off for a few minutes.
10   Lightly buff the element area with fine steel wool, then clean it thoroughly with rubbing alcohol.
11   Use masking tape to mask off the area being repaired.
12   Thoroughly mix the epoxy, following the instructions provided with the repair kit.
13   Apply the epoxy material to the slit in the masking tape, overlapping the undamaged area about 3/4-inch on either end (see illustration).
14   Allow the repair to cure for 24 hours before removing the tape and using the system.

15   Headlight bulb - replacement

❄❄ WARNING:

Halogen gas-filled bulbs are under pressure and can shatter if the surface is scratched or the bulb is dropped. Wear eye protection and handle the bulbs carefully, grasping only the base whenever possible. Do not touch the surface of the bulb with your fingers because the oil from your skin could cause it to overheat and fail prematurely. If you do touch the bulb surface, clean it with rubbing alcohol.

1   Raise the hood.
2   If necessary, remove the headlight housing (see Section 17).

➡ Note: On some models it isn't necessary to remove the headlight housing in order to access the bulbs.

3   Disconnect the electrical connector from the headlight housing (see illustration).

15.3 Remove the connector by pulling it straight away from the headlamp

4   Remove the seal cap from the headlamp housing (see illustration).

5   Remove the headlamp retaining clip (see illustration).

6   Remove the headlamp (see illustration).

7   Installation is the reverse of removal.

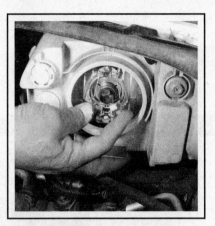

15.4 The seal aligns with the three prongs of the headlamp. Be sure to align them when reinstalling.

15.5 Grasp the retaining clip and squeeze it together to unlatch the clip

15.6 Notice the notch in the bulb base. This notch needs to be aligned in the groove before attaching the retaining clip

16 Headlights - adjustment

➡ **Note: The headlights must be aimed correctly. If adjusted incorrectly they could blind the driver of an oncoming vehicle and cause a serious accident or seriously reduce your ability to see the road. The headlights should be checked for proper aim every 12 months and any time a new headlight is installed or front end body work is performed. It should be emphasized that the following procedure is only an interim step that will provide temporary adjustment until a properly equipped shop can adjust the headlights.**

1   The vertical adjustment screws (one per housing) are located on the top of the headlight housings (see illustration). There are no horizontal adjustment screws.

2   There are several methods for adjusting the headlights. The simplest method requires masking tape, a blank wall and a level floor.

3   Position masking tape vertically on the wall in reference to the vehicle centerline and the centerlines of both headlights (see illustration).

4   Position a horizontal tape line in reference to the centerline of all the headlights.

➡ **Note: It might be easier to position the tape on the wall with the vehicle parked only a few inches away.**

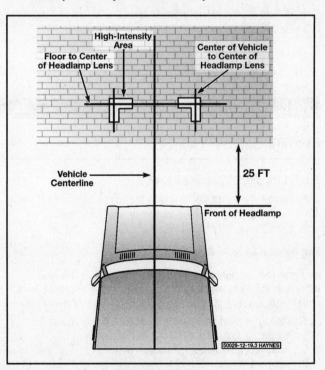

16.3 Headlight adjustment details

16.1 Headlight vertical adjuster location - right side shown, left side identical

5   Adjustment should be made with the vehicle parked 25 feet from the wall, sitting level, the gas tank half-full and no heavy load in the vehicle.

6   Starting with the low beam adjustment, position the high intensity zone so it is two inches below the horizontal line. Adjustment is made by turning the adjusting screw.

➡ **Note: It might not be possible to position the headlight aim exactly for both high and low beams. If a compromise must be** made, keep in mind that the low beams are the most used and have the greatest effect on safety.

7   With the high beams on, the high intensity zone should be vertically centered with the exact center just below the horizontal line.

8   Have the headlights adjusted by a dealer service department or service station at the earliest opportunity.

17 Headlight housing - removal and installation

1   Raise the hood.

2   Remove the fasteners securing the headlight housing (see illustration).

3   Pull the headlamp assembly out of the opening.

4   Disconnect the electrical connectors.

5   Installation is the reverse of removal.

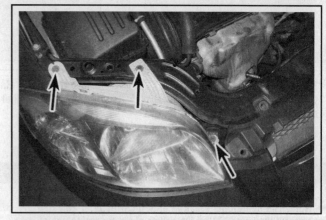

17.2 Headlight housing mounting fasteners

18 Horn - replacement

1   Remove the radiator grille (see Chapter 11).

2   Disconnect the electrical connector from the horn.

3   Remove the horn mounting bracket bolt and remove the horn with its bracket.

4   Installation is the reverse of removal.

19 Bulb replacement

EXTERIOR BULB REPLACEMENT

Front turn signal/parking light bulbs

1   Remove the appropriate headlamp housing (see Section 17).

2   Remove turn signal/parking lamp bulb (see illustration).

3   Installation is the reverse of removal.

Fog light bulbs

➡ **Note: The fog lights, if equipped, are located in the lower corners of the front bumper cover. They're easily accessed from underneath the bumper cover or through the inner fender liner.**

4   Raise the front of the vehicle and place it securely on jackstands.

5   Remove the nuts securing the fog lamp assembly.

6   Disconnect the electrical connector.

7   Remove the bulb.

8   Installation is the reverse of removal.

19.2 Twist it counterclockwise to remove the bulb

Bulb removal

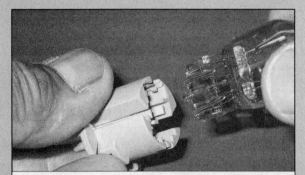

To remove many modern exterior bulbs from their holders, simply pull them out

On bulbs with a cylindrical base ("bayonet" bulbs), the socket is spring-loaded; a pair of small posts on the side of the base hold the bulb in place against spring pressure. To remove this type of bulb, push it into the holder, rotate it 1/4-turn counterclockwise, then pull it out

If a bayonet bulb has dual filaments, the posts are staggered, so the bulb can only be installed one way

To remove most overhead interior light bulbs, simply unclip them

Front side marker bulbs

9 Pry the side marker lens assembly free with a flat trim tool or equivalent.

10 Pull the side marker assembly from the vehicle. The bulb fixture will come out with it (see illustration).

11 Remove the bulb holder from the housing, then remove the bulb from the holder (see illustration).

12 Installation is the reverse of removal.

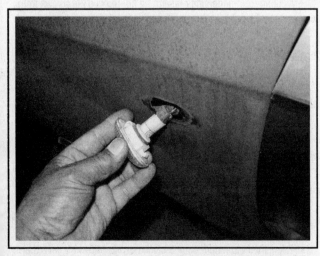

19.10 Pull the light fixture out to gain access to the bulb

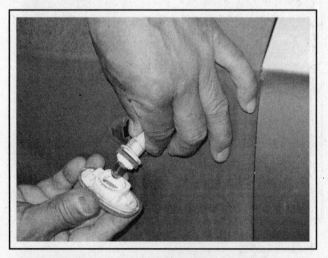

19.11 Remove the side marker bulb holder by turning it counterclockwise, then pull the bulb from the holder

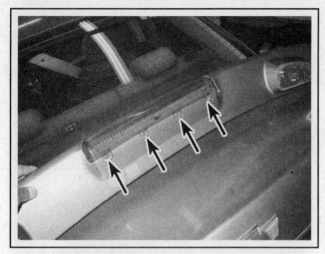

19.13a Remove the mounting screws from inside the trunk

19.13b Disconnect the electrical connector to the light

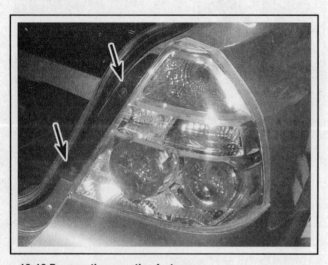

19.19 Remove the mounting fasteners

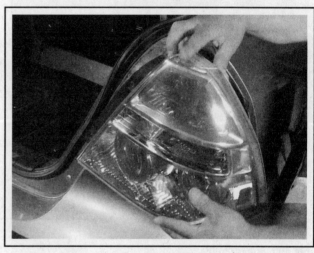

19.20 Pull it straight out to disengage the clips

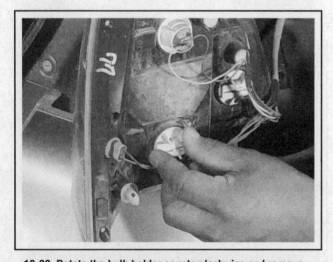

19.22 Rotate the bulb holder counterclockwise and remove the bulb holder

Center-mount brake light - Sedan models

13 Working from underside of the trunk lid, remove the screws from the center mount brake light (see illustrations).

14 Installation is the reverse of removal.

Center-mount brake light - Hatchback

15 Open the rear hatch.

16 Pry off the center mount brake lamp access panel with a small flat bladed screwdriver.

17 Remove the bulb.

18 Installation is the reverse of removal.

Rear lighting - brake/tail/turn signal

19 Open the trunk or rear hatch (whichever is applicable), then remove the mounting fasteners (see illustration).

20 Pull the tail light housing straight back to disengage the mounting studs (see illustration).

21 Disconnect the electrical connector.

22 Rotate the bulb holder counterclockwise to remove the bulb that you want to replace (see illustration).

23 Installation is the reverse of removal.

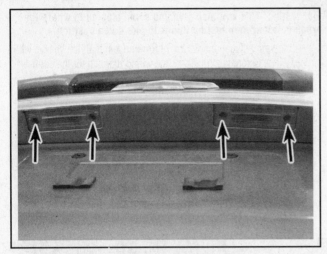

19.24 License plate light lens retaining screws

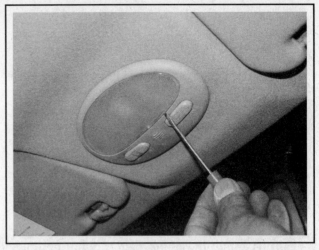

19.27 Use a small screwdriver to depress the tabs and pry the lens out

License plate light

24 Remove the screws securing the license plate lens and light to the trunk lid or hatch (whichever is applicable) (see illustration).
25 Replace the bulb by pulling straight out.
26 Installation is the reverse of removal.

INTERIOR LIGHT REPLACEMENT

Dome light, map/reading light or trunk light bulbs

27 Carefully pry the lens out (see illustration).

28 Remove the screws retaining the lamp housing to the headliner.
29 Disconnect the electrical connector.
30 To replace the bulb(s), pull the bulb from the socket.
31 Installation is the reverse of removal.

Rear compartment/trunk interior lamp

32 Open trunk or rear hatch (whichever is applicable).
33 Pry off the lens to the rear compartment interior lamp fixture.
34 Remove the bulb.
35 Installation is the reverse of removal.

20   Electric side view mirrors - description

➡ Note: These models are equipped with a Body Control Module (BCM). Several systems are linked to a centralized control module that allows simple and accurate troubleshooting, but only with a professional-grade scan tool. The Body Control Module governs the door locks, the power windows, the ignition lock and security system, the interior lights, the Daytime Running Lights system, the horn, the windshield wipers, the heating/air conditioning system and the power mirrors. In the event of malfunction with this system, have the vehicle diagnosed by a dealership service department or other qualified automotive repair facility.

1 The electric rear view mirrors use two motors to move the glass; one for up and down adjustments and one for left-right adjustments. Some vehicles are equipped with memory mirrors as well. These mirrors are an integral part of the power seat memory unit as well as incorporated with the Body Control Module (BCM). If there is a problem with these systems it is advised to seek out a qualified independent repair facility or your local dealer.

2 The control switch has a selector portion which sends voltage to the left or right side mirror. With the ignition in the ACC position and the engine OFF, roll down the windows and operate the mirror control switch through all functions (left-right and up-down) for both the left and right side mirrors.
3 Listen carefully for the sound of the electric motors running in the mirrors.
4 If the motors can be heard but the mirror glass doesn't move, there's probably a problem with the drive mechanism inside the mirror. Power mirrors have no user-serviceable parts inside - a defective mirror must be replaced as a unit (see Chapter 11).
5 If the mirrors don't operate and no sound comes from the mirrors, check the fuses (see Section 3).
6 If the fuses are OK, remove the mirror control switch. Have the switch continuity checked by a dealer service department or other qualified shop.
7 Check the ground connections.

8   If the mirror still doesn't work, remove the mirror and check the wires at the mirror for voltage.

9   If there's not voltage in each switch position, check the circuit between the mirror and control switch for opens and shorts.

➡ **Hint: If the mirror is inoperative, try holding the switch in one of the directions and swing the door open and closed. If there is a break in the door jamb you may occasionally make contact long enough to avoid removing the mirror from the door for fur-** ther testing. **This will also give you some clue as to where the break is rather than testing things in one given position.**

10 If there's voltage, remove the mirror and test it off the vehicle with jumper wires. Before testing, check the wiring diagram for the correct leads that have to be used for each position. Applying voltage to the wrong leads can damage the mirror drive motors. Replace the mirror if it fails this test (see Chapter 11).

21 Cruise control system - general information

1   These models have an electrically controlled throttle body - there is no accelerator cable or cruise control cable. The accelerator pedal communicates with the throttle body through the Powertrain Control Module (PCM). See Chapters 4 and 6 for more information about the electronic throttle control system. The PCM also controls the cruise control system, which is now an integral function of the electronic throttle control system. If the system malfunctions, take it to a dealer service department or other qualified repair shop for further diagnosis.

➡ **Note: There are several service codes associated with the operation of the cruise control. For service see a qualified repair shop that handles electrical service work and have them diagnose it with a scanner.**

➡ **Tip: The cruise control is one of the many systems on today's vehicles that a generic code reader isn't capable of extracting the codes from the vehicle. A professional level scanner is needed to diagnose the cruise control properly.**

2   Cruise control switch removal (see Section 7).

22 Power window system - description and check

➡ **Note: These models are equipped with a Body Control Module (BCM) incorporated with the window system. Several systems are linked to a centralized control module that allows simple and accurate troubleshooting, but only with a professional-grade scan tool. The Body Control Module governs the door locks, the power windows, the ignition lock and security system, the interior lights, the Daytime Running Lights system, the horn, the windshield wipers, the heating/air conditioning system and the power mirrors. In the event of malfunction with this system, have the vehicle diagnosed by a dealership service department or other qualified automotive repair facility.**

1   The power window system operates electric motors, mounted in the doors, which lower and raise the windows. The system consists of the control switches, the motors, regulators, glass mechanisms, the Body Control Module (BCM) and associated wiring.

2   The power windows can be lowered and raised from the master control switch by the driver or by remote switches located at the individual windows. Each window has a separate motor that is reversible. The position of the control switch determines the polarity and therefore the direction of operation.

3   The window motor circuits are protected by a fuse. Each motor is also equipped with an internal circuit breaker; this prevents one stuck window from disabling the whole system.

4   The power window system will only operate when the ignition switch has activated the Retained Accessory Power (RAP) relay. In addi- tion, many models have a window lockout switch at the master control switch which, when activated, disables the switches at the rear windows and, sometimes, the switch at the passenger's window also. Always check these items before troubleshooting a window problem related to any of the other windows besides the driver's window. Window lock-out does not affect the driver's window.

5   These procedures are general in nature, so if you can't find the problem using them, take the vehicle to a dealer service department or to an independent repair facility that specializes in electrical repairs.

6   If the power windows won't operate, always check the fuse and circuit breaker first.

7   If only the rear windows are inoperative, or if the windows only operate from the master control switch, check the rear window lockout switch for continuity in the unlocked position. Replace it if it doesn't have continuity.

8   Check the wiring between the switches and fuse panel for continuity. Repair the wiring, if necessary.

9   If only one window is inoperative from the master control switch, try the other control switch at each individual window.

➡ **Note: This doesn't apply to the driver's door window.**

10 If the same window works from one switch, but not the other, check the switch and/or wiring for continuity.

11 If the switch tests OK, check for a short or open in the circuit between the affected switch and the window motor.

12 If one window is inoperative from both switches, remove the switch panel from the affected door. Check for voltage at the motor while the switch is operated.

➡ **Note: There are voltage and ground signals present at the switch connector. However, on 2010 and later models, there are also two data lines to the BCM that are not true positive/negative signals. Be sure you are testing the correct leads. Do not apply voltage or ground to any leads you are not sure of. Seek professional help in diagnosing any problems with the window circuits if you are unsure.**

13 If voltage is reaching the motor, disconnect the glass from the regulator (see Chapter 11). Move the window up and down by hand while checking for binding and damage. Also check for binding and damage to the regulator. If the regulator is not damaged and the window moves up and down smoothly, replace the motor. If there's binding or damage, lubricate, repair or replace parts, as necessary.

14 If voltage isn't reaching the motor, check the wiring in the circuit for continuity between the switches and the BCM, and between the BCM (if applicable) and the motors. You'll need to consult the wiring diagram in Chapter 13. If the circuit is equipped with a relay, check that the relay is grounded properly and receiving voltage.

15 Test the windows to confirm proper repairs.

➡ **Hint: To verify if the motor is getting the needed voltage or ground, a simple but effective test is to sit in the car with** the ignition on, open a door and look at the dome light. Then operate the switch to the faulty window. If you see the dome light dimming slightly this is a good indication that the motor is getting power and is probably a stuck motor or faulty wiring. Do not hold the switch on for very long when a motor is stuck or wiring is in question or more damage may occur. Finally, in some cases, a good rap on the door panel in the general area of the window motor - while the key is on and the window switch is depressed in the direction the window needs to move - will free up a stuck motor temporarily. You can damage the door panel or more internal components if you hit it too hard or are too aggressive.

WINDOW EXPRESS DOWN PROGRAMMING

➡ **Note: Any time the battery or window motor are disconnected, you will need to perform this procedure to reestablish the auto feature.**

16 Lower the window to its lowest position, holding the switch in the Down position for an additional five seconds.

17 Raise the window to its highest position, holding the window switch in the Up position for an additional five seconds.

18 Verify proper operation.

23 Power door lock and keyless entry system - description and check

➡ **Note: These models are equipped with a remote control door lock receiver (RCDLR) located under the left side of the instrument panel. If you are not experienced in electrical diagnostics, have the vehicle diagnosed by a dealership service department or other qualified repair facility.**

1   The power door lock system operates the door lock actuators mounted in each door. The system consists of the switches, actuators, lock and unlock relays, remote control door lock receiver (RCDLR) the associated wiring, and the theft deterrent system. Diagnosis can usually be limited to simple checks of the wiring connections and actuators for minor faults that can be easily repaired.

2   Power door lock systems are operated by bi-directional solenoids located in the doors. The lock actuators are mounted as part of the door latch. Remove the door latch for access to the door lock actuator, (see Chapter 11). The lock switches have two operating positions: Lock and Unlock. These switches send a signal to the RCDLR, which in turn sends a signal to the door lock relays, (located in the car fuse box), the relays then send the needed voltage to each of the door lock solenoids.

3   If you are unable to locate the trouble using the following general steps, consult your dealer service department or qualified independent repair shop.

➡ **Note: Always check the circuit protection first. Some vehicles use a combination of circuit breakers and fuses. Check the wiring diagrams provided to determine the location and type of fuse or breaker that are used in conjunction with the door lock system.**

4   The lock switch has both positive and ground potential at the switch. The switch reverses the polarity internally and sends the appropriate signal to the door lock relays and RCDLR.

5   You can check the switch for continuity. Using the wiring diagrams provided to find the incoming lead and the prospective output lead, you want to check for continuity. Attach your ohmmeter to those leads and operate the switch in that direction. If the switch has continuity, check the wiring between the switch, RCDLR, the door lock relay and the door lock solenoid.

6   If all but one lock solenoids operate, remove the trim panel from the affected door (see Chapter 11) and check for voltage and ground signal at the solenoid while the lock switch is operated. The polarity should reverse when the switch is pushed in the opposite direction.

7   If the inoperative solenoid is receiving positive voltage on one lead and negative on the other, the solenoid is most likely defective. Check the connections for good contact; if the connection is good, replace the solenoid.

8   If the inoperative solenoid isn't receiving voltage or ground, check for an open or short in the wire between the lock solenoid and the relay. A good method of non-destructive testing is to squeeze the rubber corrugated tubing in the door jam area and search with your fingers for an individual wire that has separated.

9   If there is a broken wire in the jam, pull the rubber boot back to expose the wiring. Attach a new length of wire and feed it through the rubber boot. Now, take the other end of the rubber boot and free it from

the door. Find the new wire you added and the opposite end of the broken one. Attach the two leads together.

➡ **Note: When repairing the leads in the door jam there are several different colors and sizes of wire. Make sure you are splicing the same wire together on each end. (More than one wire can be broken.)**

➡ **Note: It's not uncommon for wires to break in the portion of the harness between the body and door (opening and closing the door fatigues the wire and eventually breaks the wire in two sections).**

10 If the above tests do not pinpoint a problem, take the vehicle to a dealer or qualified shop with the proper scan tool.

➡ **Tip: To avoid replacing good components always test thoroughly before any parts are deemed faulty.**

KEYLESS ENTRY SYSTEM

11 The keyless entry system consists of a remote control transmitter that sends a coded infrared signal to a receiver, which then operates the door lock system.

12 Replace the battery when the transmitter doesn't operate the locks at a distance of ten feet. Normal range should be about 30 feet.

➡ **Tip: If the transmitter in question as to whether or not it is functioning, take your remote/key fob/transmitter to a repair shop that has a tire monitor test tool. Most of these tools have an added feature in them to check the RF strength. This can be used to determine the battery condition and/or the actual operation of the transmitter. If the battery is a known good battery and the transmitter still fails to send a signal, chances are the transmitter will need to be replaced and reprogrammed to the vehicle.**

24 Daytime Running Lights (DRL) - general information

1 The Daytime Running Lights (DRL) system illuminates the headlights whenever the engine is running. The only exception is with the engine running and the parking brake engaged. Once the parking brake is released, the lights will remain on as long as the ignition switch is on, even if the parking brake is later applied.

2 The DRL system supplies reduced power to the headlights so they won't be too bright for daytime use, while prolonging headlight life.

25 Airbag system - general information and precautions

GENERAL INFORMATION

1 All models are equipped with a Supplemental Inflatable Restraint (SIR) system, consisting of a steering wheel airbag, a passenger's-side dash airbag, driver and front passsenger knee bolster airbags, front and rear seat-back mounted airbags, and roof rail airbags. This system is designed to protect the occupants of the vehicle from serious injury in the event of a frontal or side-impact collision. It consists of an array of external and internal (inside the SDM) information sensors (decelerometers), the Inflatable Restraint Sensing and Diagnostic Module (SDM), the inflator modules in the airbag units and the wiring and connectors tying all these components together.

AIRBAG/INFLATOR MODULES

Driver's airbag/inflator module

. 2 The steering wheel airbag and knee airbag inflator modules contains a housing incorporating the cushion (airbag), an initiating device, and a canister of gas-generating material. The initiator is part of the inflator module deployment loop. When a collision occurs, the SDM sends current through the deployment loop to the initiator. Current passing through the initiator ignites the material in the canister, producing a rapidly expanding gas, which inflates the airbag almost instanta-neously. Seconds after the airbag inflates, it deflates almost as quickly through airbag vent holes and/or the airbag fabric.

3 When the SDM sends current to the initiator, it travels through the airbag circuit to the steering column. From there, a clockspring on the steering wheel delivers the current to the module initiator. This clockspring assembly, which is the final segment of the airbag ignition circuit, functions as the bridge between the end of the airbag circuit on the (fixed) steering column and the beginning of the circuit on the (rotating) steering wheel. It's designed to maintain a closed circuit between the steering column and the steering wheel regardless of the position of the steering wheel. For this reason, removing and installing the clockspring is critical to the performance of the driver's side airbag. For information on how to remove and install the driver's side airbag, refer to *Steering wheel - removal and installation* in Chapter 10.

Passenger's airbag/inflator module

4 The passenger's airbag/inflator module is mounted above the glove compartment and a second, smaller airbag module is located just below the glove compartment. When deployed by the SDM, the passenger's airbags burst through the dashboard above the glove box and below. Although these areas look like they are simply part of the dashboard, they are actually trim covers with a perforated seam that allows the cover to separate from the dash when the passenger's airbag(s) inflates.

Side impact airbag/inflator modules

5   The side-impact airbag/inflator (roof rail) modules are mounted along the outer edges of the headliner, above the door openings. They extend from the A-pillar (front windshield pillar) to the C-pillar (rear window pillar). Each module consists of a housing, an inflatable airbag, an initiator and a canister of gas-generating material. Each roof rail module employs its own side impact sensor (SIS), which contains a sensing device that monitors changes in vehicle acceleration and velocity. This data is sent to the SDM, which compares it with its program. When the data exceeds a certain threshold, the SDM determines that the vehicle has been hit hard enough on one side or the other to warrant deployment of the roof rail on that side. The SDM doesn't deploy the roof rail airbags on both sides, just on the side being hit. Then the SDM sends current to the roof rail initiator to inflate the airbag, ripping open the headliner trim as it deploys to protect the occupant(s) on the left or right side of the vehicle. Side impact airbag/inflator modules are long enough to protect the driver and a left-side rear-seat passenger, or a front seat passenger and right-side rear-seat passenger.

6   The seats are also equipped with side-impact airbags, located in the outside cushion of each front and rear seat back.

INFLATABLE RESTRAINT SENSING AND DIAGNOSTIC MODULE (SDM)

7   The SDM is the computer module that controls the airbag system. Besides a microprocessor, the SDM also includes an array of sensors. Some of them are inside the SDM itself. Other external sensors are located throughout the vehicle. All of the sensors, internal and external, send a continuous voltage signal to the SDM, which compares this data to values stored in its memory. When these signals exceed a threshold value (the SDM determines that the vehicle is decelerating more quickly than the threshold value), the SDM allows current to flow through the circuit to the appropriate airbag module(s), which initiates deployment of the airbag(s).

8   For more information about the airbag system in your vehicle, refer to your owner's manual.

IMPACT SEAT BELT RETRACTORS

9   All models are equipped with pyrotechnic (explosive) units in the front seat belt retracting mechanisms for both the lap and shoulder belts. During an impact that would trigger the airbag system, the airbag control unit also triggers the seat belt retractors. When the pyrotechnic charges go off, they accelerate the retractors to instantly take up any slack in the seat belt system to more fully prepare the driver and front seat passenger for impact.

10 The airbag system should be disabled any time work is done to or around the seats.

✳✳ WARNING:

Never strike the pillars or floorpan with a hammer or use an impact-driver tool in these areas unless the system is disabled.

DISARMING THE SYSTEM AND OTHER PRECAUTIONS

✳✳ WARNING:

Failure to follow these precautions could result in accidental deployment of the airbag and personal injury.

11 Whenever working in the vicinity of the steering wheel, instrument panel or any of the other SIR system components, the system must be disarmed. To disarm the system:

   a) *Point the wheels straight ahead and turn the key to the Lock position.*
   b) *Disconnect the cable from the negative battery terminal. Refer to Chapter 5 for the disconnecting procedure.*
   c) *Wait at least two minutes for the back-up power supply to be depleted.*
   d) *Remove airbag fuse no. 17 from the underhood fuse/relay box and airbag fuse no. 15 from the under-dash fuse relay box (see Section 3).*

12 Whenever handling an airbag module, always keep the airbag opening (the upholstered side) pointed away from your body. Never place the airbag module on a bench or other surface with the airbag opening facing the surface. Always place the airbag module in a safe location with the airbag opening (the upholstered side) facing up.

13 Never measure the resistance of any SIR component or use any electrical test equipment on any of the wiring or components. An ohm-meter has a built-in battery supply that could trigger the airbag inflator.

14 Never dispose of a live airbag/inflator module. Return it to a dealer service department or other qualified repair shop for safe deployment and disposal.

15 Never use electrical welding equipment in the vicinity of any airbag components. The connectors for the system are easy to spot because they're bright yellow.

16 Like the PCM, the SDM has a malfunction indicator light, known as the AIR BAG indicator light, on the instrument cluster. When you turn the ignition key to ON, the SDM checks out all of the SIR components and circuits. If everything is okay, the AIR BAG indicator light goes off, just like the PCM's Malfunction Indicator Light (MIL). But if there's a problem somewhere, the light stays on, and will remain on until the problem is repaired and the DTC(s) cleared from the SDM's memory.

26 Key fob battery replacement

1   Use a small jeweler's Phillips screwdriver to separate the key fob (see illustration).

2   Remove the cover, being careful not to damage the seal (see illustration).

3   Take care to note the polarity and position of the battery. Then remove the battery.

4   Installation is the reverse of removal.

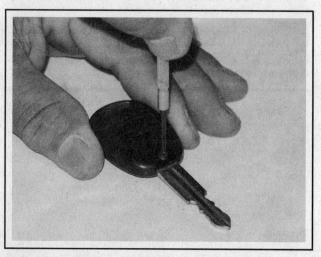

26.1 Unscrew the two halves with a jeweler's size Phillips screwdriver

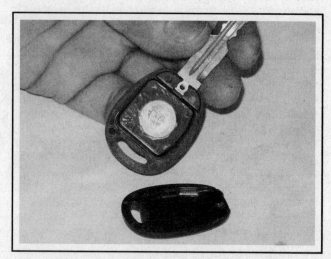

26.2 Separate the key fob halves and remove the battery

27 Key fob RF signal strength testing

➤ **Note: If for some reason your key fob fails to operate even after you've tried a replacement battery, take your key fob to a repair shop that has a tire monitor reset tool. Most of these tools have an RF strength indicator test as part of their diagnostics features. The technician can check whether or not your key fob is in working order or not. If there is no RF signal, the key fob is more than likely faulty. If the signal is weak chances are the battery needs to be replaced.**

TRANSMITTER PROGRAMMING

1   Programming replacement transmitters (key fob) requires the use of a specialized scan tool. Take the vehicle and the transmitter(s) to a dealer service department or other qualified repair shop equipped with the necessary tool to have the transmitter(s) programmed to the vehicle. Up to four key fobs can be programmed to one car. All fobs for the vehicle have to be present when reprogramming.

28 Wiring diagrams - general information

1   Since it isn't possible to include all wiring diagrams for every year covered by this manual, the following diagrams are those that are typical and most commonly needed.

2   Prior to troubleshooting any circuits, check the fuse and circuit breakers (if equipped) to make sure they're in good condition. Make sure the battery is properly charged and check the cable connections (see Chapter 1).

3   When checking a circuit, make sure that all connectors are clean, with no broken or loose terminals. When unplugging a connector, do not pull on the wires. Pull only on the connector housings.

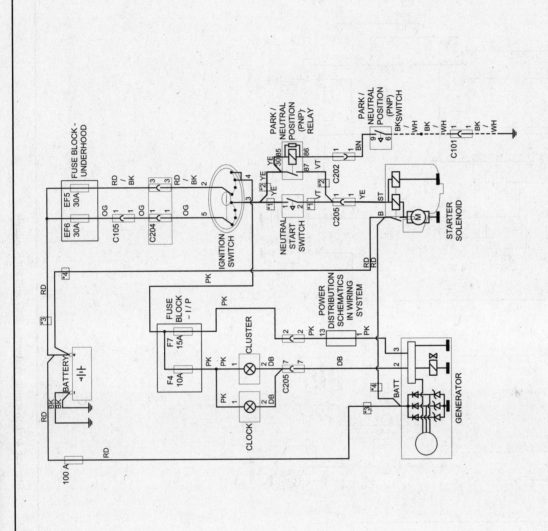

Starting and charging systems - 2004 to 2006 models

*1 Manual transmission
*2 Automatic transmission
*3 North America
*4 Except North America

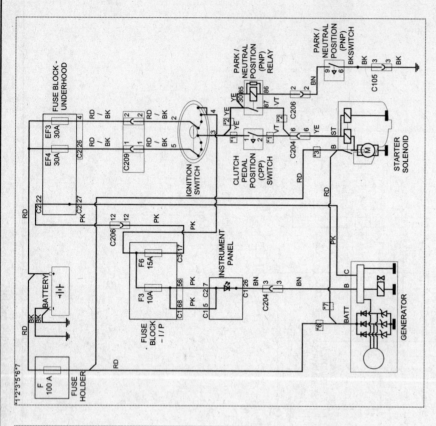

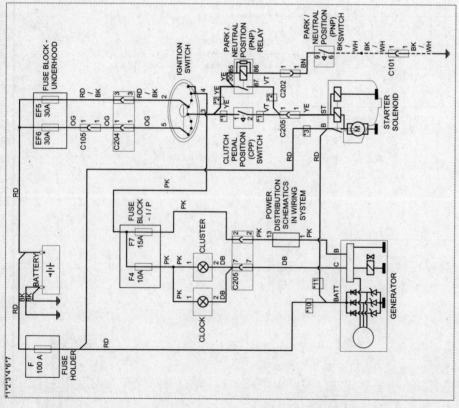

Starting and charging systems - 2007 and 2008 models

*1 Manual transmission
*2 Automatic transmission
*3 North America
*4 Hatchback
*5 Notchback
*6 Equipment code: XFE
*7 Equipment code: XFE

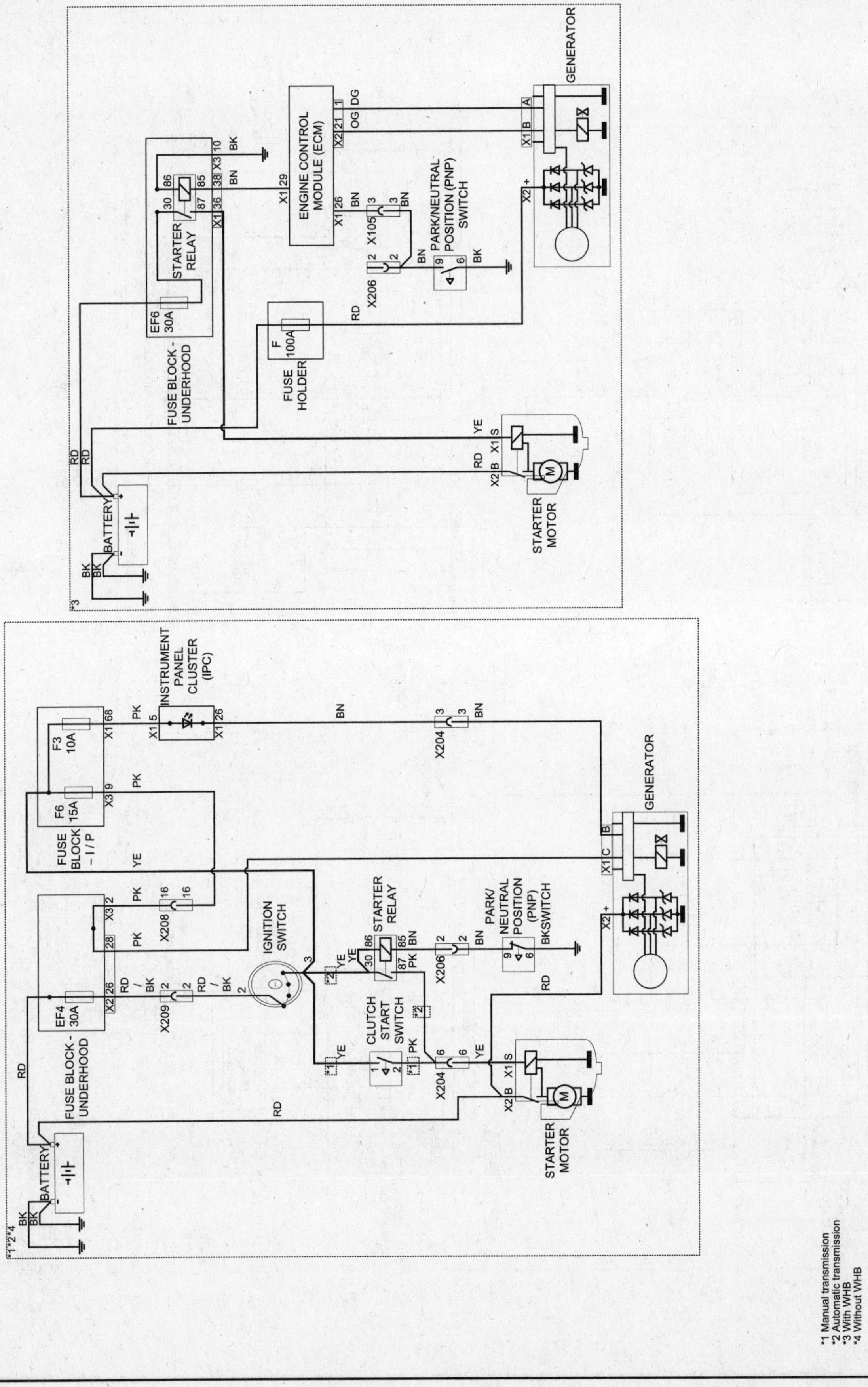

Starting and charging systems - 2009 and later models

*1 Manual transmission
*2 Automatic transmission
*3 With WHB
*4 Without WHB

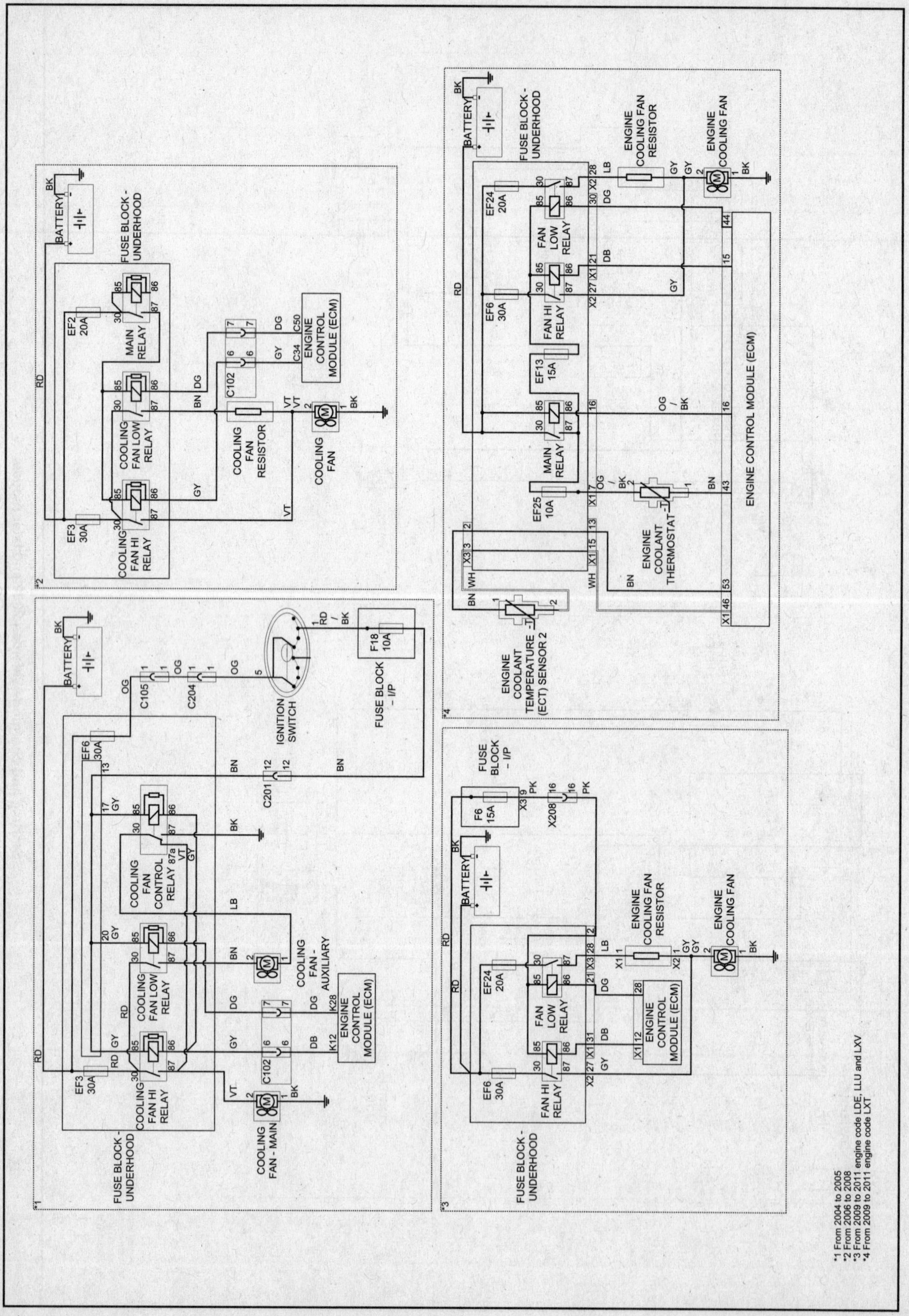

Engine cooling fan system

*1 From 2004 to 2005
*2 From 2006 to 2008
*3 From 2009 to 2011 engine code LDE, LLU and LXV
*4 From 2009 to 2011 engine code LXT

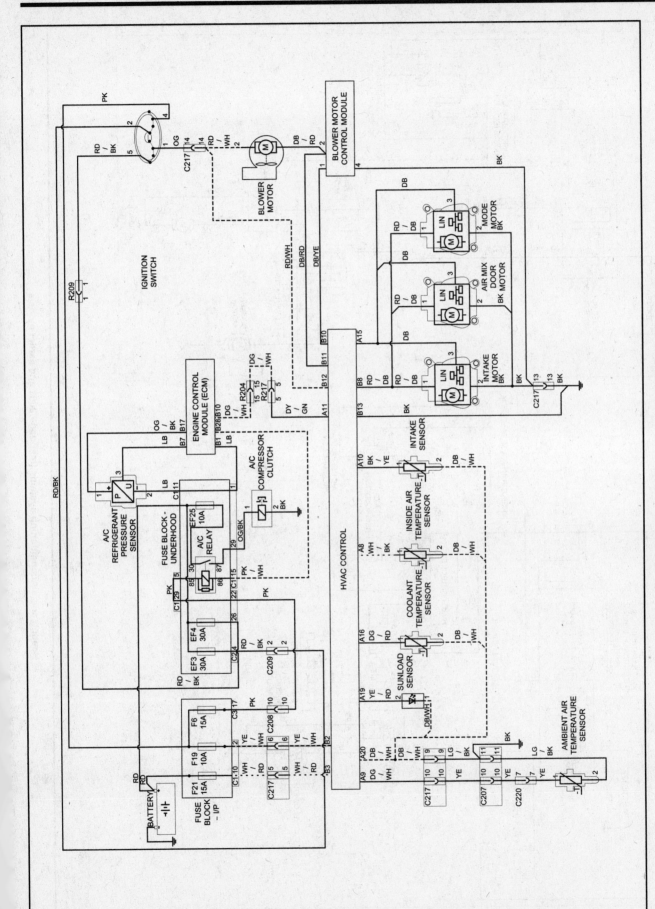

Heating and air conditioning systems (automatic) - 2008 and earlier models

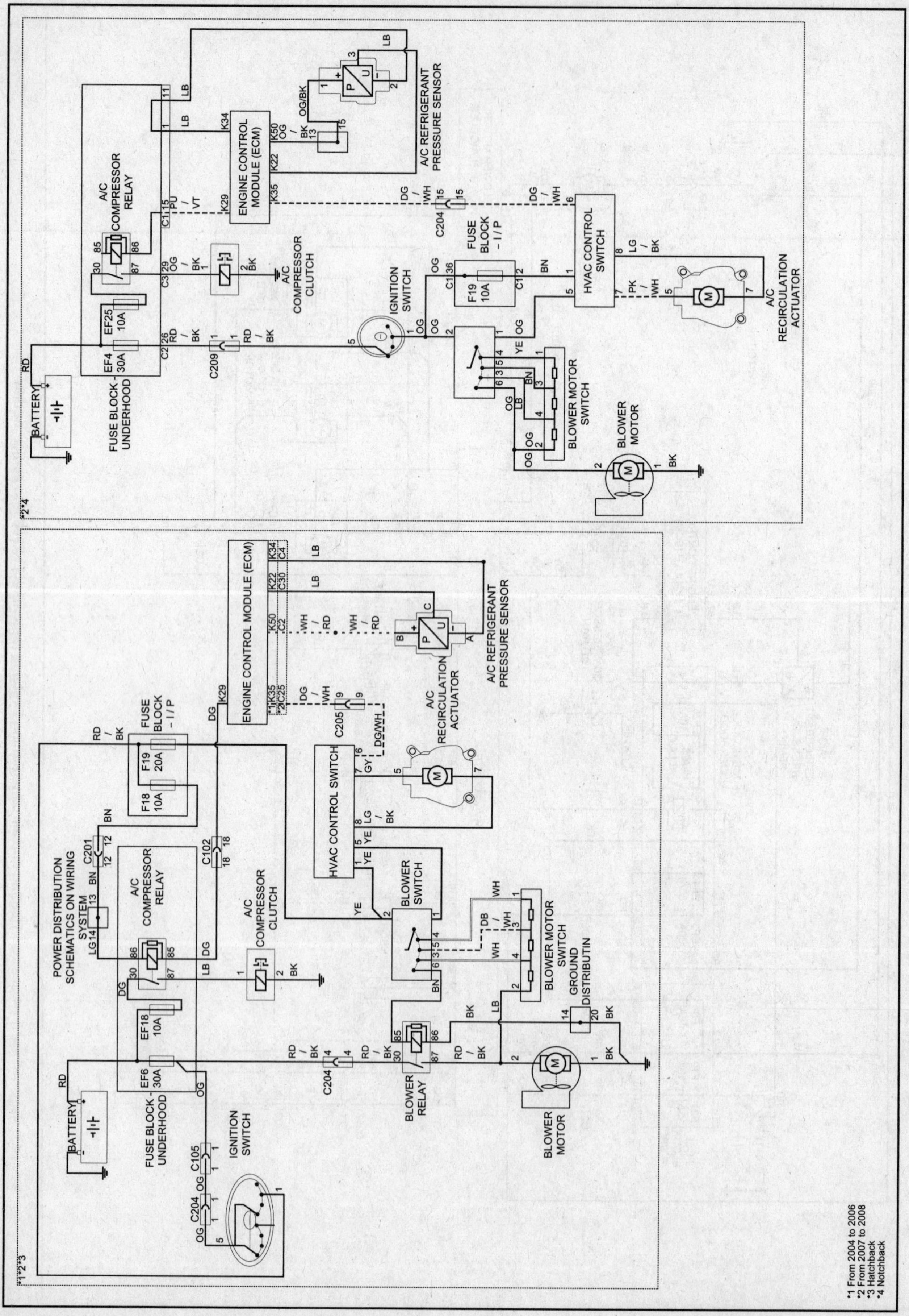

Heating and air conditioning systems (manual) - 2008 and earlier models

*1 From 2004 to 2006
*2 From 2007 to 2008
*3 Hatchback
*4 Notchback

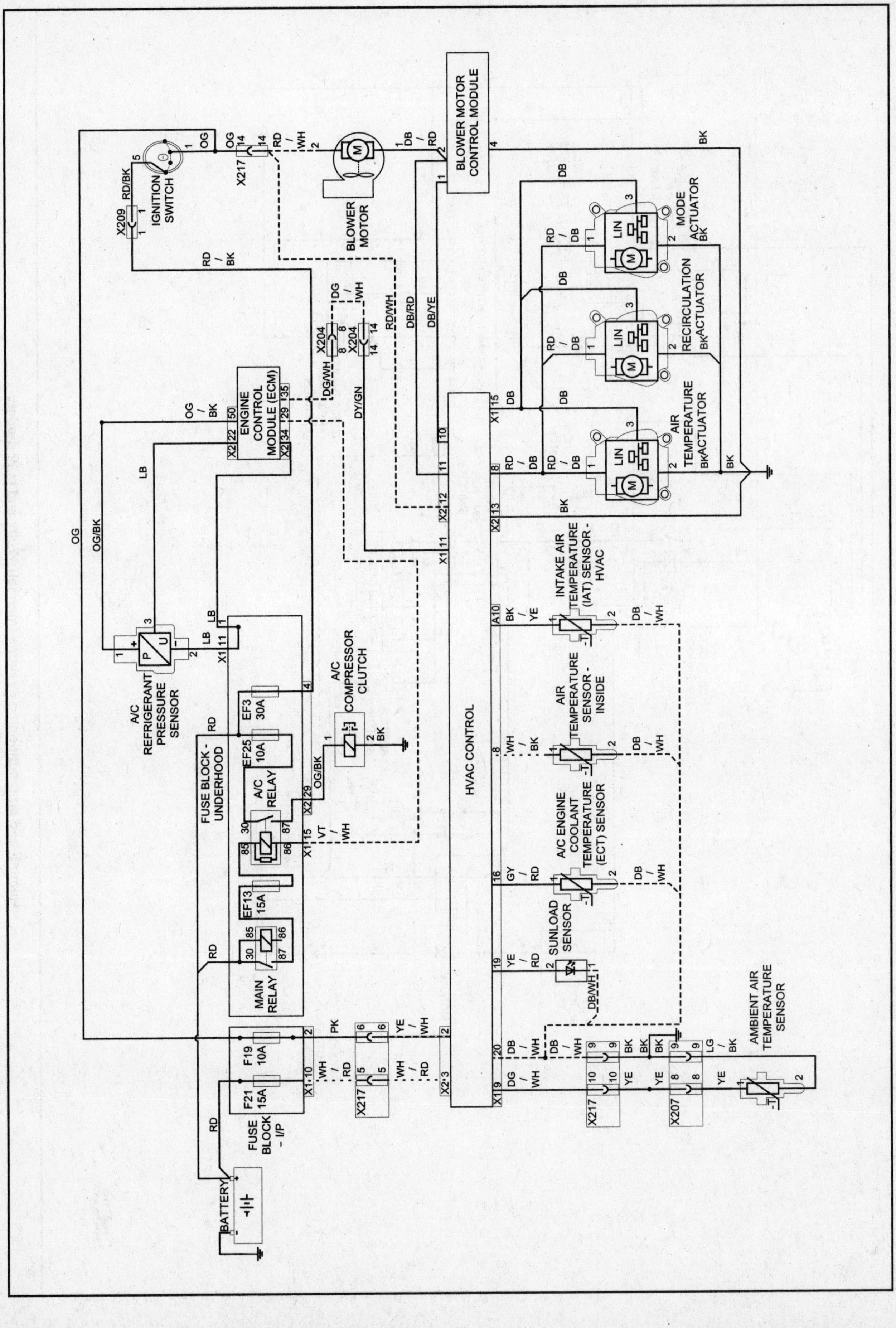

Heating and air conditioning systems (automatic) - 2009 and later models

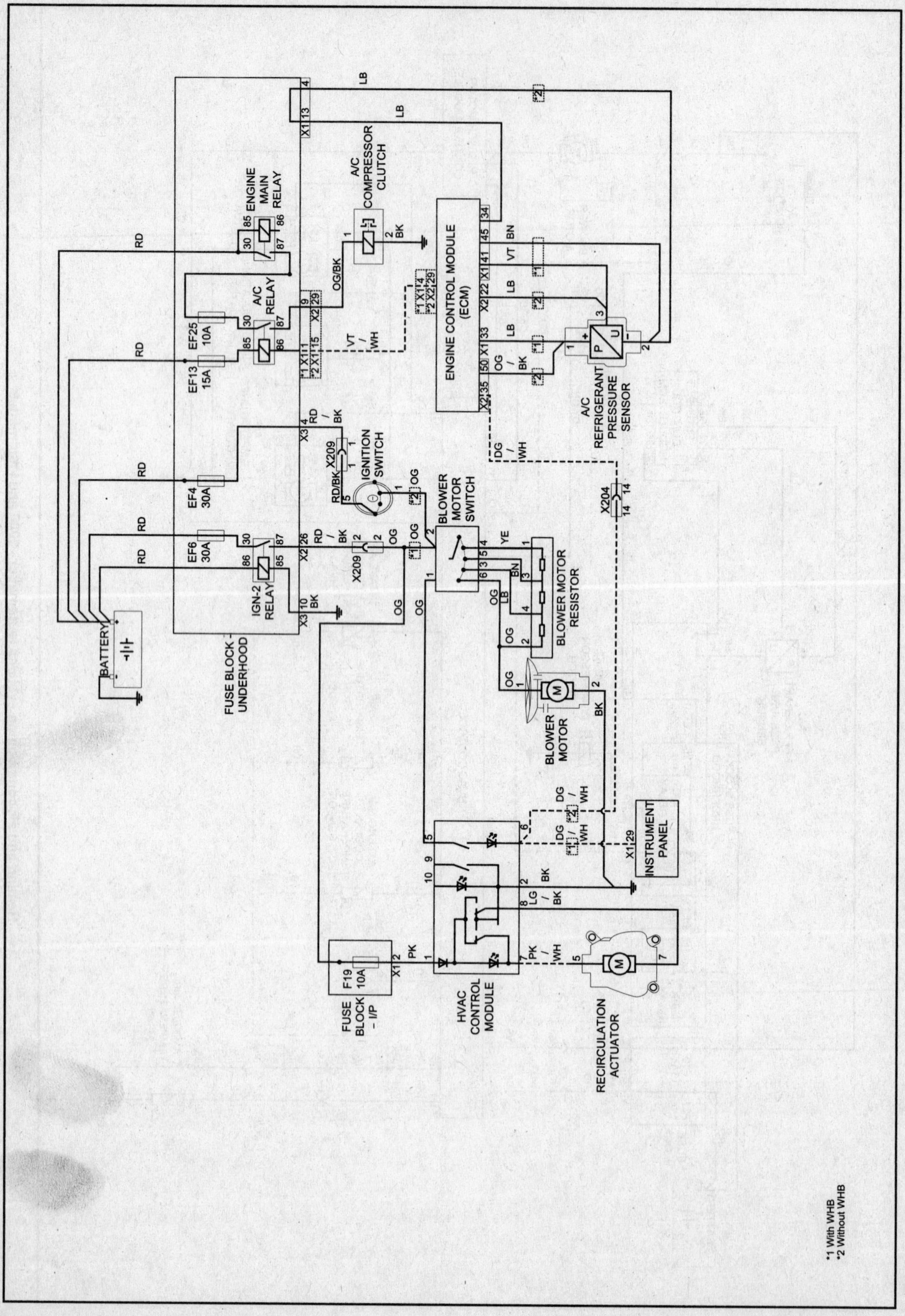

Heating and air conditioning systems (manual) - 2009 and later models

*1 With WHB
*2 Without WHB

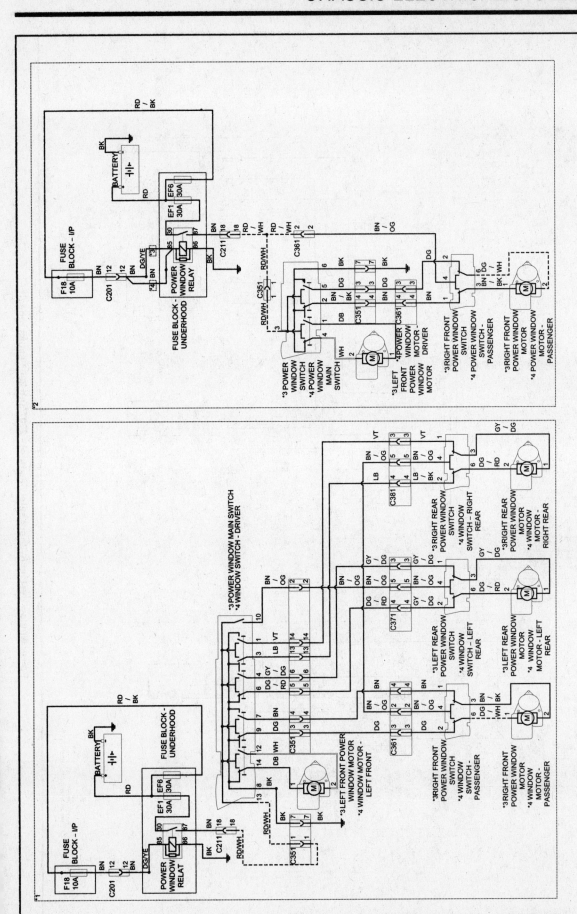

Power window system - 2008 and earlier hatchback models

*1 Front and rear power windows
*2 Front power windows
*3 From 2004 to 2006
*4 From 2007 to 2008 available on hatchbak

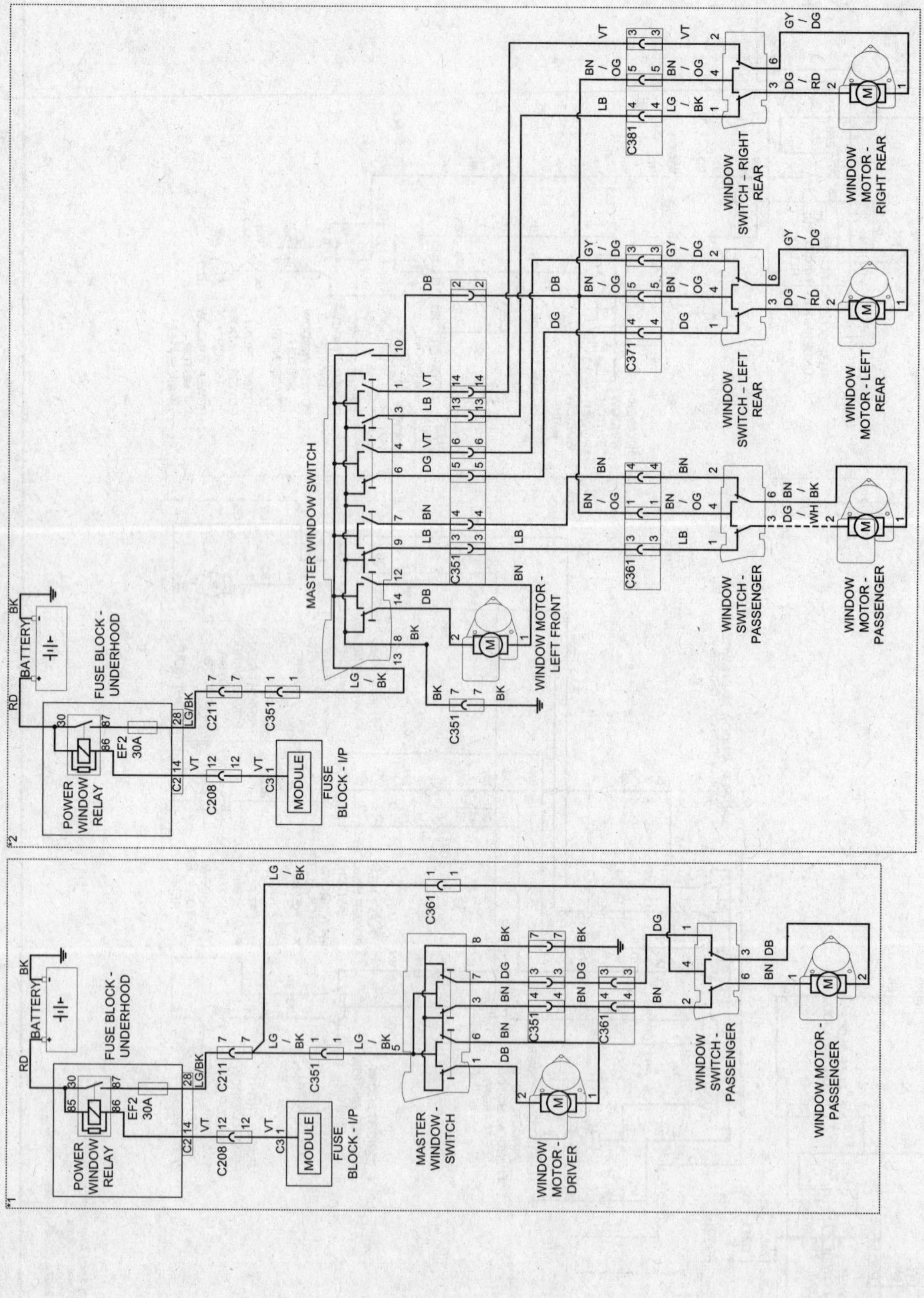

Power window system (without safety feature) - 2007 and 2008 sedan models

*1 Front power windows
*2 Front and rear power windows

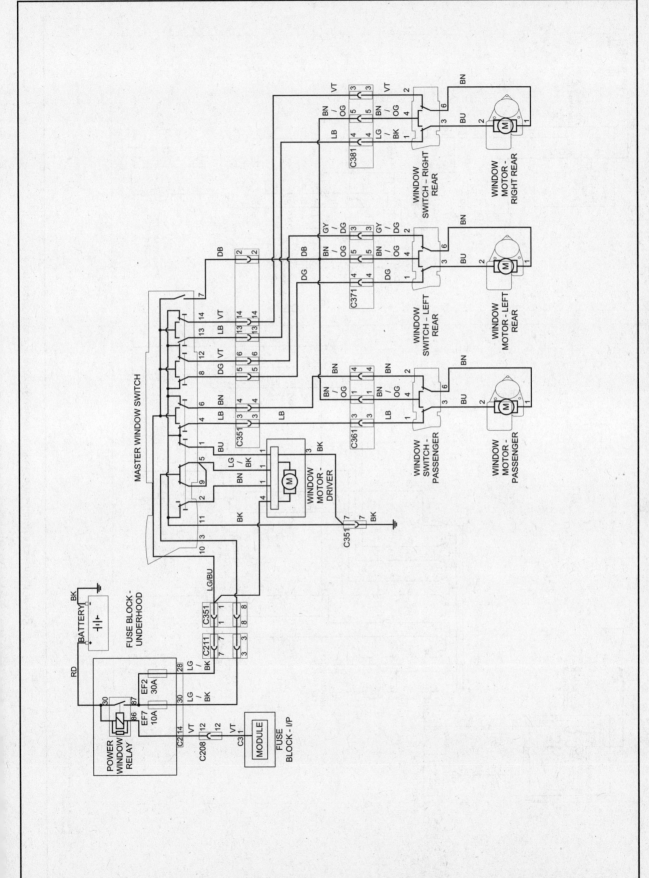

Power window system (with safety feature) - 2007 and 2008 sedan models

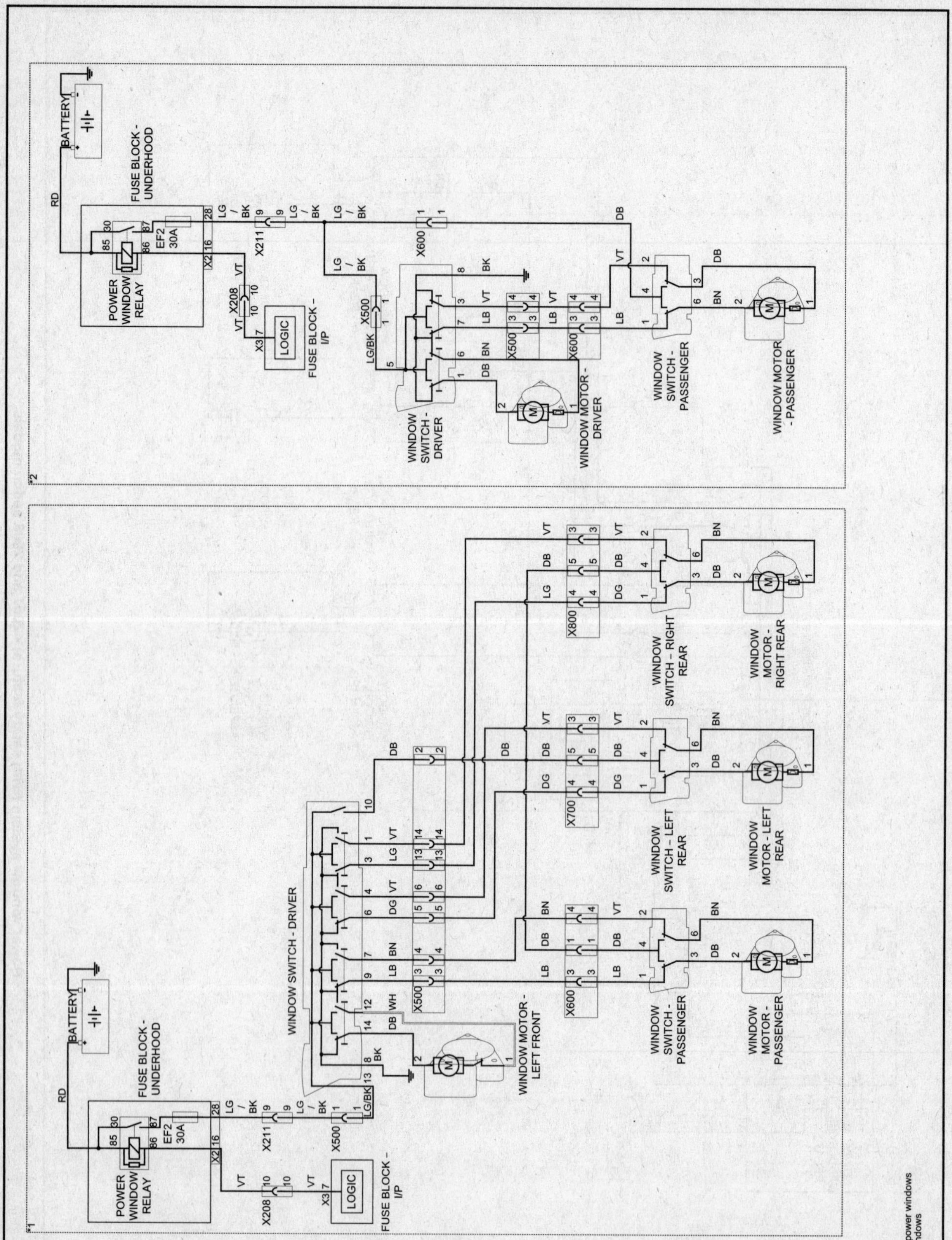

Power window system (without safety feature) - 2009 and later models

*1 Front and rear power windows
*2 Front power windows

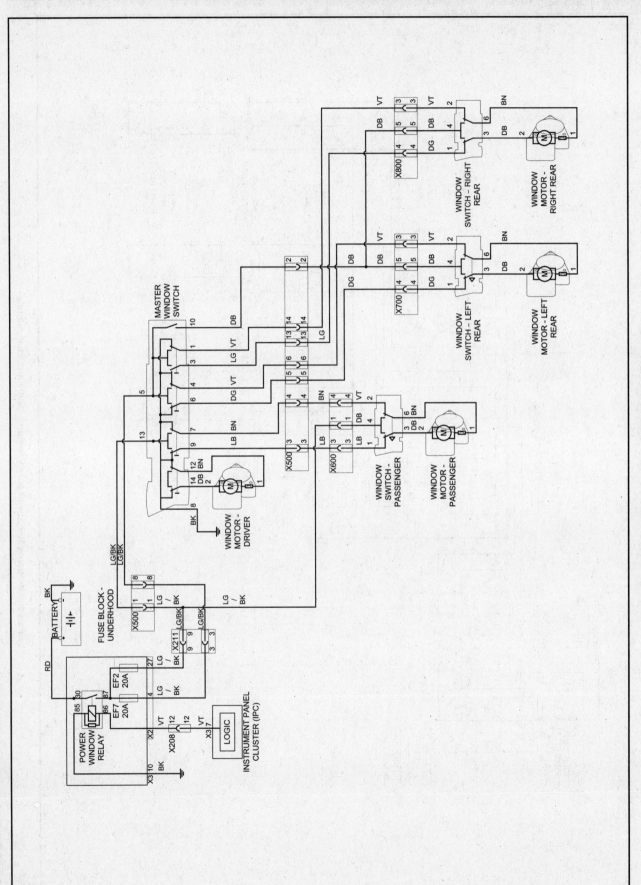

Power window system (export) - 2009 and later models

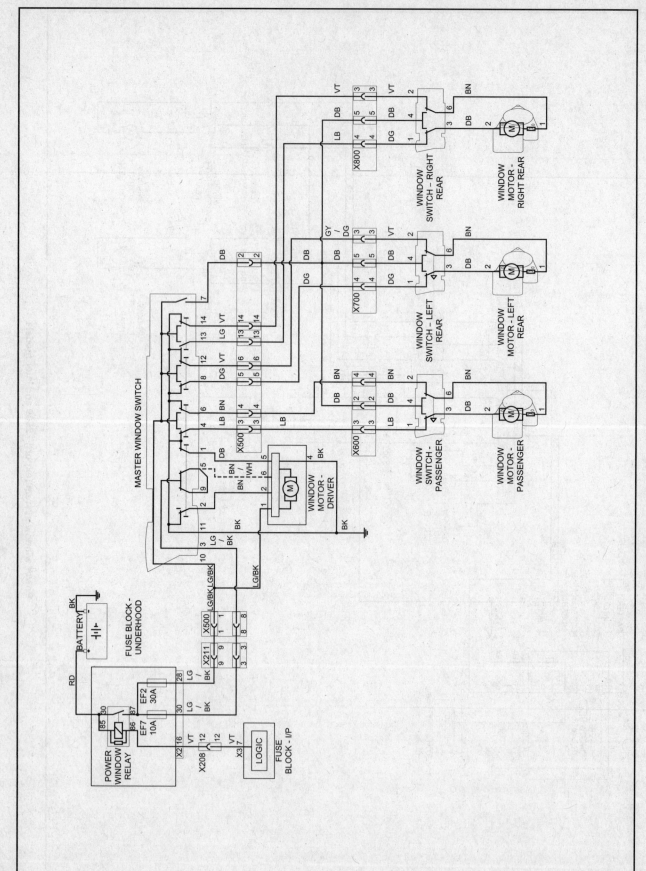

Power window system (with safety feature) - 2009 and later models

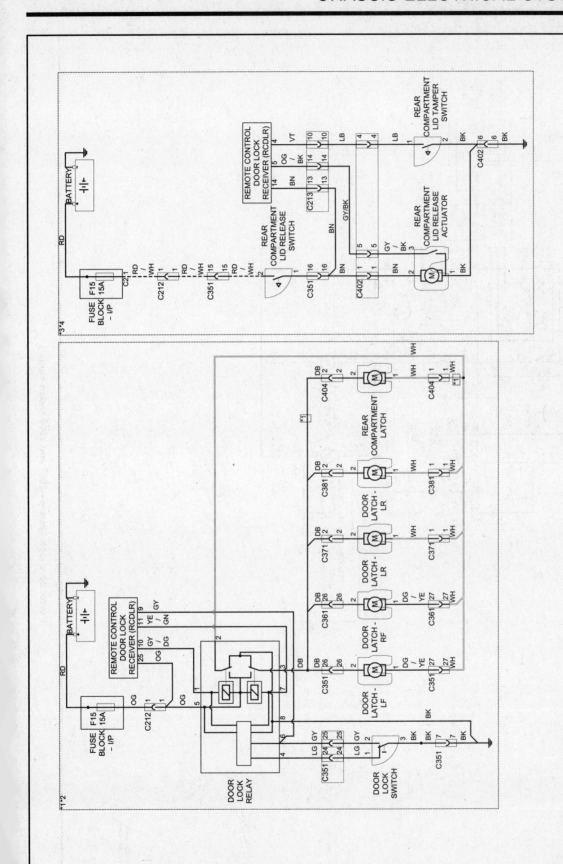

Power door lock system - 2004 to 2006 sedan models/2004 to 2008 hatchback models

*1 Hatchback
*2 From 2004 to 2008
*3 From 2007 to 2008
*4 Rear Compartment

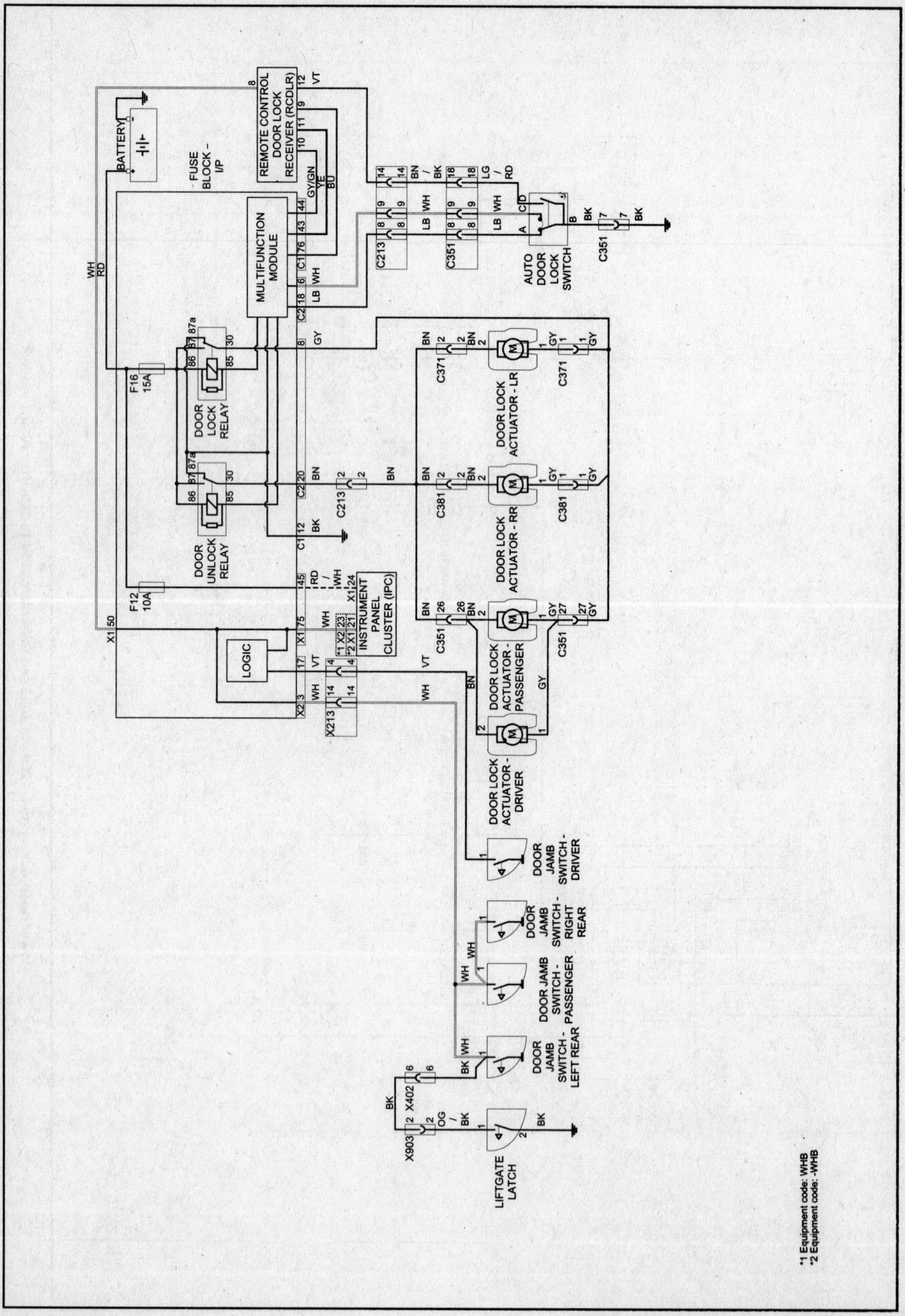

Power door lock system - 2007 and 2008 sedan models

*1 Equipment code: WHB
*2 Equipment code: -WHB

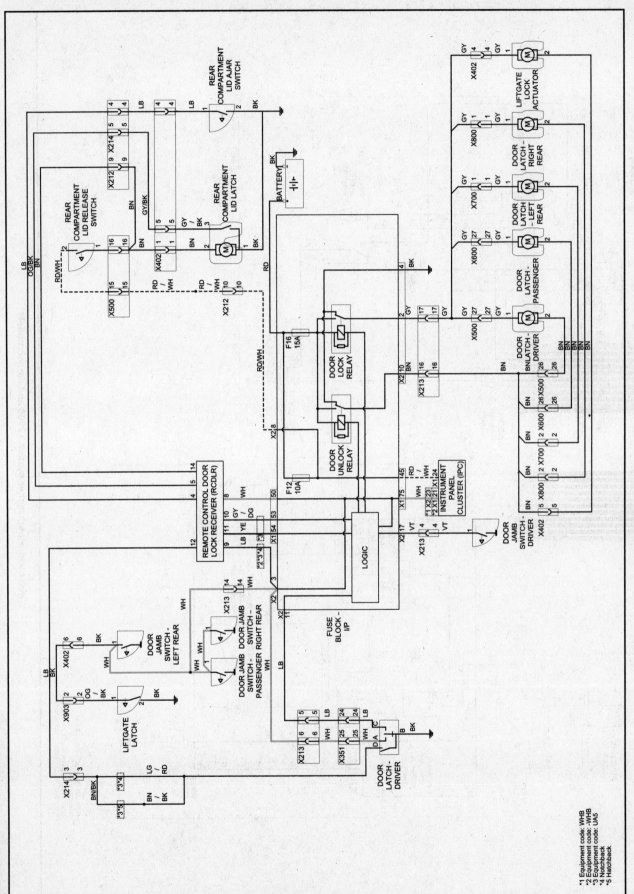

Power door lock system - 2009 and later models

*1 Equipment code: WHB
*2 Equipment code: -WHB
*3 Equipment code: UA5
*4 Notchback
*5 Hatchback

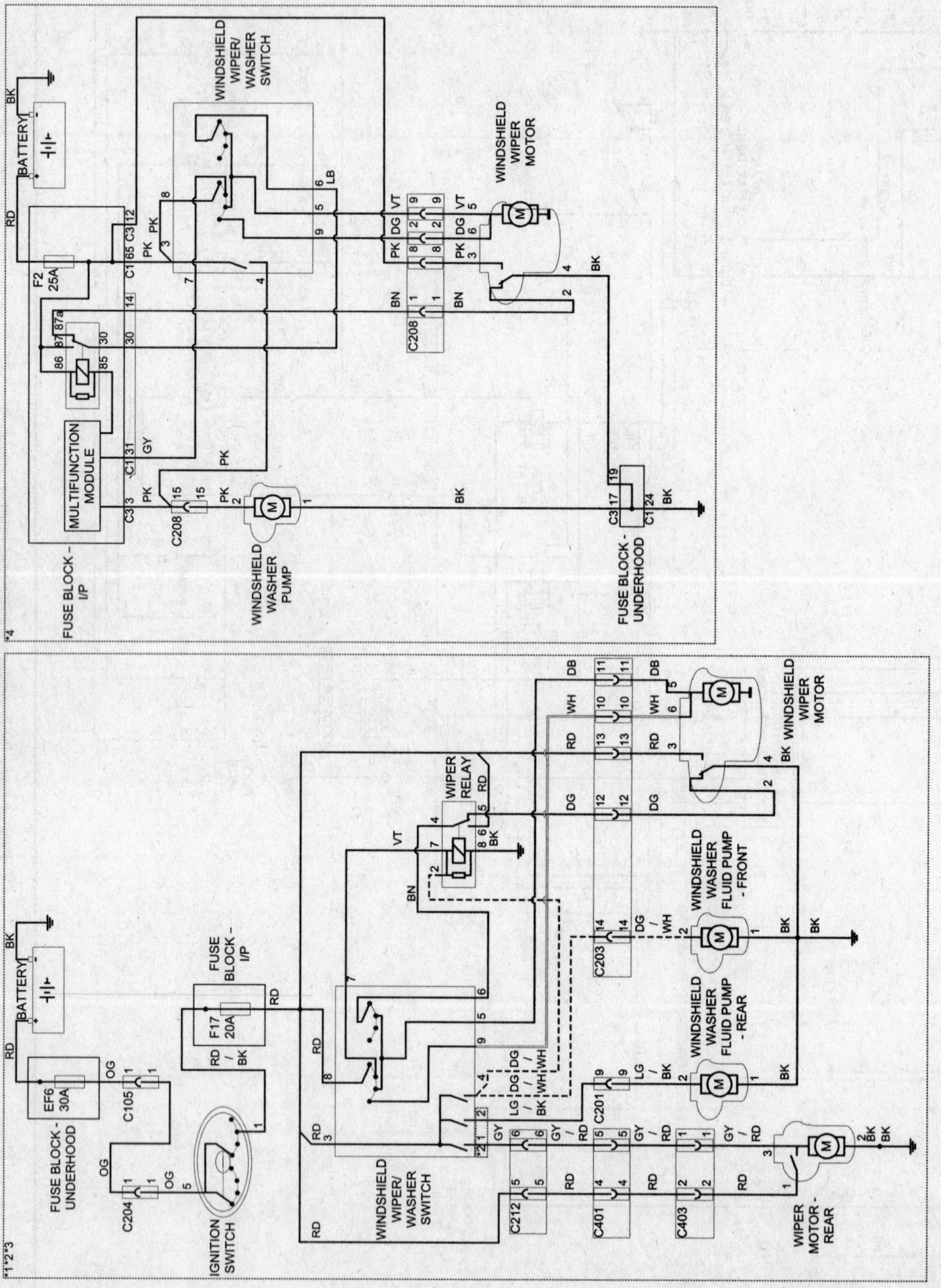

Windshield wiper/washer system - 2008 and earlier models

*1 From 2004 to 2006 available for all types
*2 Hatchback
*3 From 2007 to 2008 available for hatchback
*4 From 2007 to 2008 available for notchback

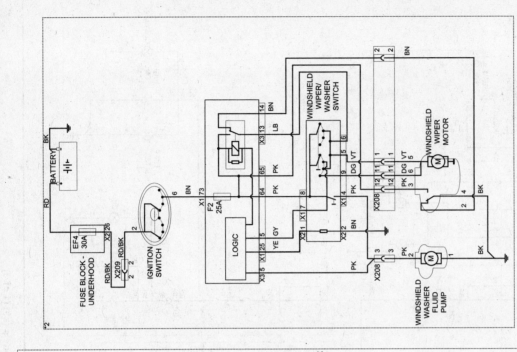

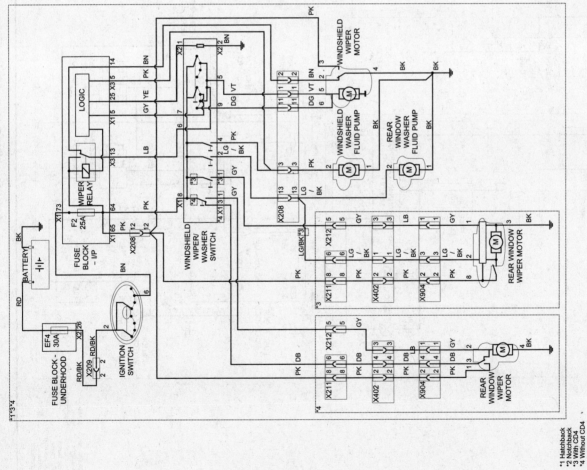

Windshield wiper/washer system - 2009 and later models

*1 Hatchback
*2 Notchback
*3 With CD4
*4 Without CD4

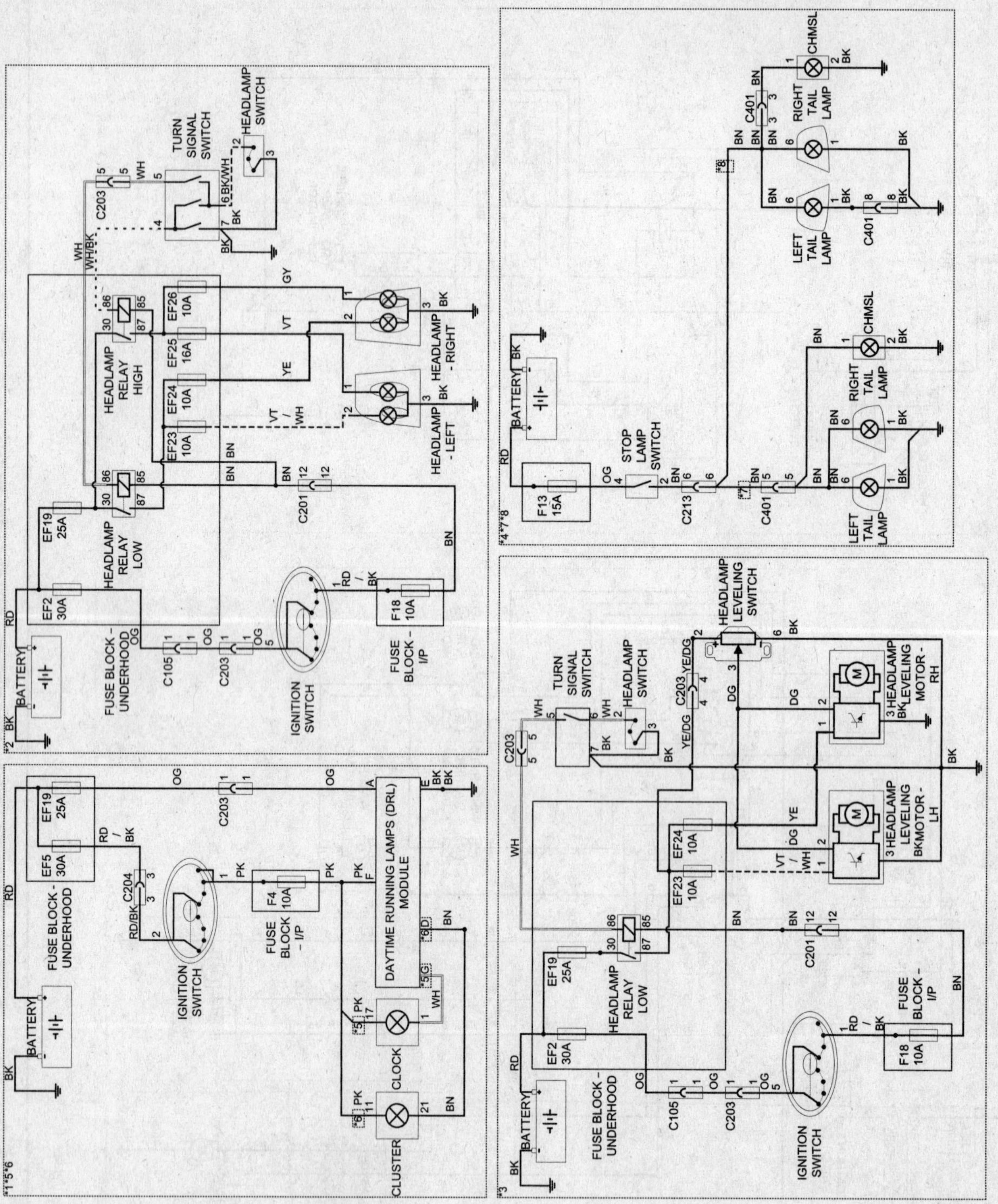

Exterior lighting system - 2004 to 2006 models (all) (1 of 3)

*1 Daytime running lights
*2 Headlight Schematics
*3 Headlight leveling Schematics
*4 Stop lamps
*5 With tach
*6 Without tach
*7 Notchback
*8 Hatchback

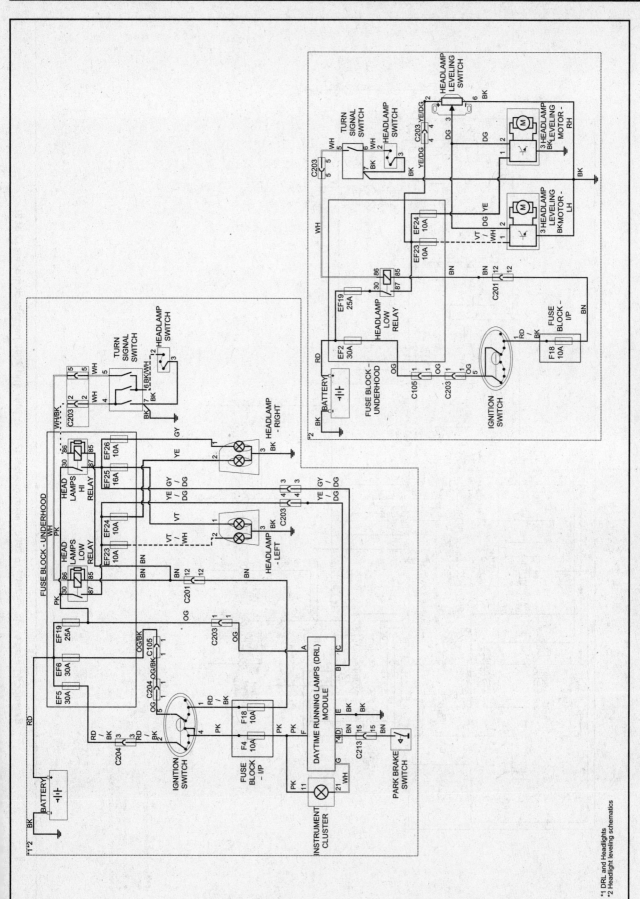

Exterior lighting system - 2007 and 2008 hatchback models (1 of 3)

*1 DRL and Headlights
*2 Headlight leveling schematics

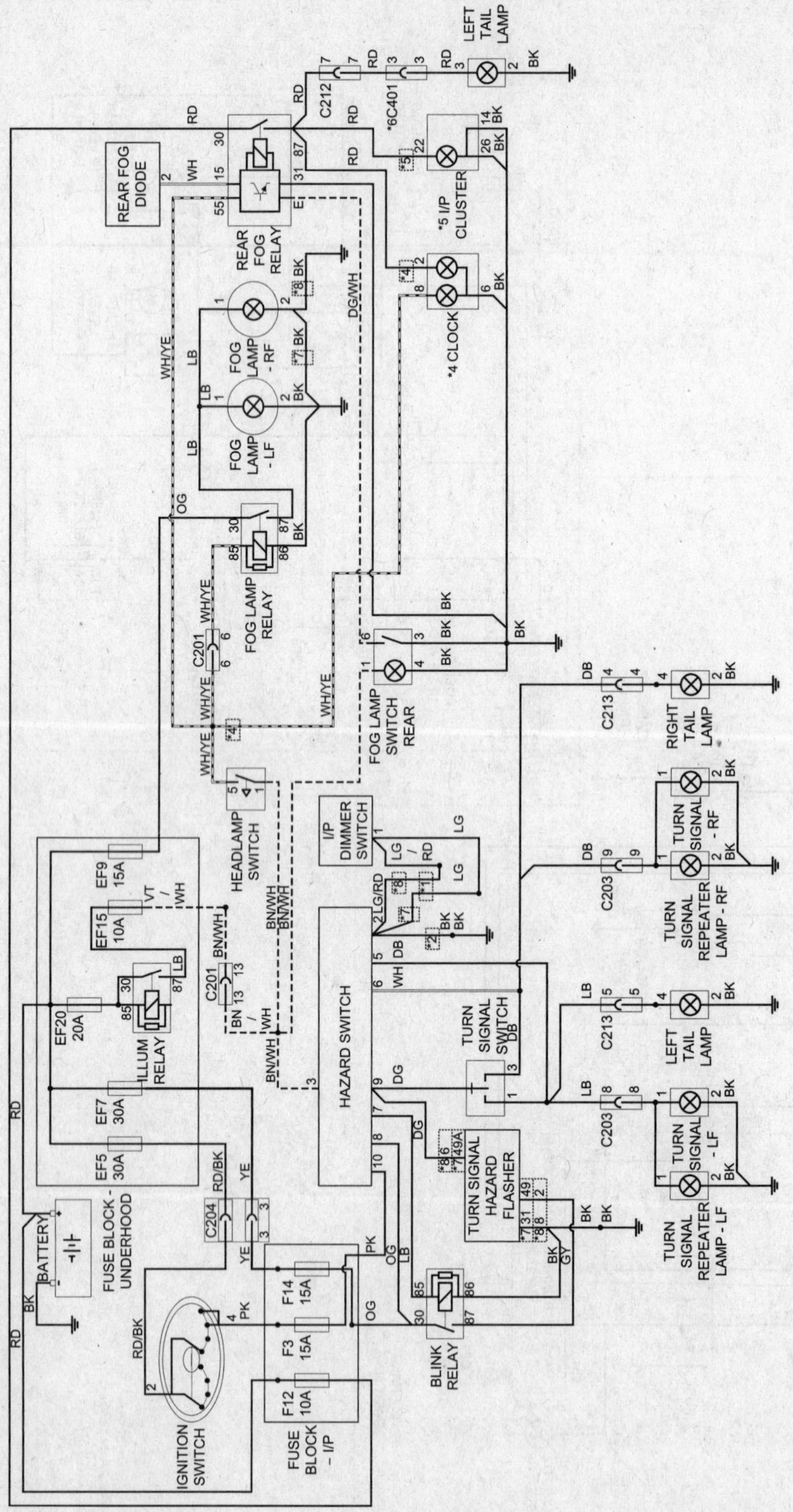

Exterior lighting system - 2004 to 2008 sedan models (2 of 3)/2007 and 2008 hatchback models (2 of 3)

LEFT TAIL LAMP

REAR FOG DIODE

REAR FOG RELAY

FOG LAMP - RF

FOG LAMP - LF

FOG LAMP RELAY

FOG LAMP SWITCH REAR

*5 I/P CLUSTER

*4 CLOCK

HEADLAMP SWITCH

I/P DIMMER SWITCH

HAZARD SWITCH

TURN SIGNAL SWITCH

TURN SIGNAL HAZARD FLASHER

ILLUM RELAY

BLINK RELAY

IGNITION SWITCH

BATTERY

FUSE BLOCK - UNDERHOOD

FUSE BLOCK - I/P

EF9 15A
EF15 10A
EF20 20A
EF7 30A
EF5 30A
F14 15A
F3 15A
F12 10A

RIGHT TAIL LAMP

TURN SIGNAL REPEATER LAMP - RF

LEFT TAIL LAMP

TURN SIGNAL - LF

TURN SIGNAL REPEATER LAMP - LF

*1 Turn hazard lamps and fog lights
*2 With Dimmer
*3 Without Dimmer
*4 Equipment code: With Tacho
*5 Equipment code: Without Tacho
*6 Notchback only available from 2004 to 2006
*7 From 2004 to 2006
*8 From 2007 to 2008

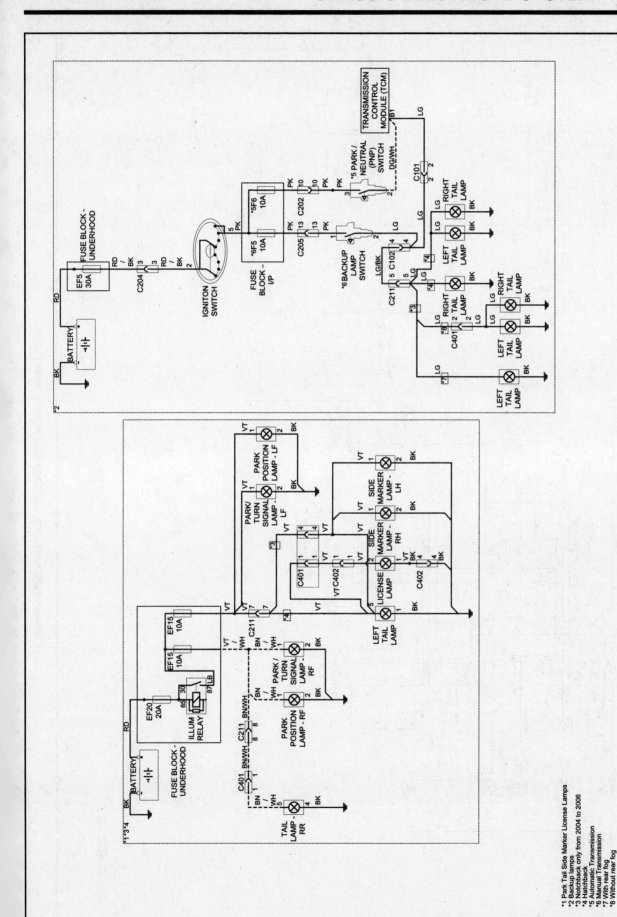

Exterior lighting system - 2004 to 2008 sedan models (3 of 3)/2007 and 2008 hatchback models (3 of 3)

*1 Park Tail Side Marker License Lamps
*2 Backup lamps
*3 Notchback only from 2004 to 2006
*4 Hatchback
*5 Automatic Transmission
*6 Manual Transmission
*7 With rear fog
*8 Without rear fog

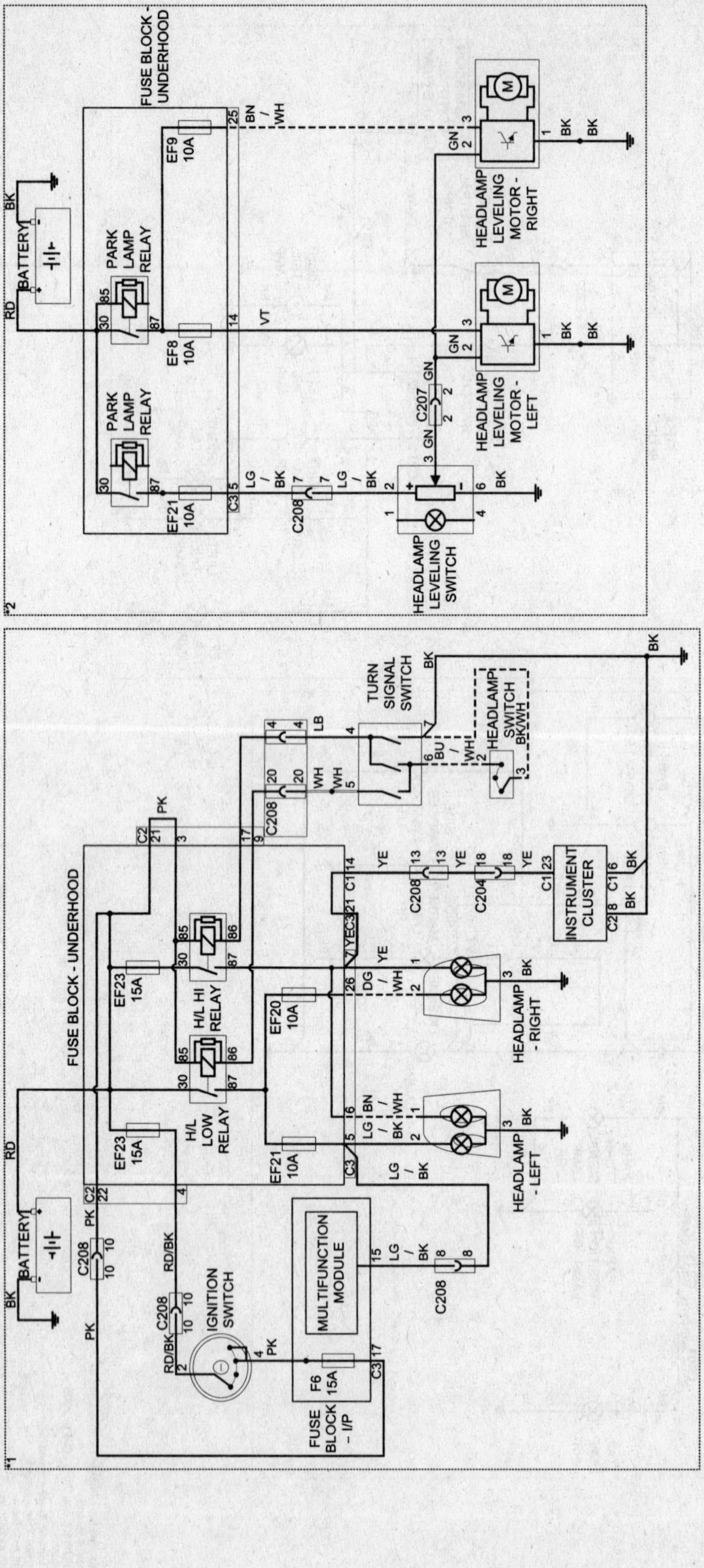

Exterior lighting system - 2007 and 2008 sedan models (1 of 3)

*1 Headlamps and turn signal switch
*2 Headlight leveling schematics

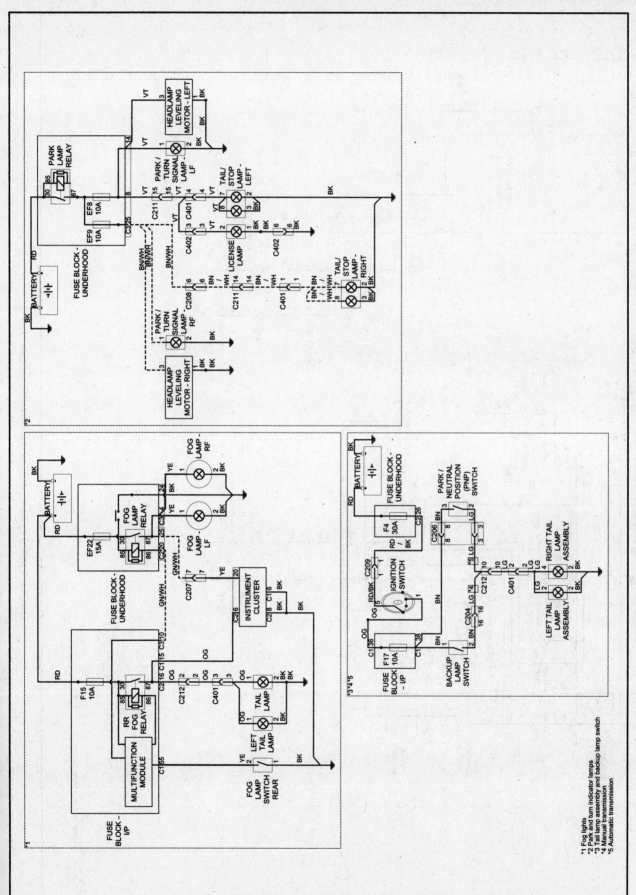

Exterior lighting system - 2007 and 2008 sedan models (2 of 3)

*1 Fog lights
*2 Park and turn indicator lamps
*3 Tail lamp assembly and backup lamp switch
*4 Manual transmission
*5 Automatic transmission

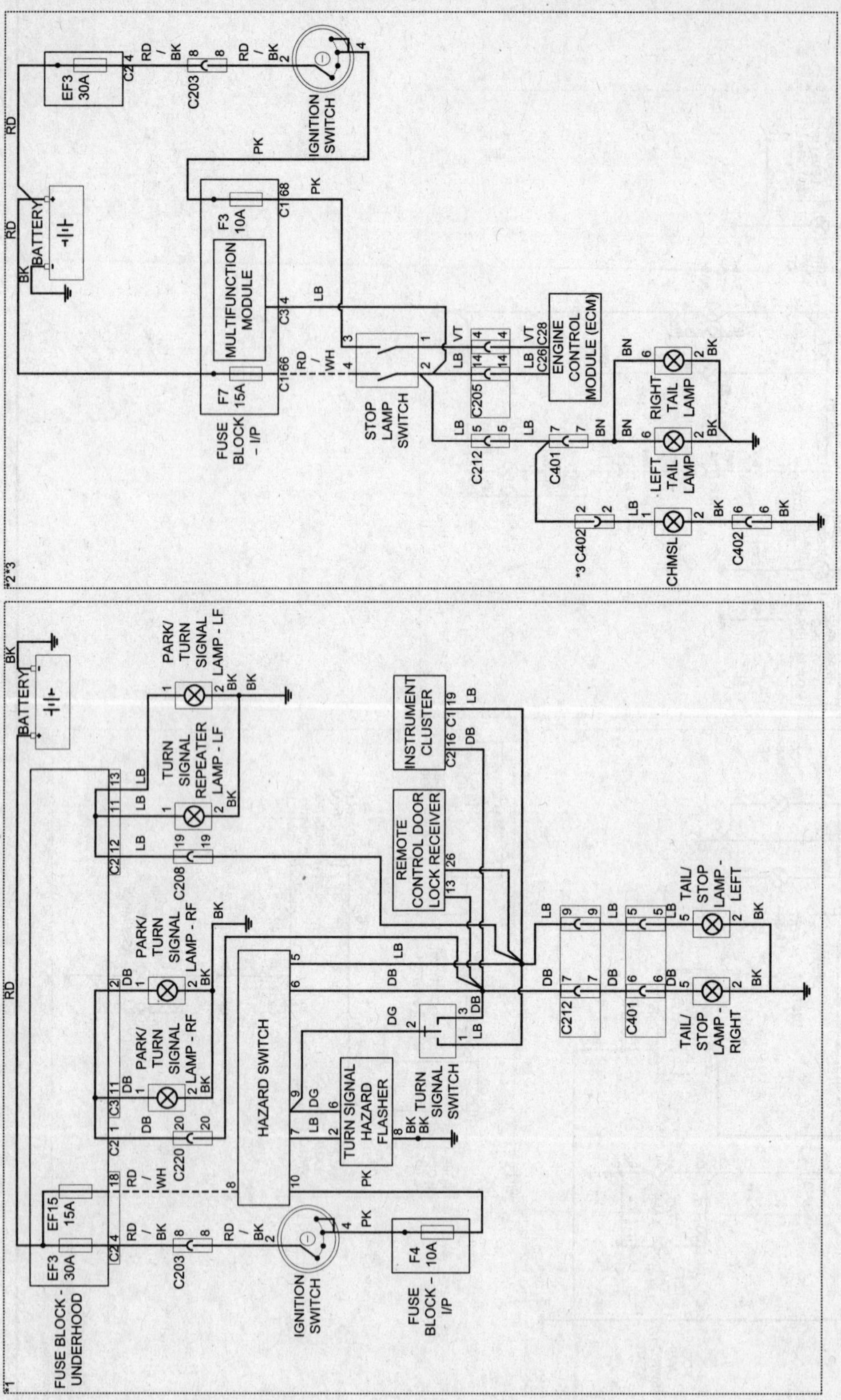

Exterior lighting system - 2007 and 2008 sedan models (3 of 3)

*1 Turn signal
*2 Tail Lamp Assembly and Stop Lamp Switch
*3 With spoiler

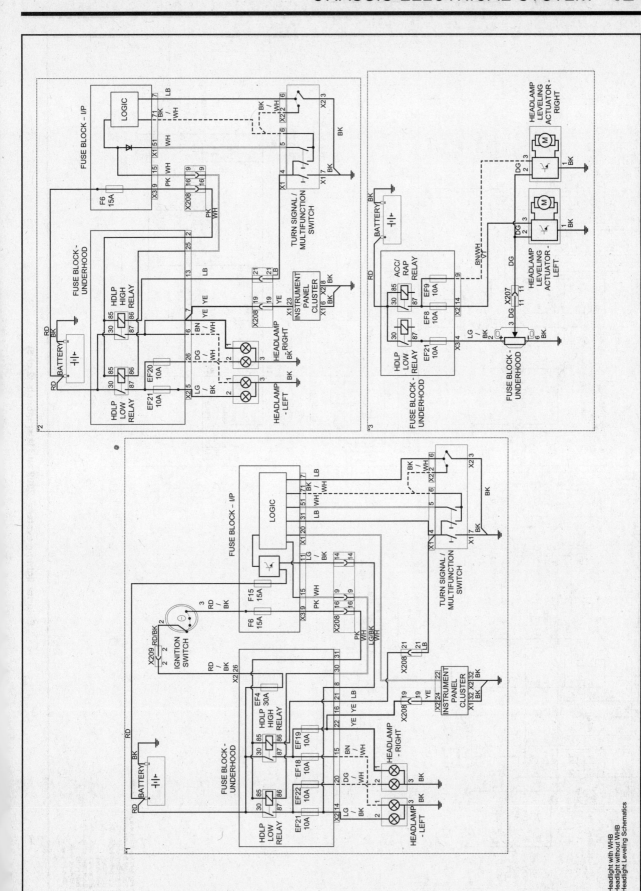

Exterior lighting system - 2009 and later models (1 of 5)

*1 Headlight with WHB
*2 Headlight without WHB
*3 Headlight Leveling Schematics

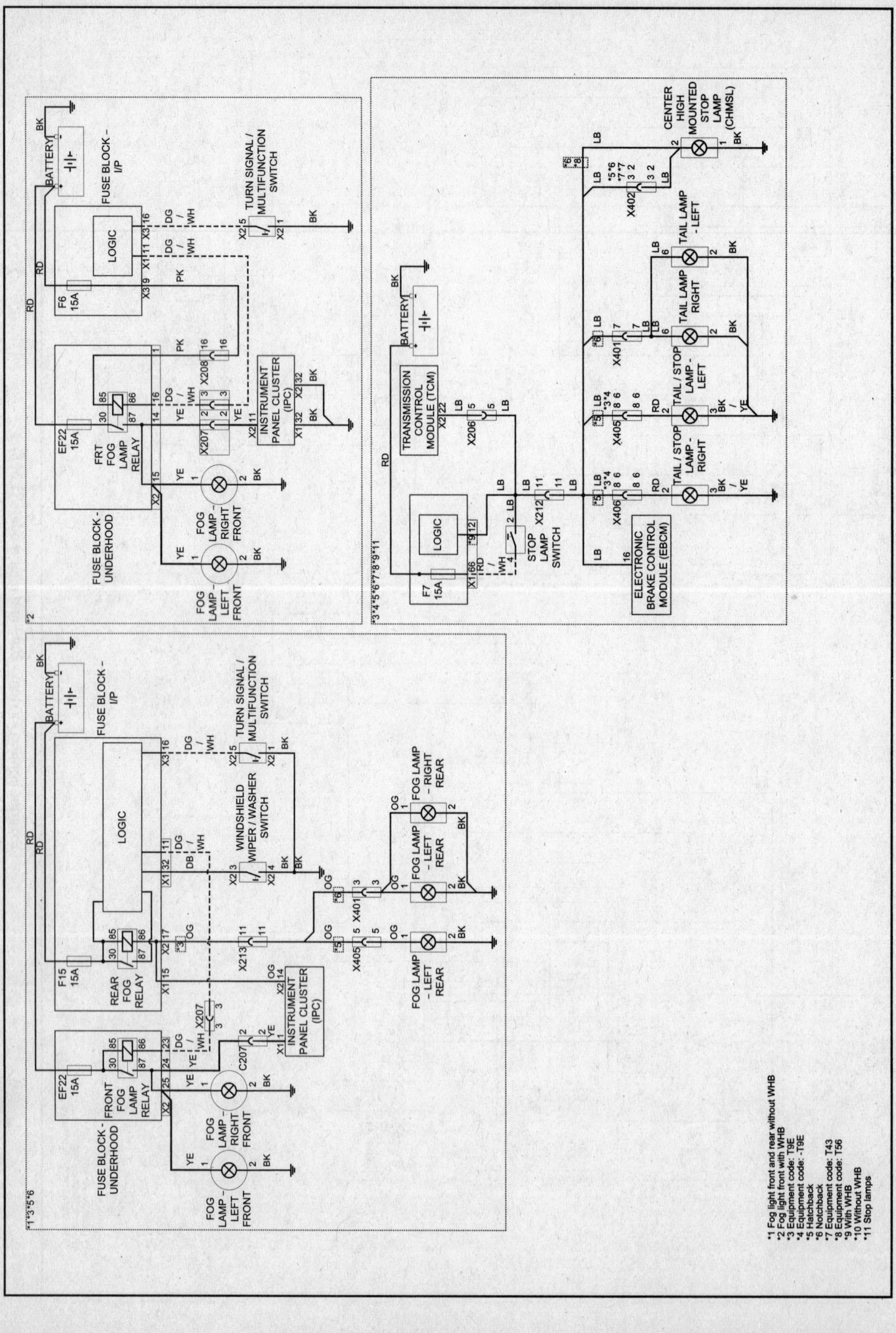

BATTERY BK

FUSE BLOCK – I/P

LOGIC

F6 15A

RD RD RD

X3 16 DG/WH

X1 11 DG/WH

X39 PK

TURN SIGNAL / MULTIFUNCTION SWITCH

X2 5

X2 1

X3 21 BK

FUSE BLOCK – UNDERHOOD

EF22 15A

30 85

87 86

FRT FOG LAMP RELAY

X2 15

16 PK

16 DG/WH

14 YE

X208 16 16

X207 2 3

X2 11

INSTRUMENT PANEL CLUSTER (IPC)

X132 X2 232 BK

YE

FOG LAMP – RIGHT FRONT 2 BK

FOG LAMP – LEFT FRONT 2 BK

*2

BATTERY BK

TRANSMISSION CONTROL MODULE (TCM) X2 122

RD

LOGIC

F7 15A

X1 66 RD

LB 5

X206 5

LB

LB 2 LB

WH 4

STOP LAMP SWITCH X212

LB 11 11 LB

LB 16

ELECTRONIC BRAKE CONTROL MODULE (EBCM)

*3 *4 *5 *6 *7 *8 *9 *11

CENTER HIGH MOUNTED STOP LAMP (CHMSL)

LB 2 1 BK

*G *8

LB *5 *6 *7 *7 3 2

X402 3 2 LB

TAIL LAMP – LEFT 6 2 BK

LB

X401 6 6

*6 LB 7 7

TAIL LAMP RIGHT 6 2 BK

LB *3 *4

8 6 8 6

X405 RD

TAIL / STOP LAMP – LEFT 3 1 BK YE

*5 LB

8 6 8 6

X406 RD

*5 LB *3 *4

TAIL / STOP LAMP – RIGHT 3 1 BK YE

BATTERY BK

FUSE BLOCK – I/P

LOGIC

RD RD

X3 16 DG/WH

X1 32 11 DG/WH

DB/WH

F15 15A

30 85

87 86

REAR FOG RELAY

X2 17

X1 15

*3 OG

TURN SIGNAL / MULTIFUNCTION SWITCH

X2 5 X2 1

WINDSHIELD WIPER / WASHER SWITCH

X2 3 X2 4 BK

FOG LAMP – RIGHT REAR

OG

X401 3 3

OG 2 BK

FOG LAMP – LEFT REAR 2 BK

OG *6

OG *5

X213 11 11

OG

X2 14

INSTRUMENT PANEL CLUSTER (IPC) X1 11

X405 5 5 OG

FOG LAMP – LEFT REAR 2 BK

OG

EF22 15A

30 85

87 86

FRONT FOG LAMP RELAY

X2 24 23

25 DG

X207 3 3

WH YE

C207 2 2

YE 1

FOG LAMP – RIGHT FRONT 2 BK

FUSE BLOCK – UNDERHOOD

YE 1

FOG LAMP – LEFT FRONT 2 BK

*1 *3 *5 *6

*1 Fog light front and rear without WHB
*2 Fog light front with WHB
*3 Equipment code: T9E
*4 Equipment code: T9E
*5 Hatchback
*6 Notchback
*7 Equipment code: T43
*8 Equipment code: T56
*9 With WHB
*10 Without WHB
*11 Stop lamps

Exterior lighting system - 2009 and later models (2 of 5)

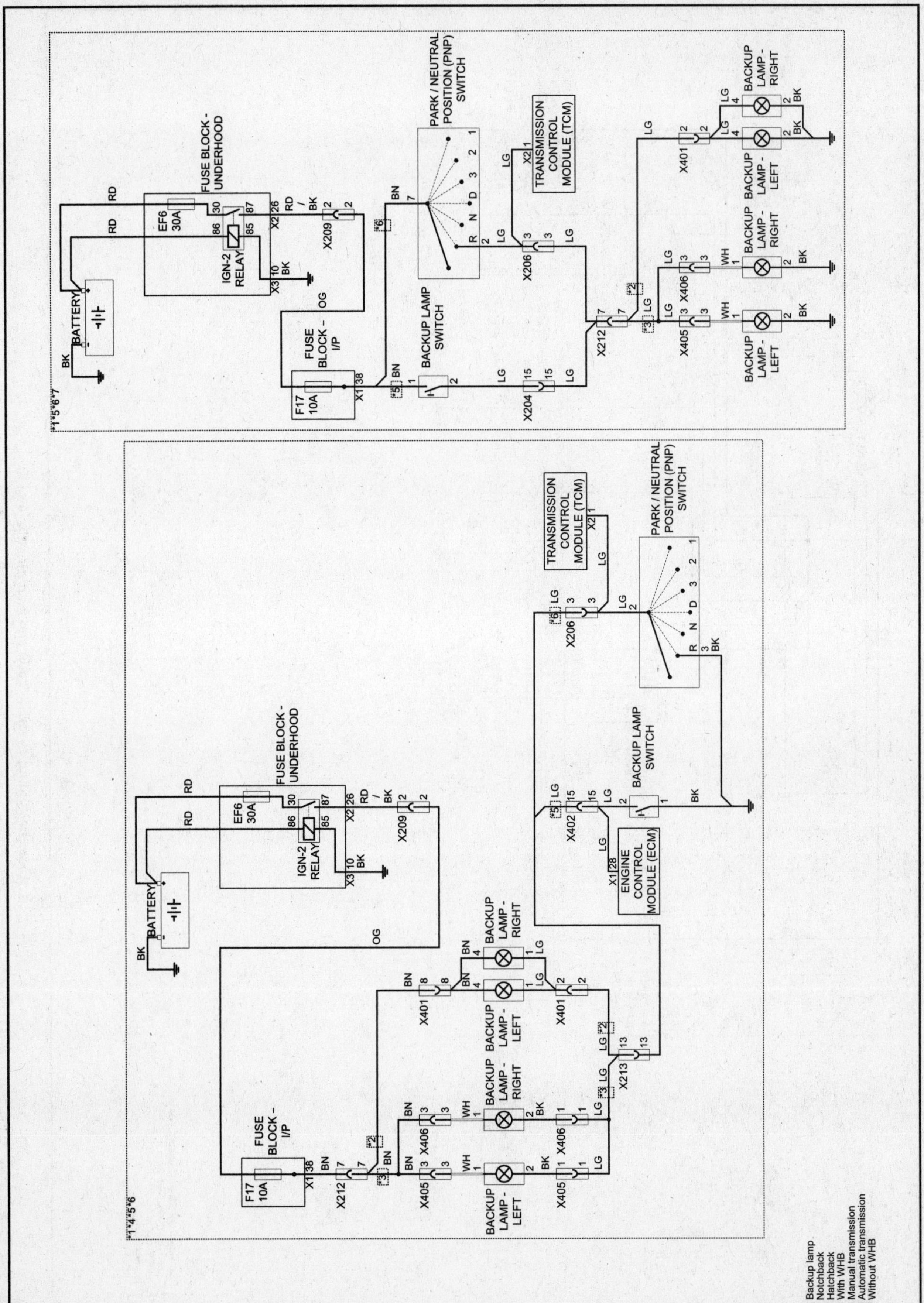

Exterior lighting system - 2009 and later models (3 of 5)

*1 Backup lamp.
*2 Notchback
*3 Hatchback
*4 With WHB
*5 Manual transmission
*6 Automatic transmission
*7 Without WHB

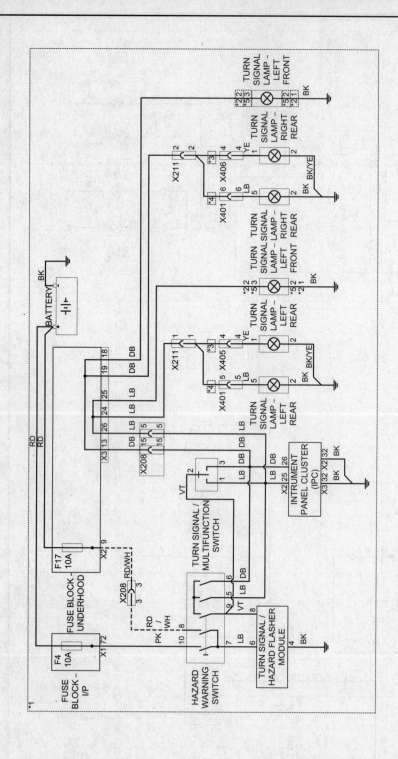

Exterior lighting system - 2009 and later models (4 of 5)

*1 Turn signal Lamps and Hazard Warning
*2 Equipment code: T84
*3 Hatchback
*4 Notchback
*5 Equipment code: FL2

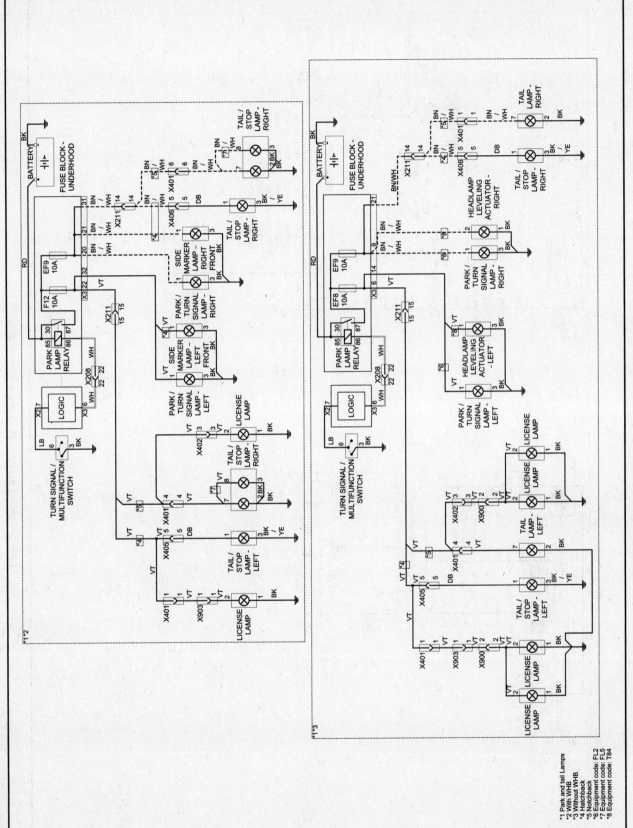

Exterior lighting system - 2009 and later models (5 of 5)

*1 Park and tail Lamps
*2 With WHB
*3 Without WHB
*4 Hatchback
*5 Notchback
*6 Equipment code: FL2
*7 Equipment code: FL5
*8 Equipment code: T84

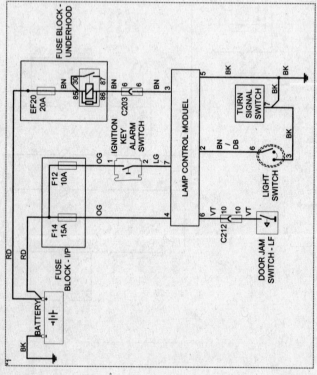

Interior lighting system - 2006 and earlier models

*1 Lamp control / Battery saver
*2 Courtesy and Trunk Lamp
*3 Hatchback
*4 Notchback
*5 With Sunroof
*6 Without Sunroof

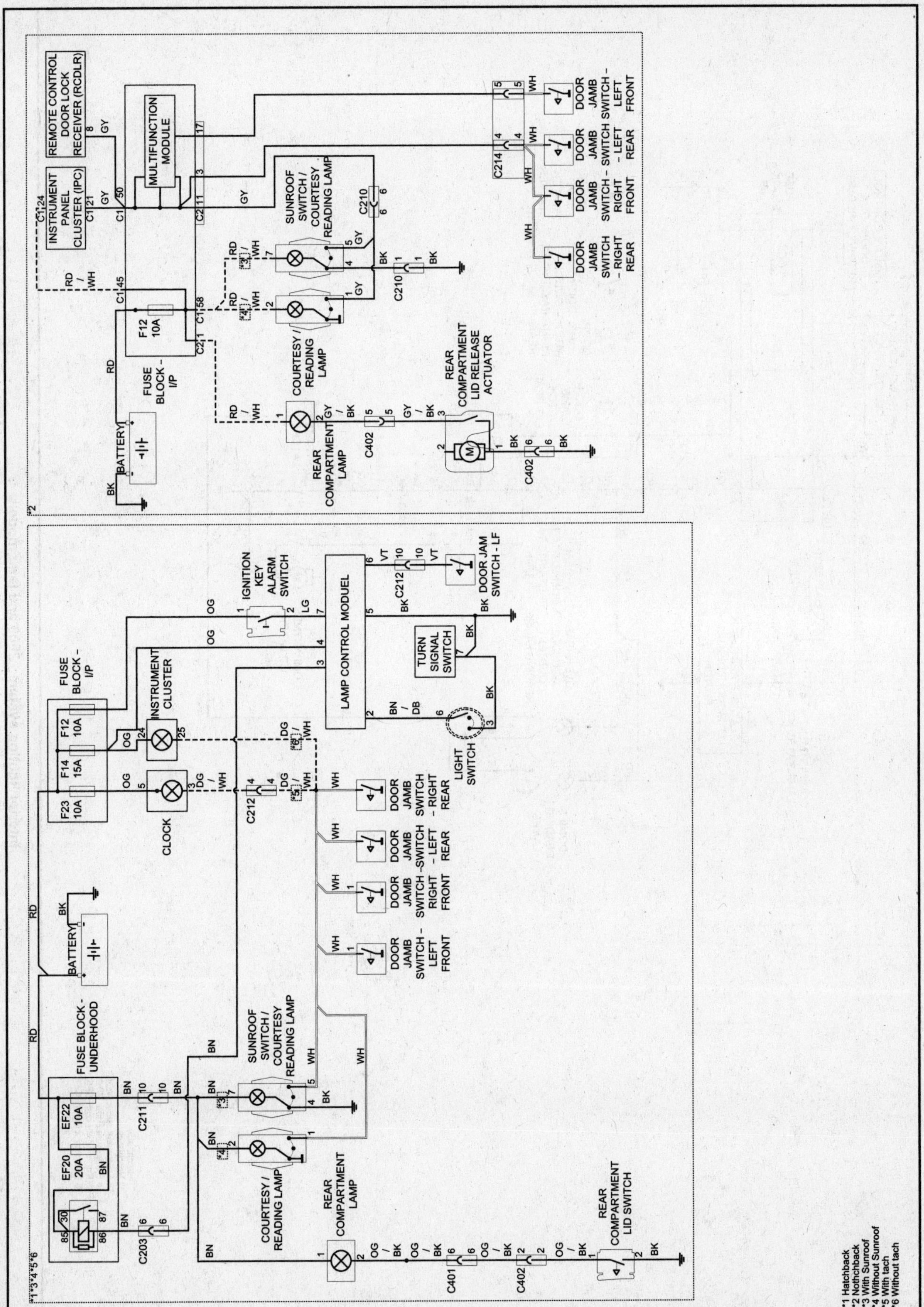

Interior lighting system - 2007 and 2008 models

*1 Hatchback
*2 Notchback
*3 With Sunroof
*4 Without Sunroof
*5 With tach
*6 Without tach

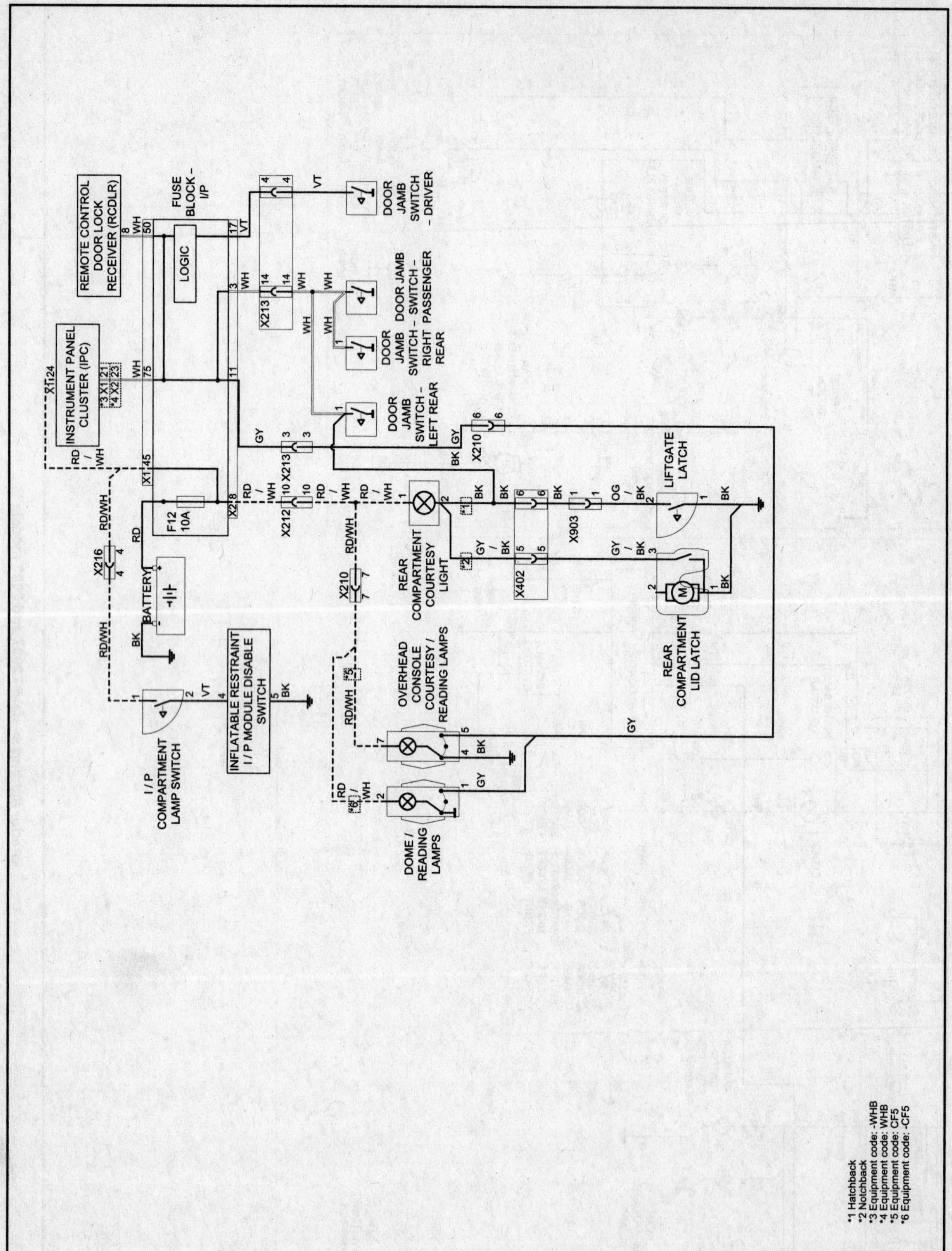

REMOTE CONTROL DOOR LOCK RECEIVER (RCDLR)

FUSE BLOCK - I/P

LOGIC

INSTRUMENT PANEL CLUSTER (IPC)

DOOR JAMB SWITCH - DRIVER

DOOR JAMB SWITCH - RIGHT PASSENGER

DOOR JAMB SWITCH - RIGHT REAR

DOOR JAMB SWITCH - LEFT REAR

LIFTGATE LATCH

REAR COMPARTMENT COURTESY LIGHT

REAR COMPARTMENT LID LATCH

I/P COMPARTMENT LAMP SWITCH

INFLATABLE RESTRAINT I/P MODULE DISABLE SWITCH

OVERHEAD CONSOLE COURTESY / READING LAMPS

DOME / READING LAMPS

BATTERY

F12 10A

Interior lighting system - 2009 and later models

*1 Hatchback
*2 Notchback
*3 Equipment code: -WHB
*4 Equipment code: WHB
*5 Equipment code: CF5
*6 Equipment code: -CF5

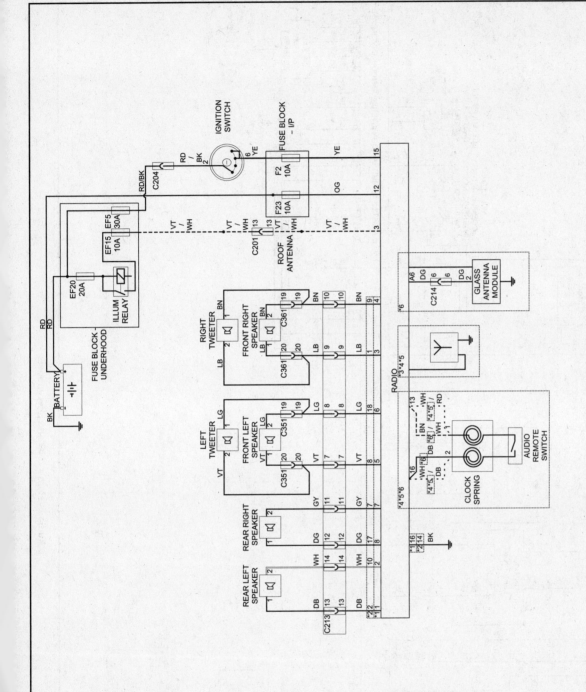

Audio system - 2008 and earlier models

*1 With RDS
*2 Without RDS
*3 From 2004 to 2006
*4 For 2006
*5 From 2007 to 2008 Hatchback
*6 From 2007 to 2008 Notchback

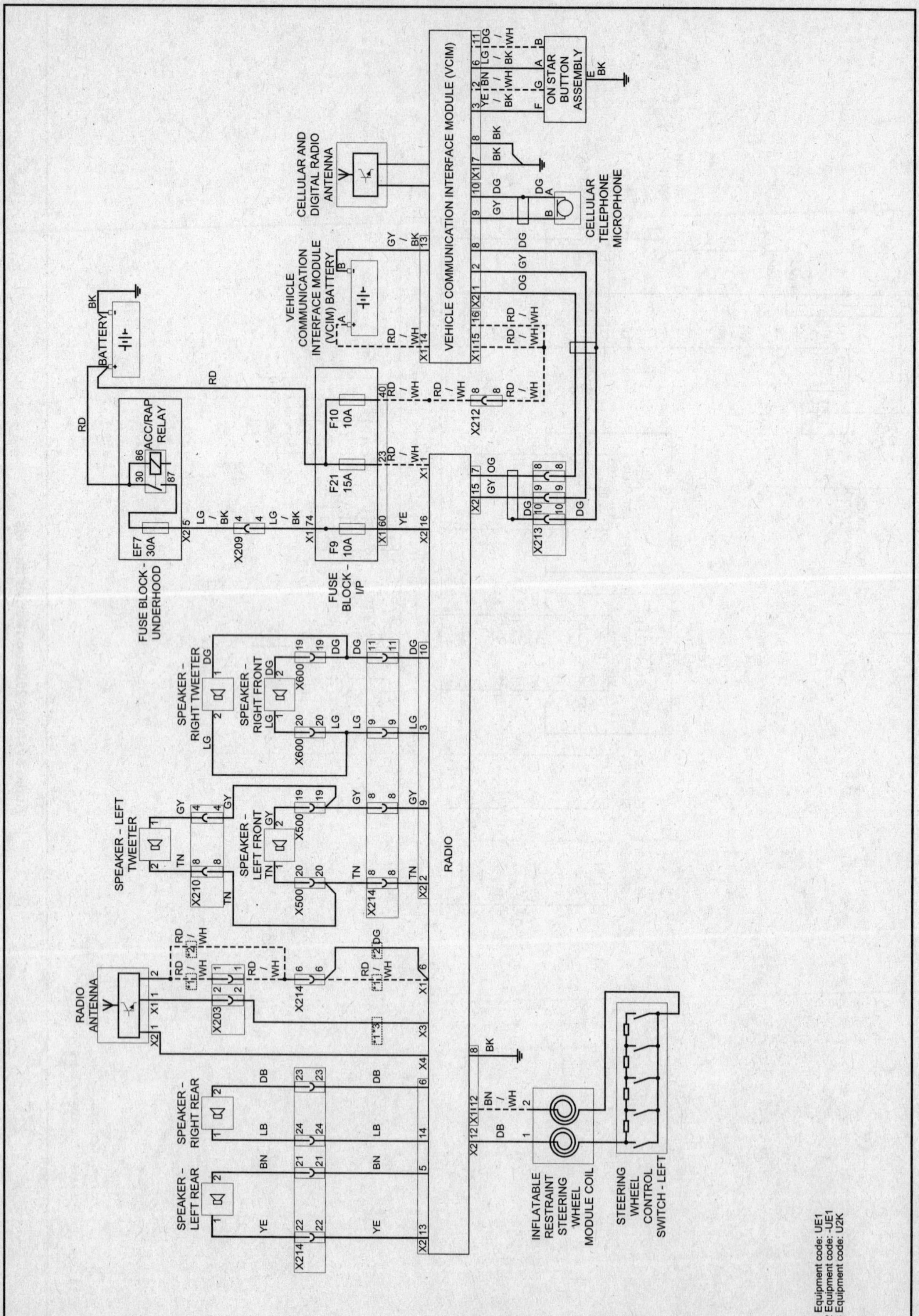

Audio system - 2009 and later models

1 Equipment code: UE1
2 Equipment code: -JE1
3 Equipment code: U2K

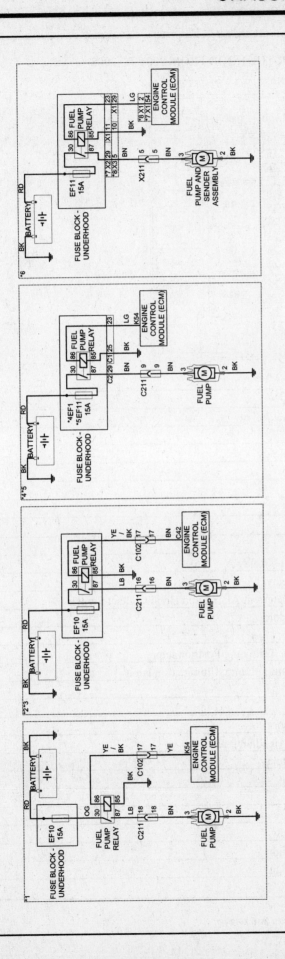

Fuel pump system

*1 From 2004 to 2005
*2 For 2006
*3 From 2007 to 2008 Hatchback
*4 From 2007 to 2008 With Throttle actuator control
*5 From 2007 to 2008 Without Throttle actuator control
*6 From 2009 to 2011
*7 Engine code: LXT
*8 Engine code: LDE, LLU and LXV

FUSE BLOCK UNDER THE HOOD FROM 2004 TO 2008

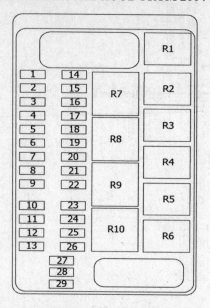

FUSE/RELAY	VALUE	DESCRIPTION
EF1	30 A	Power Window Relay
EF2	20 A	Main Relay
EF3	30 A	Cooling Fan Relay
EF4	50 A	EBCM
EF5	30 A	Ignition–1
EF6	30 A	Ignition–2
EF7	30 A	Battery Main
EF8	20 A	Blower Motor
EF9	15 A	Front Fog Lamp Relay
EF10	15 A	Fuel Pump Relay
EF11	10 A	Horn, Theft Deterrent Alarm, and Hood Contact Switch
EF12	20 A	Sun Roof Module
EF13	—	Not Used
EF14	10 A	License Lamp, Tail lamp, Position lamp
EF15	10 A	Tail lamp, Position Lamp, Illumination lamo
EF16	—	Not Used
EF17	—	Not Used
EF18	20 A	A/C compressor
EF19	25 A	DRL module, Headlamp relay
EF20	15 A	Illumination Relay
EF21	30 A	Defog
EF22	10 A	Trunk lamp
EF23	10 A	Head Lamp Low
EF24	10 A	Head Lamp Low
EF25	10 A	Head Lamp High
EF26	10 A	Head Lamp High

Fuses and relays

GLOSSARY

AIR/FUEL RATIO: The ratio of air-to-gasoline by weight in the fuel mixture drawn into the engine.

AIR INJECTION: One method of reducing harmful exhaust emissions by injecting air into each of the exhaust ports of an engine. The fresh air entering the hot exhaust manifold causes any remaining fuel to be burned before it can exit the tailpipe.

ALTERNATOR: A device used for converting mechanical energy into electrical energy.

AMMETER: An instrument, calibrated in amperes, used to measure the flow of an electrical current in a circuit. Ammeters are always connected in series with the circuit being tested.

AMPERE: The rate of flow of electrical current present when one volt of electrical pressure is applied against one ohm of electrical resistance.

ANALOG COMPUTER: Any microprocessor that uses similar (analogous) electrical signals to make its calculations.

ARMATURE: A laminated, soft iron core wrapped by a wire that converts electrical energy to mechanical energy as in a motor or relay. When rotated in a magnetic field, it changes mechanical energy into electrical energy as in a generator.

ATMOSPHERIC PRESSURE: The pressure on the Earth's surface caused by the weight of the air in the atmosphere. At sea level, this pressure is 14.7 psi at 32°F (101 kPa at 0°C).

ATOMIZATION: The breaking down of a liquid into a fine mist that can be suspended in air.

AXIAL PLAY: Movement parallel to a shaft or bearing bore.

BACKFIRE: The sudden combustion of gases in the intake or exhaust system that results in a loud explosion.

BACKLASH: The clearance or play between two parts, such as meshed gears.

BACKPRESSURE: Restrictions in the exhaust system that slow the exit of exhaust gases from the combustion chamber.

BAKELITE: A heat resistant, plastic insulator material commonly used in printed circuit boards and transistorized components.

BALL BEARING: A bearing made up of hardened inner and outer races between which hardened steel balls roll.

BALLAST RESISTOR: A resistor in the primary ignition circuit that lowers voltage after the engine is started to reduce wear on ignition components.

BEARING: A friction reducing, supportive device usually located between a stationary part and a moving part.

BIMETAL TEMPERATURE SENSOR: Any sensor or switch made of two dissimilar types of metal that bend when heated or cooled due to the different expansion rates of the alloys. These types of sensors usually function as an on/off switch.

BLOWBY: Combustion gases, composed of water vapor and unburned fuel, that leak past the piston rings into the crankcase during normal engine operation. These gases are removed by the PCV system to prevent the buildup of harmful acids in the crankcase.

BRAKE PAD: A brake shoe and lining assembly used with disc brakes.

BRAKE SHOE: The backing for the brake lining. The term is, however, usually applied to the assembly of the brake backing and lining.

BUSHING: A liner, usually removable, for a bearing; an anti-friction liner used in place of a bearing.

CALIPER: A hydraulically activated device in a disc brake system, which is mounted straddling the brake rotor (disc). The caliper contains at least one piston and two brake pads. Hydraulic pressure on the piston(s) forces the pads against the rotor.

CAMSHAFT: A shaft in the engine on which are the lobes (cams) which operate the valves. The camshaft is driven by the crankshaft, via a belt, chain or gears, at one half the crankshaft speed.

CAPACITOR: A device which stores an electrical charge.

CARBON MONOXIDE (CO): A colorless, odorless gas given off as a normal byproduct of combustion. It is poisonous and extremely dangerous in confined areas, building up slowly to toxic levels without warning if adequate ventilation is not available.

CARBURETOR: A device, usually mounted on the intake manifold of an engine, which mixes the air and fuel in the proper proportion to allow even combustion.

CATALYTIC CONVERTER: A device installed in the exhaust system, like a muffler, that converts harmful byproducts of combustion into carbon dioxide and water vapor by means of a heat-producing chemical reaction.

CENTRIFUGAL ADVANCE: A mechanical method of advancing the spark timing by using flyweights in the distributor that react to centrifugal force generated by the distributor shaft rotation.

CHECK VALVE: Any one-way valve installed to permit the flow of air, fuel or vacuum in one direction only.

CHOKE: A device, usually a moveable valve, placed in the intake path of a carburetor to restrict the flow of air.

CIRCUIT: Any unbroken path through which an electrical current can flow. Also used to describe fuel flow in some instances.

CIRCUIT BREAKER: A switch which protects an electrical circuit from overload by opening the circuit when the current flow exceeds a predetermined level. Some circuit breakers must be reset manually, while most reset automatically.

COIL (IGNITION): A transformer in the ignition circuit which steps up the voltage provided to the spark plugs.

COMBINATION MANIFOLD: An assembly which includes both the intake and exhaust manifolds in one casting.

COMBINATION VALVE: A device used in some fuel systems that routes fuel vapors to a charcoal storage canister instead of venting them into the atmosphere. The valve relieves fuel tank pressure and allows fresh air into the tank as the fuel level drops to prevent a vapor lock situation.

COMPRESSION RATIO: The comparison of the total volume of the cylinder and combustion chamber with the piston at BDC and the piston at TDC.

CONDENSER: 1. An electrical device which acts to store an electrical charge, preventing voltage surges. 2. A radiator-like device in the air conditioning system in which refrigerant gas condenses into a liquid, giving off heat.

CONDUCTOR: Any material through which an electrical current can be transmitted easily.

CONTINUITY: Continuous or complete circuit. Can be checked with an ohmmeter.

COUNTERSHAFT: An intermediate shaft which is rotated by a mainshaft and transmits, in turn, that rotation to a working part.

CRANKCASE: The lower part of an engine in which the crankshaft and related parts operate.

CRANKSHAFT: The main driving shaft of an engine which receives reciprocating motion from the pistons and converts it to rotary motion.

CYLINDER: In an engine, the round hole in the engine block in which the piston(s) ride.

CYLINDER BLOCK: The main structural member of an engine in which is found the cylinders, crankshaft and other principal parts.

CYLINDER HEAD: The detachable portion of the engine, usually fastened to the top of the cylinder block and containing all or most of the combustion chambers. On overhead valve engines, it contains the valves and their operating parts. On overhead cam engines, it contains the camshaft as well.

DEAD CENTER: The extreme top or bottom of the piston stroke.

DETONATION: An unwanted explosion of the air/fuel mixture in the combustion chamber caused by excess heat and compression, advanced timing, or an overly lean mixture. Also referred to as "ping".

DIAPHRAGM: A thin, flexible wall separating two cavities, such as in a vacuum advance unit.

DIESELING: A condition in which hot spots in the combustion chamber cause the engine to run on after the key is turned off.

DIFFERENTIAL: A geared assembly which allows the transmission of motion between drive axles, giving one axle the ability to turn faster than the other.

DIODE: An electrical device that will allow current to flow in one direction only.

DISC BRAKE: A hydraulic braking assembly consisting of a brake disc, or rotor, mounted on an axle, and a caliper assembly containing, usually two brake pads which are activated by hydraulic pressure. The pads are forced against the sides of the disc, creating friction which slows the vehicle.

DISTRIBUTOR: A mechanically driven device on an engine which is responsible for electrically firing the spark plug at a predetermined point of the piston stroke.

DOWEL PIN: A pin, inserted in mating holes in two different parts allowing those parts to maintain a fixed relationship.

DRUM BRAKE: A braking system which consists of two brake shoes and one or two wheel cylinders, mounted on a fixed backing plate, and a brake drum, mounted on an axle, which revolves around the assembly.

DWELL: The rate, measured in degrees of shaft rotation, at which an electrical circuit cycles on and off.

ELECTRONIC CONTROL UNIT (ECU): Ignition module, module, amplifier or igniter. See Module for definition.

ELECTRONIC IGNITION: A system in which the timing and firing of the spark plugs is controlled by an electronic control unit, usually called a module. These systems have no points or condenser.

END-PLAY: The measured amount of axial movement in a shaft.

ENGINE: A device that converts heat into mechanical energy.

EXHAUST MANIFOLD: A set of cast passages or pipes which conduct exhaust gases from the engine.

FEELER GAUGE: A blade, usually metal, or precisely predetermined thickness, used to measure the clearance between two parts.

FIRING ORDER: The order in which combustion occurs in the cylinders of an engine. Also the order in which spark is distributed to the plugs by the distributor.

FLOODING: The presence of too much fuel in the intake manifold and combustion chamber which prevents the air/fuel mixture from firing, thereby causing a no-start situation.

FLYWHEEL: A disc shaped part bolted to the rear end of the crankshaft. Around the outer perimeter is affixed the ring gear. The starter drive engages the ring gear, turning the flywheel, which rotates the crankshaft, imparting the initial starting motion to the engine.

FOOT POUND (ft. lbs. or sometimes, ft.lb.): The amount of energy or work needed to raise an item weighing one pound, a distance of one foot.

FUSE: A protective device in a circuit which prevents circuit overload by breaking the circuit when a specific amperage is present. The device is constructed around a strip or wire of a lower amperage rating than the circuit it is designed to protect. When an amperage higher than that stamped on the fuse is present in the circuit, the strip or wire melts, opening the circuit.

GEAR RATIO: The ratio between the number of teeth on meshing gears.

GENERATOR: A device which converts mechanical energy into electrical energy.

HEAT RANGE: The measure of a spark plug's ability to dissipate heat from its firing end. The higher the heat range, the hotter the plug fires.

HUB: The center part of a wheel or gear.

HYDROCARBON (HC): Any chemical compound made up of hydrogen and carbon. A major pollutant formed by the engine as a byproduct of combustion.

HYDROMETER: An instrument used to measure the specific gravity of a solution.

INCH POUND (inch lbs.; sometimes in.lb. or in. lbs.): One twelfth of a foot pound.

INDUCTION: A means of transferring electrical energy in the form of a magnetic field. Principle used in the ignition coil to increase voltage.

INJECTOR: A device which receives metered fuel under relatively low pressure and is activated to inject the fuel into the engine under relatively high pressure at a predetermined time.

INPUT SHAFT: The shaft to which torque is applied, usually carrying the driving gear or gears.

INTAKE MANIFOLD: A casting of passages or pipes used to conduct air or a fuel/air mixture to the cylinders.

JOURNAL: The bearing surface within which a shaft operates.

KEY: A small block usually fitted in a notch between a shaft and a hub to prevent slippage of the two parts.

MANIFOLD: A casting of passages or set of pipes which connect the cylinders to an inlet or outlet source.

MANIFOLD VACUUM: Low pressure in an engine intake manifold formed just below the throttle plates. Manifold vacuum is highest at idle and drops under acceleration.

MASTER CYLINDER: The primary fluid pressurizing device in a hydraulic system. In automotive use, it is found in brake and hydraulic clutch systems and is pedal activated, either directly or, in a power brake system, through the power booster.

MODULE: Electronic control unit, amplifier or igniter of solid state or integrated design which controls the current flow in the ignition primary circuit based on input from the pick-up coil. When the module opens the primary circuit, high secondary voltage is induced in the coil.

NEEDLE BEARING: A bearing which consists of a number (usually a large number) of long, thin rollers.

OHM: (Ω) The unit used to measure the resistance of conductor-to-electrical flow. One ohm is the amount of resistance that limits current flow to one ampere in a circuit with one volt of pressure.

OHMMETER: An instrument used for measuring the resistance, in ohms, in an electrical circuit.

OUTPUT SHAFT: The shaft which transmits torque from a device, such as a transmission.

OVERDRIVE: A gear assembly which produces more shaft revolutions than that transmitted to it.

OVERHEAD CAMSHAFT (OHC): An engine configuration in which the camshaft is mounted on top of the cylinder head and operates the valve either directly or by means of rocker arms.

OVERHEAD VALVE (OHV): An engine configuration in which all of the valves are located in the cylinder head and the camshaft is located in the cylinder block. The camshaft operates the valves via lifters and pushrods.

OXIDES OF NITROGEN (NOx): Chemical compounds of nitrogen produced as a byproduct of combustion. They combine with hydrocarbons to produce smog.

OXYGEN SENSOR: Use with the feedback system to sense the presence of oxygen in the exhaust gas and signal the computer which can reference the voltage signal to an air/fuel ratio.

PINION: The smaller of two meshing gears.

PISTON RING: An open-ended ring with fits into a groove on the outer diameter of the piston. Its chief function is to form a seal between the piston and cylinder wall. Most automotive pistons have three rings: two for compression sealing; one for oil sealing.

PRELOAD: A predetermined load placed on a bearing during assembly or by adjustment.

PRIMARY CIRCUIT: the low voltage side of the ignition system which consists of the ignition switch, ballast resistor or resistance wire, bypass, coil, electronic control unit and pick-up coil as well as the connecting wires and harnesses.

PRESS FIT: The mating of two parts under pressure, due to the inner diameter of one being smaller than the outer diameter of the other, or vice versa; an interference fit.

RACE: The surface on the inner or outer ring of a bearing on which the balls, needles or rollers move.

REGULATOR: A device which maintains the amperage and/or voltage levels of a circuit at predetermined values.

RELAY: A switch which automatically opens and/or closes a circuit.

RESISTANCE: The opposition to the flow of current through a circuit or electrical device, and is measured in ohms. Resistance is equal to the voltage divided by the amperage.

RESISTOR: A device, usually made of wire, which offers a preset amount of resistance in an electrical circuit.

RING GEAR: The name given to a ring-shaped gear attached to a differential case, or affixed to a flywheel or as part of a planetary gear set.

ROLLER BEARING: A bearing made up of hardened inner and outer races between which hardened steel rollers move.

ROTOR: 1. The disc-shaped part of a disc brake assembly, upon which the brake pads bear; also called, brake disc. 2. The device

mounted atop the distributor shaft, which passes current to the distributor cap tower contacts.

SECONDARY CIRCUIT: The high voltage side of the ignition system, usually above 20,000 volts. The secondary includes the ignition coil, coil wire, distributor cap and rotor, spark plug wires and spark plugs.

SENDING UNIT: A mechanical, electrical, hydraulic or electromagnetic device which transmits information to a gauge.

SENSOR: Any device designed to measure engine operating conditions or ambient pressures and temperatures. Usually electronic in nature and designed to send a voltage signal to an on-board computer, some sensors may operate as a simple on/off switch or they may provide a variable voltage signal (like a potentiometer) as conditions or measured parameters change.

SHIM: Spacers of precise, predetermined thickness used between parts to establish a proper working relationship.

SLAVE CYLINDER: In automotive use, a device in the hydraulic clutch system which is activated by hydraulic force, disengaging the clutch.

SOLENOID: A coil used to produce a magnetic field, the effect of which is to produce work.

SPARK PLUG: A device screwed into the combustion chamber of a spark ignition engine. The basic construction is a conductive core inside of a ceramic insulator, mounted in an outer conductive base. An electrical charge from the spark plug wire travels along the conductive core and jumps a preset air gap to a grounding point or points at the end of the conductive base. The resultant spark ignites the fuel/air mixture in the combustion chamber.

SPLINES: Ridges machined or cast onto the outer diameter of a shaft or inner diameter of a bore to enable parts to mate without rotation.

TACHOMETER: A device used to measure the rotary speed of an engine, shaft, gear, etc., usually in rotations per minute.

THERMOSTAT: A valve, located in the cooling system of an engine, which is closed when cold and opens gradually in response to engine heating, controlling the temperature of the coolant and rate of coolant flow.

TOP DEAD CENTER (TDC): The point at which the piston reaches the top of its travel on the compression stroke.

TORQUE: The twisting force applied to an object.

TORQUE CONVERTER: A turbine used to transmit power from a driving member to a driven member via hydraulic action, providing changes in drive ratio and torque. In automotive use, it links the driveplate at the rear of the engine to the automatic transmission.

TRANSDUCER: A device used to change a force into an electrical signal.

TRANSISTOR: A semi-conductor component which can be actuated by a small voltage to perform an electrical switching function.

TUNE-UP: A regular maintenance function, usually associated with the replacement and adjustment of parts and components in the electrical and fuel systems of a vehicle for the purpose of attaining optimum performance.

TURBOCHARGER: An exhaust driven pump which compresses intake air and forces it into the combustion chambers at higher than atmospheric pressures. The increased air pressure allows more fuel to be burned and results in increased horsepower being produced.

VACUUM ADVANCE: A device which advances the ignition timing in response to increased engine vacuum.

VACUUM GAUGE: An instrument used to measure the presence of vacuum in a chamber.

VALVE: A device which control the pressure, direction of flow or rate of flow of a liquid or gas.

VALVE CLEARANCE: The measured gap between the end of the valve stem and the rocker arm, cam lobe or follower that activates the valve.

VISCOSITY: The rating of a liquid's internal resistance to flow.

VOLTMETER: An instrument used for measuring electrical force in units called volts. Voltmeters are always connected parallel with the circuit being tested.

WHEEL CYLINDER: Found in the automotive drum brake assembly, it is a device, actuated by hydraulic pressure, which, through internal pistons, pushes the brake shoes outward against the drums.

Notes

A